Policing
White-Collar Crime
Characteristics of White-Collar Criminals

Advances in Police Theory and Practice Series

Series Editor: Dilip K. Das

Policing White Collar Crime: Characteristics of White Collar Criminals
Petter Gottschalk

Honor-Based Violence: Policing and Prevention
Karl Anton Roberts, Gerry Campbell, and Glen Lloyd

Policing and the Mentally Ill: International Perspectives
Duncan Chappell

Security Governance, Policing, and Local Capacity
Jan Froestad with Clifford D. Shearing

Policing in Hong Kong: History and Reform
Kam C. Wong

Police Performance Appraisals: A Comparative Perspective
Serdar Kenan Gul and Paul O'Connell

Los Angeles Police Department Meltdown: The Fall of the Professional-Reform Model of Policing
James Lasley

Financial Crimes: A Global Threat
Maximillian Edelbacher, Peter Kratcoski, and Michael Theil

Police Integrity Management in Australia: Global Lessons for Combating Police Misconduct
Louise Porter and Tim Prenzler

The Crime Numbers Game: Management by Manipulation
John A. Eterno and Eli B. Silverman

The International Trafficking of Human Organs: A Multidisciplinary Perspective
Leonard Territo and Rande Matteson

Police Reform in China
Kam C. Wong

Mission-Based Policing
John P. Crank, Dawn M. Irlbeck, Rebecca K. Murray, and Mark Sundermeier

The New Khaki: The Evolving Nature of Policing in India
Arvind Verma

Cold Cases: An Evaluation Model with Follow-up Strategies for Investigators
James M. Adcock and Sarah L. Stein

Policing Organized Crime: Intelligence Strategy Implementation
Petter Gottschalk

Security in Post-Conflict Africa: The Role of Nonstate Policing
Bruce Baker

Community Policing and Peacekeeping
Peter Grabosky

Community Policing: International Patterns and Comparative Perspectives
Dominique Wisler and Ihekwoaba D. Onwudiwe

Police Corruption: Preventing Misconduct and Maintaining Integrity
Tim Prenzler

FORTHCOMING

Crime Linkage: Theory Research, and Practice
Jessica Woodhams and Craig Bennell

Female Criminals: An Examination and Interpretation of Female Offending
Venessa Garcia

Democratic Policing
Darren Palmer

Cold Cases: Evaluation Models with Follow-up Strategies for Investigators, Second Edition
James M. Adcock and Sarah L. Stein

Women in Policing: An International Perspective
Venessa Garcia

Islamic Women in Policing: A Contradiction in Terms?
Tonita Murry

Civilian Oversight of Police: Advancing Accountability in Law Enforcement
Tim Prenzler and Garth den Heyer

Policing
White-Collar Crime

Characteristics of White-Collar Criminals

Petter Gottschalk

CRC Press
Taylor & Francis Group
Boca Raton London New York

CRC Press is an imprint of the
Taylor & Francis Group, an **informa** business

CRC Press
Taylor & Francis Group
6000 Broken Sound Parkway NW, Suite 300
Boca Raton, FL 33487-2742

Printed on acid-free paper
Version Date: 20131101

International Standard Book Number-13: 978-1-4665-9177-6 (Hardback)

Visit the Taylor & Francis Web site at
http://www.taylorandfrancis.com

and the CRC Press Web site at
http://www.crcpress.com

Contents

Series Editor's Preface   xi
Acknowledgments   xv
Author   xvii
Introduction   xix

1   White-Collar Crime Typologies   1

Financial Crime Variety   2
Financial Crime Categories   4
Fraud Crime Category   5
Theft Crime Category   10
Manipulation Crime Category   13
Corruption Crime Category   17
References   20

2   White-Collar Criminal Typologies   25

Financial Crime of Trust   27
Authority and Opportunity   31
Sample Criminals   37
Criminal Characteristics   42
    The Case of Hermansen at Spitsbergen   47
    The Case of Røkke at Aker   48
Theoretical Perspectives   49
References   51

3   White-Collar Criminal Roles   55

Corporate versus Occupational   55
Corporate Crime Theories   58
Corporate Criminal Sample   62
Leaders versus Followers   64
Leader Criminal Characteristics   65
Leader Crime Theories   67
Leader Criminal Sample   72
Rotten Apples versus Rotten Barrels   76
Rotten Criminal Characteristics   76

Rotten Crime Theories   78
Rotten Criminal Sample   82
Groups of White-Collar Criminals   86
Criminal Entrepreneurs   87
Corporate Criminals   88
Criminal Followers   91
Female Criminals   93
Comparison of Groups   94
References   96

4   Women in White-Collar Crime   99

Criminal Characteristics   104
Crime Theories   111
Criminal Sample   116
Discussion   119
References   120

5   Stage Model for Female Criminals   123

Stage Model Overview   123
Determinants of Female Criminal Fraction   124
From Population Fraction to Needs Fraction   125
From Needs Fraction to Crime Fraction   128
Women's Opportunity for Crime   128
Women's Motivation for Crime   134
Women's Justification of Crime   140
Crime Star for Women   144
From Crime Fraction to Detection Fraction   145
From Detection Fraction to Sentence Fraction   148
From Sentence Fraction to Prison Fraction   148
Discussion   149
References   150

6   Management Positions in Crime   155

Chief Executives   155
Heroic Criminals   162
Crime Theories   166
Criminal Sample   169
References   172

7   Victims, Detection, and Sector   175

Victims Criminal Characteristics   175
Victims Crime Theories   176

Victims Criminal Sample 178
Classification of Victims 179
Criminal Insiders 183
Detection of White-Collar Criminals 185
Detection Crime Theories 185
White-Collar Crime Detection 188
The Role of Journalists in Crime Detection 190
The Role of Auditors in Crime Detection 194
Crime in Private versus Public Sector 197
Sector Crime Theories 198
Sector Criminal Sample 200
References 200

8   Statistical Analyses of Crime Sample   205

Statistical Correlation Analysis 205
Statistical Regression Analysis 207
Structural Equation Modeling 210
References 217

9   Police Value Shop Configuration   219

Police Culture 220
Value Shop Work 230
Learning Organization 232
References 236

10   Police Information Management Strategy   241

Criminal Intelligence 242
Strategy Characteristics 245
Classification of Information Sources 246
Forensic Accounting 250
Crime Intelligence Analysis 252
References 255

11   Police Knowledge Management Strategy   257

Intelligence for Knowledge 257
Management Approaches 258
Police Knowledge 260
Knowledge Integration 261
Knowledge Categories 263
From Data to Wisdom 268
References 270

12   Police Information Systems Strategy   273

  Knowledge Management Systems   273
  Stage 1: Investigator to Technology   275
  Stage 2: Investigator to Investigator   277
  Stage 3: Investigator to Information   283
  Stage 4: Investigator to Application   290
  Knowledge Work   295
  References   296

Conclusion   299

A Call for Authors   303

Index   305

Series Editor's Preface

While the literature on police and allied subjects is growing exponentially, its impact upon day-to-day policing remains small. The two worlds of research and practice of policing remain disconnected, even though cooperation between the two is growing. A major reason is that the two groups speak in different languages. The research work is published in hard-to-access journals and presented in a manner that is difficult to comprehend for a layperson. On the other hand, the police practitioners tend not to mix with researchers and remain secretive about their work. Consequently, there is little dialogue between the two and almost no attempt to learn from one another. Dialogue across the globe, among researchers and practitioners situated in different continents, is of course even more limited.

I attempted to address this problem by starting the IPES (www.ipes.info), where a common platform has brought the two together. IPES is now in its 17th year. The annual meetings that constitute most major annual events of the organization have been hosted in all parts of the world. Several publications have come out of these deliberations, and a new collaborative community of scholars and police officers has been created whose membership runs into several hundreds.

Another attempt was to begin a new journal, aptly called *Police Practice and Research: An International Journal* (PPR), that has opened the gate to practitioners to share their work and experiences. The journal has attempted to focus upon issues that help bring the two on a single platform. *PPR* is completing its 12 years in 2011. It is certainly an evidence of growing collaboration between police research and practice that *PPR*, which began with four issues a year, expanded into five issues in its fourth year, and now it is issued six times a year,

Clearly, these attempts, despite their success, remain limited. Conferences and journal publications do help create a body of knowledge and an association of police activists but cannot address substantial issues in depth. The limitations of time and space preclude larger discussions and more authoritative expositions that can provide stronger and broader linkages between the two worlds.

It is this realization of the increasing dialogue between police research and practice that has encouraged many of us—my close colleagues and I connected closely with IPES and *PPR* across the world—to conceive and implement a new attempt in this direction. I am now embarking on a book series, *Advances in Police Theory and Practice*, that seeks to attract writers from all parts of the world. Further, the attempt is to find practitioner contributors. The objective is to make the series a serious contribution to our knowledge of the police as well as to improve police practices. The focus is not only in work that describes the best and successful police practices but also one that challenges current paradigms and breaks new ground to prepare a police for the 21st century. The series seeks for comparative analysis that highlights achievements in distant parts of the world as well as one that encourages an in-depth examination of specific problems confronting a particular police force.

Policing White-Collar Crime: Characteristics of White-Collar Criminals

This book offers a unique study of the contingent approach to policing white-collar criminals. Important elements in police strategy include information management strategy, knowledge management strategy, information technology strategy, and value configuration in law enforcement. A national sample of convicted white-collar criminals is presented, and a model is introduced to explain why there are so few women convicted of white-collar crime.

It is hoped that through this series, it will be possible to accelerate the process of building knowledge about policing and help bridge the gap between the two worlds—the world of police research and of police practice. This is an invitation to police scholars and practitioners across the world to come and join in this venture.

Dilip K. Das, PhD
Founding President, International Police Executive Symposium
http://www.ipes.info

Series Editor, Advances in Police Theory and Practice
(CRC Press/Taylor & Francis Group)

Series Editor, Interviews with Global Leaders in Police, Courts, and Prisons
(CRC Press/Taylor & Francis Group)

Series Editor, PPR Special Issues as Books
(Routledge/Taylor & Francis Group)

Founding Editor-in-Chief, Police Practice and Research:
An International Journal (Routledge/Taylor & Francis Group)
http://www.tandfonline.com/GPPR

Acknowledgments

Empirical research into white-collar criminals is not an easy endeavor. White-collar defense lawyers and criminals themselves have tried to stop my registration of court cases with names of convicts based on privacy laws and regulations. Fortunately, the Ombudsman for Research in Norway has concluded that the advantages of my research for society exceed the disadvantages for registered individuals. In their conclusion, the Ombudsman finds that white-collar criminals as previously high-profile individuals in business and society have to accept being registered and researched with names and other identification information. So my first thanks go to the Ombudsman.

Next, I am very impressed with Professor Dilip Das, who has created so many important arenas for crime studies linked to police research and practice. International Police Executive Symposium, Police Research & Practice, and this book series are some of the examples of the impressive achievements of Dr. Das. I would like to thank him for accepting my manuscript into his book series and for so many exciting IPES experiences in Turkey, Dubai, Argentina, Sweden, New York, and Hungary.

Furthermore, I am quite impressed with the publishing team at CRC Press Taylor & Francis, and I would like to thank Carolyn Spence and Cynthia Klivecka for all their support. We have never met, but in a virtual world, an excellent cooperation has been possible anyway.

Finally, I would like to thank my family for all their support. My wife Grethe has joined me for several IPES meetings including Dubai, Argentina, and Hungary, while our youngest daughter Mette joined me for New York. I am sure our oldest daughter Anne will join me one day for an IPES conference.

— **Petter Gottschalk**

Author

Dr. Petter Gottschalk is one of Norway's leading experts on financial crime and policing. He frequently comments on white-collar criminals and law enforcement in the media, such as on national public television and in financial newspapers. He has published extensively in research journals on crime and criminals, policing strategies, and knowledge management strategies.

Dr. Gottschalk has, for several years, conducted extensive empirical research into white-collar criminals on which this book is based. Previously, he conducted research into organized crime, knowledge management technology, information systems, and leadership issues. He is a professor in the Department of Leadership and Organizational Psychology at BI Norwegian Business School in Oslo, where he teaches courses on policing financial crime and information systems strategy.

Dr. Gottschalk has extensive experience in technology management and executive management, including positions such as chief executive officer at the Norwegian Computing Center, CEO at ABB Data Cables, and board memberships. He has held numerous positions appointed by the Norwegian government.

After high school in Norway, Petter Gottschalk studied at the Technical University of Berlin in Germany, where he completed the MBA degree. Later, he received a scholarship to study at Dartmouth College and MIT in the United States, where he completed the MSc degree. After several years of executive experience in business, he went to Brunel University in the United Kingdom, where he completed the DBA degree.

Dr. Gottschalk received, in 2012, the best paper award for his article with Dr. Holgersson on "Whistle-blowing in the police" in *Police Practice and Research,* volume 12, number 5, October 2011.

Introduction

As long as there are weaknesses that can be exploited for gain, advantage will be taken of companies and other organizations as well as private individuals. This theoretically based but practitioner-oriented book focuses on what is generally seen as financial or economic crime. Such profit-driven crime is categorized according to type as theft, fraud, manipulation, or corruption.

Financial crime is often defined as crime against property, involving the unlawful conversion of property belonging to another to one's own personal use and benefit. Financial crime is profit-driven crime to gain access to and control over property that belonged to someone else. Pickett and Pickett (2002) define financial crime as the use of deception for illegal gain, normally involving breach of trust, and some concealment of the true nature of the activities. They use the terms financial crime, white-collar crime, and fraud interchangeably.

The term financial crime expresses different concepts depending on the jurisdiction and the context. Nevertheless, Henning (2009) argues that financial crime generally describes a variety of crimes against property, involving the unlawful conversion of property belonging to another to one's own personal use and benefit, more often than not involving fraud but also bribery, corruption, money laundering, embezzlement, insider trading, tax violations, cyber-attacks, and the like. Criminal gain for personal benefit seems to be one of the core characteristics of financial crime.

Financial crime often involves fraud. Financial crime is carried out via check and credit card fraud, mortgage fraud, medical fraud, corporate fraud, bank account fraud, payment (point of sale) fraud, currency fraud, and health care fraud and involves acts such as insider trading, tax violations, kickbacks, embezzlement, identity theft, cyber-attacks, money laundering, and social engineering. Embezzlement and theft of labor union property and falsification of union records used to facilitate or conceal such larcenies remain the most frequently prosecuted Labor-Management Reporting and Disclosure Act offenses in the United States (Toner, 2009).

White-collar crime is financial crime committed by white-collar criminals. Sensational white-collar crime cases regularly appear in the international business press and studies in journals of ethics and crime. White-collar crime is financial crime committed by higher-class members of society for personal or organizational gain. White-collar criminals are individuals who tend to be wealthy, highly educated, and socially connected, and they are typically employed by, and in, legitimate organizations. Ever since Edwin Sutherland introduced the concept of "white-collar" crime in 1939, researchers have discussed what might be encompassed by this concept and what might be excluded. The discussion is summarized by scholars such as Benson and Simpson (2009); Blickle, Schlegel, Fassbender, and Klein (2006); Bookman (2008); Brightman (2009); Bucy, Formby, Raspanti, and Rooney (2008); Eicher (2009); Garoupa (2007); Hansen (2009); Heath (2008); Kempa (2010); McKay, Stevens, and Fratzi (2010); Pickett and Pickett (2002); Podgor (2007); Robson (2010); and Schnatterly (2003).

Most of these scholars apply anecdotal evidence to suggest what might be included and what might be excluded from the concepts of white-collar crime and white-collar criminals. Examples of anecdotal evidence in the United States are famous white-collar criminals, such as Bernard Madoff, Raj Rajaratnam, and Jeffrey K. Skilling. While being relevant and interesting case studies, the extent of generalization from such case studies applied by some of the scholars mentioned above is questionable. What seems to be needed is a larger sample of white-collar criminals that can be studied in terms of average values as well as variation in white-collar characteristics.

Hansen (2009) suggests that a distinction can be made between economic crime, business crime, and elite crime. Freewheeling predators who are not attached to organizations commit some white-collar crimes, but individuals employed by, and in, legitimate organizations probably commit the bulk of such crimes. Individuals or groups commit occupational or elite crime for their own purposes or enrichment, rather than for the enrichment of the organization on the whole in spite of supposed corporate loyalty. The origins of elite crime can be explored and then summarized by examining several criminology theories that offer explanations regarding why this type of crime is so prevalent among seemingly respectable individuals.

Elite crime includes acts committed by members of the higher classes, including those who head corporate and governmental organizations. It is crime committed by a person of respectability and high social status in the course of his or her occupation (Reasons, 2005).

Policing white-collar crime requires appropriate strategies that are put into action. In this book, four important strategies are presented: information management strategy, knowledge management strategy, information systems strategy, and value configuration strategy.

In general, police strategy is concerned with choices to reach policing goals:

A policing strategy is an approach to delivering police services based on specific assumptions about matters such as how police and community residents should interact, what causes crime to worsen, and how technology might be leveraged. Each strategy has unique advantages and disadvantages. Some strategies are mutually exclusive, while others complement or support one another. (Ortmeier & Davis, 2012, p. 29)

An information management strategy is concerned with issues such as sources of information and quality of information in police work. A knowledge management strategy is concerned with personnel and their knowledge areas. An information systems strategy is concerned with information and communication technology to store and retrieve electronic information. A value configuration strategy is concerned with the choice between value chain, value shop, and value network. These strategies may be partly mutually exclusive as well as partially complimentary and supportive of one another.

This book is concerned with crime, not with ethics. Normally, a criminal act is considered unethical. However, an unethical act is not always illegal. Byrne (2011) describes business ethics in this way:

Business ethics generally recognize that some actions performed by individuals in a workplace setting are unethical. These misbehaviors they variously refer to as "unethical business practices" or "unethical business behavior." These range from petty theft to deliberate mistreatment of employees or customers or suppliers; and they are studied assiduously to identify discernible patterns, causal connections, and possible remedies. (p. 500)

While business ethics at a certain point in time is subject to debate and variations in opinions, business crime is, at a certain point in time, always defined by law.

This book consists of two parts. In the first part, characteristics of white-collar criminals based on a Norwegian sample are presented. In the second part, a number of policing strategies are presented: information management strategy, knowledge management strategy, and systems strategy. The book also touches on the handling of the criminal justice of white-collar crime.

This book is focusing on white-collar crime and criminals, which is a challenge in all societies, because we find criminals among politicians, business executives, and government officials. While this is only one area among many crime areas, it has distinct challenges related to the identification and prosecution of offenders.

References

Benson, M. L., & Simpson, S. S. (2009). *White-collar crime: An opportunity perspective.* New York: Routledge.

Blickle, G., Schlegel, A., Fassbender, P., & Klein, U. (2006). Some personality correlates of business white-collar crime. *Applied Psychology: An International Review, 55*(2), 220–233.

Bookman, Z. (2008). Convergences and omissions in reporting corporate and white collar crime. *DePaul Business & Commercial Law Journal, 6,* 347–392.

Brightman, H. J. (2009). *Today's white-collar crime: Legal, investigative, and theoretical perspectives.* New York: Routledge, Taylor & Francis Group.

Bucy, P. H., Formby, E. P., Raspanti, M. S., & Rooney, K. E. (2008). Why do they do it? The motives, mores, and character of white collar criminals. *St. John's Law Review, 82*(2), 401–571.

Byrne, E. F. (2011). Business ethics should study illicit businesses: To advance respect for human rights. *Journal of Business Ethics, 103,* 497–509.

Eicher, S. (2009). Government for hire. In S. Eicher (Ed.), *Corruption in international business: The challenge of cultural and legal diversity,* Corporate Social Responsibility Series, Gower Applied Business Research. Farnham, England: Ashgate Publishing Limited.

Garoupa, N. (2007). Optimal law enforcement and criminal organization. *Journal of Economic Behavior & Organization, 63*(3), 461–474.

Hansen, L. L. (2009). Corporate financial crime: Social diagnosis and treatment. *Journal of Financial Crime, 16*(1), 28–40.

Heath, J. (2008). Business ethics and moral motivation: A criminological perspective. *Journal of Business Ethics, 83*(4), 595–614.

Henning, J. (2009). Perspectives on financial crimes in Roman-Dutch law: Bribery, fraud and the general crime of falsity. *Journal of Financial Crime, 16*(4), 295–304.

Kempa, M. (2010). Combating white-collar crime in Canada: Serving victim needs and market integrity. *Journal of Financial Crime, 17*(2), 251–264.

McKay, R., Stevens, C., & Fratzl, J. (2010). A 12-step process of white-collar crime. *International Journal of Business Governance and Ethics, 5*(1), 14–25.

Ortmeier, P. J., & Davis, J. J. (2012). *Police administration: A leadership approach.* New York: McGraw Hill.

Pickett, K. H. S., & Pickett, J. M. (2002). *Financial crime investigation and control.* New York: John Wiley & Sons.

Podgor, E. S. (2007). The challenge of white collar sentencing. *Journal of Criminal Law and Criminology, 97*(3), 1–10.

Reasons, C. E. (2005). Elite crime. In L. M. Salinger (Ed.), *Encyclopedia of white-collar and corporate crime.* Thousand Oaks, CA: Sage Publications.

Robson, R. A. (2010). Crime and punishment: Rehabilitating retribution as a justification for organizational criminal liability. *American Business Law Journal, 47*(1), 109–144.

Schnatterly, K. (2003). Increasing firm value through detection and prevention of white-collar crime. *Strategic Management Journal, 24*(7), 587–614.

Toner, G. A. (2009). New ways of thinking about old crimes: Prosecuting corruption and organized criminal groups engaged in labour-management racketeering. *Journal of Financial Crime, 16*(1), 41–59.

White-Collar Crime Typologies

1

There exists a variety of financial crime types. Money laundering is one out of many examples. Money laundering is a process by which criminals attempt to hide the origins and ownership of the proceeds of their criminal activities. It is a process of transforming illegal assets into legal assets. The aim is to enable criminals to retain control over the proceeds and to provide, ultimately, a cover for their income and wealth. There is no one way of laundering money or property. The process of money laundering is usually divided into three stages: placement, layering, and integration (Simwayi & Guohua, 2011).

Underground banking or hawala or hundi or clandestine banking is an alternative, informal value transfer system that is often associated with ethnic groups. Hawala banking is perceived as an underground system because it flies under the radar of modern supervision of financial transactions. Hawala was born centuries before Western financial systems in India and China. Currently, people in various parts of the world use it to transfer money. According to Liargovas and Repousis (2011), hawala and hawalander bankers charge lower commission rates than regular banks, and funds are transferred to the least developed regions of the world, where no proper banking services exist, without government supervision and little or no paper or electronic trail.

Thus, tracing transactions in this underground banking system is impossible without inside information. Penetrating such an operation is always difficult due to the emphasis on trusting relationships, almost invariably within a single ethnic group:

> The participants are generally reluctant to discuss their roles. Because the value of inside information is high, investigators should always seek to identify and develop potential informants. A sting operation is also a solution to fight underground banking. A sting operation is an investigative tactic in which undercover officers pose as criminals to win the confidence of suspected criminals or persons, to gather information and evidence of criminal conduct. (Liargovas & Repousis, 2011, p. 314)

Liargovas and Repousis (2011) studied the Greece-Albania remittance corridor. Albanians constitute the largest foreign community in Greece, and 46% of remitting immigrants reside in Greece. Remittance is a self-standing industry different from banking. Remittances are low value and often one-time activities. Remittances are sent to rural areas, where large banks tend not to be present. The money may be derived from drug trafficking, illegal arms sales, body part trade, corruption, tax evasion and all kinds of fraud, and moved as remittances through hawala networks.

Financial Crime Variety

There exists a great variety in white-collar crime. Miri-Lavassani, Kumar, Movahedi, and Kumar (2009) found that identity fraud is the fastest growing white-collar crime in many countries, especially in developed countries. In 2008, the number of identity fraud victims increased by 22% to 9.9 million victims from the previous year.

Bank fraud is the criminal offense of knowingly executing a scheme to defraud a financial institution. For example in China, bank fraud is expected to increase both in complexity and in quantity as criminals keep upgrading their fraud methods and techniques. Owing to the strong penal emphasis of Chinese criminal law, harsh punishment, including the death penalty and life imprisonment, has frequently been applied in cases of serious bank fraud and corruption. Cheng and Ma (2009) found, however, that the harshness of the law has not resulted in making the struggle against criminals any more effective. The uncertain law and inconsistent enforcement practices have, rather, made offenders more fatalistic about the matter, simply hoping they will not be the unlucky ones to get caught.

Fraud is generally defined as the procurement of a private asset or means of advantage through deception or through the neglect of care for the interests of an asset required by duty. In particular, fraud includes heterogeneous forms such as misappropriation, balance manipulation, insolvency, and capital investment fraud (Füss & Hecker, 2008).

Corruption might be defined as the misuse of entrusted authority for personal benefit. Business corruption is defined by the involvement of private companies and is usually motivated by corporate profits. Søreide (2006) suggests that in contrast to the term "political corruption" or the term "petty corruption," with which we focus on the interests of politicians or civil servants, we usually emphasize the perspective and the interests of the bribers when applying the term "business corruption."

The problem of business corruption can be exemplified by a number of scandals. An example is ExxonMobil in Kazakhstan, where payments were made to Kazakh officials to obtain a share in the Karachaganak oil and gas field. Another example is the Lesotho Dam project, in which eight international construction companies were charged with bribery after they allegedly used bribes to win contracts for a large dam project. Yet another example is the Titan Corporation's unofficial payments to the President of Benin to achieve important business advantages (Søreide, 2006).

We are most accustomed to thinking about corrupt behavior in organizations, primarily in micro-level terms. Ashforth, Gioia, Robinson, and Trevino (2008) argue that it is comforting to assume that one bad apple or renegade faction within an organization is somehow responsible for the corruption we observe all too often. However, organizations are important to our understanding of corruption because they influence the actions of their members. Therefore, in order to understand corruption, both micro and macro views are important.

Pinto, Leana, and Pil (2008) applied both views in their study of corruption. They focused on two fundamental dimensions of corruption in organizations: (1) whether the individual or the organization is the beneficiary of the corrupt activity and (2) whether the corrupt behavior is undertaken by an individual actor or by two or more actors.

To enable a better understanding of the similarities, distinctions, frictions, and complementarities among corruption control types and to lay the groundwork for future study of their effectiveness in combination, Lange (2008) set forth a theoretical basis for considering a corruption control type in the context of other corruption control types.

Pfarrer, DeCelles, Smith, and Taylor (2008) proposed a four-stage model of the organizational actions that potentially increase the speed and likelihood that an organization will restore its legitimacy with stakeholders following a transgression. Stage models are used to illustrate developments over time in a hierarchical fashion (Röglinger, Pöppelbuss, & Becker, 2012).

Misangyi, Weaver, and Elms (2008) draw upon theories of institutions and collective identities to present a threefold framework of institutional change—involving institutional logic, resources, and social actors—to further our understanding of the mitigation of corruption.

Corruption tends to have a deep impact on business corporations, business industries, and society as a whole. It has an important economic as well as a social impact. Dion (2010) described corruption from three basic viewpoints: the structural perspective, the social-normative perspective, and the organizational-normative perspective. In the structural perspective, corruption is a local and domestic issue, and so the best way to eradicate it would be stronger laws and regulations. In the social-normative perspective, corruption is common wherever the majority of people have dishonest practices and customs. Corruption is thereby not perceived as an immoral behavior because it has been socially institutionalized and tolerated by political authorities. In the organizational-normative perspective, corruption is dependent on organizational norms of behavior and may take three different forms, that is, procedural corruption, schematic corruption, and categorical corruption.

Collins, Uhlenbruck, and Rodriguez (2009) studied why firms engage in corruption in India. Building on a survey of 341 executives in India, they found that if executives have social ties with government officials, their firms are more likely to engage in corruption. Also, these executives are likely to reason that engaging in corruption is necessary in order to be competitive.

Financial Crime Categories

A number of illegal activities can occur in both the commercial and public sectors. So long as there are weaknesses that can be exploited for gain, companies and other organizations as well as private individuals will be taken advantage of (Pickett & Pickett, 2002).

Therefore, we find a great variety of criminal activities that are classified as financial crime. This chapter attempts to develop main categories as well as subcategories of financial crime as illustrated in Figure 1.1. The four main

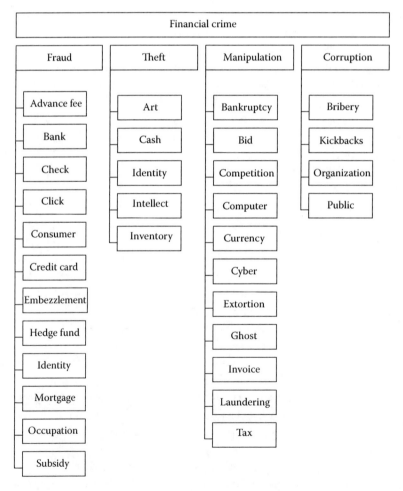

Figure 1.1 Main categories and subcategories of financial crime.

categories are labeled corruption, fraud, theft, and manipulation, respectively. A number of subcategories exist within each main category. This chapter is based on exploratory research to stimulate future research in refining and improving the categories suggested here and illustrated in the figure.

Fraud Crime Category

Fraud can be defined as an intentional perversion of truth for the purpose of inducing another in reliance upon it to part with some valuable thing belonging to him or to surrender a legal right. Fraud is unlawful and intentional making of a misrepresentation, which causes actual prejudice or which is potentially prejudicial to another (Henning, 2009).

Advance Fee Fraud. Victims are approached by letter, faxes, or e-mail without prior contact. Victims' addresses are obtained from telephone and e-mail directories, business journals, magazines, and newspapers. A typical advance fraud letter describes the need to move funds out of Nigeria or some other sub-Saharan African country, usually the recovery of contractual funds, crude oil shipments, or inheritance from late kings or governors (Ampratwum, 2009). This is an external kind of fraud, in which advance-fee fraudsters attempt to secure a prepaid commission for an arrangement that is never actually fulfilled or work that is never done.

Victims are often naïve and greedy or, at worst, prepared to abet serious criminal offenses, such as looting public money from a poor African state. The advance fee fraud has been around for centuries, most famously in the form of the Spanish prisoner scam:

> In this, a wealthy merchant would be contacted by a stranger who was seeking help in smuggling a fictitious family member out of a Spanish jail. In exchange for funding the "rescue" the merchant was promised a reward, which of course, never materialized. (Ampratwum, 2009, p. 68)

Advance fee fraud is expanding quickly on the Internet. Chang (2008) finds that this kind of fraud is a current epidemic that rakes in hundreds of millions of dollars per year. The advent of the Internet and the proliferation of its use in the last decades make it an attractive medium for communicating the fraud, enabling a worldwide reach. Advance fee fraudsters tend to employ specific methods that exploit the bounded rationality and automatic behavior of victims. Methods include assertion of authority and expert power, referencing respected persons and organizations, providing partial proof of legitimacy, creating urgency, and implying scarcity and privilege.

Bank Fraud. Fisher (2008) describes a U.S. banking fraud case. It involved Jeffrey Brett Goodin, of Azusa, California, who was sentenced to 70 months imprisonment as a result of his fraudulent activities. Goodin had sent thousands of e-mails to America Online (AOL) users that appeared to be from AOL's billing department and prompted customers to send personal and credit card information, which he then used to make unauthorized purchases. The e-mails referred the AOL customers to one of several web pages where the victims could input their personal and credit information. Goodin controlled these web pages, allowing him to collect the information that enabled him and others to make unauthorized charges on the AOL users' credit or debit cards.

Bank fraud involves purposefully executing a plot with the specific intention of defrauding some financial institution. The country of China, for example, is bracing for an anticipated increase in the crime of bank fraud. The expected rise is in the number of crimes committed as well as the complexity of the conspiracies because criminals are constantly learning new methods and techniques.

Despite potentially harsh deterrent penalties in China, which include imprisonment for life and the death penalty, for financial fraud and corruption convictions, Cheng and Ma (2009) revealed that there has been little change in the fight against the criminal element in the country. The laws themselves are unclear and enforcement practices can be unpredictable and erratic. The result is that offenders, rather than choosing not to commit crime, have developed an almost defeatist approach; they hope not to get caught, but if they are found out, they are resigned to whatever fate that might bring.

Financial fraud in the banking sector is a criminal act or acts often linked to financial instruments in that investors are deceived into investing money in a financial instrument that is said to yield a high profit. Investors lose their money because no investment actually takes place, the instrument does not exist, the investment cannot produce the promised profit, or it is a very high-risk investment unknown to the investor. The money is usually divided between the person who talked the investor into the deal and the various middlemen, who all played a part in the scheme (Økokrim, 2008).

Check Fraud. When a company check is stolen, altered, or forged, it may be diverted to an unauthorized person who accesses the funds and then closes the account or simply disappears (Pickett & Pickett, 2002).

Click Fraud. This occurs when an individual or computer program fraudulently clicks on an online ad without any intention of learning more about the advertiser or making a purchase. When you click on an ad displayed by a search engine, the advertiser typically pays a fee for each click, which is supposed to direct potential buyers to its product. Click fraud has become a serious problem at Google and other websites that feature pay-per-click online advertising. Some companies hire third parties (typically from low-wage countries) to fraudulently click on a competitor's ads to weaken them by driving up their marketing costs. Click fraud can also be perpetrated with software programs doing the clicking.

Consumer Fraud. These are attempts to coerce consumers into paying for goods not received or goods that are substandard, not as specified, or at inflated prices or fees. The growing use of Internet websites, as an alternative to unsolicited phone calls or visits to potential customers, compounds this problem (Pickett & Pickett, 2002).

Consumer fraud is a term also used with the opposite meaning, when the consumer is fraudulent. An example is consumer insurance fraud, which is defined as a deliberate deception perpetrated against an insurance company for the purpose of financial gain. Common frauds include misrepresentation of facts on an insurance application, submission of claims for injuries or damages that never occurred, arrangement of accidents, and inflation of actual claims. Insurance fraud is a global economic problem that threatens the financial strength of insurers and threatens the survival of the insurance institutions (Yusuf & Babalola, 2009).

Credit Card Fraud. This is use of stolen credit card details to secure goods or services in the name of the cardholder. Sometimes a brand new credit card is forged using known details. Cards can be stolen or details obtained from files that are not properly secured; credit card details may also be purchased from people who are able to access this information (Pickett & Pickett, 2002). Credit card fraud can be considered a subcategory of identity theft (Gilsinan et al., 2008).

One of the worst ever data thefts for credit card fraud was carried out by 11 men in five countries:

> In early August 2008, U.S. federal prosecutors charged 11 men in five countries, including the United States, Ukraine, and China, with stealing more than 41 million credit and debit card numbers. This is now the biggest known theft of credit card numbers in history. The thieves focused on major retail chains such as OfficeMax, Barnes & Noble, BJ's Wholesale Club, the Sports Authority, and T.J. Maxx.
>
> The thieves drove around and scanned the wireless networks of these retailers to identify network vulnerabilities and then installed sniffer programs obtained from overseas collaborators. The sniffer programs tapped into the retailers' networks for processing credit cards, intercepting customers' debit and credit card numbers and PINs (personal identification numbers). The thieves then sent that information to computers in the Ukraine, Latvia, and the United States. They sold the credit card numbers online and imprinted other stolen numbers on the magnetic stripes of blank cards so they could withdraw thousands of dollars from ATM machines. Albert Gonzales of Miami was identified as a principal organizer of the ring.
>
> The conspirators began their largest theft in July 2005, when they identified a vulnerable network at a Marshalls department store in Miami and used it to install a sniffer program on the computers of the chain's parent company, TJX. They were able to access the central TJX database, which stored customer transactions for T.J. Maxx, Marshalls, HomeGoods, and A.J. Wright stores in the United States and Puerto Rico, and for Winners and HomeSense stores

in Canada. Fifteen months later, TJX reported that the intruders had stolen records with up to 45 million credit and debit card numbers.

TJX was still using the old Wired Equivalent Privacy (WEP) encryption system, which is relatively easy for hackers to crack. Other companies had switched to the more secure Wi-Fi Protected Access (WPA) standard with more complex encryption, but TJX did not make the change. An auditor later found that TJX had also neglected to install firewalls and data encryption on many of the computers using the wireless network, and did not properly install another layer of security software it had purchased. TJX acknowledged in a Securities and Exchange Commission filing that it transmitted credit card data to banks without encryption, violating credit card company guidelines. (Laudon & Laudon, 2010, p. 326)

There are many different forms of credit card fraud. One of the more simple methods involves the unauthorized use of a lost or stolen card. Another form of credit card fraud is commonly known as nonreceipt fraud. This occurs when the credit card is stolen while in transit between credit issuer and the authorized account holder. A third form involves counterfeit credit cards, which is a scheme utilizing credit card-sized plastic with account numbers and names embossed on the cards. In many instances, a counterfeit crime ring will recruit waiters and waitresses from restaurants to get the necessary information from customers through the use of skimming and apply the information from the magnetic strip or chip to the counterfeit card (Barker, D'Amato, & Sheridon, 2008).

Embezzlement. This is the fraudulent appropriation to personal use or benefit of property or money entrusted by another. The actor first comes into possession of the property with the permission of the owner (Williams, 2006).

Hedge Fund Fraud. This may cause substantial losses for hedge fund investors. A hedge fund is defined by Muhtaseb and Yang (2008) as a pooled investment that is privately organized and administered by a professional management firm and not widely available to the public. The fund managers often invest a considerable amount of their own wealth in the funds they manage. They tend to refuse to discuss their trading strategies because they do not want competitors to imitate their moves.

Muhtaseb and Yang (2008) presented the following hedge fund fraud case. Samuel Israel, James Marquez, and Daniel Marino set up and managed Bayou Funds in 1996. Marquez had a good reputation and was well connected in the industry as he had been a former trader for the billionaire hedge fund manager George Soros. Customers invested more than $450 million in Bayou from 1996 to 2005. The leftover funds were approximately $100 million. To hide and perpetuate their fraudulent scheme, the managers knowingly misrepresented the value and performance of Bayou Funds and issued false and misleading financial documents to investors. In 2005, Israel sent a letter to the investors that Bayou Funds would shut down at the end of the month. He said that he wanted to spend more time with his children after his divorce. Investors started asking for their money back. Israel sent another letter to explain that the process had been slowed down by auditing work because they had to make sure that the funds closed with accurate book records. The letter also stated that investors would get 90 percent of their money back in the following week and the rest of their capital a little later. However, none of the investors ever received a single penny back. The truth was revealed by Marino's suicide note typed on six pages late 2005.

Identity Fraud. There are many reported cases in which people have had to defend themselves against claims because others have stolen their identity, using personal data, such as social security number, address, and date of birth (Pickett & Pickett, 2002).

Identity fraud is based on identity theft, which is a crime in which an imposter obtains key pieces of personal information, such as social security identification numbers, driver's license numbers, or credit card numbers, to impersonate someone else. The information may be used to obtain credit, merchandise, or services in the name of the victim or to provide the thief with false credentials (Laudon & Laudon, 2010).

Miri-Lavassani et al. (2009) found that identity fraud is the fastest growing white-collar crime in many countries, especially in developed countries. In 2008, the number of identity fraud victims increased by 22% to 9.9 million victims.

Mortgage Fraud. To obtain a mortgage for real estate acquisition by a private person, the person has to state his or her income. Before the financial crisis in 2008 in the United States, it was determined that 60% of the applicants for the loans examined overstated their income by 50% or more (Linn, 2009). Often, borrowers and real estate professionals combined to engage in fraud-for-profit schemes. Such schemes exploited the defining characteristics of subprime lending, such as 100 percent financing and weak underwriting standards. In an industry driven by commissions, lending officers were encouraged to participate in fraud schemes. The more loans the lenders' sales representatives could originate, the more money they made. Mortgage brokers and individuals inside lending institutions thus had powerful incentives to join mortgage fraud schemes by adding dirt to the loan files. They were staging loan files to include false documents as well as ignoring obvious misrepresentations on loan documents.

Occupational Fraud. Most developed countries have experienced a number of occupational fraud cases in the last decade, including the Enron, WorldCom, Société Générale, and Parmalat frauds. Peltier-Rivest (2009) defines occupational fraud as the use of one's occupation for personal enrichment through the deliberate misuse or misapplication of the employing organization's resources or assets. Any fraud committed by an employee, a manager or executive, or by the owner of an organization when the victim is the organization itself may be considered occupational fraud, which is sometimes called internal fraud. Sometimes labeled financial statement fraud, inaccurate earnings figures may be used as a basis for performance bonuses (Pickett & Pickett, 2002).

Included in occupational fraud is basic company fraud, for example, when an employee fakes sickness to obtain paid sick leave, submits inflated overtime claims, or uses company equipment for an unauthorized purpose, which may be to operate a private business (Pickett & Pickett, 2002).

Peltier-Rivest (2009) studied characteristics of organizations that are victims of occupational fraud. The most frequent category of fraud in this study in Canada was asset misappropriations (81% of cases), followed by corruption (35%), and fraudulent statements (10%). Asset misappropriations may be cash or noncash. Cash schemes include cash larceny, skimming, or fraudulent disbursements, such as billing schemes, payroll fraud, check tampering, and expense reimbursement frauds. Noncash schemes include theft of inventory, equipment, proprietary information, and securities.

The most frequent victims of occupational fraud in the Peltier-Rivest (2009) study were private companies, followed by government entities, and public companies. The mean loss suffered by private companies was U.S. $1 million. The study was based on a sample of 90 complete cases of occupational fraud investigated in Canada.

The same definition of occupational fraud is used by the Association of Certified Fraud Examiners in the U.S. (ACFE, 2008): Occupational fraud is the use of one's occupation for personal enrichment through the deliberate misuse or misapplication of the employing organization's resources or assets. The association argues that the typical organization loses 7% of its annual revenues to occupational fraud.

Subsidy Crime. This pertains to criminal offences committed when government subsidies are granted. A person or a business might provide incorrect information when applying for government subsidies or use the subsidies contrary to intentions and agreements (Økokrim, 2008). A similar kind of fraud of the public is sundry frauds; an example is illegal price-fixing cartels (Pickett & Pickett, 2002).

Theft Crime Category

Theft can be defined as the illegal taking of another person's, group's, or organization's property without the victim's consent.

Art Theft. This is art crime involving theft by burglary, robbery, or deception (frauds, fakes, forgery, and false attribution) and might involve money laundering. Hill (2008) suggests that the monetary value of stolen works of art is not as great as the value of art frauds, fakes, forgeries, dodgy attributions, and bogus provenance in the art, antiques, and antiquities world.

One kind of art theft is trophy art crime, in which some violent criminals enjoy the self-esteem, self-regard, and self-indulgence they feel when committing high-profile art crimes at specific times, often when law enforcement resources are stretched. Some examples include the following:

1. The theft of the original version of Edvard Munch's *Scream*, stolen from the National Gallery in Oslo on the first day of the 1994 Winter Olympics in Lillehammer.
2. The theft of a portrait attributed to Rembrandt, called *Rembrandt's Mother*, from Wilton House, Wiltshire on Bonfire Night, November 5, 1994.
3. The theft of Titian's *Rest on the Flight into Egypt* and two other 16th century pictures from Longleat House, Wiltshire on Twelfth Night, January 6, 1995.
4. The theft of the Ashmolean's only Cezanne in Oxford on Millennium Eve night 2000.
5. The armed robbery at the Isabella Stewart Gardner Museum in Boston, Massachusetts, on the night of St. Patrick's Day 1990 in which several Rembrandts, a Vermeer, and other highly significant works of art were stolen. (Hill, 2008, p. 445)

The financial value of stolen art varies as the market for such stolen goods is limited. Hill (2008) argues that money laundering through works of art is serious but more a matter of tax evasion rather than from the laundering of illicit drug profits.

Bowman (2008) argues that trafficking in antiques is a crime of transnational proportions because it involves the illegal removal and export of cultural material from source countries, which supplies the demand generated from developed, rich market economies. Transnational crime against culture includes looting at archaeological sites and the grey market in antiquities on a global scale.

Theft of Cash. For example, skimming occurs when cash is taken before it enters the books. Embezzlement involves direct breach of trust when someone entrusted with the cash diverts it for personal use. Lapping is a technique whereby the theft of cash or checks is covered up by using later receipts so that the gap in funds is not noticed (Pickett & Pickett, 2002).

Identity Theft. A distinction can be made between identity fraud and identity theft. While identity fraud refers to actual misuse of obtained identifiers and engaging in unlawful activities committed by impersonating victims, identity theft refers to obtaining those identifiers of an identity holder by being a thief. Typically, identity theft is an enabler of identity fraud. Identity theft is the crime of acquiring another's personal information without their knowledge. Identity theft is the acquisition of sufficient data for one individual to successfully impersonate another. It involves securing pieces of an individual's personal information (e.g., birth date, driver's license, social security number) and using the information extracted from these forms of identification to impersonate the individual (Miri-Lavassani et al., 2009).

Identity theft combined with identity fraud is the unlawful use of another's personal identifying information. It involves financial or other personal information stolen with the intent of establishing another person's identity as the thief's own. It occurs when someone uses personally identifying information, like name, social security number, date of birth, government passport number, or credit card number, without the owners' permission to commit fraud or other crimes (Higgins, Hughes, Ricketts, & Wolfe, 2008).

Higgins et al. (2008) argue that identity theft is a behavior that threatens the growth and development of economies worldwide and has been viewed as the crime of the new millennium. In their study, they found that states with more males, higher residential mobility, and more entertainment establishments are likely to have more identity theft complaints.

Intellectual Property Crime. Intellectual property crime is a serious financial concern for car manufacturers, luxury goods makers, media firms, and drug companies. Most alarmingly, according to Interpol (2009), is that counterfeiting endangers public health, especially in developing countries, where the World Health Organization estimates more than 60% of pharmaceuticals are fake goods.

Interpol (2009) launched a new database on international intellectual property crime, which was created to fill the void in seizure data collated by various international bodies and the private sector. Of 1710 entities in the database, checks against other Interpol databases revealed links to credit card and currency counterfeiting, fraud, money laundering, theft, violent crimes, trafficking in human beings, weapons, and drugs. This demonstrates the role of organized crime in large-scale counterfeiting and piracy.

Intellectual property's rising value in the production of wealth has been mirrored by its increasing vulnerability to crime. Snyder and Crescenzi (2009) found that intellectual property crime is often linked to cybercrime, and they explored the risks of crime inherent in intellectual capital and a distributed cyber environment to demonstrate that traditional legal remedies are largely ineffective to protect property rights.

Inventory Theft. This is stealing goods from a company (Pickett & Pickett, 2002).

Manipulation Crime Category

Manipulation can be defined as a means of gaining illegal control or influence over others' activities, means, and results.

Bankruptcy Crime. This is a criminal act or acts committed in connection with bankruptcy or liquidation proceedings. A person filing for bankruptcy or a business that has gone into liquidation can hide assets after proceedings have been initiated, thereby preventing creditors from collecting their claims. However, most of the criminal acts are typically committed before bankruptcy/liquidation proceedings are initiated, for example, the debtor has failed to keep accounts or has unlawfully withdrawn money from the business (Økokrim, 2008).

Bid Rigging. This is when a vendor is given an unfair advantage to defeat an open competition for a given contract. A vendor may be provided with extra information to bid low but then raise more income through many variations to the set contract. This may be linked to the receipt of kickbacks (Pickett & Pickett, 2002).

Competition Crime. This is collaborating on and influencing prices, profits, and discounts as well as tender and market-sharing collaboration. The prohibition regulations in competition laws, first of all, target cartel collaboration in which market participants in a particular industry collaborate in order to limit the competition. They may divide the market between themselves and agree about what prices to charge their customers. Prices will be higher than if real competition prevailed in the market (Økokrim, 2008).

Computer Crime. This is defined as any violation of criminal law that involves a knowledge of computer technology for its perpetration, investigation, or prosecution (Laudon & Laudon, 2010). The initial role of information and communication technology was to improve the efficiency and effectiveness of organizations. However, the quest for efficiency and effectiveness serves more obscure goals as fraudsters exploit the electronic dimension for personal profits. Computer crime is an overwhelming problem that has brought an array of new crime types (Picard, 2009). Examples of computer-related crimes include sabotage, software piracy, and stealing personal data (Pickett & Pickett, 2002).

In computer crime terminology, the term "cracker" is typically used to denote a hacker with a criminal intent. No one knows the magnitude of the computer crime problem—how many systems are invaded, how many people engage in the practice, or the total economic damage. According to Laudon and Laudon (2010), the most economically damaging kinds of computer crime are denial-of-service attacks, in which customer orders might be rerouted to another supplier.

Counterfeit Currency. Currency counterfeiting and money laundering have the potential to destabilize national economies and threaten global security as these activities are sometimes used by terrorists and other dangerous criminals to finance their activities or conceal their profits (Interpol, 2009). The crime of counterfeiting currency is as old as money itself. In the past, nations had used counterfeiting as a means of warfare. The idea was to overflow the enemy's economy with fake banknotes so that the real value of the said money was reduced, thereby attacking the economy and general welfare of a society.

Cyber Crime. Attacks on the cyber security infrastructure of business organizations can have several goals. One goal pursued by criminals is to gain unauthorized access to the target's sensitive information. Most businesses are vitally dependent on their proprietary information, including new product information, employment records, price lists and sales figures. According to Gallaher, Link, and Rowe (2008), an attacker may derive direct economic benefits from gaining access to and/or selling such information or may inflict damage on an organization by impacting upon it. Once access has been attained, attackers can not only extract and use or sell confidential information, they can also modify or delete sensitive information, resulting in significant consequences for their targets.

Cyber crime and computer crime are both related to Internet crime. The Internet is a "double-edged sword" that provides many opportunities for individuals and organizations to develop. At the same time, the Internet has brought with it new opportunities to commit crime. Salifu (2008) argues that Internet crime has become a global issue that requires the full cooperation and participation of both developing and developed countries at the international level.

Extortion. This is a criminal offense, which occurs when a person unlawfully obtains money, property, or services from a person, entity, or institution through coercion. Coercion is the practice of compelling a person or forcing him or her to behave in an involuntary way. A common abuse of public authority in some countries relates to the enforcement of road traffic regulations (or other minor infractions) where informal, on-the-spot fines (or bribes) are negotiated with the alleged offender rather than pursuing a formal prosecution or other legal process. In extreme circumstances, this can be regarded by some as the normal way of doing business. Assessors may experience this first hand.

For the first time in a published decision in the United States, the Court of Appeals approved the reach of the federal extortion statute to the operation of employee pension and health plans:

> In the *Gotti* case the organized criminal defendants were convicted of having obtained by extortion health plan participants' intangible right to have their plan trustees and fiduciaries contract with pharmaceutical and mental health service providers of their choice and discharge their duties in the best interest of the plan. The organized crime defendants were convicted of plotting to have

the health plan trustees award these contracts to mob favored companies; especially one ran by an individual who had paid substantial monies to a mob leader for support in getting a prescription drug contract. (Toner, 2009, p. 49)

In another court case in the United States, extortion victims were prosecuted (Ferrer, 2009). It started in 1997 when Carlos Castaño, head of Autodefensas Unidas Campesinas (AUC), a Colombian paramilitary group, met with the general manager of the Colombian subsidiary of Chiquita, a major banana-exporting corporation. In that meeting, Castaño informed Chiquita that the AUC was engaged in military operations in the area. Castaño sent an "unspoken but clear message" that failure to make payments to the AUC in exchange for its "protection" could result in physical harm to Chiquita's personnel and property. Chiquita paid almost $2 million to the AUC. However, the U.S. Secretary of State had designated the AUC as a terrorist organization. Chiquita, a U.S. corporation operating in Colombia and confronted with threats of life and property loss, was found liable for making illicit payments to the AUC.

Ghost Employees. This is getting extra names onto a company payroll and diverting the funds to a bank account specifically set up for this scam. If an employee can stay on the payroll after having left the company, again, extra funds can be obtained for a while (Pickett & Pickett, 2002).

Inflated Invoices. A company inflates its bills without agreement from the bill payer, who may be a customer. Conversely, an employee may arrange to pay a vendor more than is due in return for an unauthorized payment or some other gain (Pickett & Pickett, 2002). Similarly, travel and entertainment (subsistence) claims occur when claims are falsified, inflated, or there is basic abuse of the schemes. Also similar are misappropriation schemes, which involve altering sales figures, writing off income that was actually received, obtaining blank purchase orders, amending documentation, diverting vendor discounts, and writing off balances as some examples (Pickett & Pickett, 2002).

Boyrie, Nelson, and Pak (2007) studied capital movement through trade false invoicing. Data from 30 African nations were examined for deviations from average import and export prices as an indicator of capital flow. The results of the study demonstrated that capital outflow from African nations to the United States grew by more than 50% from 2000 to 2005.

Money Laundering. This is an important activity for most criminal activity (Abramova, 2007; Council of Europe, 2007; Elvins, 2003). Money laundering means the securing of the proceeds of a criminal act. The proceeds must be integrated into the legal economy before the perpetrators can use it. The purpose of laundering is to make it appear as if the proceeds were acquired legally as well as disguising its illegal origins (Financial Intelligence Unit, 2008). Money laundering takes place within all types of profit-motivated crime, such as embezzlement, fraud, misappropriation, corruption, robbery, distribution of narcotic drugs, and trafficking in human beings (Økokrim, 2008).

Money laundering has often been characterized as a three-stage process that requires (1) moving the funds from direct association with the crime, (2) disguising the trail to foil pursuit, and (3) making them available to the criminal once again with their occupational and geographic origins hidden from view. The first stage is the most risky one for the criminals because money from crime is introduced into the financial system. Stage 1 is often called the placement stage. Stage 2 is often called the layering stage, in which money is moved in order to disguise or remove direct links to the offense committed. The money may be channeled through several transactions, which could involve a number of accounts, financial institutions, companies, and funds as well as the use of professionals such as lawyers, brokers, and consultants as intermediaries. Stage 3 is often called the integration stage, in which a legitimate basis for asset origin has been created. The money is made available to the criminal and can be used freely for private consumption, luxury purchases, real estate investment, or investment in legal businesses.

Money laundering has also been described as a five-stage process: placement, layering, integration, justification, and embedding (Stedje, 2004).

It has also been suggested that money laundering falls outside of the category of financial crime. Because money-laundering activities may use the same financial system that is used for the perpetration of core financial crime, its overlap with the latter is apparent (Stedje, 2004).

According to Joyce (2005), criminal money is frequently removed from the country in which the crime occurred to be cycled through the international payment system to obscure any audit trail. The third stage of money laundering is done in different ways. For example, a credit card might be issued by offshore banks, casino "winnings" can be cashed out, capital gains on option and stock trading might occur, and real estate sale might cause profit.

The proceeds of criminal acts could be generated from organized crime such as drug trafficking; people smuggling; people trafficking; proceeds from robberies; or money acquired by embezzlement, tax evasion, fraud, abuse of company structures, insider trading, or corruption. The Financial Intelligence Unit (2008) in Norway argues that most criminal acts are motivated by profit. When crime generates significant proceeds, the perpetrators need to find a way to control the assets without attracting attention to themselves or the offense committed. Thus, the money laundering process is decisive in order to enjoy the proceeds without arousing suspicion.

The proceeds of crime find their ways into different sectors of the economy. A survey in Canada indicates that deposit institutions are the single largest recipient, having being identified in 114 of the 149 proceeds of crime (POC) cases (Schneider, 2006). While the insurance sector was implicated in almost 65% of all cases, in the vast majority, the offender did not explicitly seek out the insurance sector as a laundering device. Instead, because motor vehicles, homes, companies, and marine vessels were purchased with the proceeds of crime, it was often necessary to purchase insurance for these assets.

Income Tax Crime. The failure to comply with national income tax laws is one of the most prevalent financial crimes in many countries. The Internal Revenue Service in the United States estimated that U.S. $245 billion represents the total individual tax gap in the nation (Cecil, Placid, and Pacini, 2009). Tax evasion can be divided into three main categories (Økokrim, 2008): undeclared work/business, unlawful planning and adjustment of taxes, and exploitation of ambiguities or alleged loopholes in the legislation so as to obtain improper tax advantages.

Malkawi and Haloush (2008) distinguished between tax avoidance and tax evasion. Tax avoidance is the act of taking advantage of legally available opportunities to minimize one's tax liability. Individuals and legal entities tend to choose a tax alternative that will incur the least income tax liability. This is known as tax planning that is taking place within certain legal boundaries. However, tax-planning strategies encounter boundaries that are sometimes difficult to identify. For example, there is a grey area between tax avoidance, which is legal tax saving, and tax evasion, which is illegal.

Tax evasion is defined as the willful attempt to defeat or circumvent the tax law in order to illegally reduce one's tax liability. Tax evasion is illegal, and tax avoidance is a legal approach to saving taxes. In many legislation regions, the crime of tax evasion requires a positive action. A mere passive neglect of the statutory duty is then insufficient to establish violation—acts such as submitting incorrect statements of accounts, making false entries or alterations or false books or records, destruction of books and records, concealment of assets, or covering up sources of income constitute tax evasion (Malkawi and Haloush, 2008).

Compliance and ethics in taxation were studied by Ho and Wong (2008). They found that ethical beliefs could be an effective means to improve tax compliance, particularly for taxpayers with lower levels of moral development. Also, as tax compliance rate is found to be higher when taxpayers have a stronger moral belief that tax evasion is not ethical, a stronger enforcement effort might have a positive overall effect on tax compliance.

A special kind of tax fraud is value added tax (VAT) fraud. Pashev (2007) studied cross-border VAT fraud in terms of credit mechanisms known as missing trader or carousel fraud.

Corruption Crime Category

Corruption is defined as the giving, requesting, receiving, or accepting of an improper advantage related to a position, office, or assignment. The improper advantage does not have to be connected to a specific action or to not doing this action. It will be sufficient if the advantage can be linked to a person's position, office, or assignment (Økokrim, 2008). An individual or group is guilty of corruption if they accept money or money's worth for doing something that they are under a duty to do anyway or that they are under a duty not to do or to exercise a legitimate discretion for improper reason (Ksenia, 2008). Corruption is to destroy or pervert the integrity or fidelity of a person in his discharge of duty, it is to induce to act dishonestly or unfaithfully, it is to make venal, and it is to bribe.

Corruption involves behavior on the part of officials in the public or private sectors, in which they improperly and unlawfully enrich themselves and/ or those close to them or induce others to do so by misusing the position in which they are placed. Corruption covers a wide range of illegal activity, such as kickbacks, embezzlement, and extortion. Kayrak (2008) includes money laundering as well in his definition of corruption. The notion of corruption may be classified as sporadic or systemic corruption, bureaucratic or political corruption, grand or petty corruption, and active and passive corruption.

In recent times, corruption has become an issue of major political and economic significance when developing countries are trying to make their transition into becoming developed countries. In the past, bilateral donors, such as the United States and its allies, not only overlooked partisan self-enrichment on the part of developing country governments, they also supported many corrupt regimes in Africa and other parts of the world in return for bilateral relationship and control (Abdulai, 2009).

Bowman and Gilligan (2008) suggest that corruption may be a greater issue for the Australian public than has been assumed in the past, given the relatively low levels of reported systematic corruption in Australia. Moreover, while there may be widespread agreement that corruption in Australia is harmful and perhaps inevitable, people can find it difficult at times to differentiate between what is corrupt and what is not.

From an economic perspective, corruption is generally defined as the misuse of position of authority for private or personal benefit based on external influences. The external influence supplies benefits to solve a problem. Typically, a problem is solved by providing benefits to persons in positions of authority. Corruption, when applying the value shop configuration, reflects rational, self-interested behavior by the principal using its discretion to direct allocations to other social actors who offer rewards in return for favorable discretionary treatment. According to Misangyi et al. (2008), this approach assumes that corruption is a response to situations that present opportunities for gain and the discretionary power to appropriate that gain.

Bribery. This is corruption conducted to achieve a favorable treatment. For example, a criminal entrepreneur is dependent on a favorable treatment to succeed in organized crime. In the distinction applied by Pinto et al. (2008), an organization of corrupt individuals is a behavioral phenomenon, and a corrupt organization is a top-down phenomenon in which a group of organization members undertake corrupt actions. Corrupt actions are carried out by the dominant coalition, organizational elites, or top management team, either directly or through their subordinates, to the benefit of the organization.

Deciding to bribe is the result of a problem-solving activity. Bribery activity can involve organizations in their home country or abroad and can involve the local or foreign governments with which organizations might interact. Bribery activity differs on the basis of who is supplying as opposed to demanding the bribes, and whether public or private sector institutions are involved (Martin, Cullen, Johnson, & Parbotteeah, 2007).

Kickbacks. An employee with influence over who gets a particular contract is able and willing to obtain something for assisting the prospective contractor. Likewise, bribes may be paid to inspectors to turn a blind eye to substandard goods coming into a loading dock. If bribes do not work, the dedicated fraudster may well turn to blackmail and pose threats (Pickett & Pickett, 2002).

Modern criminal justice systems try to ensure that victims of crime are compensated for injuries and losses suffered at the hands of the defendant. Therefore, Young (2009) phrased the question, does the same apply to victims of corruption? The crime of corruption tends to be unique, and gains and losses involved can be substantial. The proceeds of corruption, if traceable, are often in another jurisdiction, thereby complicating recovery. For example, when 11 Siemens executives were prosecuted in Germany for briberies all over the world, the victims in terms of competitors and customers could not easily be identified and compensated.

Organizational Corruption. Lange (2008) defines this as the pursuit of interests by organizational actors through the intentional misdirection of organizational resources or perversion of organizational routines, which might ultimately impede the organization's ability to accomplish its legitimate purpose and may threaten its very survival.

Public Corruption. This is the abuse of entrusted power by political leaders for private gain. The corrosive effect of corruption undermines all efforts to improve governance and foster development. Corruption is just as much an economic problem as it is a political and social one because it is a "cancer" that burdens the poor in developing countries:

> Corruption works to undermine development projects in three primary ways. First, the world's poor often do not receive the full benefit of development aid because as much as 10, 20, 30 and even higher percentages of development loans are siphoned off—often in the form of bribes—by corrupt actors, such as government officials, contractors, and in rare cases, by employees of international organizations. Bribe payers in turn short-change the project by, for

example, using substandard materials or performing below specification, in order to pay these bribes.

Second, even though aid recipients may consequently receive only a fraction in benefits from every dollar or euro spent for development aid because of corruption, they nonetheless have to pay back the full amount of the development loan, often with interest. The resulting debt burdens placed on the world's poor stifle any chance they may have of freeing themselves from the vexing cycle of poverty and debt. Worse still, the poor in developing nations grow cynical of international organizations that lend money to corrupt leaders while providing little or no oversight to ensure these loans are used for the purposes intended.

Third, corruption leads to donor fatigue. Taxpayers from donor countries, along with their elected representatives responsible for approving development aid budgets, are increasingly skeptical that development projects are being effectively implemented. Pleas from international aid agencies that more aid is needed for development projects or famine relief are increasingly falling on the deaf ears of taxpayers, who perceive that international organizations either ignore, or do little to stop, the corruption that makes a mockery of international aid. (Berkman et al., 2008, p. 125)

Public corruption is found all over the world. Sato (2009) tells the story about Pacific Consultants International (PCI), a Japanese consulting firm, which had paid an $820,000 bribe to a Ho Chi Minh City official. In a highway construction project in Vietnam, PCI made the payment as a reward for helping secure a consultancy service contract of $3 million.

Corruption can play an important role in the building up of criminal organizations. Criminal entrepreneurs may expand their illegal activities by bribing local officials. An example can be found in Brazil, where the Rabelo brothers built up their criminal enterprise by corrupting a reliable network of alliances. The Rabelos' enterprise is in the cocaine business, and they have built up reliable relationships within political elites. When studying the Rabelo enterprise, Filho (2008) found that organized crime in Brazil could grow quickly because of the absence of an effective judicial system and the lack of social service delivery by the government as well as cultural factors.

References

Abdulai, A.-G. (2009). Political will in combating corruption in developing and transition economies: A comparative study of Singapore, Hong Kong and Ghana. *Journal of Financial Crime, 16*(4), 387–417.

Abramova, I. (2007). The funding of traditional organized crime in Russia. *Economic Affairs*, Institute of Economic Affairs, March 18–21.

Ampratwum, E. F. (2009). Advance fee fraud "419" and investor confidence in the economies of sub-Saharan African (SSA). *Journal of Financial Crime, 16*(1), 67–79.

Ashforth, B. E., Gioia, D. A., Robinson, S. L., & Trevino, L. K. (2008). Re-reviewing organizational corruption. *The Academy of Management Review, 33*(3), 670–684.

Association of Certified Fraud Examiners (ACFE). (2008). *2008 report to the nation: On occupational fraud & abuse.*

Barker, K. J., D'Amato, J., & Sheridon, P. (2008). Credit card fraud: Awareness and prevention. *Journal of Financial Crime, 15*(4), 398–410.

Berkman, S., Boswell, N. Z., Brüner, F. H., Gough, M., McCormick, J. T., Pedersen, P. E., Ugaz, J., & Zimmermann, S. (2008). The fight against corruption: International organizations at a cross-roads. *Journal of Financial Crime, 1*(2), 124–154.

Bowman, B. A. (2008). Transnational crimes against culture: Looting at archaeological sites and the "grey" market in antiquities. *Journal of Contemporary Criminal Justice, 24*(3), 225–242.

Bowman, D., & Gilligan, G. (2008). Public awareness of corruption in Australia. *Journal of Financial Crime, 14*(4), 438–452.

Boyrie, M. E., Nelson, J. A., & Pak, S. J. (2007). Capital movement through trade misinvoicing: The case of Africa. *Journal of Financial Crime, 14*(4), 474–489.

Cecil, H. W., Placid, R. L., & Pacini, C. (2009). Income tax crime and government responses in the United States 1998-2007. *Journal of Financial Crime, 16*(1), 97–106.

Chang, J. J. S. (2008). An analysis of advance fee fraud on the Internet. *Journal of Financial Crime, 15*(1), 71–81.

Cheng, H., & Ma, L. (2009). White collar crime and the criminal justice system: Government response to bank fraud and corruption in China. *Journal of Financial Crime, 16*(2), 166–179.

Collins, J. D., Uhlenbruck, K., & Rodriguez, P. (2009). Why firms engage in corruption: A top management perspective. *Journal of Business Ethics, 87*, 89–108.

Council of Europe. (2007). *Council conclusions setting the EU priorities for the fight against organized crime based on the 2007 organized crime threat assessment*, Brussels, Belgium: Council of the European Union.

Dion, M. (2010). Corruption and ethical relativism: What is at stake? *Journal of Financial Crime, 17*(2), 240–250.

Elvins, M. (2003). Europe's response to transnational organised crime. In A. Edwards & P. Gill (Eds.), *Crime: Perspectives on global security* (pp. 29–41). London: Routledge.

Ferrer, M. (2009). Prosecuting extortion victims: How counter-terrorist finance measure Executive Order 13224 is going too far. *Journal of Financial Crime, 16*(3), 262–288.

Filho, L. A. (2008). The dynamics of drug-related organized crime and corruption in Brazil from a development perspective. *Journal of Financial Crime, 15*(1), 49–59.

Financial Intelligence Unit. (2008). *Annual report.* Oslo, Norway: Norwegian National Authority for Investigation and Prosecution of Economic and Environmental Crime (Økokrim).

Fisher, J. (2008). The UK's faster payment project: Avoiding a bonanza for cybercrime fraudsters. *Journal of Financial Crime, 15*(2), 155–164.

Füss, R., & Hecker, A. (2008). Profiling white-collar crime: Evidence from German-speaking countries. *Corporate Ownership & Control, 5*(4), 149–161.

Gallaher, M. P., Link, A. N., & Rowe, B. R. (2008). *Cyber security: Economic strategies and public policy alternatives.* Cheltenham, UK: Edward Elgar Publishing.

Gilsinan, J. F., Millar, J., Seitz, N., Fisher, J., Harshman, E., Islam, M., & Yeager, F. (2008). The role of private sector organizations in the control and policing of serious financial crime and abuse. *Journal of Financial Crime, 15*(2), 111–123.

Henning, J. (2009). Perspectives on financial crimes in Roman-Dutch law: Bribery, fraud and the general crime of falsity. *Journal of Financial Crime, 16*(4), 295–304.

Higgins, G. E., Hughes, T., Ricketts, M. L., & Wolfe, S. E. (2008). Identity theft complaints: Exploring the state-level correlates. *Journal of Financial Crime, 15*(3), 295–307.

Hill, C. (2008). Art crime and the wealth of nations. *Journal of Financial Crime, 15*(4), 444–448.

Ho, D., & Wong, B. (2008). Issues on compliance and ethics in taxation: What do we know? *Journal of Financial Crime, 15*(4), 369–382.

Interpol. (2009). *Financial and high-tech crimes*. Lyon, France: International Criminal Police Organizaton. Retrieved from http://www.interpol.int/Public/Financial Crime/Default.asp

Joyce, E. (2005). Expanding the international regime on money laundering in response to transnational organized crime, terrorism, and corruption. In P. Reichel (Ed.), *Handbook of Transnational Crime and Justice* (pp. 79–97). London: Sage Publications.

Kayrak, M. (2008). Evolving challenges for supreme audit institutions in struggling with corruption. *Journal of Financial Crime, 15*(1), 60–70.

Ksenia, G. (2008). Can corruption and economic crime be controlled in developing countries and if so, is it cost-effective? *Journal of Financial Crime, 15*(2), 223–233.

Lange, D. (2008). A multidimensional conceptualization of organizational corruption control. *The Academy of Management Review, 33*(3), 710–729.

Laudon, K. C., & Laudon, J. P. (2010). *Management information systems: Managing the digital firm*, Eleventh Edition. London: Pearson Education.

Liargovas, P., & Repousis, S. (2011). Underground banking or hawala and Greece-Albania remittance corridor. *Journal of Money Laundering Control, 14*(4), 313–323.

Linn, C. J. (2009). The way we live now: The case for mandating fraud reporting by persons involved in real estate closings and settlements. *Journal of Financial Crime, 16*(1), 7–27.

Malkawi, B. H., & Haloush, H. A. (2008). The case of income tax evasion in Jordan: Symptoms and solutions. *Journal of Financial Crime, 15*(3), 282–294.

Martin, K. D., Cullen, J. B., Johnson, J. L., & Parbotteeah, K. P. (2007). Deciding to bribe: A cross-level analysis of firm and home country influences on bribery activity. *Academy of Management Journal, 50*(6), 1401–1422.

Miri-Lavassani, K., Kumar, V., Movahedi, B., & Kumar, U. (2009). Developing an identity measurement model: A factor analysis approach. *Journal of Financial Crime, 16*(4), 364–386.

Misangyi, V. F., Weaver, G. R., & Elms, H. (2008). Ending corruption: The interplay among institutional logics, resources, and institutional entrepreneurs. *The Academy of Management Review, 33*(3), 750–798.

Muhtaseb, M. R., & Yang, C. C. (2008). Portraits of five hedge fund fraud cases. *Journal of Financial Crime, 15*(2), 179–213.

Økokrim. (2008). *Annual Report 2007*. Oslo, Norway: Norwegian National Authority for Investigation and Prosecution of Economic and Environmental Crime.

Pashev, K. V. (2007). Countering cross-border VAT fraud: The Bulgarian experience. *Journal of Financial Crime, 14*(4), 490–501.

Peltier-Rivest, D. (2009). An analysis of the victims of occupational fraud: A Canadian perspective. *Journal of Financial Crime, 16*(1), 60–66.

Pfarrer, M. D., DeCelles, K. A., Smith, K. G., & Taylor, M. S. (2008). After the fall: Reintegrating the corrupt organization. *The Academy of Management Review, 33*(3), 730–749.

Picard, M. (2009). Financial services in trouble: The electronic dimension. *Journal of Financial Crime, 16*(2), 180–192.

Pickett, K. H. S., & Pickett, J. M. (2002). *Financial crime investigation and control.* New York: John Wiley & Sons.

Pinto, J., Leana, C. R., & Pil, F. K. (2008). Corrupt organizations or organizations of corrupt individuals? Two types of organization-level corruption. *The Academy of Management Review, 33*(3), 685–709.

Röglinger, M., Pöppelbuss, J., & Becker, J. (2012). Maturity models in business process management. *Business Process Management Journal, 18*(2), 328–346.

Salifu, A. (2008). The impact of Internet crime on development. *Journal of Financial Crime, 15*(4), 432–443.

Sato, Y. (2009). How to deal with corruption in transitional and developing economies: A Vietnamese case study. *Journal of Financial Crime, 16*(3), 220–228.

Schneider, S. (2006). Privatizing economic crime enforcement: Exploring the role of private sector investigative agencies in combating money laundering. *Policing & Society, 16*(3), 285–312.

Simwayi, M., & Guohua, W. (2011). The role of commercial banks in combating money laundering. *Journal of Money Laundering Control, 14*(4), 324–333.

Snyder, H., & Crescenzi, A. (2009). Intellectual capital and economic espionage: New crimes and new protections. *Journal of Financial Crime, 16*(3), 245–254.

Søreide, T. (2006). *Business corruption: Incidence, mechanisms, and consequences.* (Doctoral thesis). Norwegian School of Economics and Business Administration, Bergen, Norway.

Stedje, S. (2004). *The man in the street, or the man in the suite: An evaluation of the effectiveness in the detection of money laundering in Norway.* (Masters thesis). University of Manchester.

Toner, G. A. (2009). New ways of thinking about old crimes: Prosecuting corruption and organized criminal groups engaged in labour-management racketeering. *Journal of Financial Crime, 16*(1), 41–59.

Williams, C. C. (2006). *The hidden enterprise culture: Entrepreneurship in the underground economy.* Cheltenham, UK: Edward Elgar Publishing.

Young, S. N. M. (2009). Why civil actions against corruption? *Journal of Financial Crime, 16*(2), 144–159.

Yusuf, T. O., & Babalola, A. R. (2009). Control of insurance fraud in Nigeria: An exploratory study. *Journal of Financial Crime, 16*(4), 418–435.

White-Collar Criminal Typologies

2

The most economically disadvantaged members of society are not the only ones committing crime. Members of the privileged socioeconomic class are also engaged in criminal behavior (Brightman, 2009). The types of crime may differ from those of the lower classes, such as business executives bribing public officials to secure contracts, chief accountants manipulating balance sheets to avoid taxes, and procurement managers approving fake invoices for personal gain (Simpson & Weisburd, 2009).

Criminal behavior by members of the privileged socioeconomic class is labeled "white-collar crime" (Benson & Simpson, 2009). It is often argued that women commit less white-collar crime than men (Haantz, 2002; Holtfreter, Beaver, Reisig, & Pratt, 2010; Huffman, Cohen, & Pearlman, 2010). Suggested reasons for possible gender differences in white-collar crime include lack of opportunity and risk aversion.

Sutherland (1949), in his seminal work, defined white-collar crime as crime committed by a person of respectability and high social status in the course of his occupation. According to Brightman (2009), Sutherland's theory of white-collar crime from 1939 was controversial, particularly because many of the academics in the audience perceived themselves to be members of the upper echelon of American society, among which white-collar criminals can be found. Despite his critics, Sutherland's theory of white-collar criminality served as the catalyst for an area of research that continues today. In particular, differential association theory proposes that a person associating with individuals who have deviant or unlawful mores, values, and norms learns criminal behavior. Certain characteristics play a key role in placing individuals in a position to behave illegally, including the proposition that criminal behavior is learned through interaction with other criminal persons in the upper echelon as well as the interaction that occurs in small intimate groups who might be involved in corruption, money laundering, or embezzlement (Hansen, 2009).

Sutherland argued that criminal acts are illegalities that are contingently differentiated from other illegalities by virtue of the specific administrative procedures to which they are subject. Some individual white-collar offenders avoid criminal prosecution because of the class bias of the courts (Tombs & Whyte, 2007). White-collar crime is sometimes considered creative crime (Brisman, 2010).

In contrast to Sutherland, Brightman (2009) differs slightly regarding the definition of white-collar crime. While societal status may still determine access to wealth and property, he argues that the term "white-collar crime" should be broader in scope and include virtually any nonviolent act committed for financial gain, regardless of one's social status. For example, access to technology, such as personal computers and the Internet, now allows individuals from all social classes to buy and sell stocks or engage in similar activities that were once the bastion of the financial elite.

In Sutherland's definition of white-collar crime, a white-collar criminal is a person of respectability and high social status who commits crime in the course of his occupation. This excludes many kinds of crime of the higher classes, for example, most of their cases of murder, adultery, and intoxication, because these are not customarily a part of their white-collar business activities (Benson & Simpson, 2009). It also excludes lower-class criminals committing financial crime as pointed out by Brightman (2009).

What Sutherland meant by respectable and high social status individuals is not quite clear, but in today's business world, we can assume he refers to business managers and executives. They are, for the most part, individuals with power and influence that are associated with respectability and high social status. Part of the standard view of white-collar offenders is that they are mainstream, law-abiding individuals. They are assumed to be irregular offenders, not people who engage in crime on a regular basis:

> Unlike the run-of-the-mill common street criminal who usually has had repeated contacts with the criminal justice system, white-collar offenders are thought not to have prior criminal records. (Benson & Simpson, 2009, p. 39)

As part of the white-collar criminal definition, the role of class has been highly contested as the status of an offender may matter less than the harm done by someone in a trusted occupational position. Croall (2007) argues that the term "crime" is also contentious, as many of the harmful activities of businesses or occupational groups are not subject to criminal law and punishment but administrative or regulatory law and penalties and sanctions. Therefore, some have suggested a definition of white-collar crime as an abuse of a legitimate occupational role that is regulated by law, typically representing a violation of trust.

When white-collar criminals appear before their sentencing judges, they can correctly claim to be first-time offenders. They are wealthy, highly educated, and socially connected. They are elite individuals, according to the description and attitudes of white-collar criminals as suggested by Sutherland.

Therefore, very few white-collar criminals seem to be put on trial, and even fewer higher-class criminals are sentenced to imprisonment. This is in contrast to most financial crime sentences, in which financial criminals appear in the justice system typically not without being wealthy, highly educated, or socially connected. White-collar criminals are not entrenched in traditional criminal lifestyles like common street criminals. Some of them belong to the elite in society and are typically individuals employed by and in legitimate organizations.

What Podgor (2007) found to be the most interesting aspect of Sutherland's work is that a scholar needed to proclaim that crimes of the "upper socioeconomic class" were in fact crimes that should be prosecuted. It is apparent that prior to the coining of the term "white-collar crime," wealth and power allowed some persons to escape criminal liability. These individuals were characterized by high status, enjoying high levels of trust, and their criminal acts were made possible by their legitimate employment or corporate ownership.

Financial Crime of Trust

Crime of trust represents a category of criminal offenses that includes, but is not limited to, white-collar crime, in which the success of the crime depends less on concealment of the offender than concealment of the crime itself. The term "crime of trust" borrows from the concept of trust violation, which includes both civil and criminal offenses. Crime of trust focuses on the criminal and not the civil violation of trust. In contrast to conventional property crime, in which the offender may seek to avoid detection by the victim, a crime of trust involves deliberate contact with at least one of the victims. For example, the perpetrator deliberately continues to show up at work while embezzling, files the false tax or insurance forms, or signs and presents the forged check or credit card receipt. The goal of the criminal here is to gain and maintain the trust of the victim (Menard & Morris, 2012).

Next to the characteristics of criminals, the characteristics of crime are important to understanding white-collar offenders and offenses. Hasnas, Prentice, and Strudler (2010) find that federal law on white-collar crime has several distinctive features that set it apart from the traditional criminal law enforced by the state governments:

> It consists predominantly of inchoate and extraordinarily broadly defined offenses, it frequently dispenses with or dilutes the traditional requirement of intentional or reckless conduct (mens rea) for conviction, and it permits vicarious criminal liability. (p. 518)

Traditionally, criminal offenses almost always require that the accused do some harm. Inchoate offenses, such as attempt and conspiracy—offenses that are complete without the production of the contemplated harm—are the exception rather than the rule. But this proportion is reversed in the case of white-collar crime in which the vast majority of offenses consist of actions that need not produce actual harm or are innocent apart from the context in which they occur (Hasnas et al., 2010):

> For example, criminal fraud—the offense of false pretenses—traditionally required the misrepresentation of a material fact that the victim relied upon in relinquishing his or her property. This required that the victim suffer an actual loss. Federal fraud, in contrast, consists of any "scheme or artifice to defraud," which does not require misrepresentation, actual reliance, or loss, and is complete upon formation of the plan to dishonestly deprive someone of his or her money, property, or right to honest services. (p. 518)

Under traditional criminal law, there could be no vicarious criminal liability. However, corporations are held vicariously liable for the offenses of their employees committed within the scope of their employment. Furthermore, those executives within the corporation who have the power to prevent or correct the violations of other employees may be charged with and convicted of the offenses of their subordinates (Hasnas et al., 2010).

Alalehto and Larsson (2009) suggest that white-collar crime is largely understood as power and control exercised by persons in privileged positions as occupation by free entrepreneurship—persons whose criminal activity can cause great suffering among those who witness it. They argue that the roots of modern white-collar crime has its foundation in the transition from a society dominated by agriculture to one dominated by industry.

In an empirical study of white-collar crime by Bucy, Formby, Raspanti, and Rooney (2008), it was found that typical white-collar criminals might be characterized as personalities who are intelligent, arrogant, cunning, successful, greedy, willing to take risks, aggressive, narcissistic, determined, and charismatic. This is in line with eight personality characteristics that fuel white-collar criminal activity: (1) need for control, (2) bullying, (3) charisma, (4) fear of failing, (5) company ambition, (6) lack of integrity, (7) narcissism, and (8) lack of social conscience.

Greed is a characteristic often applied to white-collar criminals. Greed can be defined as socially constructed wants that can never be completely satisfied, when having more leads to wanting more again (Goldstraw-White, 2012).

Pickett and Pickett (2002) use the terms "financial crime," "white-collar crime," and "fraud" interchangeably. They define white-collar crime as the use of deception for illegal gain, normally involving breach of trust, with some concealment of the true nature of the activities. White-collar crime is often defined as crime against property, involving the unlawful conversion of property belonging to another to one's own personal use and benefit.

Financial crime is a profit-driven crime to gain access to and control over money, goods, or property that belongs to someone else.

Bucy et al. (2008) argue that white-collar crime refers to nonviolent, business-related violations of state and/or federal criminal statutes, and they make a distinction between "leaders" and "followers" in white-collar crime. This is in line with Tombs and Whyte (2003), who argue that there is a need for unmasking the crimes of the powerful. Despite the enormous economic, physical, and social impacts of crimes committed by states and corporations, they are still relatively under-researched within contemporary social science—partly because of the perpetrator's ability to evade critical scrutiny.

White-collar crime can be defined in terms of the offense, the offender, or both. If white-collar crime is defined in terms of the offense, it means crime against property for personal or organizational gain. It is a property crime committed by nonphysical means and by concealment or deception (Benson & Simpson, 2009). If white-collar crime is defined in terms of the offender, it means crime committed by higher-class members of society for personal or organizational gain. They are individuals who are wealthy, highly educated, and socially connected, and they are typically employed by and in legitimate organizations (Hansen, 2009).

One of the most famous white-collar criminals was Bernhard Ebbers, chief executive officer (CEO) of WorldCom:

> To answer why Bernard Ebbers did this, one must take a look at his personal finances. Bernard Ebbers was extremely wealthy by the time WorldCom began to experience difficulties in 2000. Unfortunately for Ebbers (and ultimately for WorldCom shareholders), his desires exceeded his income. Ebber's purchases included an enormous ranch, timber lands, and a yacht-building company, and his loans totaled over $400 million. To secure these loans, he used millions of shares of WorldCom stock as collateral. Any time the price of WorldCom stock went down he needed more cash or assets to maintain his collateral. At one of WorldCom's financial meetings, Ebbers told his employees that his "lifeblood was in the stock of the company" and that if the price fell below approximately $12 per share, he would be wiped out financially by margin calls. Bernard Ebbers could not allow WorldCom's stock price to fall even if it was realistically inevitable that this would eventually occur. As Judge Winter stated, "[t]he methods used were specifically intended to create a false picture of profitability even for professional analysts that, in Ebber's case, was motivated by his personal financial circumstances." (Wagner, 2011, p. 978)

A study in the United States concluded that two main characteristics of white-collar criminals are irresponsibility and antisocial behavior as compared to other white-collar individuals. The study by Collins and Schmidt (1993) examined the construct validity of personality scales, a personality-based integrity test, and homogeneous bio data scales as reflected in their ability to discriminate white-collar criminals from other white-collar employees. A bio data scale is a systematic method of scaling life history experiences. The sample included 365 prison inmates incarcerated in 23 federal correctional institutions for white-collar offenses and 344 individuals employed in upper-level positions of authority.

The various measures were administered to prisoners at the prison sites and to employees at their workplaces. Results show that nonoffenders scored significantly higher on performance than offenders. Individuals with high scores on the performance scale are described as dependable, reliable, responsible, motivated to perform well on the job, and rule abiding and conscientious in their work behavior.

Furthermore, results show that nonoffenders scored significantly higher on socialization than offenders. Individuals who score high on this scale are predicted to be dependable, honest, conscientious, and rule abiding and are not inclined to be opportunistic or manipulative.

The third measure was responsibility, which shares some common characteristics with socialization. The responsibility scale measures the degree to which the individual is conscientious, responsible, dependable, and has a commitment to social, civic, or moral values. Persons who score low on this scale often show antisocial behavior, and, in the workplace, higher scores predict responsibility and attention to duty. Results show that offenders scored significantly lower on the responsibility scale than nonoffenders.

The fourth and final measure was tolerance, where nonoffenders had a significantly higher score. Persons scoring high on the tolerance scale are tolerant and trusting whereas low scorers tend to be suspicious and judgmental toward others and do not believe they can depend on others.

The common theme running through these four scales applied by Collins and Schmidt (1993) is conscientiousness and positive attitudes toward responsible and pro-social behaviors and activities, suggesting that the discriminating factor between offenders and nonoffenders might be conscientiousness.

A study in Germany concluded that two main characteristics of white-collar criminals are hedonism and narcissism as compared to other white-collar individuals. The study by Blickle, Schlegel, Fassbender, and Klein (2006) examined the following hypotheses in their research:

Hypothesis 1. The greater the degree of hedonism present in a business-person, the greater the tendency to commit economic offenses.

Hypothesis 2. The more diagnostic features of a narcissistic personality disorder an individual in a high-ranking white-collar position exhibits, the higher the probability that this person will commit a white-collar crime.

Hypothesis 3. The lower the behavioral self-control of a person in a high-ranking white-collar position in business, the greater the probability that this person will commit a white-collar crime.

Hypothesis 4. The higher the rating of conscientiousness that a person in a high-ranking white-collar position gives himself/herself, the lower the probability that this person will commit a white-collar crime.

The first hypothesis concerns hedonism. People for whom material things and enjoyment generally possess a high value are called hedonists. Living in a culture in which a very high value is placed on material success and individual wealth can serve as one cause of strong hedonism. With this in mind, the first hypothesis is that, everything else being equal, the greater the degree of hedonism present in a businessperson, the greater the tendency to commit economic offenses.

The second hypothesis concerns narcissism. The essential features are a pattern of grandiosity, a need for admiration, and a lack of empathy.

The third hypothesis concerns self-control. It is argued that criminals lack self-control. Generally, criminals tend to engage in criminal and similar acts, such as school misconduct when younger, substance abuse, physical aggression, wastefulness, absenteeism and tardiness, reckless driving, antisocial problem behavior, job quitting, or promiscuous sex.

The fourth hypothesis concerns conscientiousness. This is a concept with attributes such as striving for competence, order, fulfillment of duties, achievement, self-discipline, and deliberate action.

Blickle et al. (2006) tested these hypotheses empirically by comparing results from a survey of white-collar criminal prison inmates with managers working in various companies. Their empirical test was thus a comparison of offenders with nonoffenders. Their empirical results indicate support for hypotheses 1, 2, and 3.

Hypothesis 4 was not supported. Blickle et al. (2006) discuss the lack of support for the last hypothesis by arguing that some kind conscientiousness might well be needed for individuals committing white-collar crime. Accordingly, no statistically significant difference was found between offenders and nonoffenders.

Dhami (2007) studied white-collar prisoners' perceptions of audience reaction. The study indicates that white-collar prisoners perceive the reactions of the judiciary and media as negative (e.g., punitive), but the reactions of prison staff and other inmates as positive (e.g., supportive). Offenders also neutralized their own criminal behavior.

Authority and Opportunity

White-collar crime is a broad concept that covers all illegal behavior that takes advantage of positions of professional authority and power as well as opportunity structures available within business for personal and corporate gain:

Crimes such as embezzlement, fraud and insider trading, on the one hand, and market manipulation, profit exaggeration, and product misrepresentation on the other, add up to a massive criminal domain. (Kempa, 2010, p. 252)

Collins and Schmidt (1993) apply a definition provided by the U.S. Department of Justice:

Nonviolent crime for financial gain committed by means of deception by persons whose occupational status is entrepreneurial, professional or semi-professional and utilizing their special occupational skills and opportunities; also, nonviolent crime for financial gain utilizing deception and committed by anyone having special technical and professional knowledge of business and government, irrespective the person's occupation. (p. 296)

Blickle et al. (2006) apply the same definition:

White-collar crime is non-violent crime for financial gain committed by means of deception. (p. 221)

The term white-collar refers to the characteristics of the occupational position, such as power in the executive position. Therefore, white-collar crime refers to upper-level occupational crime (Collins & Schmidt, 1993).

If white-collar crime is defined in terms of both perspectives of crime and criminals mentioned above, white-collar crime has the following characteristics:

- White-collar crime is crime against property for personal or organizational gain, which is committed by nonphysical means and by concealment or deception. It is deceitful, it is intentional, it breaches trust, and it involves losses.
- White-collar criminals are individuals who are wealthy, highly educated, and socially connected, and they are typically employed by, and in, legitimate organizations. They are persons of respectability and high social status who commit crime in the course of their occupation.

In this book, we apply this definition of white-collar crime, in which both characteristics of offense and offender identify the crime. Therefore, white-collar crime is only a subset of financial crime in our perspective: White-collar crime is violation of the law committed by one holding a position of respect and authority in the community who uses his or her legitimate occupation to commit financial crime (Eicher, 2009).

White-collar crime contains several clear components (Pickett & Pickett, 2002):

- *It is deceitful.* People involved in white-collar crime tend to cheat, lie, conceal, and manipulate the truth.
- *It is intentional.* Fraud does not result from simple error or neglect but involves purposeful attempts to illegally gain an advantage. As such, it induces a course of action that is predetermined in advance by the perpetrator.
- *It breaches trust.* Business is based primarily on trust. Individual relationships and commitments are geared toward the respective responsibilities of all parties involved. Mutual trust is the glue that binds these relationships together, and it is this trust that is breached when someone tries to defraud another person or business.
- *It involves losses.* Financial crime is based on attempting to secure an illegal gain or advantage, and for this to happen, there must be a victim. There must also be a degree of loss or disadvantage. These losses may be written off or insured against or simply accepted. White-collar crime nonetheless constitutes a drain on national resources.
- *It may be concealed.* One feature of financial crime is that it may remain hidden indefinitely. Reality and appearance may not necessarily coincide. Therefore, every business transaction, contract, payment, or agreement may be altered or suppressed to give the appearance of regularity. Spreadsheets, statements, and sets of accounts cannot always be accepted at face value; this is how some frauds continue undetected for years.
- *There may be an appearance of outward respectability.* Fraud may be perpetrated by persons who appear to be respectable and professional members of society and may even be employed by the victim.

PricewaterhouseCoopers (PwC) is a consulting firm conducting biennial global economic crime surveys. The 2007 economic crime study reveals that many things remain the same: Globally, economic crime remains a persistent and intractable problem from which U.S. companies are not immune as over 50% of U.S. companies were affected by it in the past two years.

The percentage of companies that reported suffering actual incidents of fraud were the following:

- 75% suffered asset misappropriation
- 36% suffered accounting fraud
- 23% suffered intellectual property infringement
- 14% suffered corruption and bribery
- 12% suffered money laundering

Schnatterly (2003) argued that white-collar crime can cost a company from 1% to 6% of its annual sales, yet little is known about the organizational conditions that can reduce this cost. She found that operational governance, including clarity of policies and procedures, formal cross-company communication, and performance-based pay for the board and for more employees, significantly reduces the likelihood of a crime commission.

There are a number of explanatory approaches to white-collar crime in business from scientific fields, such as economics, sociology, psychiatry, and psychology. In economics, the rational choice approach implies that if the rationally expected utility of the action clearly outweighs the expected disadvantages resulting from the action, thereby leaving some net material advantage, then every person will commit the offense in question. One of the many suppositions of this theory is that people generally strive for enjoyment and the fulfillment of desire for material goods (Blickle et al., 2006).

The sociological theory of white-collar crime postulates that managers who commit economic offenses live in a social setting, that is, a culture, in which a very high value is placed on material success and individual wealth. Both economic theory and sociological theory are of the opinion that strong striving for wealth and enjoyment in some way contributes to economic crimes committed by managers (Blickle et al., 2006).

Psychiatrists view the behavior of white-collar criminals in terms of narcissistic fantasies of omnipresence. White-collar criminals display little guilt and identify themselves with the ideal of achieving success at any price. The essential features of such individuals are a pervasive pattern of grandiosity, a need for admiration, and a lack of empathy (Blickle et al., 2006).

In psychology, people for whom material things and enjoyment generally possess a high value are called hedonists. Living in a culture in which a very high value is placed on material success and individual wealth can serve as one cause of strong hedonism (Blickle et al., 2006).

Wagner (2011) puts forward that, counter-intuitively, one way to help avoid future accounting scandals, such as WorldCom, would be the legalization of "fraud-inhibiting insider trading." Fraud-inhibiting insider trading is the subcategory of insider trading in which

1. Information is present that would have a price-decreasing effect on stock if made public.
2. The traded stock belongs to an individual who will likely suffer financial injury from a subsequent stock price reduction if the trading does not take place.
3. The individual on whose behalf the trading occurs would have the ability to prevent the release of the information or to release distorted information to the public.
4. The individual in question did not commit any fraudulent activities prior to availing himself or herself of safe harbor.

Arguing that prohibiting all insider trading incentivizes corporate fraud, Wagner's (2011) article begins by giving examples from recent cases in which insider trading could have been used to avoid significant harm. His article particularly focuses on the two most prominent arguments raised against insider trading:

1. That it erodes confidence in the market
2. That it is similar to theft and should be prosecuted accordingly

Previously unexamined empirical evidence suggests that the confidence argument may be incorrect and does not suffice to justify a prohibition on fraud-inhibiting insider trading. While the property rights rationale is the strongest position against general insider trading, it might be an insufficient basis to outlaw fraud-inhibiting insider trading.

The leadership trait perspective is an important intellectual tradition in leadership research. For white-collar criminals, we may find both light and dark sides of leadership traits although the dark sides may be the most prominent when white-collar criminals commit financial crime.

Judge, Piccolo, and Kosalka (2009) identified four dark-side personality traits:

- *Narcissism* is a personality trait that is characterized by arrogance, self-absorption, entitlement, and hostility. Narcissists exhibit an unusually high level of self-love, believing as if they are uniquely special and entitled to praise and admiration. As a self-regulatory defense mechanism against a grandiose yet shallow self-concept, narcissists tend to view others as inferior to themselves, often acting in insensitive, hostile, and self-enhancing ways. Narcissist leaders are more likely to interpret information with a self-serving bias and make decisions based on how those decisions will reflect on their reputations.
- *Hubris* exists when an individual has excessive pride, an inflated sense of self-confidence, and makes self-evaluations in terms of talent, ability, and accomplishment that are much more positive than any reasonable objective assessment would otherwise suggest. Leaders who carry an exaggerated sense of self-worth are likely to be defensive against most forms of critical feedback, and respond to negative feedback by questioning the competence of the evaluator and the validity of evaluation technique. When subordinates or peers disagree with hubristic leaders, these leaders deny the credibility and value of negative evaluations.
- *Social dominance* represents a preference for hierarchy and stability to achieve control. Dominant individuals tend to control

conversations, put pressure on others, and demand explanations for otherwise normal activities. Dominating individuals tend to be prejudiced, power hungry, and manipulative.

- *Machiavellianism* is a term used to define a personality trait characterized by cunning, manipulation, and the use of any means necessary to achieve one's political ends. These kinds of leaders are concerned with maximizing opportunities to craft their own personal power.

In summary, here are some of the characteristics of white-collar criminals as defined by our literature review:

- Members of the privileged socioeconomic class (Benson & Simpson, 2009; Collins & Schmidt, 1993; Podgor, 2007) who commit nonviolent acts for financial gain (Brightman, 2009)
- Persons of respectability and high social status (Sutherland in Benson & Simpson, 2009)
- Persons who commit crime in the course of his or her occupation (Benson & Simpson, 2009)
- Persons with power and influence (Benson & Simpson, 2009) who commit financial crime of trust (Menard & Morris, 2012), in which actions need not produce actual harm (Hasnas et al., 2010)
- Power and control exercised by persons in privileged positions (Alalehto and Larsson, 2009)
- Persons who are intelligent, arrogant, cunning, successful, greedy, willing to take risks, aggressive, narcissistic, deterministic, and charismatic (Bucy et al., 2008)
- Persons who use deception for illegal gain (Blickle et al., 2006; Pickett & Pickett, 2002)
- Individuals who are wealthy, highly educated, and socially connected and who are typically employed by, and in, legitimate organizations (Hansen, 2009)

With these characteristics in mind, we identified a substantial sample of white-collar criminals in Norway, which is described and applied for statistical analysis in this book.

It might be argued that our definition of white-collar criminals is very wide and broad, as we, among others, focus on nonviolent taking of property. On the other hand, our definition excludes violent taking of property. Some authors distinguish white-collar crime from corporate crime, for example, Croall (2007). In our definition, corporate crime can be distinguished from occupational crime, and both represent white-collar crime.

On the other hand, it might be argued as well that our definition of white-collar criminals is narrow as we only look at a subset of criminals that parallels Sutherland's initial view while leaving the possible impression that only those who are high-level executives engage in fraud and other kinds of financial crime. Therefore, it is important to stress here to readers who have had little or no exposure to white-collar crime that an important part of the definition is the characteristics of the criminals. Of course, the socioeconomic status of an offender does not determine whether a crime has occurred. It might be argued that the occurrence of white-collar crime is not contingent on the socioeconomic status of the offender, no more than a homicide is only a homicide if it is committed by someone from lower socioeconomic status because we somehow expect those from a certain background to commit homicide. However, this argument is flawed as we indeed do not count financial crime as white-collar crime unless it is committed by a white-collar person with socioeconomic status.

Furthermore, it is important to stress that these criminals do not necessarily commit crime only once. There are those offenders who are predatory in nature and seek out organizations to defraud for the reason that many organizations do not prosecute fraud offenders because they do not want to draw attention to themselves for various reasons, such as embarrassment or that they would be viewed as incompetent by others. Also, many offenders commit financial crime over a lengthy period of time before they are caught.

Sample Criminals

Several options exist to identify a substantial sample of white-collar criminals and to collect relevant information about each criminal. However, in a small country like Norway with a population of only five million people, there are limits to available sample size. One available option would be to study court cases involving white-collar crime and criminals. A challenge here would be to identify the relevant laws and sentences that cover our definition not only of white-collar crime, but also the required characteristics of white-collar criminals. Another available option is to study newspaper articles, in which the journalists already have conducted some kind of selection of higher-class, white-collar individuals convicted in court because of financial crime. An advantage of this approach is that the cases are publicly known, which makes it easier to identify cases by individual white-collar names. The selective and otherwise filtered information in newspapers might be a problem in other kinds of studies but is considered acceptable in this study. Therefore, the latter option was chosen in this research.

Based on this decision, our sample has the following characteristics as applied by newspapers when presenting news: famous individuals, famous companies, surprising stories, important events, substantial consequences, matters of principle, and significant public interest. The sample consists of high-profile and large-yield offenses. This is in line with research by Schnatterly (2003), who searched the *Wall Street Journal* for several years in her study of white-collar crime, which was published in the *Strategic Management Journal*.

The two main financial newspapers in Norway are *Dagens Næringsliv* and *Finansavisen*, both of which are conservative-leaning business newspapers. In addition, the business-friendly national daily newspaper *Aftenposten* regularly reports news of white-collar criminals. Left-wing newspapers, such as *Klassekampen*, very seldom cover specific white-collar criminal cases although they generally report on white-collar crime. It is important to understand the agenda setting and framing functions of the press and media, perhaps the two most important schemes in journalism, media, and communication studies and clearly relevant as the theme and focus of this chapter.

Dagens Næringsliv, Finansavisen, and *Aftenposten* were studied on a daily basis from 2009 to 2012, that is, for four years, to identify white-collar criminals. A total of 305 white-collar criminals were reported during those years. A person was defined as a white-collar criminal if the person satisfied the general criteria mentioned above and if the person was sentenced in court to imprisonment. Examples of newspaper accounts include Dugstad (2010), Haakaas (2011), and Kleppe (2012).

It is important to keep in mind that our data are about newspaper accounts of white-collar crime, not the distribution of white-collar crime in society, because that is not what is being measured. Using a newspaper sample is different from the population of white-collar crime cases. We argue that a newspaper account is one of the characteristics of white-collar crime as defined previously. Therefore, news reports are relevant reflections of knowledge about white-collar crime.

As suggested by Barak (2007), newsmaking criminology refers to the conscious efforts and activities of criminologists to interpret, influence, or shape the representation of newsworthy items about crime and justice. Newsmaking criminology as a perspective on the theory, practice, and representations of crime and justice is an important approach for understanding white-collar crime. However, Barak's work focused on how the media constructs images of crime. In this research, the media is used as a source of potentially objective information, from which factual information in terms of quantitative numbers is collected from newspaper accounts.

We make no distinction between prison and jail in this study. A prison or jail in Norway is a place in which people are physically confined and deprived of a range of personal freedoms. Imprisonment is a legal penalty that is imposed by the state for commission of a crime judged in court. In the United States, the difference between jail and prison is primarily a function of imprisonment length, and the use of prison over jail implies a more serious punishment.

Our operational definition of white-collar crime restricts the sample to those who receive jail time as punishment. This restriction excludes cases of fines as penal response, which is quite common. This sample restriction enables us to only study serious white-collar crime cases. Our intention is not to identify white-collar crime in reference to the law but mainly with respect to the reporting of these offenses resulting in imprisonment. If the sample would be selected as references by the law, then a number of offenses would be defined in noncriminal statutes. Noncriminal statutes cannot, by their definition, result in jail time, only in civil remedies. Thus, by taking this view, we have essentially omitted most white-collar crime cases of fines from our study because their severity is of a minor extent. Research articles edited by Gerber and Jensen (2006) suggest that only the most serious white-collar crime offenders end up in prison.

For this study, it was considered sufficient that the person was sentenced in one court even if the person represented a recent case that still had appeals pending for higher courts. A sentence was defined as a jail sentence. Therefore, cases ending with fines only were not included in the sample. Because our research is based on newspaper articles written by journalists, the reliability and completeness of such a source is a challenge in social research. However, most cases were presented in several newspapers over several days, weeks, or even months, enabling this research to correct erroneous initial facts as more information became available. Additionally, court documents were obtained whenever there was doubt about the reliability of a single newspaper report that could not be confirmed by other media. This happened in one third of the reported cases.

It must be noted that there are, of course, disadvantages in using newspapers as data sources. It has been suggested that the media present research suggests that the media present a distorted image of crime by focusing on violent, sensational events that are atypical of crime in society. They argue that the media is neglecting coverage of corporate offenses and that the media disproportionately focus on conventional crime while neglecting the impact of corporate misbehavior. This line of reasoning does not only acknowledge possible biases in our research, but it can also be understood as an argument for our research design, in which an important characteristic of our sample is that the white-collar crime cases are prominent in the media.

Nevertheless, some types of corporate crime—probably those that are more typical—maybe still go unreported more often than other types of corporate crime. For instance, the media may be biased against small corporate offenses, preferring larger, more sensational offenses.

Two methodological issues have to be kept in mind because of our decision to use newspapers as sources:

- *Bias because of press coverage.* Financial crime committed by white-collar criminals is only exposed in the press to the extent that they are sensational and possibly revealed and discovered by the press itself. Therefore, no claim is made that the sample is representative of white-collar criminals in general. Rather, there is a bias toward white-collar criminals that, for some reason, are of special interest to journalists and newspapers that cover their story. Therefore, the attribute of news coverage is explicitly added to the list of attributes for white-collar criminals, including items such as position of trust, network, and opportunity. White-collar crimes are committed by people at all levels of the social structure—all they need is the opportunity and mindset. Looking at only those reported in the newspapers, the high-visibility white-collar crimes certainly bias the results toward people at the higher social level.
- *Data errors in press coverage.* Newspaper articles tend to have some errors in them. There may be factual errors, such as offender name, offender age, imprisonment sentence, crime type, and crime year. Furthermore, there may be a disproportionate focus on the sensational aspects of both criminal and crime. Everyone who has ever read about himself or herself in the newspaper will know that there are errors or wrong impressions in the presentation. To minimize this source of error, several newspaper stories on the same case were read and cited based on investigative research. Furthermore, court sentences were obtained in most of the cases to check both factual and story elements concerning both criminal and crime.

Joshi, Chi, Datta, and Han (2010) recognized the limitation of secondary data collection in that secondary data were susceptible to media bias because of unbalanced media attention and reports about different companies across various industries. To address this limitation, they searched a wide range of data sources in terms of news outlets to reduce potential media bias.

It must be noted that journalists in Norway enjoy respectability because of their integrity and seriousness. Very few newspapers, if any, are engaged in reporting undocumented, sensational stories. In fact, during our research into financial crime by white-collar criminals, we have not found any such newspaper in Norway. Some journalists in the Norwegian financial press have developed sophisticated skills in digging for criminal cases, to which they apply robust and transparent methodologies. Every year in Norway, a prestigious prize, the SKUP award, is given to journalist(s) who has (have) conducted an investigation and reported news in a professional way. The prize is awarded by the Norwegian Foundation for a Free and Investigative Press to someone who both found and reported a good story in a respectable and professional way.

The media in other countries might find a very different public vision of the media in Norway, which enjoys and deserves public trust. For example in the United States, "it now appears clear that some prominent columnists and commentators placed that trust at risk by accepting substantial fees from Enron" (Rosoff, 2009, p. 515). Furthermore, Knottnerus, Ulsperger, Cummins, and Osteen (2006) argue that deviance at Enron could be difficult to detect because of special rituals that were an important part of corporate culture. The press, needless to say, depends on public trust.

A newspaper sample might suffer from severe selection biases that have to be taken into account when studying research results:

- Longer jail sentences than many other crime cases because newspaper articles will disproportionately discuss more serious crime cases with longer sentences.
- Selecting crime cases with sentences instead of fines will also produce cases with longer sentences and thus give skewed distribution to the data.
- The average amount involved in each crime case will be higher because newspaper articles generally focus on more serious crime cases.
- Most crime cases were committed by a group as, again, newspaper articles are more likely to discuss these crime cases because conspiracies are more newsworthy than other individual crime cases.
- A significant number of criminals in high management positions will be present in the sample, again because newspapers are more likely to discuss crime committed by higher-level employees.
- The size of the company in terms of turnover and employees will be at the higher end, and the company will tend to be profitable because crime against more successful companies is more likely to be newsworthy.

The danger of media as an information source for research into white-collar crime was wisely emphasized by Pontell and Geis (2007):

We tend to see the media as our colleagues, for in keeping with our critical stance toward the power elite, journalists tantalize us with exposés that attack the powerful. In our enthusiasm for the bounty of information that the sensational case produces, we must remind ourselves of what we know about the manufacture of news and the social construction of knowledge for public consumption. (p. viii)

Similarly, Goldstraw-White (2012) warns that journalist research is often biased, aimed at producing a good story rather than a factual report, and tends to highlight particular types of offenders, such as those regarded as famous. However, because being famous or becoming famous is part of our definition, this bias is acceptable for the current research. Goldstraw-White, in her research, applied a small convenience sample of white-collar criminals in prison who were interviewed about their offending behavior.

Newspaper articles are suitable for content analysis, which is the research method applied in the following. This can tell us a lot about how media organizations frame and depict white-collar crime, but it cannot be used as a direct reflection of the real number and/or nature of white-collar crime in Norway. It has value in its ability to examine the social construction of white-collar criminality in Norway's financial media.

Criminal Characteristics

Criminal characteristics collected for each person included gender, age when convicted, age when committing crime, number of years in prison, court level, amount of money involved in the crime, number of persons involved in the crime, crime type, position level, personal income, personal tax, personal wealth according to their income statement, organization revenue, organization employees, private *versus* public sector, internal *versus* external detection, source of detection, corporate *versus* occupational crime, leader *versus* follower, and rotten apple versus rotten apple barrel.

Most white-collar criminals are men. This is confirmed in the sample of 305 persons, which included only 26 female criminals and 279 male criminals. Thus, only 8% of the white-collar crime people identified in newspaper articles were women—sometimes labeled pink-collar criminals.

The youngest white-collar criminal in Norway was 17 years old and the oldest was 77 years. A distinction is made between age when convicted and

Table 2.1 Characteristics of Convicted White-Collar Criminals

Total 305 Criminals	Mean	Median	Minimum	Maximum
Age when convicted	48 years	47 years	17 years	77 years
Age when crime committed	43 years	42 years	16 years	73 years
Years in prison	2.2 years	1.6 years	.04 years	9 years
Crime amount	47 million kr	5 million kr	.1 million kr	1200 million kr
Personal income	335,000 kr	170,000 kr	0 kr	4,000,000 kr
Personal tax	141,000 kr	60,000 kr	0 kr	1,700,000 kr
Personal wealth	1,514,000 kr	0 kr	0 kr	62,000,000 kr
Business revenue	190 million kr	11 million kr	1 million kr	2000 million kr
Business employees	124 persons	10 persons	1 person	2000 persons

age when committing the crime. On average, a person was convicted five years after the crime; thus the average age when committing a crime is 43 years old, and the average age when convicted is 48 years old, as listed in Table 2.1.

Most anecdotal cases, such as Rajaratman and Schilling, were men in their 50s or older. This is confirmed in our sample in which the average age is 48 years old when convicted in court. These average numbers are similar to a study by Blickle et al. (2006) of 76 convicted German white-collar criminals. In their responding sample, there were six female criminals and 70 male criminals. The mean age of the offenders in Germany was 47 years. In a study reported by Benson and Simpson (2009) in the United States, the average age of common criminals was 30 years, and the average age for white-collar criminals was 40 years. It is unclear whether the age of 40 years can be compared to the age of 48 years when convicted or to the age of 43 years when committing the crime in Norway.

The average jail sentence for 305 convicted white-collar criminals in Norwegian courts was 2.2 years, with a maximum of nine years and a minimum of 15 days. The longest jail sentence of nine years was given to an executive involved in major bank fraud. In the table, there is a substantial difference between jail mean and jail median, indicating that most convicted criminals received a short sentence, and a few received a very long jail sentence.

All persons in the sample received a jail sentence for white-collar crime. Compared to the famous U.S. cases mentioned above, these sentences are quite modest. However, in a Norwegian context, these jail sentences are quite substantial, only surpassed by organized crime and murder. Also, when comparing to the sample used by Blickle et al. (2006) of white-collar criminals in Germany, there is no substantial difference, as the average was 3.9 years imprisonment in Germany in their sample of 76 convicts. In a U.S. study of several thousand white-collar crime cases, the average prison sentence was only 11 months (Schanzenbach & Yaeger, 2006).

The Norwegian court system is made up of three levels, which include the district courts, the courts of appeal, and the Supreme Court. Looking at the 305 cases we studied, 174 of them were decided finally in the district courts, 120 were received a final decision at the appellate court level, and 11 cases reached the Supreme Court before being decided finally.

The average amount involved in each financial crime case by white-collar criminals was 47 million Norwegian kroner (kr). Because U.S. $1 is approximately 6 kr, this means an average of U.S. $8 million. The smallest crime amount was less than one million, and the largest was 1200 million kr. The median value for crime amount is 5 million kr as listed in the table. This indicates that most crime amounts were low, and a few cases of white-collar crime involved very large amounts.

A total of 84 cases representing 27 percent of convicted persons were single-criminal cases. These 84 white-collar criminals were convicted alone in court, which means that it was assumed that they operated on their own when committing criminal acts. In 22 cases, there were two convicted criminals. Then follows three criminals in 15 cases, four criminals in 11 cases, five criminals in five cases, six criminals in two cases, seven criminals in one case, eight criminals in two cases, and 16 criminals in one case.

The maximum number involved in a case was 200 persons, in which an accounting firm had been fixing 200 taxi owners' accounts so that they paid less tax. To avoid bias in statistics toward this case, only four persons from the taxi fraud scandal were included in our sample as white-collar criminals: the accountant responsible, the computer programmer, and two head taxi owners.

We define four main financial crime categories by white-collar offenders: fraud, theft, manipulation, and corruption. Fraud can be defined as intentional perversion of truth for the purpose of inducing another in reliance upon it to part with some valuable thing belonging to him or to surrender a legal right (Henning, 2009). Theft can be defined as the illegal taking of another person's, group's, or organization's property without the victim's consent (Hill, 2008). Manipulation can be defined as a means of gaining illegal control or influence over others' activities, means, and results, such as tax evasion (Malkawi & Haloush, 2008). Corruption can be defined as the giving, requesting, receiving, or accepting of an improper advantage related to a position, office, or assignment (Kayrak, 2008). In our sample of 305 convicted white-collar criminals, we found 153 cases of fraud, 21 cases of theft, 73 cases of manipulation, and 58 cases of corruption.

Consulting firm KPMG (2011) tried to identify characteristics of white-collar criminals who commit fraud. They found the following characteristics of the typical fraudster: Male, 36 to 45 years old, commits fraud against his own employer, works in the finance function or in a finance-related role, holds a senior management position, employed by the company for more than 10 years, and works in collusion with another perpetrator. These characteristics are based on 348 actual fraud investigations conducted by KPMG member firms in 69 countries.

We define three white-collar levels. The first level is owners of companies, board members of companies, and chief executive officers of companies. The second level is lawyers, consultants, investors, and brokers. The third level is middle managers, independent contractors, and single-working individuals. In our sample of 305 convicted white-collar criminals, we find 91 individuals (30%) at level 1, 137 individuals (45%) at level 2, and 77 individuals (25%) at level 3.

Income figures for all taxable income are published annually by Norwegian tax authorities. Almost all 305 convicted white-collar criminals were found on the list for the year 2009. The average personal income was 335,000 kr (approximately U.S. $56,000), annual tax was 141,000 kr (approximately U.S. $24,000), and personal fortune was 1.5 million kr (approximately

U.S. $250,000). As indicated in the table by median values, there are some very rich persons in the sample, and most persons in the sample have no registered fortune at all.

White-collar offenders worked in an organization with revenues of 190 million kr and 124 employees on average. Again we see in the table that there were a few very large organizations, which is indicated by the substantial differences between means and medians.

A total of 282 criminals worked in private sector organizations, and 23 criminals worked in public sector organizations.

The financial damage of 47 million kr—the crime amount—in most cases occured outside the organization where the criminal worked. The victim of the crime was typically another organization: 247 criminals caused damage to another organization or outside individual, and only 58 caused financial damage to his or her own organization. It is interesting to note that very few (23 criminals) worked in the public sector, and the victim of the crime was very often found in the public sector.

A distinction can be made between leader and follower in crime. Followers tend to be naive and unaware of what is really happening, or they are simply taken in by the personal charisma of the leader and are intensely loyal to that person (Bucy et al., 2008). In our sample of 305 criminals, we find 175 leaders and 130 followers.

Bucy et al. (2008) found that motives for leaders are different from follower motives. Compared to the view that leaders engage in white-collar crime because of greed, followers are nonassertive, weak people who trail behind someone else even into criminal schemes. Followers may be convinced of the rightness of their cause, and they believe that no harm can come to them because they are following a leader whom they trust or fear. Followers tend to be less sophisticated and may not know or understand what is actually going on. It is also possible that these followers are persuaded by the charm and magnetism of their leader, and they can often develop a powerful allegiance to that leader.

A distinction can be made between corporate crime and occupational crime. While corporate crime is mainly for the benefit of the organization, occupational crime is mainly for the benefit of the individual (Hansen, 2009). In our 305 cases, we find 42 corporate criminals and 263 occupational criminals.

Yet another distinction can be made between the criminal as a bad or rotten apple and the criminal as a member of a bad or rotten barrel. Ashforth, Gioia, Robinson, and Trevino (2008) argue that it is often comforting to assume that one bad apple or renegade faction within an organization is somewhat responsible for the crime we too often observe. In our sample of 305 criminals, we find 112 rotten apples and 193 individuals in rotten barrels.

The average jail sentence in our sample from Norway is 2.2 years, and 3.9 years in a sample from Germany (Blickle et al., 2006). In comparison, white-collar offenders in the United States have faced sentences that far exceed those imposed in previous years. For example, Bernard Ebbers, former CEO of WorldCom, was sentenced to 25 years; Jeffrey Skilling, former CEO of Enron, was sentenced to 24 years and four months; and Adelphia founder John Rigas received a sentence of 15 years, along with his son Timothy Rigas, the chief financial officer (CFO) of the company, who received a 20-year sentence. Podgor (2007) argues that these greatly increased sentences result in part from the application of the U.S. sentencing guidelines structure, which factors in the amount of fraud loss suffered in the computation of time. Although the sentencing guidelines have a degree of flexibility, resulting from the previously mentioned Supreme Court decision in *United States v. Booker,* the culture of mandated guidelines still permeates the structure and, as such, prominently influences the judiciary. Equally influential in such sentencing is the fact that as parole no longer exists in the federal system, the time given to these individuals is likely to closely correlate with the sentence that they will serve.

Our comparison of average white-collar offenders in Norway receiving a sentence of 2.2 years and in Germany receiving 3.9 years with Ebbers, Skilling, and Rigars is not quite correct. Rather, more average U.S. offenders should be compared. Dodge (2009, p. 42) lists 40 U.S. cases involving female embezzlers in midlevel management positions who were sentenced to 30 months imprisonment, that is, 2.5 years on average. Examples include controller Carol Braun (60 months), office manager Marie Cart (36 months), bank manager Connie Hunley (41 months), and internal auditor Judith Rohr (16 months).

Despite short jail sentences, white-collar crime cases are taken seriously by the court system as well as the prison service in Norway. Also in the public, no excuses are accepted for their crime. When released from prison, very few are able to regain their positions in society in terms of prestige, network, and financial freedom. When asked what they found the worst consequence to be, whether media attention, duration of imprisonment, family collapse or financial ruin, answers differ. Many offenders seem to apply techniques based on neutralization theory (Siponen & Vance, 2010).

Jail sentences of 2.2 years on average for white-collar crime have to be compared to other kinds of crime. Murder is typically nine years, drug smuggling six years, rape four years, and child abuse one year. In a relative perspective, jail sentences for white-collar crime in Norway may seem fair.

In the Norwegian court system, there are three levels: district courts, courts of appeal, and Supreme Court. Out of 305 cases, 174 were decided finally in district courts, 120 were decided finally in courts of appeal, and 11 cases were decided finally in Supreme Court. These levels are compared in Table 2.2. One-way ANOVA statistical analysis based on post-hoc Bonferroni was applied for this analysis of three groups (Hair, Black, Babin, & Anderson, 2010).

Statistically significant differences can be found for jail sentences and crime amounts as listed in Table 2.2. A jail sentence was significantly longer

Table 2.2   Comparison of Cases at Different Court Levels

	Age	Comparison	Prison	Comparison	Amount	Comparison	Involved	Comparison
District courts	46	No significance	1.9	Significantly shorter	20	Significantly smaller	4.2	No significance
Courts of appeal	49	No significance	2.7	Significantly longer	75	No significance	2.0	No significance
Supreme Court	51	No significance	1.3	Significantly shorter	150	Significantly larger	2.4	No significance

Table 2.3   Comparison of Cases of Different Crime Types

	Age	Comparison	Prison	Comparison	Amount	Comparison	Involved	Comparison
Fraud	47	No significance	2.5	Significantly longer jail sentence	61	No significance	4.4	Significantly more people
Theft	44	No significance	1.8	No significance	10	No significance	4.3	No significance
Manipulation	48	No significance	1.8	No significance	60	No significance	2.3	Significantly less people
Corruption	50	No significance	1.7	Significantly shorter jail sentence	5	No significance	3.5	No significance

in courts of appeal and significantly shorter in district courts and Supreme Court. The crime amount was significantly larger in Supreme Court cases. This is interesting as longer jail sentences are normally associated with larger crime amounts. Here, we find that in the Supreme Court, where cases of larger crime amount were decided, shorter jail sentences resulted.

As previously mentioned, we define four main financial crime categories by white-collar offenders. In our sample of 305 convicted white-collar criminals, we find 153 cases of fraud, 21 cases of theft, 73 cases of manipulation, and 58 cases of corruption. These four categories are compared in Table 2.3. Again, one-way ANOVA statistical analysis based on post-hoc Bonferroni was applied for this analysis of four groups (Hair et al., 2010).

We see in the table that there are no statistically significant differences in criminal age when committing different kinds of crime. Different kinds of crime result in statistically significant different jail sentences. Corruption is sentenced most mildly, and fraud is sentenced most harshly. In terms of involved persons, there are significantly more individuals involved in fraud than in manipulation, when number of individuals is the number of persons prosecuted and sentenced in court.

The Case of Hermansen at Spitsbergen

The former Norwegian chairman and chief executive officer of the world's northernmost mining company, Store Norske Spitsbergen Kullkompani, has been sentenced to two years in prison for his role in a bribery scandal at the Svalbard firm.

Robert Hermansen, age 72, also faces huge debt after being ordered to repay nearly 4 million kr in what the court in Nord-Troms viewed as bribes from the Bergen-based shipping company Kristian Jebsens Rederi. Jebsens enjoyed long-term, expensive contracts to ship ore from the mines that were tied to the payments to Hermansen.

Hermansen, who had enjoyed a long career as a businessman before the bribery charges were filed, had confessed to receiving the money from Jebsens but told newspaper *Dagens Næringsliv (DN)* that he thought his sentence was much too strict. He was considering an appeal but said he didn't fear going to jail.

"I've never been in prison before, it will be a new experience," he told *DN*. "Most experiences are worth something."

Robert Hermansen was once one of Svalbard's greatest modern-day heroes. Now he faces prison after finally admitting that he accepted 4 million kr in what the court system defines as bribes.

Hermansen is the former chairman and chief executive who turned the coal company at Spitsbergen from being a heavily subsidized state company into a profitable venture, and there is even a bust of him in the city of Longyearbyen on Norway's Arctic archipelago of Svalbard.

But he ended up accepting a total of 4 million kr from the shipping company that transported Store Norske's coal from Svalbard, Kristian Jebsens Rederi, in return for dropping any bidding for the job. Jebsens secured what a consulting company hired in by Store Norske after Hermansen retired in 2008 called "remarkably long-term and expensive" contracts.

An investigation was launched in 2010 into Hermansen's dealings with Jebsens, resulting in bribery charges and his confession and conviction in 2011. "This is a relief, really, for Hermansen and for many others," his lawyer Frode Sulland told news bureau NTB. "He's humble and willing to take the punishment the court will hand out."

Hermansen, now 72, had a long and distinguished career before heading for Svalbard 20 years ago. He is the brother of Tormod Hermansen, the former chief executive of telecoms giant Telenor (News, 2011).

The Case of Røkke at Aker

Kjell Inge Røkke, one of Norway's most successful businessmen and industrialists, was spending his days in jail in Vestfold, south of Oslo, in 2007. Røkke, convicted of bribery in bypassing standard procedure to obtain a boating license, was sentenced in 2005 to 120 days in prison. He appealed but dropped it when an appeals court agreed to hear parts of his case. Røkke, age

48, only spent 30 days in actual custody, however because 90 days of his jail term were suspended.

Røkke, who built his fortune fishing off the coast of Alaska, needed the license to operate a large pleasure craft he was acquiring a few years ago. Newspaper *Dagens Næringsliv,* however, published a series of articles suggesting that Røkke obtained the license via unconventional means.

The articles led to an investigation, and Røkke and his butler were ultimately convicted of fraud and delivering false testimony. A Swedish maritime inspector was convicted of receiving bribes along with a Norwegian yacht broker.

Røkke, who controls the Aker industrial group, appealed his conviction, which resulted in a 120-day prison term with 90 days suspended. But the appeals court refused to examine the question of his actual guilt, only the length of his sentence.

Røkke's attorney Ellen Holager Andenæs told newspaper *Aftenposten* that her client thus did not see any point in moving forward with the appeal and would accept his sentence even though he maintained his innocence (Hanssen, 2007).

Theoretical Perspectives

It is difficult to overstate the importance of theory to preventive understanding of white-collar crime. Theory allows analysts to understand and predict outcomes on a basis of probability (Colquitt & Zapata-Phelan, 2007). Theory also allows analysts to describe and explain a process or sequence of events. Theory prevents analysts from being bewildered by the complexity of the real world by providing a linguistic tool for organizing a coherent understanding of the real world.

Accordingly, theory acts as an educational device that creates insights into criminal phenomena:

> A theory might be a prediction or explanation, a set of interrelated constructs, definitions, and propositions that presents a systematic view of phenomena by specifying relations among variables, with the purpose of explaining natural phenomena. The systematic view might be an argument, a discussion, or a rationale, and it helps to explain or predict phenomena that occur in the world. Some define theory in terms of relationships between independent and dependent variables, where theory is a collection of assertions, both verbal and symbolic, that identifies what variables are important and for what reasons, and that specifies how they are interrelated and why. It identifies the conditions under which variables should be related or not related. Other scholars have defined theory in terms of narratives and accounts. (Colquitt & Zapata-Phelan, 2007)

Sutton and Staw (1995) define theory in the following way:

> Theory is about the connections among phenomena, a story about why acts, events, structure, and thoughts occur. Theory emphasizes the nature of causal relationships, identifying what comes first as well as the timing of such events. Strong theory, in our view, probes underlying processes so as to understand the systematic reasons for a particular occurrence or nonoccurrence. It often burrows deeply into microprocesses, laterally into neighboring concepts, or in an upward direction, tying itself to broader social phenomena. It usually is laced with a set of convincing and logically interconnected arguments. It can have implications that we have not seen with our naked (or theoretically unassisted) eye. It may have implications that run counter to our common sense. (p. 378)

Theory is based on abstraction, representation, and refinement of general principles that apply across multiple situations. Constructs applied in theory should be precisely defined, used in a clearly explained and appropriate context, draw strength from their location within relevant semantic relationships, and cohere together in a logically consistent manner (Thompson, 2011).

In conformity with the managerial perspective in business literature, which highlights the role of managers as agents in deciding enterprise strategies and operations (Lopez-Rodriguez, 2009), as well as leading the activities required to implement corporate priorities, managers can develop and implement both legal and illegal strategies. Managers' perceptions and interpretations determine their commitment to certain goals over other goals (subgoals).

Profit-driven crime by criminal business enterprises should be understood mainly in economic rather than sociological or criminological terms. In an attempt to formulate a general *theory of profit-driven crime*, Naylor (2003) proposed a typology that shifts the focus from actors to actions by distinguishing between market crime, predatory crime, and commercial crime.

The theory of profit-driven crime suggests that financial crimes are opportunity driven, in which executives and managers identify opportunities for illegal gain. Opportunity is a flexible characteristic of financial crime and varies depending on the type of criminals involved (Michel, 2008).

Learning theories have been used to explain the onset of criminal activity. The body of research on learning theory stresses the attitudes, abilities, values, and behaviors needed to maintain a criminal career (Lyman & Potter, 2007).

Cultural deviance theories are based on the assumption that, for example, slum dwellers violate the law because they belong to a unique subculture that exists in lower-class areas. The subculture's values and norms conflict with those of the higher class on which criminal law is based (Lyman & Potter, 2007).

Entrepreneurial theory can be applied to white-collar crime, whereupon we look at the dark side of entrepreneurialism. To understand entrepreneurial behavior by white-collar criminals, important behavioral areas include modus essendi, modus operandi, and modus vivendi. Modus essendi is a philosophical term relating to modes of being. Modus operandi is method of operating, which is an accepted criminological concept for classifying generic human actions from their visible and consequential manifestations. Modus vivendi represents the shared symbiotic relationship between different entrepreneurial directions (Smith, 2009).

References

Alalehto, T., & Larsson, D. (2009). The roots of modern white-collar crime: Does the modern form of white-collar crime have its foundation in the transition from a society dominated by agriculture to one dominated by industry? *Critical Criminology, 17*, 183–193.

Ashforth, B. E., Gioia, D. A., Robinson, S. L., & Trevino, L. K. (2008). Re-reviewing organizational corruption. *The Academy of Management Review, 33*(3), 670–684.

Barak, G. (2007). Doing newsmaking criminology from within the academy. *Theoretical Criminology, 11*(2), 191–207.

Benson, M. L., & Simpson, S. S. (2009). *White-collar crime: An opportunity perspective, criminology and justice series.* New York: Routledge.

Blickle, G., Schlegel, A., Fassbender, P., & Klein, U. (2006). Some personality correlates of business white-collar crime. *Applied Psychology: An International Review, 55*(2), 220–233.

Brightman, H. J. (2009). *Today's white-collar crime: Legal, investigative, and theoretical perspectives,* New York: Routledge, Taylor & Francis Group.

Brisman, A. (2010). "Creative crime" and the phytological analogy. *Crime Media Culture, 6*(2), 205–225.

Bucy, P. H., Formby, E. P., Raspanti, M. S., & Rooney, K. E. (2008). Why do they do it? The motives, mores, and character of white collar criminals. *St. John's Law Review, 82*(2), 401–571.

Collins, J. M., & Schmidt, F. L. (1993). Personality, integrity, and white collar crime: A construct validity study. *Personnel Psychology, 46*(2), 295–311.

Colquitt, J. A., & Zapata-Phelan, C. P. (2007). Trends in theory building and theory testing: A five-decade study of the Academy of Management Journal. *Academy of Management Journal, 50*(6), 1281–1303.

Croall, H. (2007). *Victims, crime and society.* Los Angeles: Sage.

Dhami, M. (2007). White collar prisoners' perceptions of audience reaction. *Deviant Behavior, 28*, 57–77.

Dodge, M. (2009). *Women and white collar crime.* New York: Prentice Hall.

Dugstad, L. (December 28, 2010). Ber om politietterforsking (Asks for police investigation). *Dagens Næringsliv* (Norwegian Business Newspaper), p. 6.

Eicher, S. (2009). Government for hire. In S. Eicher (Ed.), *Corruption in international business: The challenge of cultural and legal diversity.* Farnham, England: Gower Applied Business Research, Ashgate Publishing Limited.

Gerber, J., & Jensen, E. L. (2006). *Encyclopedia of white-collar crime.* Westport, CT: Greenwood.

Goldstraw-White, J. (2012). *White-collar crime: Accounts of offending behaviour.* London: Palgrave Macmillan Publishing.

Haakaas, E. (September 2, 2011). Fylte konas konto med kundepenger (Filled wife's account with customer money). *Aftenposten* (Norwegian national daily newspaper, Business section), p. 16.

Haantz, S. (2002). *Women and white collar crime,* National White Collar Crime Center, Retrieved from www.nw3c.org

Hair, J. F., Black, W. C., Babin, B. J., & Anderson, R. E. (2010). *Multivariate data analysis* (7th ed.). Upper Saddle River, NJ: Pearson Education.

Hansen, L. L. (2009). Corporate financial crime: Social diagnosis and treatment. *Journal of Financial Crime, 16*(1), 28–40.

Hanssen, I. D. (April 21, 2007). Røkke vedtar dommen (Røkke agrees to sentence), *Aftenposten.* Retrieved from www.aftenposten.no

Hasnas, J., Prentice, R., & Strudler, A. (2010). New directions in legal scholarship: Implications for business ethics research, theory, and practice. *Business Ethics Quarterly, 20*(3), 503–531.

Henning, J. (2009). Perspectives on financial crimes in Roman-Dutch law: Bribery, fraud and the general crime of falsity. *Journal of Financial Crime, 16*(4), 295–304.

Hill, C. (2008). Art crime and the Wealth of Nations. *Journal of Financial Crime, 15*(4), 444–448.

Holtfreter, K., Beaver, K. M., Reisig, M. D., & Pratt, T. C. (2010). Low self-control and fraud offending. *Journal of Financial Crime, 17*(3), 295–307.

Huffman, M. L., Cohen, P. N., & Pearlman, J. (2010). Engendering change: Organizational dynamics and workplace gender desegregation. *Administrative Science Quarterly, 55*, 255–277.

Joshi, K. D., Chi, L., Datta, A., & Han, S. (2010). Changing the competitive landscape: Continuous innovation through IT-enabled knowledge capabilities. *Information Systems Research, 21*(3), 472–495.

Judge, T. A., Piccolo, R. F., & Kosalka, T. (2009). The bright and dark sides of leader traits: A review and theoretical extension of the leader trait paradigm. *The Leadership Quarterly, 20*, 855–875.

Kayrak, M. (2008). Evolving challenges for supreme audit institutions in struggling with corruption. *Journal of Financial Crime, 15*(1), 60–70.

Kempa, M. (2010). Combating white-collar crime in Canada: Serving victim needs and market integrity. *Journal of Financial Crime, 17*(2), 251–264.

Kleppe, M. K. (February 1, 2012). Tromsdal tiltalt for ti luksusbilbedragerier (Tromsdal charged for ten luxury car frauds). *Finansavisen* (Norwegian financial newspaper), pp. 16–17.

Knottnerus, J. D., Ulsperger, J. S., Cummins, S., & Osteen, E. (2006). Exposing Enron: Media representations of ritualized deviance in corporate culture. *Crime Media Culture, 2*(2), 177–195.

KPMG. (2011). *Who is the typical fraudster?* Retrieved from www.kpmg.com

Lopez-Rodriguez, S. (2009). Environmental engagement, organizational capability and firm performance. *Corporate Governance, 9*(4), 400–408.

Lyman, M. D., & Potter, G. W. (2007). *Organized crime* (4th ed.). Upper Saddle River, NJ: Pearson Prentice Hall.

Malkawi, B. H., & Haloush, H. A. (2008). The case of income tax evasion in Jordan: Symptoms and solutions. *Journal of Financial Crime, 15*(3), 282–294.

Menard, S., & Morris, R. G. (2012). Integrated theory and crimes of trust. *Journal of Quantitative Criminology, 28*(2), 365–387.

Michel, P. (2008). Financial crimes: The constant challenge of seeking effective prevention solutions. *Journal of Financial Crime, 15*(4), 383–397.

Naylor, R. T. (2003). Towards a general theory of profit-driven crimes. *British Journal of Criminology, 43*, 81–101.

News. 2011. *Convicted executive faces two years in prison, Norway International Network*, published October 5, 2011. Retrieved from www.newsinenglish.no

Pickett, K. H. S., & Pickett, J. M. (2002). *Financial crime investigation and control.* New York: John Wiley & Sons.

Podgor, E. S. (2007). The challenge of white collar sentencing. *Journal of Criminal Law and Criminology, 97*(3), 1–10.

Pontell, H. N., & Geis, G. (2007). *International handbook of white-collar and corporate crime.* New York: Springer.

Rosoff, S. M. (2009). The role of the mass media in the Enron fraud. In H. N. Pontell & G. Geis (Eds.), *International handbook of white-collar and corporate crime.* New York: Springer.

Schanzenbach, M., & Yeager, M. L. (2006). Prison time, fines and federal white-collar criminals: The anatomy of racial disparity. *Journal of Criminal Law and Criminology, 96*(2), 757–793.

Schnatterly, K. (2003). Increasing firm value through detection and prevention of white-collar crime. *Strategic Management Journal, 24*(7), 587–614.

Simpson, S. S., & Weisburd, D. (Eds.). (2009). *The criminology of white-collar crime.* New York: Springer.

Siponen, M., & Vance, A. (2010). Neutralization: New insights into the problem of employee information systems security policy violations. *MIS Quarterly, 34*(3), 487–502.

Smith, R. (2009). Understanding entrepreneural behavior in organized criminals. *Journal of Enterprising Communities: People and Places in the Global Economy, 3*(3), 256–268.

Sutherland, E. H. (1949). *White collar crime.* New York: Holt Rinehart and Winston.

Sutton, R. I., & Staw, B. M. (1995). What theory is not. *Administrative Science Quarterly, 40*, 371–384.

Thompson, M. (2011). Ontological shift or ontological drift? Reality claims, epistemological frameworks, and theory generation in organization studies. *Academy of Management Review, 36*(4), 754–773.

Tombs, S., & Whyte, D. (2003). Scrutinizing the powerful: Crime, contemporary political economy, and critical social research. In S. Tombs & D. Whyte (Eds.), *Unmasking the crimes of the powerful* (pp. 3–48). New York: Lang.

Tombs, S., & Whyte, D. (2007). *Safety Crimes.* Portland, OR: Willan Publishing.

Wagner, R. E. (2011). Gordon Gekko to the rescue? Insider trading as a tool to combat accounting fraud. *University of Cincinnati Law Review, 79*, 973–993.

White-Collar Criminal Roles

3

Largely, individuals or small groups in connection with their jobs commit occupational crime. It includes embezzling from an employer, theft of merchandise, income tax evasion, manipulation of sales, fraud, and violations in the sale of securities (Bookman, 2008). Occupational crime is sometimes labeled elite crime. Hansen (2009) argues that the problem with occupational crime is that it is committed within the confines of positions of trust and in organizations, which prohibits surveillance and accountability. Heath (2008) found that the bigger and more severe occupational crime tends to be committed by individuals who are further up the chain of command in the firm.

Corporate crime, on the other hand, is enacted by collectives or aggregates of discrete individuals. If a corporate official violates the law in acting for the corporation, it is considered a corporate crime as well. But if he or she gains personal benefit in the commission of a crime against the corporation, it is occupational crime. A corporation cannot be jailed and, therefore, the majority of penalties to control individual violators are not available for corporations and corporate crime (Bookman, 2008).

Corporate versus Occupational

Bookman (2008) regards Sutherland's original definition of white-collar crime as too restrictive and suggests that white-collar crime is an illegal act committed by nonphysical means and by concealment or guile to obtain money or property, to avoid payment or loss of money or property, or to obtain business or personal advantage. Furthermore, scholars have attempted to differentiate white-collar crime into two types: occupational and corporate. By and large, individuals or small groups in connection with their jobs commit occupational crime. This includes embezzlement from an employer; theft of merchandise; income tax evasion; and manipulation of sales, fraud, and violations in the sale of securities. Corporate crime, on the other hand, is enacted by collectivities or aggregates of discrete individuals.

According to Hansen (2009), individuals or groups commit occupational or elite crime for their own purposes or enrichment, rather than for the enrichment of the organization on a whole, in spite of supposed corporate loyalty.

White-collar crime occurs typically at higher levels in business. It is crime committed by a corporate manager, a high-ranking technical specialist, a procurement manager, an official representative of a corporation, or the owner of a corporation. Included in this term are both the possibility that the white-collar offender acted self-servingly to further private interests or the interests of a group of persons in a corporation that is typically labeled occupational crime and the possibility that the person may have acted on behalf of the corporation with the intention of protecting or enhancing the interests of the corporation (Blickle, Schlegel, Fassbender & Klein 2006).

As has been previously mentioned, there is a distinction to be made between the labels "occupational crime" and "corporate crime." Occupational crime can also be referred to as elite crime. Hansen (2009) contends that one of the issues that develops with occupational crime is that the crimes are committed by people who occupy positions of trust within organizations. The levels of confidence that these people have garnered often result in less scrutiny of their actions and higher amounts of responsibility. Heath (2008) reported occupational crimes that are greater and more serious in scope are often committed by persons who occupy the upper levels of the firm's hierarchy.

If an executive working for a corporation breaks the law while acting in a corporate capacity, then this can also be considered a corporate crime. However, if a company official somehow profits personally during the commission of a crime against the corporation itself, it is then classified as occupational crime. Because a corporation as an entity cannot be held responsible or imprisoned, most of the penalties put in place to deter people from violating the law are not options when it comes to corporations and corporate crime (Bookman, 2008). Simpson (2011) argues that thinking about corporate crime requires recognition that both organizations and individuals may be illegal actors and potential targets for crime prevention and control, such as sanctions.

Corporate crime occurs when, for example, fraud is being committed on behalf of an organization; that is, the crime is being committed to benefit the business. Other crimes would be classified as against an organization for example, occupational fraud. Perri and Brody (2011) argue that corporate crime is rationalized as a behavior acceptable to overcome financial difficulties or to make a profit for the business, and occupational crime is rationalized in other ways: I am borrowing the money and will pay it back, or the company owes me money that I never received but deserve.

Fleet and Fleet (2006) argue that corporate crime is committed by higher-ranking officers:

> Corporate crime refers to those crimes committed by members of an organization to benefit the organization. White-collar crime refers to those crimes committed by higher-ranking members of an organization to benefit themselves. Occupational or employee crime refers to those crimes committed by members of an organization (generally lower ranking) that are intended to benefit the perpetrators to the detriment of the organization.

In legal terms, a corporation is an unnatural person:

> Corporate personality functions between an insentient, inanimate object and a direct manifestation of the acts and intentions of its managers. Nowhere is this duality more problematic than in the application of traditional concepts of criminal law to business organizations. The question of whether business organizations can be criminally liable—and if so, the parameters of such liability—has long been the subject of scholarly debate. Whatever the merits of such debate, however, pragmatic considerations have led courts and legislatures to expand the panoply of corporate crime in order to deter conduct ranging from reprehensible, to undesirable, to merely annoying. In the context of organizational behavior, criminal law is the ultimate deterrent. (Robson, 2010, p. 109)

Corporations become victims of crime when they suffer a loss as a result of an offense committed by a third party, including employees and managers. Corporations become perpetrators of crime when managers or employees commit financial crime within the context of a legal organization. According to Garoupa (2007), corporations can more easily corrupt enforcers, regulators, and judges as compared to individuals. Corporations are better organized, are wealthier, and benefit from economies of scale in corruption. Corporations are better placed to manipulate politicians and the media. By making use of large grants, generous campaign contributions, and influential lobbying organizations, they may push law changes and legal reforms that benefit their illegal activities.

Occupational crime is typically motivated by greed, by which white-collar criminals seek to enrich themselves personally. Similarly, firms engage in corporate crime to improve their financial performance. Employees break the law in ways that enhance the profits of the firm but which may generate very little or no personal benefit for themselves when committing corporate crime:

> There is an important difference, for instance, between the crimes committed at Enron by Andrew Fastow, who secretly enriched himself at the expense of the firm, and those committed by Kenneth Lay and Jeffrey Skilling, who for the most part acted in ways that enriched the firm, and themselves only indirectly (via high stock price). (Heath, 2008, p. 600)

While legal corporations may commit business crime, illegal organizations are in the business of committing crime. Garoupa (2007) emphasized the following differences between organized crime and business crime: (i) Organized crime is carried out by illegal firms (with no legal status), the criminal market being their primary market and legitimate markets secondary markets; (ii) corporate crime is carried out by legal firms (with legal status), the legitimate market being their primary market and the criminal market their secondary market. Whereas organized crime exists to capitalize on criminal rents and illegal activities, corporations do not exist to violate the law. Organized crime gets into legitimate markets in order to improve its standing in the criminal market, and corporations violate the law so as to improve their standing in legitimate markets.

Criminal opportunities are now recognized as an important cause of all crime. Without an opportunity, there cannot be a crime. Opportunities are important causes of white-collar crime, in which the opportunity structures may be different from those of other kinds of crime. These differences create special difficulties for control, but they also provide new openings for control (Benson & Simpson, 2009).

While occupational crime is associated with bad apples, corporate crime is associated with systems failure. The bad apples theory represents an individualistic approach in criminology, and the systems failure theory represents a business approach in criminology:

> If the individualistic approach were correct, then one would expect to find a fairly random distribution of white collar crime throughout various sectors of the economy, depending upon where individuals suffering from poor character or excess greed wound up working. Yet, what one finds instead are very high concentrations of criminal activity in particular sectors of the economy. Furthermore, these pockets of crime often persist quite stubbornly over time, despite a complete changeover in the personnel involved. (Heath, 2008, p. 601)

Similar to the distinction between corporate and occupational crime is the distinction made by Simpson (2011) between those kinds of crime committed by companies and their managers to achieve the goals of the business, and offenses committed by individuals that may or may not involve organizational or business resources but tend to be tied more to self-interest.

Corporate Crime Theories

The *institutional theory* of morale collapse might explain the extent of corporate crime. Executives in a deteriorating business will tend to expand both occupational crime and corporate crime to make a profit both personally and for the business. This is caused by moral collapse as a consequence of business collapse. The sequence might be that corporate crime occurs ahead of occupational crime.

Shadnam and Lawrence (2011) applied institutional theory to explain moral decline and crime potential in organizations:

Our theory of moral collapse has two main elements. First, we argue that morality in organizations is embedded in nested systems of individuals, organizations and moral communities in which ideology and regulation flow "down" from moral communities through organizations to individuals, and moral ideas and influence flow "upward" from individuals through organizations to moral communities. Second, we argue that moral collapse is associated with breakdowns in these flows, and explore conditions under which such breakdowns are likely to occur. (p. 379)

Shadnam and Lawrence (2011) formulated several research hypotheses that imply the likelihood of moral decline will vary depending on several circumstances:

- Moral collapse is more likely to happen in organizations that operate in moral communities in which flows of ideology are disrupted, either through a lack of commitment to formal communication mechanisms by community leaders or the disruption of informal communication networks by high rates of membership turnover.
- Moral collapse is more likely to happen in organizations in which structures and practices diminish the organization's capacity to absorb and incorporate morally charged institutions from the organization's moral community because the organization monopolizes the attention of its members and/or because the organization delegitimizes the morally charged institutions rooted in the moral community.
- Moral collapse is more likely to happen in organizations in which accusing individuals of misconduct creates significant social and economic costs for the organization or the moral community within which it operates.
- Moral collapse is more likely to occur in organizations to the degree that employment conditions undermine enclosure and/or work arrangements diminish the effectiveness of surveillance. (p. 393)

Institutional theory is in line with dysfunctional network theory in that organizations tend to mirror the basic elements of their environments. The largest business corporations can more easily absorb the negative impact of legal sanctions that some governmental or regulatory agencies might impose on them. The largest business enterprises might have better lawyers and other resources, so they can face legal pursuits in more effective and efficient ways. Microsoft versus the United States and Microsoft versus the European Union are typical examples. Therefore, laws and regulations tend to have a much less deterrent effect in the case of large business organizations (Dion, 2009). As a consequence, and ceteris paribus, it might be suggested based on this theory that a larger organization more easily can survive corporate crime.

The *self-control theory* can explain a greater impact on occupational versus corporate crime. The lower the individual's self-control, the greater is the likelihood of his or her involvement in criminal behavior. Low self-control is defined in terms of characteristics, such as impulsive, risk-taking, and self-centered (Meneses & Akers, 2011). Thus, self-control theory proposes that individuals commit crime because of low self-control. Except in rare cases of mass fraud, such as the Enron scandal, not all the elite within a given organization or industry will commit crime. Hence, although the elite at the top of their profession and corporation differentially associate with people of equal status in their own and other corporations, not all corporate elites commit crimes and behave in an overtly deviant manner (Hansen, 2009). Self-control theory was first developed by Gottfredson and Hirschi (1990) within their general theory of crime.

Gross (1978) argued in his classical article on the *theory of organizational crime* that in a considerable number of areas of sociology, studies of crime and delinquency usually have a strong theoretical base. He suggested two important theoretical relationships. First, the internal structure and setting of organizations is of such a nature as to raise the probability that the attainment of the goals of the organization will subject the organization to the risk of violating societal laws of organizational behavior. Second, persons who actually act for the organization in the commission of crimes will, by selective processes, be associated with upward mobility in organizations; be likely to be highly committed to the organization; and, for various reasons, be willing and able to carry out crime should it seem to be required in order to enable the organization to attain its goals, to prosper, or, at least, to survive.

Executives may sometimes argue that they need to commit crime because of criminogenic market forces. For example, in some markets where corruption is the rule rather than exception, they need to pay bribes to enter into and stay in the market. This is in line with the theory of criminogenic market forces. Leonard and Weber (1970) argue that too little attention has been paid to market forces as a reason for criminal behavior:

> Insufficient attention has been focused by sociologists on the extent to which market structures—that is, the economic power available to certain corporations in concentrated industries—may generate criminal conduct. (p. 408)

Another example is price fixing cartels, which may seem to be the only way of sustaining manufacturing industries in high-cost regions.

Criminal behavior on behalf of the organization can be explained by the *theory of monopoly.* This theory is drawn from the area of organized crime. Financial crime often occurs as part of organized crime. Traditionally, a criminal organization is thought of as a monopolistic firm, and the theory of monopoly is predominantly used to analyze organized crimes. The monopolistic model implies that, upon deciding to commit a crime, potential criminals have no other choice but to join the criminal organization. Chang, Lu, and Chen (2005) find this perspective to be less than exhaustive in terms of describing criminal behavior. They argue that the determination of the market structure for crime should be endogenous, something which has notable implications for the optimal crime enforcement policies and crime itself.

To exhume the conventionally neglected facts and provide a more complete picture regarding organized crime, Chang et al. (2005) developed a model in terms of a criminal decision framework in which individual crime and organized crime are coexisting alternatives to a potential offender. The model makes the size of a criminal organization a variable and explores interactive relationships between varying sizes of criminal organization, the crime rate, and the government's law enforcement strategies. Model runs showed that the method adopted to allocate the criminal organization's payoffs and the extra benefit provided by the criminal organization play crucial roles in an individual's decision to commit a crime and the way in which he or she commits that crime.

Some researchers argue that corporate crime should be studied at the organizational rather than the individual level, arguing that it is crime committed to benefit the organization. Other researchers argue that it should be studied at the individual level, so individual responsibility for financial crime is made explicit. This discussion among researchers was summarized by MacLean (2007) in the following way:

> Studies of organizational misconduct have roots in many different disciplines, including criminology, sociology, psychology, economics, and organization studies. The cross-disciplinary nature of this domain has led to a veritable theoretical thicket of terminology describing different niches of corporate wrongdoing. Illegal organizational behavior, corporate crime, unlawful organizational behavior, white-collar crime, occupational crime, and organizational deviance are all concepts overlapping, or relating to organizational misconduct.
>
> Recent theorizing describes organizational misconduct as a subset of organizational deviance. From this perspective, organizational misconduct is defined as "acts of omission or commission committed by individuals or groups of individuals acting in their organizational roles who violate internal rules, laws, or administrative regulations on behalf of organizational goals."
>
> This conceptualization offers several advantages. First, it builds on and broadens earlier conceptual work on illegal organizational behavior, which is defined as "legally prohibited action of organization members that is taken primarily on behalf of the organization." Thus, it encompasses a broader spectrum of rule violations, not limiting misconduct to the violation of civil and criminal law. It is also broad enough to include both intentional and

unintentional acts under its umbrella. This is significant because organization members who are unaware of rules prohibiting their action may commit acts of organizational misconduct. Finally, this definition highlights the role of the individual as well as the organization in misconduct. This particular point bears further discussion.

The appropriate level of analysis for measuring organizational misconduct is debatable. Throughout the history of this domain of research, scholars have argued whether misconduct by individuals on behalf of the organization should be viewed as individual acts, emphasizing individual accountability, or organizational acts, emphasizing the power of environmental and organizational pressures, thus diminishing the role of agency. (p. 4)

Legislation may vary from country to country because some nations prosecute organizations and sentence them to a fine or some other measure. In Norway, individuals are always prosecuted in corporate crime. Therefore, the following sample of corporate criminals is studied at the individual level.

Corporate Criminal Sample

In our criminal sample of 305 cases, we find 42 corporate criminals and 263 occupational criminals as listed in Table 3.1.

In this table, we see that age when convicted was 47 years for occupational criminals and 52 years for corporate criminals, and this difference is statistically significant. Corporate criminals are significantly older than occupational criminals. Similarly, there are differences for age when the crime was committed.

Years in prison are statistically not significant even though it is worth noting that occupational criminals served 2.2 years in prison while corporate

Table 3.1   Comparison of Characteristics of Occupational Crime versus Corporate Crime

Total 305 Criminals	42 Corporate Criminals	263 Occupational Criminals	t Statistical Difference	Significance of t Statistic
Age convicted	52 years	47 years	2.934	.004
Age crime	47 years	42 years	2.778	.006
Years prison	2.0 years	2.2 years	−.782	.435
Crime amount	186 million kr	24 million kr	6.457	.000
Involved individuals	3.4 persons	3.9 persons	−.767	.444
Personal income	352,000 kr	333,000 kr	.209	.835
Personal tax	166,000 kr	137,000 kr	.735	.463
Personal wealth	2,164,000 kr	1,411,000 kr	.711	.478
Business revenue	507 million kr	140 million kr	6.827	.000
Business employees	362 persons	86 persons	5.335	.000

criminals served only 2.0 years. This is particularly interesting, when the next item on the list in the table is taken into account. It is concerned with the amount of money that was involved in the crime. While occupational criminals on average abused "only" 24 million kr, corporate criminals on average abused as much as 186 million kr. So even if the magnitude of the financial crime in terms of money was substantially and significantly larger for corporate crime, occupational crime was nevertheless judged more severely in terms of imprisonment. This is particularly interesting as the crime amount has proven to be a significant predictor of jail sentence. A higher crime amount leads to longer prison terms. Here, even when the crime amount is significantly higher, prison sentence is nevertheless shorter for corporate crime, indicating that Norwegian judges—rather than Norwegian laws—treat corporate criminals more mildly.

Involved individuals are calculated on a personal rather than case basis, that is, the number of persons sharing criminal activities on average. The number of persons involved in financial crime is not significantly different between the two groups. While 3.7 persons on average were involved in occupational crime, the average for corporate crime is 3.4 persons. This result may seem counterintuitive as crime on behalf of the corporation would seem to need more involvement of others than is necessary for occupational crime. However, we have to remind ourselves that only convicted criminals are included in this sample.

The next item in the table is personal income of the offender. Although there is no statistically significant difference, in monetary terms the corporate criminal made a little more money than the occupational criminal. While making more money, the corporate criminal pays a little more money in tax to the government. Corporate criminals are a little wealthier than occupational criminals. Again, this was statistically not significant.

Corporate criminals work in significantly larger organizations than occupational criminals. This is visible both in terms of business revenue and in terms of business employees in the organization.

In summary, based on a sample of 305 convicted white-collar criminals in Norway, of which 263 individuals were occupational criminals and 42 individuals were corporate criminals, we find some interesting differences between the two groups. In statistical terms, significant differences can be found in terms of a person's age, crime amount, and organization size. Corporate criminals are older, they are involved in more severe crime when measured in the money amount involved, and they work in larger organizations than occupational criminals.

Another interesting aspect is the number of corporate criminals versus occupational criminals in the sample. There were 42 corporate and 263 occupational criminals, that is, more than six times as many occupational criminals. This is in line with a survey in Norway that we conducted earlier, in which we had CFOs as respondents. Almost all responses in this survey implied that the respondents were thinking of occupational crime rather than corporate crime when responding to the following open-ended question: How will you proceed on suspicion of white-collar crime in your company? Only a few responses could be interpreted as being concerned with corporate crime, for example, when respondents would only discuss their suspicions with colleagues they trusted and when they would undertake controls and investigate before contacting outside experts.

It is indeed possible to imagine that the number of persons involved in corporate crime is actually greater than 3.4 persons. The limited number can be explained by the theory of rotten apples. This theory argues that corporate crime is considered to be acts of individuals who represent rotten apples. According to this theory, some involved persons are overlooked when criminals are prosecuted. Ashforth, Gioia, Robinson, and Trevino (2008) argue that it is comforting to assume that one bad apple or renegade faction within an organization is somewhat responsible for the crime we too often observe. However, organizations are important to our understanding of crime, because they influence the actions of their members. Therefore, both micro and macro views are important to understanding crime.

It is certainly an interesting issue whether to view white-collar misconduct and crime as acts of individuals perceived as rotten apples or as an indication of systems failure in the company, the industry, or the society as a whole. MacLean (2007) argues that while organizational misconduct can indeed be perceived as an organization-level outcome, it is important to remember that groups and individuals carry out the acts of organizations. The perspective of occupational crime is favoring the individualistic model of deviance, which is a human failure model of misconduct and crime. This rotten apple view of white-collar crime is a comfortable perspective to adopt for business organizations as it allows them to look no further than suspect individuals. It is only when other forms of group (O'Connor, 2005) and/or systemic (Punch, 2003) corruption and other kinds of crime erupt upon a business enterprise that a more critical look is taken of white-collar criminality. Furthermore, when serious misconduct occurs and is repeated, there seems to be a tendency to consider crime as a result of bad practice, lack of resources, or mismanagement rather than acts of criminals.

We will return to the issue of rotten apples versus rotten apple barrels later in this book.

Leaders versus Followers

White-collar criminals can either take on the role of leader or take on the role of follower. Bucy, Formby, Raspanti, and Rooney (2008) argue that white-collar crime refers to nonviolent, business-related violations of state and/or federal criminal statutes, and they make a distinction between leaders and followers in white-collar crime.

McKay, Stevens, and Fratzi (2010) examined the psychopathology of the white-collar criminal acting as a corporate leader. They looked at the impact of a leader's behavior on other employees and the organizational culture developed during his or her reign. They proposed a 12-step process to explain how an organization can move from a legally operating organization to one in which unethical behavior is ignored and wrongdoing promoted.

Leader Criminal Characteristics

Bucy et al. (2008) found that motives for leaders are different from follower motives. Compared to the view that leaders engage in white-collar crime because of greed, followers are nonassertive, weak people who trail behind someone else even into criminal schemes. Followers may be convinced of the rightness of their cause, and they believe that no harm can come to them because they are following a leader whom they trust or fear. Followers tend to be naive and unaware of what is really happening, or they are simply taken in by the personal charisma of the leader and are intensely loyal to that person. However, leadership in general and the application of different styles of leadership in particular are not primarily a one-way process but are often the result of dynamics in which the behavior of followers might influence the style as well as the intensity of the leaders' behavior. Accordingly, followers may play a much more active part in such relationships contrary to what is suggested above.

Charisma is defined as a certain quality of an individual by which he or she is considered extraordinary and treated as endowed with superhuman or exceptional powers or qualities. Charismatic authority arises from the charisma or gift of grace of the leader. It is up to the followers to recognize this characteristic in leaders and to act accordingly (Aguilera & Vadera, 2008).

When leadership behavior in general is studied, differences can be found between leaders and followers. For example, Glasø and Einarsen (2008) studied emotion regulation in leader-follower relationships. They found that negative emotions, such as disappointment, uncertainty, and annoyance, are typically suppressed, and positive emotions, such as enthusiasm, interest, and calmness, are typically expressed or faked. When leaders and followers referred to experience or expressed emotions, the most highly scored emotions were "glad," "enthusiastic," "well," and "interested." The reported level of emotion regulation was higher for leaders than for followers.

According to Glasø, Ekerholt, Barman, and Einarsen (2006), emotional control can be defined as a process in which individuals influence the emotions that they experience, when they have them, and how they perceive and express them. In this line of reasoning, people can modify their emotions and the emotional expressions connected with them. Emotional control in the workplace is called emotional labor or emotion work. Emotion work takes place in face-to-face or voice-to-voice interactions, and its purpose is to influence other people's perceptions, emotions, attitudes, and behaviors.

Leaders tend to be more domineering and assertive and less social avoidant, distrustful, and exploitable than followers. Glasø, Einarsen, Matthiesen, and Skogstad's (2010) study shows that 30% of leaders exhibit elevated profiles of personality characteristics regarding interpersonal problems on a level comparable to that of a sample with psychiatric patients, thus indicating that severe problems may arise in social interactions between leaders and followers.

Leaders can use different behaviors, actions, and practices directed at followers to make them cooperate. Bullying and harassment by leaders are examples of a practice reported to happen on a regular basis in many work organizations. Bullying and harassment are carried out deliberately to cause humiliation, offense, and distress (Hoel, Glasø, Hetland, Cooper, & Einarsen, 2010).

White-collar crime involves some form of social deviance and represents a breakdown in social order. According to Heath (2008), white-collar criminals tend to apply techniques of neutralization used by offenders to deny the criminality of their actions. Examples of neutralization techniques are (a) denial of responsibility, (b) denial of injury, (c) denial of the victim, (d) condemnation of the condemners, (e) appeal to higher loyalties, (f) everyone else is doing it, and (g) claim to entitlement. The offender may claim an entitlement to act as he did, either because he was subject to a moral obligation or because of some misdeed perpetrated by the victim. These excuses are applied both for occupational crime and for corporate crime at both the rotten apple level and the rotten barrel level.

Followers may plan, initiate, and perform criminal acts on their own, thus indicating that followers may not be that passive, unaware, or naive as suggested by Bucy et al. (2008). On the contrary, it is quite thinkable that some followers may reinforce or even activate destructive and criminal behaviors from their leaders. According to Padilla, Hogan, and Kaiser (2007), there are two types of destructive followers; namely conformers and colluders. Conformers act along with destructive leaders out of fear, whereas colluders vigorously take part in destructive behaviors. Both groups are motivated by self-interest, but their concerns are different (Higgins, 1997). Conformers try to minimize any consequences of not behaving as expected, and colluders search for personal gratification through their relationship with a destructive leader. Conformers are motivated by unmet basic needs, negative self-evaluation, and psychological immaturity. Colluders, on the other hand, are ambitious, selfish, and share the values of the destructive leader (Padilla et al., 2007). They act together secretly to achieve a fraudulent, illegal, or deceitful purpose. As such, criminal leadership may, partly, be explained by follower behavior, thus limiting the influence of leaders' individual characteristics and responsibility.

When leadership behavior in general is studied, differences can be found between leaders and followers. For example, Glasø and Einarsen (2008) studied emotion regulation in leader-follower relationships. They found that negative emotions, such as disappointment, uncertainty, and annoyance, are typically suppressed, and positive emotions, such as enthusiasm, interest, and calmness, are typically expressed or faked. When leaders and followers referred to experienced or expressed emotions, the most highly scored emotions were "glad," "enthusiastic," "well," and "interested." The reported level of emotion regulation was higher for leaders than for followers.

According to Glasø et al. (2006), emotional control can be defined as a process in which individuals influence the emotions that they experience, when they have them, and how they perceive and express them. In this line of reasoning, people can modify their emotions and the emotional expressions connected with them. Emotional control in the workplace is called emotional labor or emotion work. Emotion work takes place in face-to-face or voice-to-voice interactions, and its purpose is to influence other people's perceptions, emotions, attitudes, and behaviors.

Leader Crime Theories

Obedience theory has the potential of explaining follower behavior. Obedience theory is related to the fraud triangle that consists of pressure, opportunity, and rationalization. Obedience theory can be useful in explaining pressures and rationalizations providing the motives for individuals to commit acts of occupational fraud:

> Perceived need or pressure often comes from personal financial problems or living beyond one's means, but it can also come from direct pressure from someone in authority in the workplace and the threat of losing one's job for failure to go along with the boss's scheme. Obedience theory posits that individuals may engage in behaviors that conflict with their personal values and beliefs if they are subjected to pressures to obey someone in authority. According to this theory, the individuals rationalize this behavior by essentially placing full responsibility on the authority figure rather than taking any individual responsibility for the action themselves. (Baird & Zelin, 2009, p. 1)

Obedience pressure is considered a form of social influence pressure, and there are two other types of social influence pressure: compliance pressure and conformity pressure:

> Compliance pressure is similar to obedience pressure, except that compliance pressure can come from one's peers as well as from superiors, while obedience pressure must come from an authority figure. Conformity pressure refers to pressure to conform to perceived or societal norms. (Baird & Zelin, 2009, p. 2)

Of the three forms of social influence pressure, Baird and Zelin (2009) argue that obedience pressure can be especially potent because of the power that persons in authority have over their underlings. People within an organization quietly follow the orders of top executives and rationalize their actions by denying responsibility for their behaviors. The pressures to commit crime are often overt requests of management but can also be based on perceptions from reward and incentive structures.

An even stronger argument for follower behavior can be found when obedience theory is linked to self-control theory. Self-control theory proposes that individuals commit crime because of low self-control. Except in rare cases of mass fraud, such as the Enron scandal, not all elites within a given organization or industry will commit crime. Hence, although elites at the top of their profession and corporation differentially associate with the people of equal status in their own and other corporations, not all corporate elites commit crimes and behave in an overtly deviant manner (Hansen, 2009).

Criminal leaders versus criminal followers can be studied in the context of *agency theory*. Agency theory has broadened the risk-sharing literature to include the agency problem that occurs when cooperating parties have different goals and division of labor. The cooperating parties are engaged in an agency relationship defined as a contract under which one or more persons (the principal[s]) engage another person (agent) to perform some service on their behalf, which involves delegating some decision making authority to the agent (Jensen & Meckling, 1976). Agency theory describes the relationship between the two parties using the metaphor of a contract.

In a principal-agent perspective on white-collar crime, both the agent and/or the principal can be a criminal. This kind of twofold principal-agent dilemma is discussed by Bricker and Chandar (2000). A principal-agent model consists of at least two individuals, namely, a principal and an agent, who have goals, preferences, and a set of available actions. It is clear that a principal-agent model of white-collar crime should have actions on the part of the agent that involve committing a crime, which of course, is not in the interest of the principal. It should also be the case that the payoffs to the actions of the agent take into account the probability of being caught, and the corresponding punishment. Ideally, committing the crime should not be a dominating strategy so that the question regarding the incentives set by the principal is not a vacuous one. Typically one should think of a crime as a risky strategy with two types of outcomes: one that outperforms the payoff of conforming to the law (which is earned if the crime goes undetected) and another, which underperforms that lawful payoff (which is earned if the crime is discovered). The incentives set by the principal can influence the relative outcomes as suggested by Baumol (1990), who was concerned with the role of incentives as an explanation for unproductive and destructive entrepreneurship.

We can think of the principal as the victim and the agent as the criminal, or we can think of the principal as the criminal and the agent as the victim. Each crime clearly has both. Alternatively, we can think of the principal as always being the victim. A principal is an individual who wants a certain agent to do something the agent is not interested in doing, a problem that may be difficult to overcome due to asymmetric information. In this perspective, each crime has a criminal (the agent) and a victim (the principal) regardless of the jobs the individuals involved actually have. Examples of criminals (i.e., agents) could be (i) chairmen; (ii) entrepreneurs; (iii) servants; and (iv) officials, regulators, and so forth, and the victims (i.e., principals) could be (a) the government; (b) customers; (c) stakeholders; (d) investors; (e) business partners; and (f) the general public, innocents, and so forth.

According to Eisenhardt (1985), agency theory is concerned with resolving two problems that can occur in agency relationships. The first is the agency problem that arises when the desires or goals of the principal and agent conflict, and it is difficult or expensive for the principal to verify what the agent is actually doing. Because both leader and follower are criminals, the agency problem arises for both of them in terms of conflicting goals and desires. The second is the problem of risk sharing that arises when the principal and agent have different risk preferences. Typically in white-collar crime, the leader will tend to be more risk willing, and the follower will tend to be more risk averse.

The first agency problem arises especially when the two parties do not share productivity gains. The risk-sharing problem might be the result of different attitudes toward the use of illegal means. Because the unit of analysis is the agreement governing the relationship between the two parties, the focus of the theory is on determining the most efficient criminal actions governing the principal-agent relationship given assumptions about people (e.g., self-interest, bounded rationality, risk aversion), organizations (e.g., goal conflict of members), and information (e.g., information is a commodity that can be purchased).

Garoupa (2007) applied agency theory to criminal organizations. He modeled the criminal firm as a family business with one principal and several agents. He has in mind an illegal monopoly in which it is difficult to detect and punish the principal unless an agent is detected. Furthermore, it is assumed that agents work rather independently, so the likelihood of detection of one agent is fairly independent from another. An example of such agents is drug dealers in the street with the principal being the local distributor. Another example would be agents as extortionists or blackmailers distributed across the city with the principal being the coordinator of their activities providing them information or criminal know-how.

In a white-collar crime setting, for example, money laundering might be conducted by an agent, such as a restaurant owner or law firm employee, but it is initiated by a leader, such as a drug wholesaler or smuggling organization. Bank fraud can be initiated by a leader in the real estate agency and helped by followers who are in the business of producing fake real estate values.

Gross (1978) discussed criminals as agents for a criminal organization in the following way:

> Although organizations are here held to be criminogenic and although courts no longer exhibit much hesitation in charging the organization itself with crime, organizations of course cannot themselves act—they must have agents who act for them. Who will the persons be who will act for organizations in their criminal behavior? (p. 65)

In general, agency models view corruption and other kinds of financial crime as a consequence of the principal's inability to effectively prevent the agent from abusing its power for his or her personal gain. The main reasons for this inability are the principal's lack of information about the agent's work, lack of effective checks and balances, and ineffective enforcement and punishment for criminal executives (Li & Ouyang, 2007). In our context of leader versus follower, agency models are applied to understand the criminal principal's ability to effectively make the agent abuse its power for his or her personal gain while, at the same time, receiving a shorter jail sentence if caught.

Strain theory proposes that individuals are pressured or feel pressured into crime and deviant behavior as a way of coping with or responding to strain and stress—such as failure to achieve goals and negative experiences—they encounter. The more a person has experienced stress and strain as a follower from a leader, the greater is the likelihood that he or she will be willing to commit crime (Meneses & Akers, 2011).

Similar to strain theory, *social bonding theory* can explain bonding between leader and follower. The four main explanatory concepts in social bonding theory are the individual's attachment (strength of affective ties to individuals and groups), commitment (investment of effort and resources in conventional lines of activity), involvement (amount of engagement and time spent in conforming activities), and belief (subscribing to general norms and laws of society). The theory hypothesizes that the stronger these bonds to society are, the less likely the individual is to engage in any type of crime (Meneses & Akers, 2011). Conversely, delinquent acts result when an individual's bond to society or to the organization is weak or broken. Lack of attachment to conventional others, lack of commitment to conventional lines of action, lack of involvement in conventional activities, and lack of belief in a common value system weaken the societal bond and, therefore, make criminal behavior more likely (Lasley, 1988).

As the criminal sample in this chapter will show, white-collar crime including followers involves significantly more persons. This phenomenon might be studied using *transaction cost theory*. Transaction costs include both costs associated with conflicts and costs associated with misunderstandings:

> Transaction costs apply both to legitimate business and to illicit enterprises. They include the costs of conflicts and misunderstandings that lead to delays, to breakdowns and to other malfunctions. They can include such things as the costs of incentives, of ensuring coordination and the enforcement of regulations, rules or customs. In the case of a criminal organization, controlling transaction costs is necessary to keep it protected from betrayal and from prosecution. This includes the need to protect the organization from informers and from others (such as law enforcement agencies) who threaten its profits and stability. For such organizations, the use of violence and coercion is often the most effective way of reducing transaction costs. (Wright, 2006, p. 58)

For example, mafia groups consider transaction costs before criminal acts are carried out:

> Mafia groups consider the costs of each transaction in estimating the risk involved in their drug dealing operations. Betrayal of the group by informers leading to disruption of operations, seizure of drugs and arrest of group members is the predominant transaction cost in such cases. (Wright, 2006, p. 58)

Differential association theory (a social learning theory) proposes that a person associating with individuals who have deviant or unlawful mores, values, and norms learns criminal behavior. Certain characteristics play a key role in placing individuals in a position to behave unlawfully, including the proposition that criminal behavior is learned through interaction with other persons as well as interaction occurring in small intimate groups (Hansen, 2009).

Social bonding theory proposes that the presence of four key elements of belief, attachment, commitment, and involvement may lead to elite misdeeds based on the strength of the bonds formed between corporate "bad boys" (Hansen, 2009).

Exchange theory suggests that micro-level actors are involved in economic exchanges in which white-collar crime might be the consequence of attraction, competition, differentiation, integration, and opposition (Hansen, 2009). The basic assumption of social exchange theory is that individuals establish social relationships because such relationships are expected to be rewarding, and individuals sustain those relationships because they experience them as being rewarding. Social exchange entails a series of exchanges that produce obligations to reciprocate. Trusting, loyal, mutually committed social exchange relationships might evolve over time with exchange partners trusting each other to eventually reciprocate benefits received. In order for them to do so, they must abide by the rules of exchange. One such rule, or underlying mechanism, is the norm of reciprocity (Buch, 2012).

Control balance theory measures the potential for individuals to commit corporate crimes. Control balance theory utilizes a ratio of control exercised relative to degree of control experienced. Control balance surpluses, rather than deficits, lead to white-collar and corporate deviance (Hansen, 2009).

Leader Criminal Sample

In our sample of 305 white-collar criminals, 175 persons could be identified as leaders, and 130 persons could be identified as followers as listed in Table 3.2. A typical leader-follower case in our sample is the CEO who told his CFO to make expenditures for corruption as part of the regular accounting. Another example is the woman (follower) who impersonated a rich widow to withdraw money from a bank after having been told how to do so by an insider in the bank (leader).

Leaders and followers are compared in Table 3.2. Leaders and followers are about the same age. They receive significantly different jail sentences: The average for leaders is 2.8 years and the average for followers is only 1.3 years.

An example might illustrate this significant difference. The CEO of Sponsor Service, Terje Bogen, received a jail sentence of 4.5 years. The CFO, Mark Sjuve, who had helped manipulate accounting figures so that Sponsor Service got more bank loans, received a jail sentence of one year. Two external auditors from KPMG, Jan Olav Korsmo and Erland Ødegard Stenberg, who approved the manipulated accounting, received jail sentences of only a few months each. In this case, Bogen was defined as a leader, and Sjuve, Korsmo, and Stenberg were defined as followers.

Table 3.2 Comparison of Characteristics of Criminal Leaders versus Criminal Followers

Total 305 Criminals	175 Criminal Leaders	130 Criminal Followers	*t* Statistical Difference	Significance of *t* Statistic
Age convicted	48 years	47 years	.946	.345
Age crime	43 years	43 years	.335	.738
Years prison	2.8 years	1.3 years	8.277	.000
Crime amount	49 million kr	43 million kr	.357	.721
Involved individuals	2.7 persons	5.4 persons	−7.289	.000
Personal income	357,000 kr	307,000 kr	.758	.449
Personal tax	157,000 kr	119,000 kr	1.379	.169
Personal wealth	1,712,000 kr	1,248,000 kr	.629	.530
Business revenue	185 million kr	198 million kr	−.308	.759
Business employees	102 persons	155 persons	−1.576	.116

It is not surprising to find in the table that there are significantly more criminals involved when there are followers. In the concept of followers, there must be more persons. On average, there were 5.4 persons involved in the crime when followers had roles in the crime.

As discussed earlier, an interesting distinction can be made between occupational crime and corporate crime as illustrated in the following figure. Occupational crime is crime committed by individuals for their own purposes and enrichment rather than for the enrichment of the organization as a whole in the case of corporate crime (Hansen, 2009). When a person commits an occupational crime, he or she is acting self-servingly with the goal of advancing his or her own financial well being and gratifying his or her own desires. On the contrary, a corporate criminal is working on behalf of the corporation, and he or she is often either defending or improving the welfare of the corporation (Blickle et al., 2006). Perri and Brody (2011) claim that corporate crime is explained away as acceptable conduct in the face of a corporation's monetary problems or in order to increase earnings specifically for the business. Occupational crime is often justified in different ways: a person looks at the act as "borrowing" with the intention of someday returning the funds, or these criminals may be convinced that there is remuneration due to them that the company is wrongly withholding.

Occupational versus corporate crime is combined with leaders versus followers in Figure 3.1. Here, distinction is made between occupational crime as leader versus follower and corporate crime as leader versus follower.

Figure 3.2 shows the distribution of white-collar criminals in the four categories. Most offenders are found within occupational crime when the white-collar criminal assumes the leadership role.

Table 3.3 shows that leaders—both corporate and occupational leaders—receive the longest jail sentences (2.9 and 2.8 years). In both groups, criminal followers receive significantly shorter jail sentences as indicated with an asterisk in the table. Crime amount is about the same for corporate leaders and corporate followers. Crime amount is significantly smaller for

Actor \ Role	Leader	Follower
Occupational	Occupational crime as leader	Occupational crime as follower
Corporate	Corporate crime as leader	Corporate crime as follower

Figure 3.1 Categories of white-collar crime depending on role and actor.

Actor \ Role	Leader	Follower	Total
Occupational	155	108	263
Corporate	20	22	42
Total	175	130	305

Figure 3.2 Criminals in each category of white-collar crime depending on role and actor.

occupational followers compared to occupational leaders. For followers in both groups, there are more involved persons. This difference is statistically significant for occupational criminals.

The present study has again shown that white-collar crime is a serious and prevalent problem, in organizations and in society at large. Regarding the criminals, the distinction made between leaders and followers, in terms of agency, may seem, however, blurred—the present study clearly shows that followers may plan, initiate, and perform criminal acts on their own, indicating that followers may not be as passive, unaware, or naive as suggested by Bucy et al. (2008). On the contrary, it is quite conceivable that some followers may reinforce or even activate destructive and criminal behaviors in their leaders.

Padilla et al. (2007) describes two kinds of of potentially damaging followers; these are labeled "conformers" and "colluders." Conformers are people who follow or assist destructive leaders because they are fearful of the possible consequences of not going along. On the other hand, colluders actively and willingly participate in their leaders' destructive actions. While both types of followers are driven by their own self-regard, their concerns are dissimilar (Higgins, 1997). Conformers make an effort to reduce the impact of any results of their not performing in the way others think they will, and colluders are looking to satisfy their own needs through this association with a destructive leader. Conformers are spurred by the quest to meet some fundamental needs, which are not being met; they are often experiencing low levels of self-esteem and are mentally and/or emotionally immature. In contrast, colluders are usually determined, sometimes to the point of ruthlessness, and greedy, and they frequently have the same principles as the destructive leader (Padilla et al., 2007). They surreptitiously work with the leader to accomplish their duplicitous and unlawful aims. As such, the behavior of the criminal leader might

Table 3.3   Comparison of Characteristics of Criminal Leaders versus Criminal Followers

Total 305 Criminals	20 Corporate Leaders	22 Corporate Followers	155 Occupational Leaders	108 Occupational Followers
Age convicted	54 years	51 years	48 years	46 years
Age crime	49 years	46 years	42 years	42 years
Years prison	2.9 years	1.1 years*	2.8 years	1.3 years*
Crime amount	182 million kr	189 million kr	32 million kr	13 million kr*
Involved individuals	3.1 persons	3.8 persons	2.6 persons	5.7 persons*
Personal income	397,000 kr	312,000 kr	351,000 kr	306,000 kr
Personal tax	208,000 kr	128,000 kr	150,000 kr	118,000 kr
Personal wealth	3,905,000 kr	582,000 kr	1,429,000 kr	1,384,000 kr
Business revenue	355 million kr	645 million kr*	163 million kr	106 million kr
Business employees	185 persons	522 persons*	240 persons	230 persons

possibly, at least in part, be a result of the followers' actions, and this somewhat restricts the degree to which the leaders' personal persuasive qualities may have influenced their followers and, hence, may limit responsibility.

Leaders in crime, both corporate leaders and occupational leaders, receive a significantly longer jail sentence when convicted in court than corporate and occupational followers in crime. To date, followers seem to have been studied less frequently than leaders despite the fact that their role in the criminal process is clearly essential. The result of the present chapter is that a new and interesting perspective on the notion of leader-follower exchange dynamics may be gained. The present study indicates that that there are also leader-follower exchange dynamics of a sinister kind, in which criminal leaders may form alliances with colluders in order to achieve goals that more greatly concern personal need satisfaction, and the colluders are rewarded for helping them in these endeavors. Although (owing to the design of the present study) we have not established a relationship between the criminal leaders and their followers in all cases, this study clearly indicates that there is a strong need to focus more on both criminal followership and criminal leadership as well as on potential criminal leader-follower exchange dynamics in future studies.

The aim of this chapter was to provide a sample of white-collar criminal leaders and followers and to examine differences between the two groups. The sample consists of 305 white-collar criminals in total, of which there are more leaders than followers in crime. A comparison of average values as well as variations in white-collar characteristics of the leaders and followers reveals significant differences between the two groups, regarding the number of persons involved in the crime and years of imprisonment. Leaders committing corporate crime (as opposed to occupational crime) receive a jail sentence that is three times as long as followers do. The present study clearly indicates that, contrary to statements that claim followers are passive and naïve, they may plan and commit criminal acts independently. Nevertheless, followers are, on average, treated mildly in court.

Rotten Apples versus Rotten Barrels

Ashforth et al. (2008) reason that it can be reassuring for the general public to think that one bad apple or a destructive group within an organization can to some extent be held accountable for the violations of the law that we frequently hear about. However, it's important to understand that organizations also have an effect on the activities of their members. Therefore, we have to examine both micro and macro views to gain an understanding of illegal behavior.

Without a doubt, it can be fascinating to analyze the question of whether we should look at white-collar wrongdoing and criminality as actions perpetrated by specific persons thought of as "rotten apples" or whether is should be considered to be indicative of a breakdown of the whole system within a corporation, an industry, or society in its entirety. The general assessment of occupational crime supports the first representation, the one that says the individual is responsible for his or her own criminal misconduct and behavior. This rotten apple view of white-collar crime is a standpoint that creates a feeling of security for businesses and corporations because it tolerates their only investigating certain suspicious persons. However, when other types of group (O'Connor, 2005) and/or systemic (Punch, 2003) dishonesty and other varieties of crime happen within a firm that a more serious examination of white-collar criminal behavior is undertaken. In addition, at times when a significant transgression happens, and it occurs again, there can develop the inclination to think of crime as the consequences of inappropriate practice, an absence of needed resources, or bad management as opposed to the actions of criminals.

When white-collar crime occurs in a rotten barrel, it is typically caused by a combination of pressures and opportunities. Characteristics of the business environment and of the organization combine to create scarcity or even blocked access to desirable and needed resources, creating pressure on the organization to violate laws or norms and the opportunity to do so without detection. An example might be the need for corruption to establish an enterprise in a developing country. Given the combination of enough pressure and opportunity, organizations pursue illegitimate avenues to gain resources (MacLean, 2007).

Rotten Criminal Characteristics

A rotten apple is a person who succumbs to the temptations inherent in the work environment, and a rotten barrel is a work environment that provides many opportunities to learn and develop patterns of deviant behavior (Arjoon, 2008). The rotten apple metaphor has thereby been extended to include the group level view of cultural deviance in organizations with the rotten barrel metaphor (O'Connor, 2005). Furthermore, Punch (2003) has pushed the notion of rotten orchards to highlight deviance at the systemic level. Punch (2003, p. 172) notes, "the metaphor of 'rotten orchards' indicate(s) that it is sometimes not the apple, or even the barrel, that is rotten but the *system* (or significant parts of the system)."

When the system is rotten, we can talk about systemic crime or systems crime:

> ... in some way encouraged, and perhaps even protected, by certain elements in the system. ... "Systems" refers both to the formal system—the police organization, the criminal justice system and the broader socio-political context—and to the informal system of deals, inducements, collusion and understandings among deviant officers as to how the corruption is to be organized, conducted and rationalized. (Punch, 2003, p. 172)

Rotten apples and rotten barrels are sometimes linked to the concepts of slippery slope and continuum of compromise. Slippery slope addresses the issue of why good people do bad things:

> As commonsense experience tells us, it is the small infractions that can lead to the larger ones. An organization that overlooks the small infractions of its employees creates a culture of acceptance that may lead to its own demise. This phenomenon is captured by the metaphor of the slippery slope. Many unethical acts occur without the conscious awareness of the person who engaged in the misconduct. Specifically, unethical behavior is most likely to follow the path of a slippery slope, defined as a gradual decline in which no one event makes one aware that he or she is acting unethically. The majority of unethical behaviors are unintentional and ordinary, thus affecting everyone and providing support for unethical behavior when people unconsciously lower the bar over time through small changes in their ethical behavior. (Arjoon, 2008, p. 78)

Arjoon (2008) argues that the continuum of compromise (CoC) provides a plausible explanation of the slippery-slope phenomenon:

> It explains how over a period of time mild job frustrations develop into a pathological, materialistic attitude and behavior that leads to devastating consequences. This phenomenon is also known by the metaphors "the thin edge of the wedge" and "the camel's nose" (once a camel has managed to place its nose within a tent, the rest of the camel inevitably follows). The CoC reflects a framework that demonstrates the potential for radical deterioration of socio-moral inhibitions and a perceived sense of permissibility for deviant conduct. In other words, if something relatively harmless is allowed or accepted, it may lead to a downward trend that ends with the unthinkable. (p. 78)

Rotten Crime Theories

Social learning theory can explain criminal behavior of rotten barrel members. This theory proposes that for individuals who are more likely to begin and continue in criminal behavior, the greater is the extent to which they have been in differential association with others who are involved in and hold attitudes supportive of such behavior. The more positive or neutralizing definitions or attitudes they hold with regard to such behavior, the greater the balance of rewarding over punishing consequences for such behavior they have experienced or perceived (differential reinforcement), the greater they are exposed to or influenced by observing such behavior by others (Meneses & Akers, 2011).

Another relevant explanatory approach is *integrated theory*. The integrated theory combining strain, social control, and social learning theories has the potential of explaining a variety of crime types. According to integrated theory, social and demographic background variables influence perceived and objective opportunities to attain goals and may also be associated with differences in socialization (Menard & Morris, 2012).

Bruinsma and Bernasco (2004) used *social network theory* to describe and tentatively explain differences in social organization between criminal groups that perform three types of transnational illegal activities: smuggling and large-scale heroin trading, trafficking in women, and trading in stolen cars. Groups that operate in the large-scale heroin market tend to be close-knit, cohesive, and ethnically homogeneous. Groups active in the trafficking of women have a chain structure, and three clusters of offenders in a chain characterize those that operate in the market for stolen cars. Both groups are less cohesive than criminal groups in the large-scale heroin market. The differences in social organization between the three types of illegal activities appear to be related to the legal and financial risks associated with the crimes in question and thereby to the required level of trust between collaborating criminals.

In white-collar crime, rotten barrels consist of organizational members who network their criminal activities or at least find no threat in their organization toward financial crime. Social network theory suggests that white-collar criminals join and participate in exchanges with others without any fear of being abandoned.

Dysfunctional network theory suggests that corporate crime emerges as a consequence of the dysfunction of value networks. A value network is the context within which a firm identifies and responds to customers' needs, solves problems, procures input, reacts to competitors, and strives for profit. Within this context, the firm may choose deviant behavior in line with their competitors in the industry. Dion (2009) argues that organizational culture makes it possible to adopt organizational purposes or objectives, which are basically deviant in comparison with social norms but in line with the competition. Deviant purposes can be chosen when business corporations are trapped within doubtful, immoral, or disloyal means that are used by competitors. They could also be trapped by the business milieu as a social institution. They could finally be trapped by their own sector-based morality, which is oriented towards profit maximization.

Dysfunctional network theory makes clear that the mission of the business corporation cannot be isolated from three basic components of any capitalistic system: making profits, responding to customers' needs, and reacting to competitors. Values in the value network have four basic meanings:

- Organizational values refer to what the company considers as an ethical behavior or decision.
- Organizational values reflect the criteria that employees use when they must prioritize various alternatives of action.
- Organizational values determine the basic strategic decisions taken by top managers.
- Organizational values are the criteria that give guidance throughout the resource-allocation process. (Dion, 2009)

Within the corporate culture, the tendency to commit financial crime is influenced by a number of factors. If the business corporation is having a poor financial performance, if the organization is large and unstable, and if the level of concentration of the market is high, then corporate crime is more likely to occur. According to Dion (2009), business corporations having a greater power in the market tend to commit more illegalities. In this context, bad apples tend to be replaced by and expanded to bad barrels to save the future of the firm.

Value networks define what companies can and cannot do. Value networks are focusing on values and attitudes from an ethical viewpoint. Competitors that are involved in given value networks contribute to define how each enterprise in an industry can strive for profit. Dion (2009) argues that the capacity to convert corporate intangibles, such as corporate reputation, into a negotiable value could contribute to prevent corporate crime.

According to dysfunctional network theory, the way a given enterprise defines its strategies and justifies past choices of markets determines its perceptions of the economic value it gives to alternative legal and illegal actions. Value networks constitute the cultural mix that explains how different strategic elements play a decisive role in the way an organization looks at ethical considerations. Organizations tend to mirror the basic elements of their environments. Therefore, an industry where financial crime is part of the game will tend to have more rotten barrels than industries where financial crime is not part of the game.

Socialization theory argues that learning how to commit financial crime and getting to know persons in the criminal trade will increase the likelihood of white-collar crime:

> Many lower-class male adolescents experience a sense of desperation surrounding the belief that their position in the economic structure is relatively fixed and immutable. As a result of failing to meet cultural expectations of achieving upward mobility, conditions become ideal for socialization functions such as recruitment, screening, and training for organized crime to occur at the community level. (Lyman & Potter, 2007, p. 69)

Rotten apples may think they do nothing wrong. Their thinking can be based on neutralization techniques derived from *neutralization theory*. Criminals apply techniques in order to make them feel as though they have done nothing wrong. These techniques are called neutralization techniques, whereby the feeling of guilt is neutralized. Neutralization theory encompasses all these techniques. In their original formulation of neutralization theory, Sykes and Matza (1957) proposed five techniques of neutralization: denial of responsibility, denial of injury, denial of the victim, condemnation of the condemners, and appeal to higher loyalties. Later, other researchers added the metaphor of the ledger and a technique named the defense of necessity (Siponen & Vance, 2010).

The following neutralization techniques are included in neutralization theory:

1. *Denial of responsibility.* The offender here claims that one or more of the conditions of responsible agency were not met. The person committing a deviant act defines himself or herself as lacking responsibility for his or her actions. In this technique, the person rationalizes that the action in question is beyond his or her control. The offender views him- or herself as a billiard ball, helplessly propelled through different situations. For example, the pressure to sell, the threat of competition and other brutal market forces often lead us to act in ways that we would rather not. However, in the end, it is not we who make this choice or decide how the world is.

2. *Denial of injury.* The offender seeks to minimize or deny the harm done. Denial of injury involves justifying an action by minimizing the harm it causes. The misbehavior is not really serious because no party suffers directly as a result of it. For example, the nature of damage caused by fraud and corruption cannot be compared to, for

example, violent or serious crime. Often nobody gets hurt. All we are doing is following the rules of the game in the market.

3. *Denial of victim.* The offender acknowledges the injury but claims that the victim is unworthy of concern. Any blame for illegal actions are unjustified because the violated party deserves whatever injury they receive. For example, sometimes a little bit of corruption is the only way to progress matters. It is like lubrication in an engine, and it can be argued that more good is done than bad. Anyway, at least our ethical standards are better than our competitors.

4. *Condemnation of the condemners.* The offender tries to accuse his or her critics of questionable motives for criticizing him. According to this technique, one neutralizes his or her actions by blaming those who are the target of the action. The offender deflects moral condemnation onto those ridiculing corporations by pointing out that they engage in similar disapproved behavior. For example, many of the people who condemn corruption are in fact naïve idealists who have no idea how the world really works.

5. *Appeal to higher loyalties.* The offender denies the act was motivated by self-interest, claiming that it was instead done out of obedience to some moral obligation. This technique is employed by those who feel they are in a dilemma that must be resolved at the cost of violating a law or policy. In the context of an organization, an employee may appeal to organizational values or hierarchies. For example, an employee could argue that he or she has to violate a policy in order to get his or her work done. Altruistic behavior seems to accord with appealing to higher loyalties, that is, sacrificing personal demands to the benefit of higher loyalties (Goldstraw-White, 2012). For example, our job as managers is to take care of the profits and the company. Let the state take care of the social aspects.

6. *Normality of action.* The offender argues that everyone else is doing it; thus he or she has done nothing wrong.

7. *Claim to entitlement.* The offender claims he or she was in his right to do what he or she did perhaps because of a very stressful situation or because of some misdeed perpetrated by the victim. This is defense of necessity, which is based on the justification that if the rule breaking is viewed as necessary, one should feel no guilt when committing the action.

8. *Legal mistake.* The offender argues that the law is wrong, and what he or she did should indeed not be illegal. One may therefore break the law because the law is unreasonable.

9. *Acceptable mistake.* The offender argues that what he or she did is acceptable given the situation and given his or her position. The person feels he or she has been doing so much good for the organization

that he or she should be excused for more wrongdoings than other people otherwise would. He or she feels that he or she has done so much good, that his or her crime is a relatively minor matter that should be ignored. This is in line with the metaphor of the ledger, which uses the idea of compensating bad acts with good acts. That is, an individual believes that he or she has previously performed a number of good acts and has accrued a surplus of good will and, as a result of this, can afford to commit some bad actions. Executives in corporate environments neutralize their actions through the metaphor of the ledger by rationalizing that their overall past good behavior justifies occasional rule breaking.

10. *Dilemma tradeoff.* The offender argues a dilemma arose whereby he or she made a reasonable tradeoff before committing the act. Tradeoff between many interests therefore resulted in the offense. The dilemma represents a state of mind in which it is not obvious what it is right and wrong to do. For example, the offense might be carried out to prevent a more serious offense from happening. (Bock & Kenhove, 2011; Heath, 2008; Iyer & Kvalnes, 2012; Siponen & Vance, 2010)

In a study of white-collar prisoners, Dhami (2007) found that they all neutralized their own criminal behavior. Justifications are socially constructed accounts that individuals who engage in criminal acts adopt to legitimate their behavior. Justifications are beliefs that counteract negative interpretations by articulating why the acts are justifiable or excusable exceptions to the norms (Aguilera & Vadera, 2008).

Rotten Criminal Sample

Out of 305 identified white-collar criminals, 112 emerged as individual rotten apples, and 193 emerged as members of rotten apple barrels as listed in Table 3.4.

In the table, we see that age upon conviction was 49 years for rotten apples and 47 years for members of rotten barrels although this difference is statistically not significant. Similarly, the difference in age when the crime was committed was not significant either. Rotten apples received a jail sentence of 2.6 years on average, and rotten barrel members received only 1.9 years. This difference is statistically significant as indicated by $p = .003$.

The shorter jail sentence for barrel members is particularly interesting when comparing crime amount because crime amount is substantially (although not significantly) larger for barrel members. So, even though the

Table 3.4 Comparison of Characteristics of Rotten Apples versus Rotten Barrel Persons

Total 305 Criminals	112 Rotten Apples	193 Rotten Barrel Persons	t Statistical Difference	Significance of t Statistic
Age convicted	49 years	47 years	1.203	.230
Age crime	44 years	42 years	1.372	.171
Years prison	2.6 years	1.9 years	2.958	.003
Crime amount	31 million kr	56 million kr	−1.289	.198
Involved individuals	2.7 persons	4.5 persons	−4.323	.000
Personal income	399,000 kr	299,000 kr	1.494	.136
Personal tax	166,000 kr	126,000 kr	1.426	.155
Personal wealth	1,493,000 kr	1,527,000 kr	−.044	.965
Business revenue	237 million kr	164 million kr	1.784	.075
Business employees	151 persons	108 persons	1.244	.214

crime amount is larger, the jail sentence is shorter—as rotten apple criminals, on average, abused 31 million kr, and rotten barrel criminals, on average, abused 56 million kr.

A greater number of persons are involved in barrel crime: 4.5 versus 2.7 persons. This difference is statistically significant.

The next item in the table is personal income of offender; although there is no statistically significant difference, in monetary terms the barrel criminal made less money than the individual criminal. The two groups have approximately the same personal wealth although individual criminals are slightly less wealthy.

The size of the organization is approximately the same in terms of both revenue and number of employees. Although statistically not significant, rotten apples commit white-collar crime in organizations that are slightly larger in terms of business revenue and number of employees than rotten barrel members.

In summary, we find that criminals in rotten barrels are involved in more serious crime in terms of crime amount. Criminals in rotten barrels involve more persons in the crime, but they receive shorter jail sentences than rotten apples.

A contingent approach to crime response has been discussed in previous chapters as being dependent on whether it is occupational or corporate crime and whether it constitutes leader or follower crime. A third situational factor is here whether rotten apple or rotten barrel is suspected as illustrated in Figure 3.3.

When a rotten apple commits occupational crime, it is interesting to study whether the rotten apple as a leader is more harshly judged than a follower is judged. As a follower, the rotten apple may have acted according to obedience pressure. Baird and Zellin (2009) conducted such a study, in which they utilized written scenarios to examine whether persons committing fraud in situations involving obedience pressure are judged less harshly by others than persons committing fraud of their own volition. Participants in their study were also asked how likely they would be, in the same circumstances, to commit the same fraudulent acts—higher expectations were predicted for participants receiving the scenarios involving obedience pressure. In their study, they found empirical support for the hypothesis that followers from obedience pressure are less harshly judged.

The matrix of leader versus follower, rotten apple versus rotten barrel, and occupational versus corporate crime shown in Figure 3.4 provides a useful framework with which to study white-collar crime. Based on a sample of 305 convicted white-collar criminals in Norway, of which 112 individuals were rotten apple criminals and 193 rotten barrel criminals, we find some interesting differences in the size of the groups as illustrated in Figure 3.4.

The largest group we find is the category of occupational crime/rotten barrel member/follower criminal with a total of 83 criminals. These criminals are involved in financial crime for personal profit and benefit; they did not initiate the crime themselves, and they were acting with others in a system accepting misconduct. The second largest group we find is the category of occupational crime/leader in crime/rotten apple criminal with a total of 81 criminals. These criminals are involved in financial crime for personal profit and benefit; they have initiated the crime, and they are acting alone or with a few others.

Actor \ Role		Leader	Follower
Occupational	Rotten apple	Occupational apple leader	Occupational apple follower
	Rotten barrel	Occupational barrel leader	Occupational barrel follower
Corporate	Rotten apple	Corporate apple leader	Corporate apple follower
	Rotten barrel	Corporate barrel leader	Corporate barrel follower

Figure 3.3 Categories of white-collar crime depending on role, actor, and level.

Role Actor		Leader	Follower	Total
Occupational	Rotten apple	81	25	106
	Rotten barrel	74	83	157
Corporate	Rotten apple	3	3	6
	Rotten barrel	17	19	36
Total		171	134	305

Figure 3.4 Occurrences of white-collar criminals depending on role, actor, and level.

The third largest group can be found in the category of occupational crime/leader/rotten apple with a total of 74 criminals. These criminals are doing it for personal profit involving none or few others.

In the corporate crime group, the largest category is found for leaders in rotten barrels.

The average age among all 305 convicted white-collar criminals in the sample is 48 years. Depending on role (leader or follower), actor (rotten apple or rotten barrel member), and level (occupational crime and corporate crime), there might be differences in offender age. This is illustrated in Figure 3.5, in which we find the oldest criminals in the group of corporate criminals who are leaders and rotten apples. This group is very small, only consisting of three criminals. Their average age was 58 years. The youngest criminals are found among occupational criminals who are followers belonging to rotten barrels. Their average age was 45 years. This is a major group of criminals as 83 persons belong to this group. Another major group of criminals with 81 criminals is the occupational/apple/leader group. Their average age is 48 years.

Another relevant comparison among groups is prison term. Average prison sentence for the total sample is 2.2 years. As listed in Figure 3.6, most serious sentences are passed to occupational criminals who are leaders and rotten apples. They received a jail sentence of 2.8 years. This group is quite large. The shortest sentences were passed to corporate criminals who are followers and rotten apples. They received jail sentences of only .9 years. This group is small. The largest group of occupational/follower/barrel criminals received low jail sentences of 1.1 years on average.

Finally, a comparison of crime amount among criminal groups is relevant in Figure 3.7. Average crime amount for the total sample is 47 million

Actor \ Role		Leader	Follower
Occupational	Rotten apple	48	57
	Rotten barrel	47	45
Corporate	Rotten apple	58	46
	Rotten barrel	53	52

Figure 3.5 Age of criminals depending on role, actor, and level.

Actor \ Role		Leader	Follower
Occupational	Rotten apple	2.8	2.0
	Rotten barrel	2.8	1.1
Corporate	Rotten apple	1.3	.9
	Rotten barrel	3.1	1.1

Figure 3.6 Prison sentence in years depending on role, actor, and level.

kr, which is about U.S. $9 million. The largest crime amount can be found in the group of corporate criminals who were followers belonging to a rotten barrel. Their amount was 215 million kr. The smallest crime amount can be found in the group of occupational criminals who were followers belonging to a rotten barrel. Their amount was 12 million kr as listed in Figure 3.7.

Groups of White-Collar Criminals

Criminal behavior among executives is a complicated challenge in human resource management. White-collar crime is financial crime committed

Actor \ Role		Leader	Follower
Occupational	Rotten apple	35	16
	Rotten barrel	30	12
Corporate	Rotten apple	67	22
	Rotten barrel	203	215

Figure 3.7 Crime amount in million kr depending on role, actor, and level.

by trusted and potentially reliable persons in important business positions. Research on white-collar crime is often based on anecdotal evidence, in which famous white-collar criminals serve as examples for case studies (Baird & Zelin, 2009; Bookman, 2008; Bucy et al., 2008; Dodge, 2009; Fleet & Fleet, 2006; Friedrichs, 2009; Garoupa, 2007; Hansen, 2009; Heath, 2008; Messerschmidt, 1997; Perri & Brody, 2011; Simpson, 2011). While being relevant and interesting cases, the extent of generalization from such studies is questionable. What is needed is a larger sample of white-collar criminals that can be studied in terms of average values as well as variation in criminal characteristics.

With this larger sample, we can then study white-collar convicts using statistical techniques to identify and study groups of white-collar criminals. Therefore, this section is concerned with the following research questions: *What groups of white-collar criminals can be identified, and what differences can be found between white-collar groups?*

When studying newspaper reports as well as court documents for all 305 convicts, four groups of white-collar criminals emerge: criminal entrepreneurs, corporate criminals, criminal followers, and female criminals as defined and described in the following sections.

Criminal Entrepreneurs

Most of the entrepreneurship literature seems to engage in a positive enthusiasm about the role of the entrepreneur. There is a need to take a neutral look at how some entrepreneurs engage in white-collar crime and how entrepreneurship is not always a wholesome and clean endeavor. An entrepreneur is a person who operates a new enterprise or venture and assumes some accountability for the inherent risk (Symeonidou-Kastanidou, 2007). The new and modern view on entrepreneurial talent is a person who takes the risks involved to undertake a business venture. Entrepreneurship is often difficult and tricky as many ventures fail. In the context of for-profit enterprises, "entrepreneur" is often synonymous with "founder." Most commonly, the term entrepreneur applies to someone who creates value by offering a product or service in order to obtain certain profit.

Entrepreneurship is the practice of starting new organizations or revitalizing mature organizations, particularly new businesses generally in response to identified opportunities. Entrepreneurship is sometimes labeled entrepreneurialism. Entrepreneurship is often a difficult undertaking as a vast majority of new businesses fail. Entrepreneurial activity is substantially different from operational activity as it is mainly concerned with creativity and innovation. Entrepreneurship ranges from small individual initiatives to major undertakings creating many job opportunities.

Self-control theory can explain can explain criminal entrepreneurs. The lower the individual's self-control, the greater is the likelihood of his or her involvement in criminal behavior. Low self-control is defined in terms of characteristics, such as impulsive, risk-taking, and self-centered (Meneses & Akers, 2011). Thus, self-control theory proposes that individuals commit crime because of low self-control. Except in rare cases of mass fraud, such as the Enron scandal, not all the elite within a given organization or industry will commit crime. Hence, although the elite at the top of their profession and corporation differentially associate with people of equal status in their own and other corporations, not all corporate elites commit crimes and behave in an overtly deviant manner (Hansen, 2009).

Corporate Criminals

Corporate crime is financial crime enacted by executive individuals or executive groups for the benefit of the organization (Hansen, 2009). If a corporate official violates the law in acting for the corporation, it is considered a corporate crime. A corporation cannot be jailed, and therefore, the majority of penalties to control individual violators are not available for corporations as such (Bookman, 2008). Simpson (2011) argues that thinking about corporate crime requires recognition that both organizations and individuals may be illegal actors and potential targets for crime prevention and control, such as sanctions.

Corporate crime concerns those particular types of financial crime that is perpetrated by top-tier members of an organization with the specific goal of gaining something for that organization (Fleet and Fleet, 2006). Corporate crime arises, for example, in instances when fraud or corruption is happening on behalf of the corporation itself as in when the infraction is being executed for the gain of the company. Growth in profits, acquiring building permits, and creating a local monopoly are instances of advantages garnered as a result of fraud. Perri and Brody (2011) contend that corporate crime is justified as actions that are tolerable when done to surmount monetary problems or to boost the financial standing or the company.

From a legal point of view, a corporation is not an actual human being. Robson (2010) says that while a corporation may have a "personality," it is still insentient and inanimate, and it only exists as a manifestation of the actions and objectives of the executives and managers that comprise it. Robson adds that this dichotomy becomes evident when we try to apply the concepts of criminal law in cases of corporate crime. Can a business organization be criminally liable? Regardless of the answer, says Robson, courts and legislatures have expanded the visibility of corporate criminal prosecution to ensure it is a deterrent to all types of criminal behavior.

Often companies indulge in corporate crime to enhance their economic performance. Workers may behave illegally in ways that increase the earnings of the company, but in corporate crime, these actions might create very little or no personal advantage for the workers themselves. In reviewing the Enron case, Heath (2008) points out key differences between the crimes committed by Andrew Fastow, who benefited himself without anyone knowing and at the firm's expense versus those committed by Kenneth Lay and Jeffrey Skilling, who primarily acted to enrich the firm; they were rewarded only indirectly (via rising stock prices).

In contrast to legal corporations that may perpetrate business crime, illegal organizations were specifically created to commit crime. Garoupa (2007) highlights this list of distinctions between organized crime and business crime: (i) organized crime is committed by illegitimate firms (that have no legal standing), and the criminal market is their main area of activity followed by authentic business arenas as their secondary markets; (ii) corporate crime is done by legal companies (with legitimate status), and they primarily operate within the legal marketplace, and the criminal environment is only a secondary option for business. The reason behind organized crime is to make the most of unlawful endeavors, but corporations are not in existence to break the law. Organized crime enters into legitimate markets for the purpose of bettering its position within the criminal market, and corporations break the law in order to enhance their reputation among valid markets.

The Institutional theory of ethical breakdown may work to elucidate the level of corporate crime. Executives in a failing company have a tendency to get involved in both occupational crime and corporate crime when they need to increase revenue both for their personal gain and for the company. The reasons behind this include failure of decency that follows on the heels of commercial ruin. It is possible that the order is possibly that corporate crime happens before the occupational crime.

Shadnam and Lawrence (2011) used this institutional theory to describe the ethical deterioration and likeliness for crime to occur within organizations: Their hypothesis in regard to moral collapse is twofold. They say the morality of an organization is rooted in nested systems of the employees, the organization, and the overall ethical community and that these moral philosophies and guidelines "flow down" through the organization to the employees, and ethical concepts and inspiration "flow upward" to the larger community. In addition, Shadnam and Lawrence say moral collapse can be a result of interruptions in this flow.

Shadman and Lawrence (2011) have articulated some research hypotheses that support this theory and suggest that the probability of moral failure varies, contingent on the following conditions:

- Moral collapse is increasingly likely to occur in organizations in which the above-mentioned flows are interrupted, which can be the result of waning commitment to official communication channels by those at the top or interference of more casual communication because of high employee or member turnover.
- Moral collapse is more likely to occur when an organization features configurations and systems that weaken the organization's ability to recognize and integrate ethical ideology from the moral community because the organization is dominating its members' attention and/or because the organization challenges the authenticity of these ideologies.
- Moral collapse is more probable in organizations where charging people with any transgression generates considerable personal and financial costs for the organization of the moral community in which it exists.
- Moral collapse is more apt to happen within organizations to the extent that the work environment undermine enclosure and/or the situation lessen the efficiency of any surveillance.

Institutional theory is very similar to dysfunctional network theory in that organizations are likely to reflect the fundamental components of their surroundings. The biggest enterprises are better able to grasp the adverse effects of legal penalties that the government or other supervisory agencies might levy. The biggest corporations often employ better legal teams and other applicable means, so they can take on any legal challenges more efficiently and effectively than smaller companies. Two examples of this are Microsoft's antitrust and anticompetition lawsuits in the United States and the European Union. The result is that laws and regulations are often far less effective deterrents to crime when it comes to these large companies (Dion, 2009). As a result of this theory, and with all other things being equal, it is reasonable to think that bigger organizations are more likely to endure corporate crime.

Criminal Followers

In contrast to criminal entrepreneurs and many corporate criminals, criminal followers are not the originators of criminal activities (Bucy et al., 2008). Followers are generally timid and weak-willed individuals who follow others, sometimes following them directly into criminal plots. Followers may be fervent supporters of the correctness of their scheme, and they are also certain that nothing bad will happen to them because they are in the shadow of a leader whom they have faith in or whom they are afraid of. Followers tend to be unsophisticated and trusting and may be oblivious to what is really happening. Sometimes, they are just overwhelmed by the charm and magnetism of the leader, and this spawns an powerful loyalty to the leader. However, leadership in general, and the function of varying approaches to leadership in particular, are not necessarily a one-way progression. In fact they are frequently the result of an arrangement in which the conduct of the followers possibly have an effect on the intensity and the style of the leaders' actions. As such, followers may be far more involved in such associations, which is in contrast to the above suggestions.

Charisma is defined as personal magnetism, a specific trait of a person by which he or she seems to be very special and may be regarded as being gifted with phenomenal or remarkable abilities or characteristics. Charismatic leadership is often borne out of the charisma or personal magnetism of the leader. It then falls to the followers to understand the implications of this charisma in leaders and to respond with appropriate behavior (Anguilera and Vadera, 2008).

When we study leadership behavior in general, some strong dissimilarities between leaders and followers are uncovered. As an example, Glasø and Einarsen (2008) researched emotional control in leader-follower relationships. They learned that adverse feelings, such as dissatisfaction, doubt, and irritation, are often muffled, and optimistic emotions, such as eagerness, attraction, and peacefulness are those that are genuinely voiced or may be feigned. When leaders and followers talk about emotions that they have actually felt and/or expressed, the most highly scored feelings in the study were "glad," "enthusiastic," "well," and "interested." The reported degree of emotional regulation was higher for leaders than for followers.

Leaders are frequently more dominant and self-confident, and they can be less likely to avoid social interactions and to be mistrustful and gullible than followers. A study by Glasø et al. (2010) shows 30% of leaders display higher profiles of personality traits when it comes to social and relational issues, which is similar to a sample taken of psychiatric patients. This suggests that very serious issues may come up in interpersonal dealings between followers and leaders.

Leaders will emply a diverse array of actions, manners, and practices aimed toward followers they are trying to convince to collaborate. Leaders engaging in persecution and bullying are instances of activity that has been recounted as occurring regularly in many work environments. Harassment and intimidation are done intentionally to cause embarrassment, insult, and suffering (Hoel et al., 2010).

Obedience theory can possibly clarify some follower behavior. Obedience theory is connected to the triangle of fraud comprised of rationalization, pressure, and opportunity. Obedience theory may be helpful when it comes to understanding the stresses and justifications that are behind the reasons cited by people who commit occupational crime (Baird and Zelin, 2009). Baird and Zelin say that these pressures may come from individual financial need, or it may come from being coerced by a person in a position of authority at one's workplace, which may be accompanied by a threat of unemployment. They posit that obedience theory can explain people who get involved in occupational fraud against their own beliefs and values because of this pressure to obey a person in authority—this behavior is then excused by placing blame for the wrongdoing entirely on the authority figure.

Pressure to obey is deemed a form of social influence pressure, of which there are two other types: compliance pressure and conformity pressure as described by Baird and Zelin (2009). They define compliance pressure as comparable to obedience pressure, but compliance pressure is as likely to come from peers as from superiors. Baird and Zelin define obedience pressure as coming only from an authority figure, and conformity pressure is pressure to conform to apparent or social standards.

Baird and Zelin (2009) claim that of these three types of social influence pressure, obedience pressure is particularly powerful because of the influence that indivuduals with authority have over their subordinates. Employees in a company complacently follow the directions of the executives at the highest levels and justify their behavior by not being accountable for their actions. The pressure to commit fraud can often take the form of explicit instructions from a company executive, but it can also be a result of on beliefs garnered from an understanding of the company's compensation and incentive configurations.

A more powerful case for follower behavior is rooted in obedience theory combined with self-control theory. Self-control theory suggests people commit fraud because they have low levels of self-control. Except in some unusual circumstances involving mass fraud, such as the Enron case, not all executives in a specific organization or industry will commit crime. Although managers at the height of their careers and corporate structures socialize with the executives of comparable standing in their own and other companies, not every corporate elite is likely to commit crimes and act in an openly aberrant way (Hansen, 2009).

Female Criminals

There are few cases of convicted women in white-collar crime. Even though women are found in the categories of criminal entrepreneurs, corporate criminals, and criminal followers, they are treated as a separate group because of their own characteristics. Female white-collar criminals are sometimes labeled pink-collar criminals. Traditionally, typical pink-collar crime types were embezzlement and fraud (Dodge, 2009).

Friedrichs (2009) argues that it is widely understood that males greatly outnumber females among conventional crime offenders. He claims that men outnumber women by six to one. Furthermore, he argues that all available evidence indicates that a parallel situation exists for white-collar crime offenders. His data indicate that the female arrest rate for white-collar crime has been one quarter or one fifth of the male arrest rate.

Similarly, Messerschmidt (1997) argues that gender is the strongest predictor of criminal involvement—it is boys and men who dominate in crime. Arrest, self-report, and victimization data all reflect that boys and men perpetrate more conventional crime and the more serious such crime than do girls and women. He suggests that men have a virtual monopoly on the commission of syndicated, corporate, and political crime.

Dodge (2009) argues that the role of women in white-collar crime has emerged as a major topic in the 21st century, but it remains a controversial and neglected area of criminological study. In her book, Dodge explores the topic of women and white-collar crime by encompassing theoretical, historical, and critical accounts of female perpetrators, victims, and whistle-blowers. Through the examination of numerous real-life case studies, the book provides insights into the personal and societal characterizations of women who cross the line into elite deviance or become victims of corporate or occupational crime.

Steffensmeier and Allan (1996) suggested a *gendered theory* of female offending. The theory attempts to explain female criminality and gender differences in crime. The theory focuses on the following elements and interactions between them:

- Organization of gender: Gender norms, moral development, and social control.

- Biological factors: Physical, sexual, and affiliate differences.
- Criminal opportunities: Sexism in the criminal underworld, access to skills, crime associates, and settings.
- Gender differences in crime: Women avoid more serious white-collar crime, such as insider trading, price-fixing, restraint of trade, dumping of toxic waste, fraudulent product commerce, bribery, and official corruption, as well as large-scale governmental crimes.
- Context of offending: Many of the most profound differences between the offenses committed by men and women involve the context of offending, in which context refers to the characteristics of a particular offense. It might be the setting, whether the offense is committed with the assistance of others, the offender's role in initiating and committing the offense, the type of victim, the victim-offender relationship, whether a weapon is used, the extent of injury, the value or type of property destroyed or stolen, and the purpose of the offense.
- Motivation for crime: Tastes regarding risk, likelihood of shame or embarrassment, self-control, and assessment of costs versus rewards of crime.

Comparison of Groups

In the sample of 305 convicted white-collar criminals in Norway from 2009 to 2012, we find 144 criminal entrepreneurs, 39 corporate criminals, 96 criminal followers, and 26 female criminals. In terms of age, corporate criminals are significantly older than criminals in other groups. In terms of prison sentence, entrepreneurs receive significantly longer jail sentences than criminals in other groups. This was confirmed in statistical analysis using dummy variables in regression analysis. Some results are presented in Table 3.5.

Crime amount in terms of Norwegian kroner is highest for corporate criminals and lowest for female criminals. It is interesting to note than even if crime amount for corporate criminals is higher than for criminal entrepreneurs, the corporate criminals received shorter jail sentences than the criminal entrepreneurs. It seems that crime on behalf of the business is treated more mildly in court when compared to crime on behalf of the person himself.

When followers are involved in the crime, there are more persons participating in the crime. The lowest number of participants is found in cases of criminal entrepreneurship.

Published figures from the public tax authorities indicate that female criminals have the lowest taxable income among criminal groups.

Table 3.5 Empirical Comparison of Characteristics of White-Collar Criminal Groups

Total 305 Criminals	144 Criminal Entrepreneurs	39 Corporate Criminals	96 Criminal Followers	26 Female Criminals
Age when convicted	47 years	52 years	47 years	47 years
Prison term	2.8 years	2.0 years	1.4 years	1.7 years
Crime amount	34 million kr	198 million kr	14 million kr	9 million kr
Involved persons	2.6 persons	3.3 persons	5.8 persons	3.9 persons
Taxable income	361,000 kr	363,000 kr	326,000 kr	182,000 kr
Organization size	95 persons	357 persons	88 persons	73 persons

In terms of organization size, the table shows that corporate crime is committed within larger organizations. Organization size is measured in terms of employees, and corporate criminals were found in organizations with an average of 357 employees.

The sample of 305 convicted Norwegian white-collar criminals based on media coverage from 2009 to 2012 indicates significant differences between conceptual groups of criminals as suggested in this article. General comparison of group characteristics is presented in Table 3.6.

In conclusion, white-collar criminals can be categorized into distinct groups. In our empirical research, criminal entrepreneurs represent the largest group of white-collar criminals. Criminal entrepreneurs are convicted at the average age of 47 years, they receive an average prison term of almost three years, and they work in organizations with an average of 95 employees. In comparison, corporate criminals receive shorter jail sentences even when the amount of money involved in the crime is larger. Criminal followers receive the shortest jail sentences, and female criminals have the lowest crime amount.

Table 3.6 General Comparison of Characteristics of White-Collar Criminal Groups

Total 305 Criminals	144 Criminal Entrepreneurs	39 Corporate Criminals	96 Criminal Followers	26 Female Criminals
Age when convicted	Younger	Older	Younger	Younger
Prison term	Long	Medium	Short	Medium
Crime amount	Medium	Large	Small	Small
Involved persons	Few	Some	Many	Some
Taxable income	Medium	Medium	Medium	Low
Organization size	Medium	Large	Medium	Medium

References

Aguilera, R. V., & Vadera, A. K. (2008). The dark side of authority: Antecedents, mechanisms, and outcomes of organizational corruption. *Journal of Business Ethics, 77*, 431–449.

Arjoon, S. (2008). Slippery when wet: The real risk in business. *Journal of Markets & Morality, 11*(1), 77–91.

Ashforth, B. E., Gioia, D. A., Robinson, S. L., & Trevino, L. K. (2008). Re-reviewing organizational corruption. *The Academy of Management Review, 33*(3), 670–684.

Baird, J. E., & Zelin, R. C. (2009). An examination of the impact of obedience pressure on perceptions of fraudulent acts and the likelihood of committing occupational fraud. *Journal of Forensic Studies in Accounting and Business, 1*(1), 1–14.

Baumol, W. J. (1990). Entrepreneurship: Productive, unproductive and destructive. *Journal of Political Economy, 98*(5), 893–921.

Benson, M. L., & Simpson, S. S. (2009). *White-collar crime: An opportunity perspective.* New York: Routledge.

Blickle, G., Schlegel, A., Fassbender, P., & Klein, U. (2006). Some personality correlates of business white-collar crime. *Applied Psychology: An International Review, 55*(2), 220–233.

Bock, T. D., & Kenhove, P. V. (2011). Double standards: The role of techniques of neutralization. *Journal of Business Ethics, 99*, 283–296.

Bookman, Z. (2008). Convergences and omissions in reporting corporate and white collar crime. *DePaul Business & Commercial Law Journal, 6*, 347–392.

Bricker, R., & Chandar, N. (2000). Where Berle and Means went wrong: A reassessment of capital market agency and financial reporting. *Accounting, Organizations and Society, 25*(6), 529–554.

Bruinsma, G., & Bernasco, W. (2004). Criminal groups and transnational illegal markets. *Crime, Law and Social Change, 41*(1), 79–94.

Buch, R. (2012). *Interdependent Exchange Relationships: Exploring the socially embedded nature of social exchange relationships in organizations.* (Series of Dissertations, No. 9 – 2012). BI Norwegian Business School, Oslo, Norway.

Bucy, P. H., Formby, E. P., Raspanti, M. S., & Rooney, K. E. (2008). Why do they do it? The motives, mores, and character of white collar criminals. *St. John's Law Review, 82*(2), 401–571.

Chang, J. J., Lu, H. C., & Chen, M. (2005). Organized crime or individual crime? Endogeneous size of a criminal organization and the optimal law enforcement. *Economic Inquiry, 43*(3), 661–675.

Dhami, M. (2007). White collar prisoners' perceptions of audience reaction. *Deviant Behavior, 28*, 57–77.

Dion, M. (2009). Corporate crime and the dysfunction of value networks. *Journal of Financial Crime, 16*(4), 436–445.

Dodge, M. (2009). *Women and white collar crime.* New York: Prentice Hall.

Eisenhardt, K. M. (1985). Control: Organizational and economic approaches. *Management Science, 31*(2), 134–149.

Fleet, D. D. van, & Fleet, E. W. van (2006). Internal terrorists: The terrorists inside organizations. *Journal of Managerial Psychology, 21*(8), 763–774.

Friedrichs, D. O. (2009). *Trusted criminals: White collar crime in contemporary society.* Belmont, CA: Wadsworth.

Garoupa, N. (2007). Optimal law enforcement and criminal organization. *Journal of Economic Behavior & Organization, 63*(3), 461–474.

Glasø, L., & Einarsen, S. (2008). Emotion regulation in leader-follower relationships. *European Journal of Work and Organizational Psychology, 17*(4), 482–500.

Glasø, L., Einarsen, S., Matthiesen, S. B., & Skogstad, A. (2010). The dark side of leaders: A representative study of interpersonal problems among leaders. *Scandinavian Journal of Organizational Psychology, 2*(2), 3–14.

Glasø, L., Ekerholt, K., Barman, S., & Einarsen, S. (2006). The instrumentality of emotion in leader-subordinate relationships. *International Journal of Work Organisation and Emotion, 1*(3), 255–276.

Goldstraw-White, J. (2012). *White-collar crime: Accounts of offending behaviour.* London: Palgrave Macmillan Publishing.

Gottfredson, M. R., & Hirschi, T. (1990). *A general theory of crime.* Stanford, CA: Stanford University Press.

Gross, E. (1978). Organizational crime: A theoretical perspective. *Studies in Symbolic Interaction, 1*, 55–85.

Hansen, L. L. (2009). Corporate financial crime: Social diagnosis and treatment. *Journal of Financial Crime, 16*(1), 28–40.

Heath, J. (2008). Business ethics and moral motivation: A criminological perspective. *Journal of Business Ethics, 83*(4), 595–614.

Higgins, E. T. (1997). Beyond pleasure and plain. *American Psychologist, 52*, 1280–1300.

Hoel, H., Glasø, L., Hetland, J., Cooper, C. L., & Einarsen, S. (2010). Leadership styles as predictors of self-reported and observed workplace bullying. *British Journal of Management, 21*, 453–468.

Iyer, N., & Kvalnes, Ø. (2012). The battle against fraud, corruption and bribery. *Fraud Intelligence.* Retrieved from www.counter-fraud.com

Jensen, M. C., & Meckling, W. H. (1976). Theory of the firm: Managerial behavior, agency costs and ownership structures. *Journal of Financial Economics, 3*(4), 305–360.

Lasley, J. R. (1988). Toward a control theory of white-collar offending. *Journal of Quantitative Criminology, 4*(4), 347–362.

Leonard, W. N., & Weber, M. G. (1970). Automakers and dealers: A study of criminogenic market forces. *Law & Society Review, 4*(3), 407–424.

Li, S., & Ouyang, M. (2007). A dynamic model to explain the bribery behavior of firms. *International Journal of Management, 24*(3), 605–618.

Lyman, M. D., & Potter, G. W. (2007). *Organized crime* (4th ed.). Upper Saddle River, NJ: Pearson Prentice Hall.

MacLean, T. L. (2007). Framing and organizational misconduct: A symbolic interactionist study. *Journal of Business Ethics, 78*, 3–16.

McKay, R., Stevens, C., & Fratzi, J. (2010). A 12-step process of white-collar crime. *International Journal of Business Governance and Ethics, 5*(1), 14–25.

Menard, S., & Morris, R. G. (2012). Integrated theory and crimes of trust. *Journal of Quantitative Criminology, 28*(2), 365–387.

Meneses, R. A., & Akers, R. L. (2011). A comparison of four general theories of crime and deviance: Marijuana use among American and Bolivian university students. *International Criminal Justice Review, 21*(4), 333–352.

Messerschmidt, J. M. (1997). *Crime as structured action: Gender, race, class, and crime in the making*. Thousand Oaks, CA: Sage Publications.

O'Connor, T. R. (2005). *Police deviance and ethics, megalinks in criminal justice*. Retrieved from http://faculty.ncwc.edu/toconnor/205/205lect11.htm

Padilla, A., Hogan, R., & Kaiser, R. (2007). The toxic triangle: Destructive leaders, susceptible followers, and conducive enviroments. *The Leadership Quarterly, 18*, 176–194.

Perri, F. S., & Brody, R. G. (2011). The Sallie Rohrbach story: Lessons for auditors and fraud examiners. *Journal of Financial Crime, 18*(1), 93–104.

Punch, M. (2003). Rotten orchards: "Pestilence", police misconduct and system failure. *Policing and Society, 13*(2), 171–196.

Robson, R. A. (2010). Crime and punishment: Rehabilitating retribution as a justification for organizational criminal liability. *American Business Law Journal, 47*(1), 109–144.

Shadnam, M., & Lawrence, T. B. (2011). Understanding widespread misconduct in organizations: An institutional theory of moral collapse. *Business Ethics Quarterly, 21*(3), 379–407.

Simpson, S. S. (2011). Making sense of white collar crime: Theory and research. *The Ohio State Journal of Criminal Law, 8*(2), 481–502.

Siponen, M., & Vance, A. (2010). Neutralization: New insights into the problem of employee information systems security policy violations. *MIS Quarterly, 34*(3), 487–502.

Steffensmeier, D., & Allan, E. (1996). Gender and crime: Toward a gendered theory of female offending. *Annual Review of Sociology, 22*, 459–487.

Sykes, G., & Matza, D. (1957). Techniques of neutralization: A theory of delinquency. *American Sociological Review, 22*(6), 664–670.

Symeonidou-Kastanidou, E. (2007). Towards a new definition of organized crime in the European Union. *European Journal of Crime, Criminal Law and Criminal Justice*, 83–103.

Wright, A. (2006). *Organised Crime*. Devon, UK: Willan Publishing.

Women in White-Collar Crime

4

The purpose of this chapter is to present an empirical study of white-collar crime conducted in Norway to create insights into perceptions of potential offenders within a gender perspective. In the popular press, white-collar crime committed by women is sometimes labeled pink-collar crime. Traditionally, typical pink-collar crime types were embezzlement and fraud (Dodge, 2009). This chapter documents that women are substantially less involved in white-collar crime, and it explores why it is so. The research attempts to explain why women are less involved, including reasons such as lack of women in management and criminological explanations for lower crime rates among women. We address and explore female participation in white-collar crime.

Media coverage of individual criminals was again used as identification for crime cases, which were then found in court rulings. This chapter is based on empirical research of convicted white-collar criminals. Out of 305 convicts presented in newspaper articles, most of them were men. There were very few women. Women convicted of white-collar crime had significantly lower management positions than convicted men. It is indeed hard to believe that Norwegian men commit 10 times more white-collar crime than Norwegian women also because Norway is seen as a salient egalitarian country. Therefore, it is a question of whether the detection rate for female white-collar criminals is lower than that for male white-collar criminals. More attention needs to be paid to characteristics of female white-collar crime in the future. Rather than presenting some cases and anecdotal evidence, this chapter presents some statistical evidence to suggest and make conclusions about gender differences in white-collar crime conviction. It is about female participation in white-collar crime.

Friedrichs (2009) claims there is conventional wisdom indicating that women are vastly outnumbered by men when it comes to the majority of criminals. He argues that females are outnumbered by male offenders by six to one. In addition, he maintains that much existing evidence shows comparable statistics in the arena of white-collar crime. His data reveals that the white-collar arrest rate for women has been one quarter or one fifth of the rate for men.

Likewise, Messerschmidt (1997) says gender is the most clear-cut forecaster of criminal activity, men and boys are dominant in crime statistics.

Data from victims as well as arrest records and self-reports all indicate that males commit more conventional crime and more serious crime than women and girls. He says men have a near monopoly when it comes to perpetrating of corporate, syndicated, and political crime.

Dodge (2009) argues that the role of women in white-collar crime has emerged as a major topic in the 21st century, but it remains a controversial and neglected area of criminological study. In her book, Dodge explores the topic of women and white-collar crime by encompassing theoretical, historical, and critical accounts of female perpetrators, victims, and whistle-blowers. Through the examination of numerous real-life case studies, the book provides insights into the personal and societal characterizations of women who cross the line into elite deviance or become victims of corporate or occupational crime.

Research on leadership and citizenship has established that the men and women performing the same behavior are judged differently and that women are often penalized when they act in ways counter to social expectations (Heilman & Chen, 2005; Heilman & Okimoto, 2007). Social role theory states that socially shared expectations exist about how men and women should behave, and when women or men contradict these expectations, they face negative consequences (Heilman & Chen, 2005; Heilman & Okimoto, 2007; Moss-Racusin, Phelan, & Rudman, 2010). Eagly and Carli (2007) have argued that there are fewer women in leadership because of this prejudice. Norms about male behavior lead to approval for men being agentic (e.g., ambitious, aggressive, dominant, forceful, independent, self-confident, and prone to act as a leader) whereas women are expected to act in a communal manner (e.g., affectionate, helpful, kind). The implications of these findings are that there will be fewer women in leadership positions, and men will be rewarded for behaving in a more aggressive and ambitious way. Both of these conclusions lend support to the gender differences found in white-collar crime—fewer women in leadership leads to less opportunity, and male/female socialization makes it more acceptable for men to be ambitious and assertive, which could more easily result in men committing white-collar crime.

Similar findings about behavioral differences between men and women emerge in the organizational research on negotiation. Negotiation is a fundamental form of coordination and influence over resources in organizations and affects the process of work, the resolution of conflict, and the advancement of careers. Gender differences found include men outperforming women in competitive negotiations (Stuhlmacher & Walters, 1999), initiating more negotiations (Babcock & Laschever, 2003), and facing fewer social consequences for pursuing negotiations (Bowles, Babcock, & Lai, 2007). From this research, indications are that whether due to social expectations or individual differences, it appears that men in organizations tend to behave more competitively and face fewer social sanctions for doing so than women.

In addition to men being in more positions of leadership, being rewarded for leadership and competitive behavior differences are also found between men and women with regard to ethical behavior. In the past decades, there has been an increased focus on the relationship between gender and ethical perceptions. A recent review of the empirical ethical decision-making literature by O'Fallon and Butterfield (2005) concluded that women make more ethical decisions than men. These findings are consistent with earlier meta studies in which women demonstrated stronger ethical attitudes than men.

Although women tend to express more ethical responsibility than men, recent research also suggests that women's responses to ethical issues might be attributed to the social desirability response bias. The social desirability response bias appears to account for a significant portion of the relationship between gender and ethical decision-making, because of which females consistently report more ethical responses than males. However, these findings also speak to women's social sensitivity and perhaps the strong influence that social expectations can have on their behavior.

From the above research, we can conclude that men and women behave differently and are not treated the same in organizational settings. Socialization pressures and social roles influence the extent to which a woman can survive with a deviant behavior or, specifically, behaviors that are more competitive or display agency. Men, on the other hand, are expected to be ambitious and competitive (Moss-Racusin et al., 2010), which may prime them for white-collar crime.

White-collar crime not only requires the individual to act but that the opportunity presents itself. The fact that men may have more opportunities to commit white-collar crime might also explain the gender differences found. According to Huffman, Cohen, and Pearlman (2010), workplace power inequality still exists, and women are not in the elite positions; this also means that women will have fewer opportunities to commit white-collar crime. It is commonly recognized that, on average, women's career prospects are poorer than those of men. This is supported by public statistics on both wages and vocational positions as stated by Jonnergård, Stafsudd, and Elg (2010):

> Previous studies have also stressed these differences and women have been found to have lower positions and less promising career prospects as well as a lower or at least different organizational commitment. Often, the differences have referred to variations in career patterns between the genders. (p. 723)

Research on women and management and social role theory have had as their aim to explain why so few women are in top positions in organizations. It could be concluded that women still lack the opportunity to commit white-collar crime rather than that women do not engage in this behavior.

However, in an old study by Hill and Harris (1981), no support was found for the opportunity theory's suggestion that similar male-female criminal profiles emerge even as opportunities for females expand. The findings indicate that other factors must be involved.

Steffensmeier and Allan (1996) suggested a gendered theory of female offending, which encompasses both individual differences and opportunity. The theory attempts to explain female criminality and gender differences and focuses on the following elements and interactions between those elements:

- Female crime is different than male crime.
  - Women avoid more serious white-collar crime, such as insider trading, price fixing, restraint of trade, toxic waste dumping, fraudulent product commerce, bribery, and official corruption, as well as large-scale governmental crimes. However, it should be noted that a recent study in Finland by Kankaanranta and Muttilainen (2010) found that 9% of economic criminals in the construction industry were females, which is a modestly higher proportion than is generally working in the construction sector (7%).
  - Context of offending: Many of the most profound differences between the offenses committed by men and women involve the context of offending, in which context refers to the characteristics of a particular offense. It might be the setting, whether the offense is committed with others, the offender's role in initiating and committing the offense, the type of victim, the victim-offender relationship, whether a weapon was used, the extent of injury, the value or type of property destroyed or stolen, and the purpose of the offense.
- Why is female crime different than male crime?
  - Organization of gender: Gender norms, moral development, and social control.
  - Criminal opportunities: Underworld sexism, access to skills, and crime associates and settings.
  - Biological factors: Physical, sexual, and affiliate differences.
  - Motivation for crime: Tastes for risk, likelihood of shame or embarrassment, self-control, and assessment of costs versus rewards of crime.

Social control and self-control could be more developed among women than men, causing less crime by women. This phenomenon of gender difference is explained by Worthen (2011) in terms of parent-child bonding. She suggests that adolescents who have healthy relationships with their parents are less likely to be involved in delinquency. She found that gender differences in delinquency can be partially explained by gender differences in mean values of each element of the parental bond, that is, emotional attachment to parents, time spent with parents, and parental monitoring. Gender differences can, in addition, be partially explained by examining the effects of the elements of the parental bond on delinquent involvement as they differ by gender.

Explanations for gender differences when they are uncovered range from the biological, which emphasizes the evolved dispositions of men and women (Buss, 1995), to social explanations, which focus on the dissimilar placement of men and women in the social structure and with different social role expectations.

The social perspective was applied by Becker and McCorkel (2011) in their study of the impact of male co-offenders on women's crime. They examined how gender affects access to criminal opportunities in terms of the effect a male co-offender has on women's offending. They found that the presence of a male co-offender broadens women's criminal involvement in distinctive ways.

The social perspective could explain the mixed results of research on ethical behavior as the context and social structure might enhance or diminish the differences found between men and women. Given the nature of white-collar crime and the importance of context and social roles we are interested in investigating the relationship previously found between gender and white-collar crime in the Norwegian context.

The Norwegian gender regime is viewed as leading in the emancipation of women. Norway ranks among the top countries on the United Nations Development Programme's gender empowerment measure of women's participation in economic and political life. Women's participation in the labor force has steadily increased in a process closely intertwined with the development of family policies. Women's labor participation is around 70%, which is nearly as high as men's. Compared to most other countries, this is a high proportion (Seeberg, 2012).

However, as pointed out by Seeberg (2012), gender segregation in the labor market is also high. While family life is increasingly gender equal, paid employment outside the family shows a discrepancy among men and women. A large proportion of women work part time, there is a significant gender pay gap, and over 90% of employees within care work and cleaning services are women. Care work can be defined as a series of embodied tasks (counseling, referrals, bathing, cooking, and cleaning) and emotional states (relationships, support, and nurturing) provided to an individual or group of individuals, aimed at enhancing functionality and day-to-day living (Baines, Charlesworth, Cunningham, & Dassinger, 2012).

Criminal Characteristics

Several studies have focused on gender patterns (e.g., Pillay, Tones, & Kelly, 2011) and gender gaps (e.g., Sörlin, Ohman, Blomstedt, Stenlund, & Lindholm, 2011) in organizations and in management. The issue of gender in relation to white-collar criminality is an under-researched area of the criminological literature. Exceptions to this rule include Steffensmeier and Allan (1996), Haantz (2002), and Robb (2006). It must be stressed that when we refer to gender in this chapter we make reference to the participation of women in white-collar crime and the issue of male bias. Women are underrepresented in the statistics that cover white-collar crime. We will argue that this is not to say that women do not participate in such crime, and in this chapter, we will present some theoretical and structural factors that help to explain this apparent underrepresentation of women in the commission of white-collar crime. It also helps to explain gaps in the literature of gender, crime, and entrepreneurship. The very term "entrepreneur" conjures up images of a male businessman and of a masculine persona. This chapter sets these issues in a gendered context. For example, stereotypes in business and in crime are biased toward the masculine as in the term "businessman gangster."

Criminal behavior by members of the privileged socioeconomic class is labeled white-collar crime (Benson & Simpson, 2009). It is often argued that women commit less white-collar crime than men (Haantz, 2002; Holtfreter, Beaver, Reisig, & Pratt, 2010; Huffman et al., 2010). Suggested reasons for possible gender differences in white-collar crime include lack of opportunity and risk aversion.

This chapter reports findings from a study of white-collar criminals. It is based on the following research question: What differences can be found between male and female white-collar criminals?

This chapter makes a contribution to the literature on gender in management, as it presents a comparison of male and female white-collar criminals adding to previous research on crime in a gender perspective (e.g., Gatrell, 2010; Madichie & Nkamnebe, 2010).

It must be stressed at the outset that white-collar crime as envisaged and posited by Edwin Sutherland (1949) is primarily a business-oriented criminological category. Sutherland envisaged a white-collar crime to be a crime committed by a person of respectability and high social status in the course of his occupation and, in particular, by entrepreneurs. This dictates that we need to take greater cognizance of business and, in particular, its operational structure conventions when discussing gendered aspects of white-collar crime. This is necessary because the apparent nonparticipation of women in the crime may be explained by social issues, which are not captured in the official statistics. As a result, it is possible that their participation and the roles they play in joint business ventures are underrepresented.

Because white-collar criminality is often conflated with particular occupationally orientated crimes and with corporate criminality (Clinard and Yeager, 2005; O'Grady, 2011), it is easy to lose sight of the white-collar crimes committed by members of family businesses and small and medium-sized enterprises. For example, crimes such as bribery, computer crime, copyright infringement, embezzlement, fraud, forgery, insider trading, identity theft, money laundering, and tax-evasion are clearly more easily perpetrated by, and more easily concealed by, owners of businesses and white-collar employees. Nevertheless, despite the continuing debate on gender discrimination and glass ceilings in corporations, a small number of women do achieve positions of power and authority and, as such, have considerable autonomy. The fact that they have more to lose may dictate that they are less likely to commit corporate crimes than men.

Also, as the term "white-collar criminal" has expanded; it could include crimes committed by employees of such businesses and crimes against such businesses irrespective of their social class or standing, which runs contrary to Sutherland's initial exposition. Moreover, at the time when Sutherland formulated his *theory of white-collar criminality*, the social system of patriarchy was more powerful than it is today, and there were fewer acknowledged female entrepreneurs.

Issues of gender in relation to white-collar criminality are important because, from our reading and from anecdotal evidence, there are other issues at play, which can skew the gender bias and lead to a higher representation of men among the official statistics:

- Businessmen may register the business (or assets) in their wife's name to avoid legal consequences or for tax-avoidance purposes. We assume this may be a two-way process and that women may run a business but register it in their husband's name. This is a legal cut-out mechanism as a spouse cannot normally be legally compelled to give evidence against the other.
- Often the registered owners of businesses are actually fronts for the real owners, again as a legal avoidance mechanism. This too may disguise the true number of female-owned business.
- Women may act as the caretaker manager of a business in the absence of their male partners or may play a role in the business but not have direct ownership.
- Women may think more about the consequences of their actions and are generally less impulsive than men. Research conducted by the Financial Services Authority in the UK in 2001 suggests that men

take more financial risks and are more likely than women to have ISAs, credit cards, mortgages, shares, unit trusts, and life insurance.

- Lower numbers of women investing in financial products is seen as indicative of a more cautious attitude. It seems that while fewer women choose to invest in financial products, they actually do better than men. A study carried out by the National Association of Investors Corporation (NAIC) for the University of California found that the share portfolios of women earned, on average, 1.4% more per year than those of men (BBC, 2001, http://news.bbc.co.uk/1/hi/business/1337830.stm).

- Men potentially commit more serious white-collar offenses, increasing their likelihood of imprisonment. Because the sample only includes criminals convicted and sent to jail, fewer women will occur in the sample.

These points are important because white-collar criminality is not the perfect crime, and people who commit it face a chance of their crime being detected by others. This means that it is not always possible to cover one's tracks evidentially. Both white-collar partners in a marriage/business may be equally guilty, but as long as the authorities can prove a charge against the alleged perpetrator of the crime, then accusations of complicity may not be pursued. Additionally, because women do not fit the official profile of a criminal, investigative chivalry may occur in which the authorities look no further than the man in charge. Our point is that studies based purely on statistical data might miss the point because they provide statistical profiles and approximations and not nuanced qualitative configurations, such as those presented in this book.

Based on the discussion above, it is natural to focus on the difficulties of accessing white-collar female offenders and how this area might be made accessible in future research. The research question might simply be stated: Why are women so underrepresented in the official statistics and in the media on white-collar crime?

Another angle would be to take a celebrity case and discuss it. One immediate thought is the American tycoon Martha Stewart and the insider trading scandal:

In 2001, Martha Stewart's name recognition expanded beyond the domestic and corporate spheres after allegations of insider trading emerged in the national media. Stewart, who was lauded as the perfect combination of homemaker and business tycoon, entered the world of convicted white-collar criminals in a stunning turn of events as federal prosecutors dropped charges of insider trading to pursue a trial based primarily on perjury. The Stewart case, in many respects, represents the penultimate example of how and why the involvement of women in crime has changed historically and conceptually. (Dodge, 2009, p. xii)

But then the celebrity angle would cloud the issue. Alternatively there is the Bernie Madoff affair in which his wife and family obviously knew more than they let on.

Over the past few decades, there has been an increased focus on the relationship between gender and ethical perceptions. A review of the empirical ethical decision-making literature by O'Fallon and Butterfield (2005) concluded that often there are no differences found between men and women. Across a large sample of countries, Dollar, Fisman, and Gatti (2001) discovered that the greater the representation of women in parliament, the lower the level of corruption. Explanations for gender differences, once they are uncovered, range from the biological, which emphasize evolved or innate dispositions of men and women (Buss, 1995) to social explanations, which focus on the dissimilar placement and ranking of men and women in the social structure. The social perspective could well explain the mixed research results on ethical behavior as context and social structure might enhance or diminish differences between men and women.

Closely related to the discourses surrounding female conduct and behavior is law's construction of the potentially natural woman who possesses a maternal instinct, longs to have children, and actively embraces the role of a caring person within the domestic setting:

> She is emotional, irrational, and passive by nature in contrast to the natural male who is rational, objective and active. Because of law's alignment to scientific discourses it speaks the voice of reason and rationality; hence its construction of femininity becomes self-evident—it is obvious what a woman is. (Ballinger, 2003, p. 225)

However, given that differences have been detected in ethical behavior, the question arises whether gender differences have also been found in specific areas, such as white-collar crime? Before we address this crime area, we can look at other areas of crime, such as police misconduct and crime. One study from the United States indicates that the answer is yes, gender differences exist. In a study using both internal and external complaints of crime in a large police agency in the United States, Lersch and Mieczkowski (2000) found male officers were over-represented. Another recent research article examined citizen complaints filed against police and revealed that female officers were less likely, compared to male officers, to become the subject of citizen complaints. Male officers were more likely to be repeat offenders, that is, officers who receive multiple complaints within a short time frame (Hassell & Archbold, 2010). A study conducted by the National Center for

Women and Policing in the United States revealed that male officers were more than eight times more likely to have sustained allegations of excessive force, and a male officer is more than twice as likely to have a citizen name him in a complaint of excessive force (NCWP, 2002).

Police officers represent an interesting analogy to our topic of white-collar criminals because they are on the other side and because several gender studies have been carried out in police forces. For example, Salo and Allwood (2011) studied gender, decision-making styles, and stress among police investigators. Their study found that women applied less rational and more dependent decision-making styles. Dependent in this context means dependence on advice from others before making important decisions. Female investigators also displayed higher levels of stress and performance-based self-esteem.

At present we are unaware of any studies that have investigated gender and white-collar crime in Norway. Norway is ranked as the second best country in the world for gender equality (Hausmann, Tyson, & Zahidi, 2010) and has one of the highest participation rates of women in the workforce. Still looking at gender and police crime, the first female police officer in Norway was in 1910 (Politidirektoratet, 2010), and the director of the Norwegian police force for the last 11 years has been a woman. Today, almost half of the police force is women. There are a total of 13,000 police employees in Norway, out of which 8000 are police officers and 5000 are civilians. While the majority of police officers are male, the majority of civilians are female.

Research investigating Norwegian police officers has found that male police officers are older, at higher organizational levels, experience higher autonomy, have less education, and work more hours and in smaller forces. The findings were dissimilar to previous research as both male and female officers indicated similar levels of work outcomes, policing attitudes toward use of force, and social skills to solve problems. Few differences between male and female officers were found on job demands, work satisfaction, social and coping resources, and psychological and physical health. Male officers did experience more violence and threats whereas female officers encountered more harassment and discrimination. From the egalitarian social context of Norway and our previous research on the Norwegian police, we might expect to find more similarities than differences between male and female officers' crime.

However, the empirical cases examined in our previous police crime research from Norway demonstrate that men are over-represented in crime cases and convictions. This finding is in line with research on citizen complaints and convictions of excessive force in other countries (Hassell & Archbold, 2010; Lersch & Mieczkowski, 2000; NCWP, 2002). Although

Norway is known for gender equality, it appears that gender differences occur within crime.

Benson and Simpson (2009) argue that one of the oldest and most widely accepted findings in criminology is that males are more likely to be offenders than females. However, in regard to traditional street crime, the gap between male and female offending is not the same for all offenses. It is smaller for some offenses than it is for others. For example, one study showed that the female percentage of arrests for minor property crime was 35%. For crime such as robbery, females accounted for only 8% of arrests.

Therefore, Benson and Simpson (2009) argue that the gender gap is narrower for minor property offenses and wider for more violent offenses. Similarly, the size of the gender gap depends on the type of white-collar crime. Women made up less than 5% in a study of those convicted of antitrust or securities fraud, and they accounted for almost 50%—half—of the convicted bank embezzlers in a Yale study cited by Benson and Simpson (2009, p. 169).

Traditionally, crimes committed by women were associated and ingrained in separate spheres of femininity and masculinity and intrinsically linked to distinct motives and opportunities:

> Women were more likely to be engaged in prostitution, shoplifting, check kiting, and small-scale embezzlement as a means of financial support. The expansion of opportunities for women in the workplace, however, has changed perceptions that corporate and occupational criminal activities are delineated by gender. (Dodge, 2009, p. xii)

Data from other studies show similar variations in the gender gap. One study showed that women constituted only 10% of those convicted of bribery and tax offenses, but again 50% of the bank embezzlers. Another study showed that individuals who committed asset misappropriation were significantly less likely to be male than those who committed fraudulent statements. In other words, females were more significantly represented among those charged with asset misappropriation as compared to those charged with fraudulent statements (Benson & Simpson, 2009).

Traditionally, women were considered victims of white-collar crime:

> Considerable evidence exists that women were sought out as victims by frauds and embezzlers who well understood their vulnerability. During the 1860s, for example, the shady company promoter Albert Grant compiled lists of widows, unmarried women and other small investors to whom he sent circulars advertising his dubious speculations. (Robb, 2006, p. 1062)

Benson and Simpson (2009) challenge this traditional view of women as primarily victims of white-collar crime:

Most criminological work on gendered white-collar victimization focuses on women as victims. Few, however, take a comprehensive look at the ways in which gendered opportunities to engage in white-collar crime affect victimization patterns that are also gendered. (p. 173)

Moreover, women tend to express more ethical responsibility than men. However, women's responses to ethical issues might be attributed to the social desirability response bias. The social desirability response bias appears to be driving a significant portion of the relationship between gender and ethical decision-making, by which females consistently report more ethical responses than males.

Dodge (2009) argues that there is little evidence that women who manage to climb the corporate ladder will act more ethically or legally compared to their male counterparts:

Given the opportunity, women are just as likely to commit white-collar crime. Illegal opportunities to jettison careers, earn more money, and gain respect in the corporate world, more often than not, outweigh the risks of getting caught. Doing gender in the world of business equates to being tough, taking risks, and playing aggressively. (p. 72)

When offenders are asked to explain their crimes, they typically portray themselves as decent people despite their wrongdoings. They tend to apply neutralization techniques as defined by neutralization theory (Bock & Kenhove, 2011; Siponen & Vance, 2010; Sykes & Matza, 1957). To be effective at managing the stigma of crime, motivational accounts must be believable to the social audience. Thus, Klenowski, Copes, and Mullins (2011) found that variation in patterns of accounts is likely due to the social position of the actors. They examined whether gender constrains the way individuals describe their crimes by analyzing the motivational accounts of male and female white collar offenders. Results show that while men and women both elicit justifications when discussing their crimes, they do differ in the frequency with which they call forth specific accounts and in the rhetorical nature of these accounts. When accounting for their crime, white-collar offenders draw on gendered themes to align their actions with cultural expectations of masculinity and femininity. These findings suggest that gender does constrain the accounts that are available to white-collar offenders.

Cauffman (2008, p. 126) found that:

on average, males tend to have longer criminal careers than females. Because it is difficult to assess when a criminal career is 'finished,' convincing evidence about the duration of criminal careers is sparse. A long-term study by Roger Tarling followed a sample of male and female offenders who were born in 1958 through age thirty-one, finding that the average duration of offending was 4.9 years for females, and 7.4 years for males.

Crime Theories

When we now turn to the literature on of gender differences in white-collar crime, we first have to look at the extent to which women have the opportunity to commit this kind of crime. According to Huffman et al. (2010), women's access to organizational power structures matters in organizations because, as a significant source of internal pressure, the characteristics of leaders can shape organizational adaptation and strongly influence workplace inequality. As long as workplace power inequality exists, then women have less opportunity to commit white-collar crime.

Research conducted in the 1980s by Daly (1989) supports this contention. Daly compared men's and women's socioeconomic profiles and occupations and the nature of their offending. The results showed that a minority of men but only a handful of women fit the image of a high-status white-collar offender. Most employed women were clerical workers, and most employed men were managers or administrators. Women were more likely to be nonwhite, less likely to have completed college, and owned less in economic assets. Men were more likely to work in crime groups and to use organizational resources in carrying out crimes, and their attempted economic gains were higher. Daly suggests that occupational marginality, not mobility, better explains the form that women's white-collar crime takes.

A fairly consistent finding in the emotions literature is that women are both expected to, and do, display greater emotional intensity and emotional expressiveness than men, and such differences apply to both positive and negative emotions. The root of such differences may lie in role development whereby females are socialized to be more emotionally expressive and men are socialized to be more emotionally restrained. Socialization pressures influence the extent to which a woman can survive with deviant behavior in the organizational power structure and thereby the extent to which white-collar crime is a pertinent and attractive option.

Another relevant gender perspective is persistence, whereby men may be more persistent and thus more willing to carry out both legal and illegal acts. When Bowles and Flynn (2010) studied gender and persistence, they focused on persistence in negotiations. Negotiation is a fundamental form of coordination in organizations that affects the process of work, the resolution of conflict, and the advancement of careers. Their findings challenge sex-stereotypic perspectives, showing that women persist more with male naysayers than with female naysayers, but they do so in a stereotypically low-status (more indirect than direct) manner. Persistence here is the willingness to continue to seek a compromise with a naysaying counterpart.

Opportunity theory suggests that as women's opportunities to commit white-collar crime increase, so will their deviant behavior, and the types of crime they commit will much more closely resemble those that men commit. However, in an old study, Hill and Harris (1981) found no support for the suggestion that similar male-female criminal profiles emerge as opportunities for females expand.

Schwartz and Steffensmeier (2007) applied opportunity theory to explain the gender gap:

> Lack of opportunity helps explain the negligible female involvement in serious white-collar crime. Female representation in high-level finance, corporate leadership, and politics is simply too limited to provide much chance for women to become involved in insider trading, price-fixing, restraint of trade, toxic waste dumping, fraudulent product production, bribery, official corruption, or large-scale governmental crimes such as the Iran-Contra affair or the Greylord scandal. (p. 65)

Opportunity means the presence of a favorable combination of circumstances that renders a possible course of action relevant. Opportunity arises when individuals or groups can engage in illegal and unethical behavior and expect, with reasonable confidence, to avoid detection and punishment. Opportunity to commit crime may include macro- and micro-level factors. Macro-level factors encompass the characteristics of the industries in which the organization is embedded, such as the market structure; organizational sets of an industry, that is, companies whose actions are visible to each other; and variations in the regulatory environment (Aguilera & Vadera, 2008).

Goldstraw-White (2012) argues that white-collar criminals not only have the opportunity to commit crime, but also have the ability to identify situations where opportunity arises. The opportunity and ability to identify these situations are different for white-collar criminals than for other types of offenders.

Steffensmeier and Allan (1996) suggested a *gendered theory* of female offending. The theory attempts to explain female criminality and gender differences in crime. The theory focuses on the following elements and interactions between them:

- Organization of gender: Gender norms, moral development, and social control.
- Biological factors: Physical, sexual, and affiliate differences.

- Criminal opportunities: Sexism in the criminal underworld, access to skills, crime associates, and settings.
- Gender differences in crime: Women avoid more serious white-collar crime, such as insider trading, price-fixing, restraint of trade, dumping of toxic waste, fraudulent product commerce, bribery, and official corruption, as well as large-scale governmental crimes.
- Context of offending: Many of the most profound differences between the offenses committed by men and women involve the context of offending, in which context refers to the characteristics of a particular offense. It might be the setting, whether the offense is committed with the assistance of others, the offender's role in initiating and committing the offense, the type of victim, the victim-offender relationship, whether a weapon is used, the extent of injury, the value or type of property destroyed or stolen, and the purpose of the offense.
- Motivation for crime: Tastes regarding risk, likelihood of shame or embarrassment, self-control, and assessment of costs versus rewards of crime.

Gender theory allows for interactions among these five factors. For example, criminal motivation will be influenced by both gender organization and criminal preference (Steffensmeier & Allan, 1996):

> Gender norms, social control, lack of physical strength, and moral and relational concerns also limit female willingness to participate in crime at the subjective level—by contributing to gender differences in tastes for risk, likelihood of shame or embarrassment, self-control, and assessment of costs versus rewards of crime. Motivation is distinct from opportunity, but the two often intertwine, as when opportunity enhances temptation. As in legitimate enterprise, being able tends to make one more willing, just as being willing increases the prospects for being able. Like male offenders, female offenders gravitate to those activities that are easily available, are within their skills, provide a satisfactory return, and carry the fewest risks. (p. 478)

A study in Finland showed no difference between male and female crime rates when correcting for occupation fraction. Kankaanranta and Muttilainen (2010) found that 9% of economic criminals in the construction industry were females, which is a modestly higher proportion than that of women generally working in the construction sector (who account for 7%).

Obedience theory is related to the fraud triangle that consists of pressure, opportunity and rationalization. Obedience theory can be useful in explaining the pressures and rationalizations that provide the motives for individuals to commit acts of occupational fraud:

Perceived need or pressure often comes from personal financial problems or living beyond one's means, but it can also come from direct pressure from someone in authority in the workplace and the threat of losing one's job for failure to go along with the boss's scheme. Obedience theory posits that individuals may engage in behaviors that conflict with their personal values and beliefs if they are subjected to pressures to obey someone in authority. According to this theory, the individuals rationalize this behavior by essentially placing full responsibility on the authority figure rather than taking any individual responsibility for the action themselves. (Baird & Zelin, 2009, p. 1)

In a gender perspective, it might be argued that women and men not only differ in terms of opportunity. They also differ in terms of pressure and rationalization. While financial problems may cause female white-collar crime, the threat of losing one's job may cause male white-collar crime.

Obedience pressure is considered to be one of three forms of social influence pressure, the two other types being compliance pressure and conformity pressure:

Compliance pressure is similar to obedience pressure, except that compliance pressure can come from one's peers as well as from superiors, while obedience pressure must come from an authority figure. Conformity pressure refers to pressure to conform to perceived or societal norms. (Baird & Zelin, 2009, p. 2)

It might be argued that both compliance pressure and conformity pressure are felt more strongly among women than men, thereby preventing female crime if the pressure is of a positive character.

The obedience effect tends to be especially strong if an individual subscribes to a moral foundation, such as the importance of respect toward authority figures. The classical study of obedience to authority consisted of an experiment in which an authority figure told an individual to administer increasingly powerful electric shocks to a learner in the next room when the learner answered a question incorrectly. When the shocks reached a certain level, the learner began calling for help and asking that the experiment stop while the authority figure calmly instructed the individual to continue. All individuals involved in the experiment administered shocks up to the 300V level, and 65% of subjects administered them to the strongest shock label available that was labeled "Danger, Severe Shock."

Of the three forms of social influence pressure, Baird and Zelin (2009) argue that obedience pressure can be especially potent owing to the power that persons in authority have over their subordinates. People within an organization simply quietly follow the orders of top executives and rationalize their actions by denying responsibility for their behaviors. The pressures to commit crime are often overt requests of management, but they can also be based on perceptions of reward and incentive structures.

In a sample of convicted white-collar criminals in prison, Goldstraw-White (2012) found some offenders who claimed to have committed their crimes as a result of being pressurized in some way. These individuals claimed to have felt compelled to behave in particular ways, driven to react when a certain set of circumstances were presented to them. They claimed that they felt overwhelmed by the issues they were facing, particularly financial ones, whether these related to their own expectations, to the business, or to their family.

Authority can be defined as domination, when the probability is high that a certain specific command will be obeyed by a given group of persons. Authority assumes voluntary compliance or an interest in obedience. Obedience is an obligation that is formal and one follows it without regard to one's own attitude or lack of value of its content. It is often essential that the authority is believed to be legitimate, and there needs to be an immediate relationship between command and obedience (Aguilera & Vadera, 2008).

Another theoretical perspective on gender and white-collar crime is Quinney's Social Reality of Crime, which was applied by Moyer (2001). This perspective might help understand gender patterns in exploring how white-collar crime is defined, labeled in the media, and adjudicated. Similarly, Chamlin and Cochran's (1997) social altruism principle applies differently between male and female white-collar offenders.

Furthermore, *labeling theory* could be used to consider whether offenses are labeled differently by the media based on the gender of white-collar offenders. Labeling theory is closely related to social-construction analysis, in which deviance is not inherent to an act but instead focuses on the tendency of majorities of influential forces, such as the media, to label criminals from standard cultural norms. Labeling theory is concerned with how the self-identity and behavior of individuals may be determined or influenced by the terms used to describe or classify them. Labeling theory has been criticized for only focusing on the deviance of the poor, while the rich commit serious crime. It has been argued that the cost of crime committed by white-collar criminals far exceeds those imposed by the lower classes. Becker (1963) developed his theory of labeling—also known as social reaction theory—during a period of social and political power struggle.

Feminist theory is concerned with female offending, females as victims, and females in the prison system (Britton, 2000). Hurwitz and Smithey (1998) discuss the gender gap in terms of feminist theory:

> Despite extensive documentation of the gender gap across a range of political issues, little is known about gender differences toward issues of crime and punishment. In this study, we systematically examine how, and why, women and men approach the issue of crime. We find that women are more afraid of crime

and more supportive of prevention efforts than men, though fear of crime and women's policy attitudes are not related in a causal sense. These findings are consistent with differences in women's and men's socialization experiences. They have important implications for both feminist theory and the ability of the political parties to use the crime issue to their advantage. (p. 89)

Postwar views on female crime emphasized sexuality as well as biological and sociological influences. A classic book—*The Criminality of Women*—by Otto Pollak, argues that females are inherently manipulative and deceitful, characteristics of their physiological and social attributes. Pollak's theory, as well as other, earlier theories of female crime, has been criticized. Researchers have begun to rely more heavily on sociological explanations of women's lower criminality (Denno, 1994).

Criminal Sample

As suggested in the research literature, most white-collar criminals are men. This is confirmed in the sample of 305 persons, which included only 26 female criminals and 279 male criminals. Thus, only 9% of the white-collar crime sample from newspaper articles was women.

Characteristics of male versus female white-collar criminals are listed in Table 4.1. There are no significant differences between women and men when equal variances are assumed (Hair, Black, Babin, & Anderson, 2010). However, because of the large number of males versus the small number of females, equal variances do not have to be assumed from a statistical point of view. Rather, equal variances might not be assumed. Then some significant differences between women and men can indeed be found.

Table 4.1 Comparison of Characteristics of Male versus Female White-Collar Criminals

Total 305 Criminals	279 Male Criminals	26 Female Criminals	*t* Statistical Difference	Significance of *t* Statistic
Age convicted	48 years	47 years	.574	.566
Age crime committed	43 years	42 years	.560	.576
Years prison	2.2 years	1.7 years	1.395	.164
Crime amount	50 million kr	9 million kr	1.263	.207
Personal income	350,000 kr	182,000 kr	1.454	.956
Personal tax	148,000 kr	70,000 kr	1.601	.147
Personal wealth	1,654,000 kr	12,435 kr	1.257	.110
Involved persons	3.8 persons	3.9 persons	−.056	.210
Business revenue	200 million kr	92 million kr	1.521	.129
Business employees	129 persons	73 persons	.939	.348

First, crime amount differs significantly, from an average of 50 million kr among men to an average of nine million among women. Next, personal income among female criminals is significantly lower than personal income among male criminals. Similarly, men pay more tax and have more financial wealth according to public figures.

Three position levels were defined in this research: 1) top management (chairman of the board, chief executive officer, etc.), 2) middle management (procurement officer, accounting manager, etc.), and 3) other white-collar criminals (consultants, clerks, etc.). Female white-collar criminals—pink-collar criminals, Gucci criminals, or Louis Vuitton criminals—are at a significantly lower management level as compared to men. While men had an average score of 1.9, women had only 2.6 on a scale from 1 (high) to 3 (low).

Although not statistically significant, jail sentences are, on average, shorter for women, which matches that the crime amount, in terms of millions of Norwegian kroner, is substantially lower. It is also interesting to note some similarities. First, they are about the same age, both when committing crime and receiving court sentence. Next, they work in organizations of about the same size. Furthermore, there are about the same number of persons involved in white-collar crime and pink-collar crime (3.8 versus 3.9).

Crime categories are compared in a gender perspective in Table 4.2. On average, women committed 9% of all criminal acts in the sample. Women are more involved in fraud, theft, and manipulation and less in corruption. It is interesting to note that none of the detected cases of corruption involved women.

When addressing the low fraction of female white-collar criminals (a mere 9%) to qualified audiences, the following reasons are typically mentioned:

- Women have less opportunity to commit white-collar crime.
- Women are less opportunistic as they are more committed to relationships and rules.

Table 4.2 Comparison of Crime Categories of Male versus Female White-Collar Criminals

Category	Total	Men	Women	Share
Fraud	153	136	17	11%
Theft	21	19	2	10%
Manipulation	73	66	7	10%
Corruption	58	58	0	0%
Total	305	279	26	9%

- It is more seldom that women are invited by criminals to participate in crime. For example, a criminal will prefer to bribe a man rather than a woman.
- Women have a greater sense of risk aversion rather than risk willingness.
- Companies are typically registered in the name of the husband rather than the wife.
- Women are more readily perceived as victims of crime rather than perpetrators.
- Female criminal acts tend to carry lesser legal penalties.
- Women are not as efficient as men are in terms of successfully applying neutralization techniques.

It is conventionally understood that women are offered fewer occupational opportunities than men have. This is reinforced by data about both salaries and business options, as argued by Jonnergård et al. (2010), who cite studies that show women often hold lower ranking jobs and have fewer encouraging prospects for the future as well as differing levels of commitment to their organization. Jonnergård et al. say these disparities sometimes denote alternatives in career paths between the sexes.

This statement supports the opportunity argument, according to which women are less likely to commit white-collar crime because they are not in the position to do so. Thoroughgood, Hunter, and Sawyer (2011) argue that although women occupy an increasing number of leadership roles in supervisory and middle management capacities they are seldom at the top when it comes to the majority of large organizations.

Haantz (2002) found that females comprise 17% of the individual perpetrators identified and reported by victims of fraud. However, there has been an increase in the number of women convicted of fraud felonies over time. Over the past few decades, political, social, economic, and technological changes have impacted the role of women at home and in the workplace. These same changes have also brought about increased participation among women in certain types of criminal behavior. It seems that nowhere are these trends more pronounced than in the arena of white-collar criminality. However, Holtfreter et al. (2010) argue that this trend might be modified by potentially higher levels of self-control among women.

There are several avenues for future research based on this study. Our intent for this chapter was to conduct an empirical study of white-collar crime to create insights into perceptions of potential offenders with a gender perspective. However, future research needs to develop a more focused account than white-collar offenders identified by Norwegian newspapers between 2009 and 2012. Only 26 female offenders were identified, thereby making comparisons quite difficult. The description of the cases does not include our attempt to disentangle gender or gender roles. Given our interest in examining gendered differences in white-collar offending, we might in the future seek data that will allow for such an exploration in more depth. Therefore, for future research based on news accounts to find the few women's cases of white-collar crime, we may need to visit the court documents again and analyze the legal information pertaining to their cases, engage in interviews with attorneys and businesses affected, interview the women, or perform other sound social science research practices to better inform the analysis that we perform.

Although we claim that the data are not a major concern for this study, the data are generally problematic and have a substantial dark figure. We acknowledge that the information is selective and filtered. Newspapers are going to cover large cases of crime with larger damages. Also, courts are going to filter cases along the same lines. As the data here show, women's financial crime produces less gain than men's crime. This is a finding echoed in Klenowski et al. (2011). Thus the absence of female cases in the newspaper is in part a product of less female white-collar crime, but it is also a function of female crime being filtered out of both the justice and media systems.

Discussion

Only 26 out of 305 white-collar criminals presented in Norwegian newspapers in the years from 2009 to 2012 were women. In this chapter, a number of reasons for this result are discussed. Women's access to organizational power structures is rising, but remains still limited. This is in line with opportunity theory. Women may have a greater sense of risk aversion rather than risk willingness, and women may more easily be perceived as victims of crime. It is indeed hard to believe that Norwegian men commit 10 times more white-collar crime than Norwegian women. Therefore, it is a question of whether the detection rate for female white-collar criminals is lower than for males. As a consequence, more attention should be paid to characteristics of female white-collar crime and criminals in future criminology research and law enforcement.

A total of 26 out of 305 convicted persons represents 9%. This percentage can be compared to the current female conviction rate of 15% in Norway. This female conviction rate has more than doubled over the last 30 years. In 1980, only 6% of all those who were sentenced to prison were women. In Norwegian prisons in 2012, only 7% of all inmates were women while the conviction rate has risen to 15%. This is because women receive shorter jail sentences as a result of less severe crime (Tilseth, 2012). The next chapter will build a stage model based on these empirical findings.

References

Aguilera, R. V., & Vadera, A. K. (2008). The dark side of authority: Antecedents, mechanisms, and outcomes of organizational corruption. *Journal of Business Ethics, 77*, 431–449.

Babcock, L., & Laschever, S. (2003). *Women don't ask.* Princeton: Princeton University Press.

Baines, D., Charlesworth, S., Cunningham, I., & Dassinger, J. (2012). Self-monitoring, self-blaming, self-sacrificing workers: Gendered managerialism in the non-profit sector. *Women's Studies International Forum, 35*, 362–371.

Baird, J. E., & Zelin, R. C. (2009). An examination of the impact of obedience pressure on perceptions of fraudulent acts and the likelihood of committing occupational fraud. *Journal of Forensic Studies in Accounting and Business, 1*(1), 1–14.

Ballinger, A. (2003). Researching and redefining state crime: Feminism and the capital punishment of women. In S. Tombs & D. Whyte (Eds.), *Unmasking the crimes of the powerful: Scrutinizing states & corporations.* New York: Peter Lang.

Becker, H. S. (1963). *Outsiders: Studies in the sociology of deviance.* New York: The Free Press.

Becker, S., & McCorkel, J. A. (2011). The gender of criminal opportunity: The impact of male co-offenders on women's crime. *Feminist Criminology, 6*(2), 79–110.

Benson, M. L., & Simpson, S. S. (2009). *White-collar crime: An opportunity perspective.* New York: Routledge.

Bock, T. D., & Kenhove, P. V. (2011). Double standards: The role of techniques of neutralization. *Journal of Business Ethics, 99*, 283–296.

Bowles, H. R., & Flynn, F. (2010). Gender and persistence in negotiation: A dyadic perspective. *Academy of Management Journal, 53*(4), 769–787.

Bowles, H. R., Babcock, L., & Lai, L. (2007). Social incentives for gender differences in the propensity to initiate negotiations: Sometimes it does hurt to ask. *Organizational Behavior and Human Decision Processes, 103*, 84–103.

Britton, D. M. (2000). Feminism in criminology: Engendering the outlaw. *Annals of the American Academy of Political and Social Science, 571*, 57–76.

Buss, D. M. (1995). Evolutionary psychology: A new paradigm for psychological science. *Psychological Inquiry, 6*(1), 1.

Cauffman, E. (2008). Understanding the female offender. *The Future of Children, 18*(2), 119–142.

Chamlin, M. B., & Cochran, J. K. (1997). Social altruism and crime. *Criminology, 35*(2), 203–226.

Clinard, M. B., & Yeager, P. C. (2005). *Corporate Crime.* Somerset, NJ: Transaction Publishers.

Daly, K. (1989). Gender and varieties of white collar crime. *Criminology, 27*(4), 769–794.

Denno, D. W. (1994). Gender, crime, and the criminal law defenses. *The Journal of Criminal Law and Criminology, 85*(1), 80–180.

Dodge, M. (2009). *Women and white collar crime.* New York: Prentice Hall.

Dollar, D., Fisman, R., & Gatti, R. (2001). Are women really the "fairer" sex? Corruption and women in government. *Journal of Economic Behavior & Organization, 46*(4), 423–429.

Eagly, A. H., & Carli, L. L. (2007). Women and the labyrinth of leadership. *Harvard Business Review, 85*(9), 63–71.

Friedrichs, D. O. (2009). *Trusted criminals: White collar crime in contemporary society*. Belmont, CA: Wadsworth.

Gatrell, C. (2010). Who rules the game? An investigation of sex-work, gender, agency and the body. *Gender in Management: An International Journal, 25*(3), 208–226.

Goldstraw-White, J. (2012). *White-collar crime: Accounts of offending behaviour*. London: Palgrave Macmillan.

Haantz, S. (2002). *Women and white collar crime*. National White Collar Crime Center. Retrieved from www.nw3c.org

Hair, J. F., Black, W. C., Babin, B. J., & Anderson, R. E. (2010). *Multivariate data analysis* (7th ed.). Upper Saddle River, NJ: Pearson Education.

Hassell, K. D., & Archbold, C. A. (2010). Widening the scope on complaints of police misconduct. *Policing: An International Journal of Police Strategies and Management, 33*(3), 473–489.

Hausmann, R., Tyson, L., & Zahidi, S. (2010). *The global gender gap 2008*. Geneva: World Economic Forum.

Heilman, M. E., & Chen, J. J. (2005). Same behavior, different consequences: Reactions to men's and women's altruistic citizenship behavior. *Journal of Applied Psychology, 90*(3), 431–441.

Heilman, M. E., & Okimoto, T. G. (2007). Why are women penalized for success at male tasks? The implied communality deficit. *Journal of Applied Psychology, 92*(1), 81–92.

Hill, G. D., & Harris, A. R. (1981). Changes in the gender patterning of crime, 1953–77: Opportunity vs. identity. *Social Science Quarterly, 62*(4), 658–671.

Holtfreter, K., Beaver, K. M., Reisig, M. D., & Pratt, T. C. (2010). Low self-control and fraud offending. *Journal of Financial Crime, 17*(3), 295–307.

Huffman, M. L., Cohen, P. N., & Pearlman, J. (2010). Engendering change: Organizational dynamics and workplace gender desegregation. *Administrative Science Quarterly, 55*, 255–277.

Hurwitz, J., & Smithey, S. (1998). Gender differences on crime and punishment. *Political Research Quarterly, 51*(1), 89–115.

Jonnergård, K., Stafsudd, A., & Elg, U. (2010). Performance evaluations as gender barriers in professional organizations: A study of auditing firms. *Gender, Work and Organization, 17*(6), 721–747.

Kankaanranta, T., & Muttilainen, V. (2010). Economic crimes in the construction industry: Case of Finland. *Journal of Financial Crime, 17*(4), 417–429.

Klenowski, P. M., Copes, H., & Mullins, C. W. (2011). Gender, identity and accounts: How white collar offenders do gender when making sense of their crimes. *Justice Quarterly, 28*(1), 49–69.

Lersch, K. M., & Mieczkowski, T. (2000). An examination of the convergence and divergence of internal and external allegations of misconduct filed against police officers. *Policing: An International Journal of Police Strategies & Management, 23*(1), 54–68.

Madichie, N. O., & Nkamnebe, A. D. (2010). Micro-credit for microenterprises? A study of women "petty" traders in Eastern Nigeria. *Gender in Management: An International Journal, 25*(4), 301–319.

Messerschmidt, J. M. (1997). *Crime as structured action: Gender, race, class, and crime in the making*. Thousand Oaks, CA: Sage Publications.

Moss-Racusin, C. A., Phelan, J. E., & Rudman, L. A. (2010). When men break the gender rules: Status incongruity and backlash against modest men. *Psychology of Men & Masculinity, 11*(2), 140–151.

Moyer, I. L. (2001). *Criminological theories: Traditional and non-traditional voices and themes.* Thousand Oaks, CA: Sage.

NCWP. (2002). *Men, women, and police excessive force: A tale of two genders, a content analysis of civil liability cases, sustained allegations & citizen complaints.* National Center for Women & Policing, a division of the feminist majority foundation. Retrieved from www.womenandpolicing.org/pdf/2002_excessive_Force.pdf.

O'Fallon, M., & Butterfield, K. D. (2005). A review of the empirical ethical decision-making literature: 1996–2003. *Journal of Business Ethics, 59*(4), 375–413.

O'Grady, W. (2011). *Crime in Canadian context.* Don Mills, ON: Oxford University Press Canada.

Pillay, H., Tones, M., & Kelly, K. (2011). Gender patterns for aspirations for transitional employment and training and development in local government. *Gender in Management: An International Journal, 26*(5), 367–379.

Politidirektoratet. (2010). *100 år med kvinnelig politi (100 years with female police officers),* Norwegian Police Directorate, Oslo, Norway. Retrieved from www.politi.no/politidirektoratet/aktuelt/nyhetsarkiv/2010_06/Nyhet_8743.xhtml.

Robb, G. (2006). Women and white-collar crime. *British Journal of Criminology, 46,* 1058–1072.

Salo, I., & Allwood, C. M. (2011). Decision-making styles, stress and gender among investigators. *Policing: An International Journal of Police Strategies & Management, 34*(1), 97–119.

Schwartz, J., & Steffensmeier, D. (2007). The nature of female offending: Patterns and explanations. In R. Sheehan, G. McIvor & C. Trotter (Eds.), *What works with women offenders.* Devon, UK: Willan Publishing.

Seeberg, M. L. (2012). Immigrant careworkers and Norwegian gender equality: Institutions, identities, intersections. *European Journal of Women's Studies, 19*(2), 173–185.

Siponen, M., & Vance, A. (2010). Neutralization: New insights into the problem of employee information systems security policy violations. *MIS Quarterly, 34*(3), 487–502.

Sörlin, A., Ohman, A., Blomstedt, Y., Stenlund, H., & Lindholm, L. (2011). Measuring the gender gap. *Gender in Management: An International Journal, 26*(4), 275–288.

Steffensmeier, D., & Allan, E. (1996). Gender and crime: Toward a gendered theory of female offending. *Annual Review of Sociology, 22,* 459–487.

Stuhlmacher, A. F., & Walters, A. E. (1999). Gender differences in negotiation outcome: A meta-analysis. *Personnel Psychology, 52*(3), 653–677.

Sutherland, E. H. (1949). *White collar crime.* New York: Holt Rinehart and Winston.

Sykes, G., & Matza, D. (1957). Techniques of neutralization: A theory of delinquency. *American Sociological Review, 22*(6), 664–670.

Thoroughgood, C. N., Hunter, S. T., & Sawyer, K. B. (2011). Bad apples, bad barrels, and broken followers? An empirical examination of contextual influences on follower perceptions and reactions to aversive leadership. *Journal of Business Ethics, 100,* 647–672.

Tilseth, T. O. (April 24, 2012). Flere kvinner straffes (More women are sentenced). *Aftenposten* (Norwegian daily newspaper), p. 7.

Worthen, M. G. F. (2011). Gender differences in parent-child bonding: Implications for understanding the gender gap in delinquency. *Journal of Crime and Justice, 34*(1), 3–23.

Stage Model for Female Criminals
5

White-collar crime is financial crime committed by trusted persons in important business positions. White-collar crime committed by women is sometimes labeled pink-collar crime.

When half of the general population is women, why do women only comprise 6% of the inmates in prison for white-collar crime? This chapter provides an answer to this question by means of a stage model that suggests, step by step, how a 50% female fraction of the population is reduced to a 6% female fraction in prison for white-collar crime. The model presents an organizing framework for explanations found in the research literature.

Stage Model Overview

Figure 5.1 illustrates a model with factors that determine the fraction of women in prison. This is an overview model for illustration purposes only. A complete model is presented later in this chapter.

The model starts with a female fraction in the population of 50%. It is assumed that women, relative to men, have an 80% need for self-realization by means of earning money. Therefore, the potential percentage of women committing white-collar crimes is reduced to 40%. The model further includes factors that assume women have a relative opportunity to commit white-collar crime of 70%, have a relative motivation for white-collar crime of 90%, and have a relative crime justification ability of 80%, when the percentages are compared to those for men.

The combination of these determinants results in a female fraction of white-collar crime—the pink-collar crime fraction—of 20%. Furthermore, it is assumed that the relative detection rate for female criminals versus male criminals is only 40%, which implies that substantially fewer women involved in financial crime are detected. Therefore, only 9% of all court sentences are female convictions.

Finally, the model suggests that women receive shorter jail sentences than men, approximately 70% of men's imprisonment times. This results in a fraction of women in prison of 6%.

These numbers are estimated based on theories and common reasoning, which will be presented later in this chapter. There are no known empirical

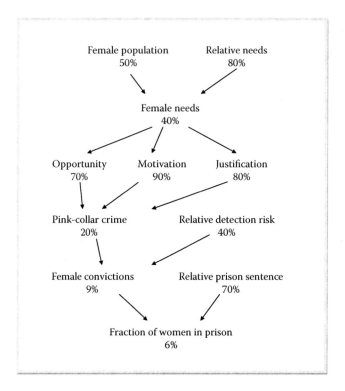

Figure 5.1 Model with factors to determine the fraction of women in prison.

studies that can confirm such numbers. Nevertheless, it is useful to indicate reasonable magnitudes of differences between men and women in terms of percentages and thus derive quantitative numbers because it is so difficult to understand why one half of the total population can end up as only one 17th of the prison population in terms of women in prison.

Determinants of Female Criminal Fraction

Figure 5.2 includes the same factors as Figure 5.1, but this time, the model is illustrated clearly by stages. It shows how the female fraction is reduced stage by stage on the left-hand side caused by factors on the right-hand side.

There are a total of five stages, which are discussed in the following section. The only difference between Figures 5.1 and 5.2 is the explicit representation of conviction rate, in which it is assumed that a larger fraction of prosecuted women relative to men are convicted in court.

The purpose of the model is to illustrate and explain how common opinions documented in theoretical thoughts can predict the decreasing female fraction from general population fraction to imprisonment fraction.

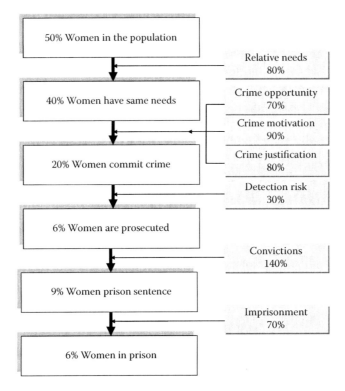

Figure 5.2 Model for estimation of female fraction of white-collar crime.

The common opinion in society is that men represent the large majority within all kinds of crime, including white-collar crime (Friedrichs, 2009). The model supports Messerschmidt's (1997) suggestion that gender is an important predictor of criminal involvement—males dominate criminal activity in society. Both Friedrichs (2009) and Messerschmidt (1997) receive support from Steffensmeier and Allan (1996), who list a number of empirical studies in different countries in which men commit far more crimes than women. Additionally, Blickle, Schlegel, Fassbender, and Klein (2006) show that men were the dominant majority among white-collar criminals in Germany.

From Population Fraction to Needs Fraction

The Russian-American psychologist Abraham Maslow (1908–1970) developed a thought-inspiring *theory of human needs*. His theory is used to explain human behavior and motivation by means of a hierarchy of needs. His basic assumption was that the individual cannot move higher in the pyramid before the need below is satisfied.

Personal needs are at the following levels: physiological needs (breathing, food, water, sex, sleep, homeostasis, excretion), safety needs (security of body, employment, resources, morality, health, property), social needs (love, belonging, friendship, family, intimacy), respectability needs (self-esteem, confidence, achievement, respect for others, respect by others), and self-actualization needs (morality, creativity, spontaneity, problem solving, lack of prejudice, acceptance of facts).

White-collar crime can be found at the top two levels, that is, the need for self-esteem and self-realization, mostly referred to as self-actualization. Undetected white-collar crime can result in personal achievement, respect by others, and problem solving. All humans have a need to be respected and to have self-esteem and self-respect. Esteem represents the normal human desire to be accepted and valued by others. Where wealth helps in being included in desirable social circles, then white-collar crime can be an option. Self-actualization might be linked to white-collar crime, when the outcome of crime enables a person to realize his or her full potential. For example, an executive might have the strong desire to become a shareholder or owner of the firm. According to Maslow, needs at the top two levels always exceed the available coverage and will therefore never be completely met.

In a gender perspective, we find differences between men and women at the top of Maslow's hierarchy of needs. Women spend more money on children and vacations, and men spend more on cars and houses. Already here we see differences in priorities and self-actualization between women and men. Because women are seldom convicted relative to men, one might phrase the question whether women have less desire than men to satisfy their needs for self-esteem and self-actualization by means of money in their profession? Or maybe the priority on self-esteem and self-actualization based on job position is less so for women who prioritize self-esteem and self-actualization on other platforms, such as domination in family and among friends?

We are assuming here that the hierarchy of needs, as such, is equal for men and women and just as important for both genders; however, female needs are achieved by different means. If this is the case, then financial crime is a less desirable option for women. Power and money is associated more with status among men than among women. The feminine morale emphasizes social dimensions more than material dimensions although materialism has recently been introduced into feminism (Sullivan, 2012).

This is in line with results from a study by Dodge (2007), in which men prioritized material goods and privileges, and women prioritized family and safety. Men have higher materialistic values linked to professional careers as compared to women. Dodge's study in Canada with the participation of 515 women and 608 men from companies with more than 1000 employees indicated clearly that women's self-actualization was linked to family and home, justice and equality, team and cooperation, friends and relationships, and also fame and reward—in contrast to men who emphasized money, income, privileges, power, status, and authority.

It is not at all certain that all women voluntarily emphasize family and friends or if many feel obliged to put family and friends first. This is exemplified by the following statement from a presidential candidate in Iceland who recently had become a mother again:

> Something tells me that I should stay home with my children. A man would never be exposed to such criticism, says Icelandic Thora Arnorsdottir, a mother of three. (Moe, 2012, p. 14)

The fact that men, on average, have higher materialistic values linked to their position in the workforce is also explained by gender and income. Income is interpreted and used as a measure of work value. Wages and income differences that are established in the labor market are expressions of market values of work. Income is important because it signals the competencies in which there are shortages and in which competencies there are surpluses. Such signals are noticed by colleagues, family, and friends. That women, to a larger extent, work in low-income professions might be explained by the lower relative value assigned to goods and services associated with activities of family and friends.

This is supported by Birkelund, Gooderham, and Nordhaug (2000), who found that women prioritize values, such as interesting work, good interpersonal relationships, the possibility of learning new things, and substantial variation during the day. Men, on the other hand, prioritize income, prestige, and power. This is also confirmed by Jacobsen (2009), who studied women who chose not to become top executives.

Overall, these arguments lead us to believe that the motivation to commit financial crime is less prominent among women, both because money does not have the same importance at the top of the hierarchy of needs and because crime can lead to the loss of valuable relationships and learning possibilities.

When women have the need for financial gain, it might be for other reasons than men. For example, the woman has promised her children an exciting and expensive summer vacation, and she enters into embezzlement at work. The driving force would be that as a mother, she would like to keep her promises. The father, on the other hand, has longed for a better car, a bigger boat, or a bigger house so that the children can all have their own bedrooms. He asks carpenters and electricians to bill his employer, with which he is in a position to expedite the invoices and get them paid by the company.

Overall then, these arguments lead us to an estimation of 80% in the model, and women do not have the same (100%) but less (80%) desire for financial gain. When there are 50% women in the general population, and they have an extent of 80% desire, then the female crime needs fraction will be 40%, and the male fraction of white-collar crime needs will be 60%. In Figure 5.2, this is the calculation of women in the population combined with relative needs, leading to 40% of women that have the same needs as men.

From Needs Fraction to Crime Fraction

In the model, 40% of the people who have a need for financial crime are women, but only 20% of the people who actually commit financial crime are women. This is the difference between needs fraction and crime fraction. Several reasons for this drop can be found in the literature. It has to do with opportunity, motivation, and justification. Women have less opportunity and lower motivation to commit white-collar crime. Additionally, they are less able to justify white-collar crime. This is in agreement with the fraud triangle (Aguilera & Vadera, 2008).

In criminology, opportunity is often mentioned as one of three pillars to explain criminal acts. The other pillars are motivation to carry out the act and rationalization or justification of the act. These three pillars must work together before the criminal act can take place (Aguilera & Vadera, 2008).

In the fraud triangle, these pillars are explained:

- Opportunity to commit crime: Women are in a position to commit white-collar crime.
- Motivation in terms of incentives or pressures to commit crime: Women want to or have to commit white-collar crime.
- Acceptance of crime: Women find justification for white-collar crime (Ilter, 2009).

Risk for fraud is thus a combination of opportunity and possibility, incentives and pressures, and rationalization and justification. These three elements are discussed in our gender perspective in the following sections.

Women's Opportunity for Crime

In the model, it is assumed that women have only a 70% opportunity to commit white-collar crime when compared to men. Thus, the female fraction is reduced from 40% to 28%. This decline is caused by the fact that there are far fewer female executives than male executives, about 10%, when financial crime is an available option. Some female executives also reduce their own crime chances by practicing a transparent leadership style. If a crime requires several participants to be successful, a woman may not have the network to carry it out. An estimated opportunity factor of 70% thus represents many different circumstances in addition to the lack of gender equality in society.

Opportunity theory is concerned with situations emerging in which there is a possibility for actors and groups to carry out illegal and unethical acts with little detection risk and low likelihood of punishment (Aguilera & Vadera, 2008). The theory suggests that when there is a criminal temptation, someone will explore and exploit the opportunity to make a profit, either for themselves as an occupational crime or for the company as a corporate crime. For example, Haantz (2002) argues that the main reason for women being responsible only for 17% of all convicted fraud is "the lack of opportunity." She argues that white-collar crime among women is rising because of growing opportunity.

Aguilera and Vadera (2008, p. 434) define criminal opportunity as "the presence of a favorable combination of circumstances that renders a possible course of action." They explain the opportunity to commit crime by both micro and macro factors. Micro factors are such issues as gender, occupation, position, and characteristics of the organization. Macro factors include as industry, market structure, market actors, and regulating mechanisms in society.

Limited opportunity for women can partly be explained by *transaction cost theory.* Criminals, as well as noncriminals, prefer transaction costs to be as low as possible. Transaction costs include the risk for negative outcome. It might be considered more risky to involve a woman than a man in criminal activity because women may lack competence or position or they more easily blow the whistle. In an experiment of an audience of both men and women, in which the audience is asked whether they would bribe a man or a woman in equal positions, audiences always favor bribing the man. As a consequence, women are excluded from criminal opportunities by others, who prefer to involve men. Men prefer to involve men, and women prefer to involve men as our later experiment indicates.

The exclusion of women from criminal opportunities might be explained by the exclusion of women generally from male colleagues' social networks. This is documented in a Swedish study of female managers (Lindgren & Theandersson, 2000). A U.S. study documents that female white-collar crime increases when women are invited by men to participate, but the invitation rarely happens (Becker & McCorkel, 2011).

Female opportunities for financial crime, such as corruption, are reduced by male behavior. A study in Australia provides support for this view. Bowman and Gilligan (2008) found that women have less chance of getting involved in corruption than men. They found that women are perceived to be more responsible and ethical than men and that women to a lesser extent are invited to participate in financial crime. Here, one might include *moral theory*, where we find moral luck for women. This theory is concerned with moral tests to which humans are exposed. Moral tests are mainly determined by external factors outside an individual's control. People do not know what they would do in different situations if they have not been exposed to these situations. Based on this theory, one cannot postulate that women are more law-abiding than men. They have simply not been in the same kind of situations, which characterizes women's limited opportunity to commit white-collar crime.

According to transaction cost theory, the individual's tendency to commit crime depends on opportunity and opportunism, which means that actors cautiously exploit financial possibilities at the expense of transaction partners. It is assumed that it is difficult, if not impossible, to predict another person's attitude toward and take advantage of opportunistic possibilities. Therefore, a part of transaction costs are the costs associated with the control of others to detect and prevent opportunism (Dibbern, Winkler, & Heinzl, 2008). Here, it is again assumed those women's opportunities to commit white-collar crime are more limited compared to men.

That women neither have the same opportunity to be bribed nor have the same opportunity to participate in other kinds of white-collar crime might also be explained by *participation theory*. For example, one needs to sit behind the steering wheel to be able to drive too fast. If the woman has no chance to be chauffeur, then she cannot be caught for speeding. Another example is a woman who doesn't have the authority to approve fake invoices cannot get involved in this kind of fraud. Participation theory emphasizes that women do not have the opportunity rather than women do not have the willingness to participate in crime (Becker & McCorkel, 2011).

It can be easier for women than men to avoid job careers because it is accepted by the environment. A man expects from himself that he shall have success, and the environment expects him to succeed. If he does not succeed, he will dislike getting up in the morning, and he will dislike looking at himself in the mirror. He would not like to be seen by others because they may judge him as a failure. The first question a man often gets is in what job he is. For a woman, it might even be status to have chosen not to make a career because it is not at all perceived as egoistic. On the contrary, it may be understood that the woman has discarded an egocentric career to the advantage of care for others, particularly family. If the man has discarded his career, it is either considered a failure or an ego trip, and one may think that he has some kind of extreme hobby, such as sailing the world solo or climbing world mountains, with which nobody has pleasure but himself.

Opportunities are obviously an important reason why crime occurs. Without criminal opportunities, no criminal acts will occur (Clinard & Yeager, 2005; O'Grady, 2011). Opportunity is an important reason for white-collar crime, especially when the potential outcome is significant and the risk of detection is insignificant. Detection risk may be insignificant because white-collar crime occurs within structures and cultures that are usually closed and outside general control. At the same time, corporate structures in legal organizations are open to control that is nonexistent in criminal organizations (Benson & Simpson, 2009).

In *agency theory*, opportunities for financial crime can be found in the relationship between principal and agent. The relationship influences the danger of the principal and/or the agent committing crime. Opportunity is determined by the potential profit, which becomes more attractive when it is easily obtained or when the profit is large. Another person's or organization's property becomes attractive if it is moveable, valuable, and usable (Benson & Simpson, 2009). We assume that women, less often than men, are in principal-agent relationships, in which the woman has such an independent and free position that she can abuse the relationship in terms of white-collar crime.

Many companies apply a goal-oriented approach in their business planning. Some goals may be ambitious, and some goals may be too ambitious and thus unrealistic. Goals can be for profit, market share, or turnover in a global environment. More ambitious goals combined with strong personal responsibility for goal achievement can increase the tendency to commit white-collar crime when crime is considered a means to achieve a goal.

Dodge (2009) suggests that it is the competitive environment that generates pressure to commit crime:

> The competitive environment generates pressures on the organization to violate the law in order to attain goals. (p. 15)

In this line of reasoning, Goldstraw-White (2012) interviewed convicted white-collar criminals:

> Twenty-three of the offenders in the sample consisted of individuals who owned, or part-owned, businesses. The success of these businesses, especially where the income generated was their main livelihood, was of paramount importance to these offenders and an immediate consideration in terms of economic survival for themselves, their family, their co-workers and their employees. (p. 91)

Here, *goal theory* is in line with the *theory of profit-driven crime*. Naylor (2003) argues that profit-driven crime is best understood on financial premises rather than in sociological or criminological perspectives. The theory of profit-driven crime implies that financial crime is governed by opportunity, with which leaders and other employees identify possibilities for illegal profit. Michel (2008) argues that opportunity is definitely a characteristic of white-collar crime.

Goal theory argues that unrealistic goal setting can cause more crime. Even realistic goals can be harmful to businesses if goals go wild. It was Ordonez, Schweitzer, Galinsky, and Bazerman (2009) who wrote that goals can go wild:

> We identify specific side effects associated with goal setting, including a narrow focus that neglects non-goal areas, distorted risk preferences, a rise in unethical behavior, inhibited learning, corrosion of organizational culture, and reduced intrinsic motivation. (p. 6)

Goal-oriented management can cause financial crime because management is mainly judged—rewarded or punished—based on short-term financial results. A study in Sweden by Jonnergård, Stafsudd, and Elg (2010) found that goal-oriented management was more suited to male careers than to female careers. Goal theory can lead to two gender differences when it comes to white-collar crime. The first occurs when women, to a lesser extent than men, are willing to apply illegal means to achieve goals. The second difference occurs when women avoid employment and association with organizations that apply extreme goal orientation because women are not especially attracted to organizations that are mainly run by goal achievement, according to the Swedish study.

Women's limited opportunity to commit white-collar crime can also be explained by *resource theory*. Women seldom have access to the same resources in the same magnitude and of the same quality as men that make it possible for them to succeed in crime (Becker & McCorkel, 2011). Resources include, for example, competence, access to systems, staff, trading partners, or money to bribe someone. Resource, in this context, means enabler, when the resource enables criminal acts (Barney, 2002).

Resource theory or resource-based theory applied to white-collar crime implies that executives and employees are potential white-collar criminals who commit financial crime to the extent that they have access to resources that are needed for criminal acts. There is an internal as well as external angle on resource-based theory. The traditional angle focuses on internal analysis, and resource dependency analysis focuses on the external environment and argues that an organization always finds itself in a dependent relationship with its external environment in many respects. According to Løwendahl (2000), the essence of the resource-based perspective is found in the attention paid to internal rather than external resources. To commit crime, strategic resources are sometimes needed. Strategic resources are characterized by being valuable, rare, nonsubstitutable, inimitable, combinable, and exploitable.

Knowledge is a typical resource. An OECD study showed that 52% of all men and only 29% of all women in Norway have knowledge of finance at an acceptable level. A reason might be that men still are the main caretakers of finances and that men are more interested in finance than women.

Executive management in an organization typically has great power, status, and influence over resources. They have control over resources to do both good and bad things. They also have control over resources to hide crime and delete traces of crime. To be a top executive is based on trust and not control. It is easy to abuse trust without being detected.

One reason for women's lack of access to criminal resources is that very few of them make it through the glass ceiling. The glass ceiling is a metaphor for the final career step into executive management and the board. The glass ceiling is an invisible barrier that prevents women from reaching the top. It is above the glass ceiling, and not below, that free access to resources, such as bank accounts and experts, enable potential pink-collar criminals to carry out major financial crime over time without being detected. Because most women hit the ceiling and do not make it through the ceiling, their opportunity for white-collar crime is limited (Adams, 2012).

Culture theory can explain why women hit the glass ceiling (Dollar, Fisman, & Gatti, 2001). When men are occupying the leading positions, then it will be men's ethics that are the basis for the dominant corporate culture. Women may form their own subculture based on their own ethical guidelines. Because this subculture may be in contradiction to the dominating male culture, it becomes problematic for women to make it to top positions. The result then will be that women have to adapt to the dominant culture or risk hitting the glass ceiling.

Related to resource theory is *core competence theory*, in which competence can be one of the resources that is necessary to commit white-collar crime. Core competence is the expertise that enables work to be successful. For example, competence is needed to succeed in fake invoicing, money laundering, or tax evasion. Whether women have less competence in these areas will depend on their position and work assignments.

Many researchers have emphasized lack of opportunity when explaining the low extent of female criminality. For example, Schwartz and Steffensmeier (2007) formulate it in this way:

> Lack of opportunity helps explain the negligible female involvement in serious white-collar crime. Female representation in high-level finance, corporate leadership, and politics is simply too limited to provide much chance for women to become involved in insider trading, price-fixing, restraint of trade, toxic waste dumping, fraudulent product production, bribery, official corruption, or large-scale governmental crimes such as the Iran-Contra affair or the Greylord scandal. (p. 65)

Thus, relatively few women have the opportunity to commit pink-collar crime. These women are characterized by enjoying complete trust by their employers, important control over resources, and ample opportunity for crime. Even if they can, women will typically not steal as large an amount of money as men. The difference here can be explained by what Kelly Paxton at www.pinkcollarcrime.com calls men's three w's: wine, women, and wagers.

Women's Motivation for Crime

In the model, it is assumed that women's motivation represents only 90% of men's motivation to commit white-collar crime. One potential reason is that women are exposed to less pressure in terms of money and material wealth. They may also be less greedy, manipulate smaller amounts, and cover passing needs only. Women's motivation can be to secure daily bread and clothing, and men have greater needs, such as cars and boats that are more luxurious than that of their neighbor, colleague, or brother-in-law. Another reason is that women can be less ambitious than men. While the typical motivation for white-collar crime in general can be status, pressure, ambitions, and goal achievements, it can be argued that these are typical male values.

Stanton Wheeler's (1992) research into white-collar crime motivation illustrates how psychological factors can work together with situational factors. He asks why persons who are already extremely wealthy take the chance to involve themselves in white-collar crime when they earn little from the crime compared to what they already possess. One answer is that they fear falling off the financial cliff and losing their wealth and status. Therefore, they work constantly to remain successful, preferably more successful than others, while not having the time to relax and enjoy their wealth because of the fear of failure. It is this struggle for financial success and maintenance of that success that are important.

The traditional view concerning motivation and gender seems to be that women commit financial crime out of problems and concern for others, and men do it out of personal greed. This view says that women commit crime for profit because of financial problems involving others, and they choose theft, social security abuse, and embezzlement as crime categories. Poverty is less seldom the reason among men to commit crime.

Motivation is, like most concepts in work psychology, an abstract term that cannot be directly measured; it emerges differently from person to person and is impossible to observe. Motivation is an incentive to action. Motivation consists of three components: direction (what a person is trying to do), energy (how hard the person is trying), and endurance (how long the person is trying). Often a distinction is made between inner and outer motivation, with which there can be gender differences as well. Inner motivation tells us to do what we would like to do. Outer motivation tells us to do what others provide us with incentives to do.

Both men and women in executive positions have a strong motivation to succeed. Because female executives tend to receive more attention from the organization, they also tend to have a stronger motivation to succeed. On average, women in executive positions have a stronger motivation than men because only the really strongest get past the glass ceiling. Included in success is to behave both ethically and lawfully. On the other hand, if success is not achievable in legal ways, women may choose illegal means to reach ambitious objectives.

Women, more than men, tend to see a threat of being caught as a ruin not only for their careers but also for relationships in life. The threat of separation from loved ones is a fear carried by many women. The risk is considered too large because female risk calculations tend to put more emphasis on worries and ramifications. Furthermore, women tend to be watched more closely in society, in the organization, and in the family; thus they do not deviate too much from stereotypes. If they do, the environment may sanction them. Gender-specific circumstances, such as relationships and stereotypes, reduce the probability of women taking risks according to *rational choice theory*.

Rational choice theory argues that it is indeed rational to be a criminal providing two conditions are satisfied: The potential profit is great and the likelihood of punishment is small:

> Rational choice theory suggests that people who commit crimes do so after considering the risks of detection and punishment for the crimes (risk assessment), as well as the rewards (personal, financial, etc.) of completing these acts successfully. On the other hand, persons who do not commit crime decide that completing the act successfully is too risky or not worth the benefits. (Lyman & Potter, 2007, p. 62)

Examples of rational choice theory include a man who discovers that his wife is having an affair and chooses to kill her, her lover, or both; the bank teller who is experiencing personal financial difficulty and decides to embezzle funds from the bank to substantially increase her earnings; and an inner-city youth who decides that social opportunities are minimal and that it would be easier to make money by dealing crack cocaine (Lyman & Potter, 2007).

In our gender perspective, rational choice theory may result in different outcomes for women and men. For example, the likelihood of being caught is part of the equation. While the likelihood might be the same for both men and women, subjective probabilities can be different. In speed control studies, for example, fewer women are caught. This is partly because women believe in a more frequent speed control rate than men, therefore obeying the posted speed as opposed to men. Gender differences in how risk is perceived and judged will thus influence what is the rational choice. If women perceive the risk of crime detection as greater than men, then rational choice theory suggests that women will commit less crime than men.

Dobash, Dobash, and Cavanagh (2009) applied rational choice theory to explain white-collar crime among men and women in cases in which it might be rational to commit crime in a difficult financial situation:

> Here, crisis, stress, and opportunity explain how previously conventional individuals commit crimes of fraud and deception. Individual characteristics, adverse childhoods, and difficult adult lives do not aid in the understanding of these offenders who do something wrong to deal with some perceived crisis that threatens them, their families, or their companies. Within this framework, middle-class, white-collar offenders are best understood as men and women who make a rational choice to commit an offence in the context of a situational crisis. (p. 203)

In our model, we are not concerned with absolute detection rates for crime. Rather, we are interested in relative detection rates depending on gender. At the same time, we know that white-collar crime is seldom detected, and this can lead to more men than women committing such crime. Although we here assume that the detection rate for women is even lower than the detection rate for men, it is still plausible that women perceive detection risk as being higher than men do. It is all about perceived risk, which is subjective, as opposed to actual risk, which is objective. Subjective risk is about an individual's belief in something going wrong.

With relatively lower risk willingness among women, *deterrence theory* might explain why women are less motivated to commit white-collar crime. Detection is considered important to prevent crime according to *deterrence theory*. Some theorists believe that crime can be reduced through the use of deterrents. Crime prevention (the goal of deterrence) is based on the assumption that criminals or potential criminals will think carefully before committing a crime if the likelihood of getting caught and/or the fear of swift and severe punishment are present. Based on such a belief, *general deterrence theory* holds that crime can be thwarted by the threat of punishment, while *special deterrence theory* holds that penalties for criminal acts should be sufficiently severe that convicted criminals will never repeat their acts (Lyman & Potter, 2007). Deterrence theory postulates that people commit such crime on the basis of rational calculations about perceived personal benefits and that the threat of legal sanctions will deter people owing to fear of punishment (Yusuf & Babalola, 2009). According to Comey (2009), deterrence works best when punishment is swift and certain. White-collar sentencing in the United States in the years since Sarbanes-Oxley, however, has been anything but fast. This is the case in other countries as well. For example, in Norway white-collar crime investigations typically take more than a year before the suspected white-collar criminal is brought to trial.

Deterrence theory argues that more severe punishment will deter potential criminals from committing crime:

> Special deterrence theory holds that penalties for criminal acts should be sufficiently severe that convicted criminals will never repeat their acts. For example, if a person arrested on a first-time marijuana possession charge is sentenced to spend sixty days in a boot camp designed for first-time offenders, the punishment is to convince him or her that the price for possessing marijuana is not worth the pleasure of using it. (Lyman & Potter, 2007, p. 62)

Given the broad range of potential sentences provided after conviction within which judges essentially have complete discretion, the sentence can range from mere months in prison to more than 10 years. Moreover, unlike the average aspiring criminal actor, white-collar offenders usually know that they will have access to a lenient plea bargaining system in countries such as the United States. They are also often well aware of instances in which a court has departed downward from a guideline sentence that touched the conscience of the court, according to Comey (2009).

There is, of course, the alternative argument that deterrence is at its height when potential punishments are severe but unpredictable. Comey (2009) argues that such punishments may be imposed relatively randomly against some perpetrators but not others and would theoretically provide a greater deterrent effect than a predictable but lower sentence—the probability of sentencing might be lower, but the risk would be much higher. An adherent to this view would see the Sarbanes-Oxley system, with all its disparities and broad-ranging discretion, as a step in the right direction.

Deterrence theory can be traced back to Jeremy Bentham (1748–1832) and Cesare Beccaria (1738–1794). They argued that individuals weigh costs and benefits when deciding whether or not to commit a crime, and individuals choose crime when it pays. If an individual believes that the risk of getting caught is high, especially if there is a certainty of sanctions and severe penalties that will be applied should one be caught (severity of sanctions), then deterrence theory posits that individuals will not commit crime (Siponen & Vance, 2010). Informal sanctions and shame are included in today's sanctions. Examples of informal sanctions are disapproval of friends or peers for a given action, personal media exposure of a negative kind, family breakup, and loss of position in the local society. Shame refers to a feeling of guilt or embarrassment that arises should others know of one's socially undesirable actions. Shame adversely affects an individual's self-esteem.

Deterrence theory suggests that longer jail sentences for financial crime will cause less financial crime. Longer jail sentences might work relatively more as a deterrent on female crime. One reason is that it is more unusual for women to be prisoners, and thus it is a more severe punishment for women to serve long jail sentences. Furthermore, social contacts and care obligations make it extra problematic for a woman to think of herself as a jail inmate. Hansen (2009) mentions the *theory of social bonding* in which four main factors can lead an individual in an organization to become a criminal as a consequence of tight bonding to other criminals in the company. The four main explanatory concepts in social bonding theory are the individual's attachment (strength of affective ties to individuals and groups), commitment (investment of effort and resources in conventional lines of activity), involvement (amount of engagement and time spent in conforming activities), and belief (subscribing to general norms and laws of society). Generally, the theory hypothesizes that the stronger these bonds are to society, the less likely the individual is to engage in any type of crime (Meneses & Akers, 2011). On the other hand, delinquent acts result when an individual's bond to society or to the organization is weak or broken. Lack of attachment to conventional others, lack of commitments to conventional lines of action, lack of involvement in conventional activities, and lack of belief in a common value system weaken the societal bond and, therefore, make criminal behavior more likely (Lasley, 1988).

Deterrence theory indicates that women and men have fundamentally different views of crime:

> Despite extensive documentation of the gender gap across a range of political issues, little is known about gender differences toward issues of crime and punishment. In this study, we systematically examine how, and why, women and men approach the issue of crime. We find that women are more afraid of crime and more supportive of prevention efforts than men, though fear of crime and women's policy attitudes are not related in a causal sense. These findings are consistent with differences in women's and men's socialization experiences. They have important implications for both feminist theory and the ability of the political parties to use the crime issue to their advantage. (Hurwitz & Smithey, 1998, p. 89)

Feminist theory is referred to in this quote, and feminist criminology is concerned with female offending, females as victims, and females in the prison system (Britton, 2000).

Women tend to be more fearful toward crime because they feel more vulnerable toward the consequences of crime. They are more vulnerable because of their perceived or actual protection role. It is reasonable to assume that the fear of others' criminal acts will influence the fear of one's own criminal acts.

Motivation to commit financial crime can be influenced by the glass ceiling for women (Adams, 2012). When a woman has made it through the glass ceiling, maybe after many years of hitting their head on it, and now occupies a top executive position in the corporation, it might very well be that she is intensely focused on convincing others that she is the right person for the job. She wants to demonstrate to those who offered her the job that she will make it in a legal way so that her sponsors do not get disappointed. Needs for pleasing and impressing lead women, who have opportunities for white-collar crime, to abstain from crime to a larger extent than men, again explaining why women are less motivated toward financial crime.

Of course, not all mechanisms that influence motivation for crime work in only one direction for women, that is, women will be less motivated to commit crime. Some—although few—mechanisms work in the opposite direction, which cause women to be more motivated than men. One example is *normality theory*. According to normality theory, the offender argues that everyone else is doing it; thus she has done nothing wrong (Siponen & Vance, 2010). If misconduct or crime is normal behavior, then it might be even easier for women than men to do it, mainly because women do not wish to deviate from all others, one way or the other. In some business areas, embezzlement is seen as normal practice. In other business areas, bribes or tax evasion are seen as normal practice. For example, hairdressing studios run by women tend to register only some of the pay received while other amounts are put aside. When this has been normal practice for generations, it is considered acceptable to continue doing so. Women are over-represented in the hair-dressing business, and if normality theory is valid, this mechanism suggests that the female fraction of white-collar crime is rising rather than declining.

Entrepreneurial theory can be applied to white-collar crime, whereupon we look at the dark side of entrepreneurialism. To understand entrepreneurial behavior by white-collar criminals, important behavioral areas include *modus essendi, modus operandi,* and *modus vivendi*. Modus essendi is a philosophical term relating to modes of being. Modus operandi is a method of operating, which is an accepted criminological concept for classifying generic human actions from their visible and consequential manifestations. Modus vivendi represents the shared symbiotic relationship between different entrepreneurial directions (Smith, 2009). Most business entrepreneurs are men. An entrepreneur is characterized by risk taking, creativity, and the ability to see opportunities where others find problems. Entrepreneurs are not always aware of the border between legal and illegal activities.

It is a common impression in Norwegian culture that men have greater trust in their own abilities and competence. Tabloid phrased, men apply for job positions for which they are 80% qualified, and women apply for positions for which they are 120% qualified. This suggests that men fail more often than women and that men more often have to choose criminal means to compensate for their own lack of competence if they want to succeed.

Men's over-ambitions lead them to the wrong side of the law. Men's unsubstantiated faith and belief in their own competence was confirmed in a study by Barber and Odean (2001), who found that men have greater trust in their own skills and therefore fail more often than women.

Yet another theory, *alliance theory,* can shed light on female motivation being lower than male motivation for white-collar crime. An alliance implies mutual dependence based on trust, comfort, understanding, flexibility, cooperation, shared values, goals, problem solving, personal relationships, and regular contacts. An alliance is, to a greater extent, based on trust, understanding, and respect and, to a lesser extent, on agreements, expectations, and hierarchical roles. Women seek, to a greater extent, social acceptance in their immediate environment and are more socially active than men. There may be strong reasons for not breaking trust. Men, on the other hand, can be more calculating and distant. Men can be more conflict seeking, and women are more conflict avoiding in upholding an alliance. Alliance theory can thus explain why women commit relatively fewer financial crimes in their professions.

A final theory to explain gender difference in crime motivation is *learning theory,* which explains why girls learn to take responsibility for others. High moral, conscientious behavior and silence are often expected more of girls than boys. Learning theory assumes that criminal behavior is learned both from parents and from other boys. When growing up, boys are more often encouraged to be tough, not to cry, to be fast, and to become members of a cool gang. Learning theory assumes that criminal behavior is learned. In its explanations, learning theory emphasizes attitudes, abilities, values, and behavior as requirements for successful financial crime (Lyman & Potter, 2007). By interactions with other potential and actual criminals, men learn how it is done and develop an attitude telling them that it is neither dangerous nor risky (Hansen, 2009).

Attitudes are socially constructed rather than fixed attributes of individuals. They have the potential to influence men's and women's behavior as part of a context in which gender roles are produced and reproduced. Attitudes are relevant indicators of individuals' latent tendencies to respond to opportunities and constraints that are posed by conditions of life. Attitudes are not fixed, and changes in behavior may lead to attitudinal changes (O'Sullivan, 2012).

Women's Justification of Crime

The female fraction is further reduced in our model because of limited risk willingness among women after attempted justifications and because of somewhat lower motivation for financial crime. It is the female fear of being caught because of which women perceive a greater subjective risk than men, and the consequences of imprisonment are perceived worse by women than men, mainly because of the social collapse that follows after time in prison. Campbell, Muncer, and Bibel (2001) argue that women have a lower level of acceptable fear than men. It means that women generally experience more fear than men when they are exposed to the same objective risk. The level of acceptable fear, combined with perceived risk—which is subjective—has an impact on actions (Gass & Seiter, 2011), and women with more fear at higher risk will avoid criminal activities.

In an experiment with boys and girls, differences were found in risk willingness. They participated in a lottery. When buying a ticket, there was a 50% chance of winning $100 and a 50% chance of winning nothing. The expected value in the lottery was thus $50. Participants also had a definite alternative. This alternative started at $25 and moved upwards. Girls stopped participating in the lottery at $37, and boys stopped at $45, which indicates a greater extent of risk willingness among boys than among girls.

Risk is an element in our model as part of both motivation and justification. That women generally have a higher degree of risk aversion than men does not necessarily apply to the specific group of pink-collar criminals. For example, Adams (2012) found that more female board members do not necessarily lead to greater risk aversion in decision making:

> A large literature documents that women are different from men in their choices and preferences, but little is known about gender differences in the boardroom. If women must be like men to break the glass ceiling, we might expect gender differences to disappear among directors. Using a large survey of directors, we show that female and male directors differ systematically in their core values and risk attitudes, but in ways that differ from gender differences in the general population. These results are robust to controlling for differences in observable characteristics. Consistent with findings for the population, female directors are more benevolent and universally concerned, but less power oriented than male directors. However, in contrast to findings for the population, they are less tradition and security oriented than their male counterparts. They are also more risk loving than male directors. Thus, having a woman on the board need not lead to more risk-averse decision making. (p. 219)

A study in Sweden confirms the finding that having a woman on the board does not necessarily lead to more risk-averse decision making. On the contrary, the Swedish study indicates that women are more risk willing than previously assumed. One reason for the greater risk willingness was that women are more in favor of change. It was Adams and Funk (2012) who studied differences among a total of 1800 female and male board members in companies registered on the stock exchange in Sweden. The result of the study was that female board members take greater risks than men on the board. Men are more concerned with competition, and women like change and being independent.

Justification of crime takes place by applying neutralization techniques. White-collar crime generally encompasses some type of nonconformity societal norms and often indicates a failure within the social order. Heath (2008), based on Sykes and Matza (1957), says white-collar criminals frequently to use nullification methods to try to negate the criminality of their behaviors. Some instances of these methods are (a) denial of accountability; (b) denial of any damage; (c) denial of anyone being hurt; (d) condemnation of the condemners; (e) a call to greater allegiances; (f) the idea that lots of people are doing the same thing; and (g) an assertion of prerogative. An offender might claim authorization for a criminal act, perhaps as the result of an ethical imperative or in retaliation for some wrongdoing committed by the victim. Family as a neutralization argument is applied more frequently by women than men. Women tend to justify their crime by pointing to basic needs of the family, and men, to a larger extent, argue in business terms. However, research by Klenowski, Copes, and Mullins (2011) shows that both men and women tend to justify financial crime by family needs and more generally commit crime for the benefit of others.

When accused criminals are required to offer an explanation for their crimes, they quite often try to paint themselves as good people in spite of any transgressions they may have perpetrated. They frequently use the neutralization techniques that have been elucidated in neutralization theory (Bock and Kenhove, 2011; Siponen and Vance, 2010; Sykes and Matza, 1957). In order to successfully handle the disgrace that accompanies crime, explanations of inspiration have to be credible to those who comprise the social audience. Klenowski et al. (2011) found that disparities in people's stories are often the result of the place the person holds in the social heirarchy. They researched whether gender limits how people portray their crimes by examining the reports of incentive as told by white-collar criminals who are men versus women. The outcome was that the data indicated males and females both develop rationalizations when they talk about the crimes they have committed, but they vary in the number of times they divulge particular statements and in the linguistic character of these stories. When talking about their crime, white-collar criminals derive gendered arguments to align their behavior with social beliefs about femininity and masculinity. These results support the idea that gender defines the optional excuses used by white-collar offenders.

Cauffman (2008) discovered that men usually experience more lengthy criminal careers than women do. However, it can be hard to pinpoint when a criminal career is actually over, solid substantiation concerning the length of criminal careers is hard to come by. A long-lasting research project by Tarling examined a sample of male and female offenders, born in 1958, and followed them through age 31. His findings indicated that the average length of criminal activity was 4.9 years for women and 7.4 years for men.

The idea that women to a lesser extent than men are able to justify white-collar crime might be explained by *moral theory* (Bowman & Gilligan, 2008) combined with *slippery slope theory*. Slippery slope theory implies that a person or an organization is sliding from legal to illegal activities (Arjoon, 2008). This theory attempts to explain why good people do bad things. The explanation is that people do not really notice when they slide over the border to crime. Many unethical and criminal acts happen without involved persons knowing or understanding that they are doing something wrong. Criminal behavior can follow a downward slope, and sliding downward is a continuous deterioration in the organization not caused by any specific event. It is a development, a trend, a path that leads the wrong way. Gender differences can be found in men realizing grey zones, and women see more black or white. Therefore, women will, to a lesser extent, be able to justify activities that are on the wrong side of the law because it is black to them, and it is grey to men.

Women find it more difficult than men to justify criminal acts based on an ethical perspective, according to Ruegger and King (1992):

> The findings suggest that gender is a significant factor in the determination of ethical conduct and that females are more ethical than males in their perception of business ethical situations. (p. 181)

Yet another theory can explain gender differences in justification. It is the *theory of self-control*. The lower the individual's self-control, the greater is the likelihood of his or her involvement in criminal behavior. Low self-control is defined in terms of characteristics, such as impulsive, risk-taking, and self-centered (Meneses & Akers, 2011). While most scholars—such as Haantz (2002), Holtfreter, Beaver, Reisig, and Pratt (2010), and Huffman, Cohen, and Pearlman (2010)—argue that the main reason for less female white-collar crime is lack of opportunity, they also mention gender differences in self-control. They argue that even if women over time have the same opportunities as men, they will not commit as much crime because lack of justification leads them to more self-control.

Self-control theory simply states that white-collar people with a low degree of self-control will tend to commit more financial crime than white-collar people with a high degree of self-control:

> Self-control theory proposes that individuals commit crime because of low self-control. Except in rare cases of mass fraud such as the Enron scandal, not all elites within a given organization or industry will commit crime. Hence, though elites at the top of their profession and corporation differentially associate with the people of equal status in their own and other corporations, not all corporate elites commit crimes and behave in an overtly deviant manner. (Hansen, 2009)

It is possible that social control and self-control are better developed in females than in males; when relating this finding to learning theory, it points to a reason why there is less crime committed by women. This concept of gender disparity is described by Worthen (2011) in relation to the bond between parent and child. She says teenagers who have nurturing relationships with their parents are more unlikely to find themselves wrapped up in aberrant or criminal behavior. Worthen learned that gender disparities in law-breaking can be somewhat understood in terms of gender differences in degrees assigned to the elements of the parent-child bond; these include emotional connection with the parents, amount of time spent with parents, and parental supervision. Gender differences also can be partly clarified by looking at the consequences these components have on the parent-child connection and criminal behavior differentiated by gender.

Crime Star for Women

The crime triangle consists of pressure, opportunity, and rationalization (Aguilera & Vadera, 2008; Ilter, 2009). The triangle was applied above in our model to explain the reduction from fraction of needs to fraction of crime. Female crime is reduced compared to male crime because of less opportunity, lower motivation, and harder justification—which are the three elements or corners of the crime triangle. Our presentation so far, however, indicates that the triangle is not really optimal when it comes to illustrating a transformation from needs to actions.

One problem with only three elements in the triangle is the treatment of risk and risk willingness versus risk aversion. Risk is an element included in motivation as well as opportunity and indeed also in justification. Because aspects of risk seem to be a clear indication of gender differences, risk as a

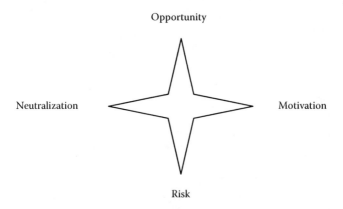

Figure 5.3 Crime star for factors affecting the extent of white-collar crime.

factor deserves an equal place at the level of opportunity, motivation, and rationalization.

Another problem with the triangle is rationalization. This term is not very well suited for the case of white-collar crime and maybe not for other kinds of crime either. The term rationalization might be replaced by the term neutralization, which has received increased attention in recent years (e.g., Bock & Kenhove, 2011; Heath, 2008; Siponen & Vance, 2010).

Here, we propose an alternative to the crime triangle in terms of a crime star. Two known elements are included, opportunity (Haantz, 2002; Lindgren & Theandersson, 2000) as well as motivation (Hurwitz & Smithey, 1998; Wheeler, 1992). A completely new element is risk (Campbell et al., 2001; Yusuf & Babalola, 2009), and a revised element is neutralization (Klenowski et al., 2011; Sipponen & Vance, 2010) as illustrated in Figure 5.3. As in the triangle, the elements in the star are indeed dependent on each other. For example, opportunity without motivation leads to no crime, and opportunity with too great a risk, leads to no crime.

When risk is separated from the three other factors, we can then estimate the following fractions based on the presented theories:

- Opportunity increases from 70% in the crime triangle to 75% in the crime star.
- Motivation increases from 90% in the crime triangle to 95% in the crime star.
- Rationalization increases from 80% in the crime triangle to 85% in the crime star in terms of neutralization.
- Based on the changes above, there is room to estimate that risk represents 85% in the crime star, meaning that, on average, women's risk willingness is only 85% of men's risk willingness.

In this way, we still achieve a model-based reduction from 40% criminal needs to 20% criminal actions among women for white-collar crime. Again, we need to emphasize that these numbers are estimated from theoretical perspectives and empirical studies as well as anecdotal evidence rather than from actual measurements in the real world.

From Crime Fraction to Detection Fraction

The next element in our model is detection likelihood in terms of detection risk when committing white-collar crime. We assume in the model that the relative detection risk for women compared to men is only 30%. This means, for example, that when the detection rate for men is 10%, then the detection rate for women is 3%. Out of 100 white-collar criminals among men, 10 men will be brought to justice. Out of 100 pink-collar criminals, three women will be brought to justice. Theories and studies are used in the following to argue the case of relatively lower detection likelihood for women.

The environment is generally less suspicious of women than men. The environment tends to decriminalize women. To the extent crime is detected, a woman is not considered or treated as the main suspect. She is either treated as a criminal follower or as a criminal victim in a typical criminal investigation when there are more people involved in the crime. Detection risk is linked to general reasons why women to a far lesser extent than men are convicted of white-collar crime, namely that women generally are not convicted of crime when compared to men.

A simple experiment we have often performed in different audiences is the question of who you would bribe. You would like to build a new home on a property that is regulated for recreation. You have the choice of bribing a female or male official in the municipality. Considering all the audiences, a large majority vote almost exclusively chooses men. Almost no one would bribe a female official. There are two learning points here. First, very few people think that a woman is corrupt, thereby reducing the detection rate. Second, because almost no one would bribe a woman, then a woman has less opportunity to be a criminal, which is relevant in the crime star discussed above.

Possibly women are smarter criminals than men. Again, when an experiment is carried out in an audience, most agree with this statement. One reason for relative smartness is that women may tend to stop criminal activities before it is too late. They are smart and manipulating and often get their way through indirect means. Women are usually brought up and thought of as the weaker sex in society and thus have to resort to other ways to accomplish things. It may seem that they only do work and carry out tasks that are indeed important for the company to get done, and men only do what they would like to do. Women monopolize areas in which they seem innocent, such as care, health, and environment. Women tend to talk most strongly about ethics, morals, and social responsibility. It is almost impossible for others to think at the same time that they are criminals. Thus, the detection fraction for women will be lower than men's. That it is women that most often talk about ethics is confirmed by a study carried out by Dodge (2007). She refers to her Canadian study in which 94% of all companies with an executive board with three or more female members had established guidelines for conflict of interest. In companies with only male board members, the fraction was 68%. Studies such as this can help confirm that women to a larger extent than men are concerned that the company should follow rules and policy lines to develop and maintain a good reputation.

Some make a distinction between ethics and being ethical. Research by O'Fallon and Butterfield (2005) shows no difference between women and men when it comes to making ethical and unethical decisions. Dollar et al. (2001) found, nevertheless, that a greater fraction of women in parliament is associated with a lower extent of corruption. But here, detection rate can play a role. Research findings that woman are more occupied with ethics and demonstrate stronger ethical attitudes than men is confirmed in earlier studies as well.

Lower relative detection rate can also be explained by the tendency that white-collar crime only captures financial crime of a large magnitude. This leads to a smaller female fraction because the average amount in female crime tends to be lower than the average amount in male crime. In addition, women may be cleverer in staying under the radar and avoiding attention by keeping quiet and stopping commiting crime at an earlier stage. A relatively low detection rate might also be explained because investigators and detectives misunderstand female roles in crime and tend to perceive women as victims of crime. Women typically present themselves as victims by claiming to be abused by men.

On the other hand, men have a reputation of being the gender that takes initiatives at high risk, and therefore, they are more easily detected. They are also detected because they like to show their material success. The police also contribute to the low detection fraction for women. We can here compare with other kinds of crime. When the police come home to a family because of home disorder, the main suspect is always the man, and the man is typically removed from the situation. If the police find documents in the home, it is assumed that they belong to the man.

In a historical perspective, we may find that society has accepted a gender culture in which it is more normal for men to be criminals. This can be explained by the confirmation trap, in which humans tend to try to confirm what they already think they know. When there are so few convicted women, then there must be fewer female criminals. When there are fewer female criminals, the police will hunt male criminals. When female criminals are not hunted, then fewer women will be convicted.

Yet another reason for a relatively lower detection fraction is that organizations internally treat suspicion as well as detection differently for women. Maybe it is because it is more normal for the board, management, and auditor to hand cases of male misconduct and crime over to the police. One might be more afraid of taking the wrong steps in terms of discrimination by accusing female employees of crime. It can be most convenient to forget about female misconduct and concentrate on male misconduct in internal investigations. It can be argued that traditional investigations are more suited to male suspects than to female suspects.

While some women may stop in time and not to be detected, men typically have a longer criminal career than women. However, it is not easy to tell exactly when a criminal career should be described as being "finished," and there is little evidence in the literature. A previously cited study by Tarling looked at male and female offenders over 31 years and found women's average criminal career lasted just under 5 years and men's lasted more than 7 years.

In our model, crime detection leads to prosecution. However, sometimes this is not the case. Therefore, it is not only the detection rate that is gender dependent but also the prosecution rate in court. If detection occurs within a business enterprise, the enterprise may decide not to go ahead with prosecution. Maybe it wants to protect its reputation, keep it internal, and not have the public lose confidence in the company. Anecdotal evidence suggests that only three out of 10 serious financial crime cases are reported to the police by companies. This number is probably even lower for female crime in the enterprise.

From Detection Fraction to Sentence Fraction

How many white-collar criminals detected and prosecuted, are convicted and given jail sentences by the court? Again, we are looking for gender differences. It seems that a larger fraction of prosecuted women are convicted in court. Therefore, our model includes an estimate of 140% as the relative sentence fraction for women compared to men.

One possible explanation for this gender gap is due to a feeling of guilt. Women may perceive and feel more guilt for a crime, for example, in terms of regret, shame, and depression (Hay, 2003). Another reason is keeping a secret, and women would like to be honest to their closest relationships.

At this stage in our model, we reach 9% convicted women and 91% convicted men. This is in line with the empirical study reported earlier in this chapter, in which 9% of convicted white-collar criminals were women.

From Sentence Fraction to Prison Fraction

The final stage in our model is the fraction of women in jail. There are 6% women and 94% men in prison. Why do we have 9% convicts but only 6% inmates among women? The reason is that women serve shorter and fewer sentences. To move from 9% court convictions to 6% prison inmates, we estimate that women only serve 70% relative to men.

One explanation is that women more often are given alternative sentences than prison. Ten percent of women are given alternatives to prison, but only 4% of men are given such alternatives.

Another explanation is that women are convicted and given shorter jail sentences. An empirical study by Schanzenbach and Yaeger (2006) confirms that women who are convicted are given shorter jail sentences:

> The sex disparity, on the other hand, consistently disfavors men. (p. 792)

Discussion

In theoretical terms, Pollak's (1978) classic book, *The Criminality of Women*, is interesting. He argues that women are not at all more law abiding than men, but they are treated differently by the justice system in society. Davis, Croall, and Tyrer (1999, pp. 225–226) wrote the following about Pollak's research:

> Writing in 1950, Otto Pollak argued that official statistics on gender and crime were highly misleading. He claimed that the statistics seriously under-estimated the extent of female criminality. From an examination of official figures in a number of different countries he claimed to have identified certain crimes that are usually committed by women but are particularly likely to be unreported.
>
> Pollak went on to give reasons as to why there should be an under-recording of female crime.
>
> 1. He argues that the police, magistrates, and other law-enforcement officials tend to be men. Brought up to be chivalrous, they are usually lenient with female offenders so that fewer women appear in the statistics. However, he regards this as only a minor factor.
> 2. Second, and to Pollak more important, women are particularly adept at hiding their crimes. He attributes this to female biology. Women have become accustomed to deceiving men according to Pollak.

Of course, Pollak's theory has been criticized. Other researchers have put more emphasis on sociological explanations for women's crime rate and crime detection. They focus on society's gender differences in raising girls versus boys:

> Pollak's theory, as well as other earlier theories of female crime has been criticized. Moreover, researchers have begun to rely more heavily on socio-logical explanations of women's lower criminality. They focus in particular on the propensity for society to more strongly persuade girls than boys to avoid delinquent behavior and risk taking. Essentially, society expects girls to follow biologically and culturally based "gender norms." (Denno, 1994, p. 89)

Our model for the calculation of women's share in white-collar crime, step by step, results in the following calculation, in which the starting point is 50% of the population and the ending point is 6% in prison:

$$0.50 \times 0.80 \times 0.70 \times 0.90 \times 0.80 \times 0.40 \times 0.70 = 0.06.$$

References

Adams, R., & Funk, P. (2012). Kvinna eller mann: Gör det skillnad i styrelsesrummet? (Woman or man: Does it make any difference in the boardroom?). SNS Analys nr 3, Studieförbundet, Retrieved from http://www.sns.se/nyheter/2012/04/sns-analys-nr-3-kvinna-eller-man-gor-det-skillnad-i-styrelserummet.

Adams, R. B. (2012). Beyond the glass ceiling: Does gender matter? *Management Science, 58*(2), 219–235.

Aguilera, R. V., & Vadera, A. K. (2008). The dark side of authority: Antecedents, mechanisms, and outcomes of organizational corruption. *Journal of Business Ethics, 77*, 431–449.

Arjoon, S. (2008). Slippery when wet: The real risk in business. *Journal of Markets & Morality, 11*(1), 77–91.

Barber, B. M., & Odean, T. (2001). Boys will be boys: Gender, overconfidence and common stock investment. *The Quarterly Journal of Economics*, February, 261–292.

Barney, J. B. (2002). *Gaining and sustaining competitive advantage.* Upper Saddle River, NJ: Prentice Hall.

Becker, S., & McCorkel, J. A. (2011). The gender of criminal opportunity: The impact of male co-offenders on women's crime. *Feminist Criminology, 6*(2), 79–110.

Benson, M. L., & Simpson, S. S. (2009). *White-collar crime: An opportunity perspective.* New York: Routledge.

Birkelund, G. E., Gooderham, P., & Nordhaug, O. (2000). Fremtidens næringslivsledere: Kjønn, karriere og skjebne (Future business leaders: Gender, career and destiny). *Tidsskrift for Samfunnsforskning, 41*, 594–619.

Blickle, G., Schlegel, A., Fassbender, P., & Klein, U. (2006). Some personality correlates of business white-collar crime. *Applied Psychology: An International Review, 55*(2), 220–233.

Bock, T. D., & Kenhove, P. V. (2011). Double standards: The role of techniques of neutralization. *Journal of Business Ethics, 99*, 283–296.

Bowman, D., & Gilligan, G. (2008). Public awareness of corruption in Australia. *Journal of Financial Crime, 14*(4), 438–452.

Britton, D. M. (2000). Feminism in criminology: Engendering the outlaw. *Annals of the American Academy of Political and Social Science, 571*, 57–76.

Campbell, A., Muncer, S., & Bibel, D. (2001). Women and crime: An evolutionary approach. *Aggression and Violent Behavior, 6*(5), 481–497.

Cauffman, E. (2008). Understanding the female offender. *The Future of Children, 18*(2), 119–142.

Clinard, M. B., & Yeager, P. C. (2005). *Corporate crime.* Somerset, NJ: Transaction Publishers.

Comey, J. B. (2009). Go directly to jail: White collar sentencing after the Sarbanes-Oxley act. *Harvard Law Review, 122*, 1728–1749.

Davis M., Croall H., & Tyrer J. (1999). *Investigating the relationships between women and crime.* Retrieved from http://www.123helpme.com/view.asp?id=149551.

Denno, D. W. (1994). Gender, crime, and the criminal law defenses. *The Journal of Criminal Law and Criminology, 85*(1), 80–180.

Dibbern, J., Winkler, J., & Heinzl, A. (2008). Explaining variations in client extra costs between software projects offshored to India. *MIS Quarterly, 32*(2), 333–366.

Dobash, R. E., Dobash, R. P., & Cavanagh, K. (2009). "Out of the blue": Men who murder an intimate partner. *Feminist Criminology, 4*(3), 194–225.

Dodge, M. (2007). Women who commit white-collar crimes. In H. N. Pontell & G. Geis (Eds.), *International handbook of white-collar and corporate crime* (pp. 379–405). New York: Springer Science + Business Media.

Dodge, M. (2009). *Women and white collar crime.* New York: Prentice Hall.

Dollar, D., Fisman R., & Gatti, R. (2001). Are women really the "fairer" sex? Corruption and women in government. *Journal of Economic Behavior & Organization, 46*(4), 423–429.

Friedrichs, D. O. (2009). *Trusted criminals: White collar crime in contemporary society.* Belmont, CA: Wadsworth.

Gass, R. H. & Seiter, J. S. (2003). *Persuasion: Social influence and compliance gaining.* Harlow: Pearson.

Goldstraw-White, J. (2012). *White-collar crime: Accounts of offending behaviour.* London: Palgrave Macmillan.

Haantz, S. (2002). *Women and white collar crime.* National White Collar Crime Center. Retrieved from www.nw3c.org.

Hansen, L. L. (2009). Corporate financial crime: Social diagnosis and treatment. *Journal of Financial Crime, 16*(1), 28–40.

Hay, C. (2003). Family strain, gender, and delinquency. *Sociological Perspectives, 46*(1), 107–135.

Heath, J. (2008). Business ethics and moral motivation: A criminological perspective. *Journal of Business Ethics, 83*(4), 595–614.

Holtfreter, K., Beaver, K. M., Reisig, M. D., & Pratt, T. C. (2010). Low self-control and fraud offending. *Journal of Financial Crime, 17*(3), 295–307.

Huffman, M. L., Cohen, P. N., & Pearlman, J. (2010). Engendering change: Organizational dynamics and workplace gender desegregation. *Administrative Science Quarterly, 55*, 255–277.

Hurwitz, J., & Smithey, S. (1998). Gender differences on crime and punishment. *Political Research Quarterly, 51*(1), 89–115.

Ilter, C. (2009). Fraudulent money transfers: A case from Turkey. *Journal of Financial Crime, 16*(2), 125–136.

Jacobsen, M. A. (2009). *Kvinner og toppledelse: Et verdivalg? (Women and executive management: A value choice?).* (Master's thesis). Universitetet i Tromsø.

Jonnergård, K., Stafsudd, A., & Elg, U. (2010). Performance evaluations as gender barriers in professional organizations: A study of auditing firms. *Gender, Work and Organization, 17*(6), 721–747.

Klenowski, P. M., Copes, H., & Mullins, C. W. (2011). Gender, identity and accounts: How white collar offenders do gender when making sense of their crimes? *Justice Quarterly, 28*(1), 49–69.

Lasley, J. R. (1988). Toward a control theory of white-collar offending. *Journal of Quantitative Criminology, 4*(4), 347–362.

Lindgren, S. Å., & Theandersson, C. (2000). *Från storsvindel til småfiffel: Teman i internationell ekobrottsforskning*, BRÅ-rapport 2000: 23, Brottsförebyggande rådet. Retrieved from http://www.bra.se/download/18.cba82f7130f475a2f1800017409/2002_3_fran_storsvindel_till_smafiffel.pdf.

Løwendahl, B. R. (2000). *Strategic management of professional service firms* (2nd ed.). Copenhagen: Copenhagen Business School Press.

Lyman, M. D., & Potter, G. W. (2007). *Organized crime* (4th ed.). Upper Saddle River, NJ: Pearson Prentice Hall.

Meneses, R. A., & Akers, R. L. (2011). A comparison of four general theories of crime and deviance: Marijuana use among American and Bolivian university students. *International Criminal Justice Review, 21*(4), 333–352.

Messerschmidt, J. M. (1997). *Crime as structured action: Gender, race, class, and crime in the making*. Thousand Oaks, CA: Sage Publications.

Michel, P. (2008). Financial crimes: The constant challenge of seeking effective prevention solutions. *Journal of Financial Crime, 15*(4), 383–397.

Moe, S. (April 24, 2012). Liv Løberg dømt til 14 måneders fengsel (Liv Løberg convicted to 14 months' prison). *Dagbladet*. Retrieved from www.dagbladet.no.

Naylor, R. T. (2003). Towards a general theory of profit-driven crimes. *British Journal of Criminology, 43*, 81–101.

O'Fallon, M., & Butterfield, K. D. (2005). A review of the empirical ethical decision-making literature: 1996–2003. *Journal of Business Ethics, 59*(4), 375–413.

O'Grady, W. (2011). *Crime in Canadian context*. Don Mills, ON: Oxford University Press Canada.

O'Sullivan, S. (2012). "All changed, changed utterly"? Gender role attitudes and the feminization of the Irish labour force. *Women's Studies International Forum, 35*, 223–232.

Ordonez, L. D., Schweitzer, M. E., Galinsky, A. D., & Bazerman, M. H. (2009). Goals gone wild: The systematic side effects of overprescribing goal setting. *Academy of Management Perspectives, 23*(1), 6–16.

Pollak, O. (1978). *The criminality of women*. Wesport, CT: Greenwood Press.

Ruegger, D., & King, E. W. (1992). A study of the effect of age and gender upon student business ethics. *Journal of Business Ethics, 11*, 179–186.

Schanzenbach, M., & Yeager, M. L. (2006). Prison time, fines and federal white-collar criminals: The anatomy of racial disparity. *Journal of Criminal Law and Criminology, 96*(2), 757–793.

Schwartz, J., & Steffensmeier, D. (2007). The nature of female offending: Patterns and explanations. In R. Sheehan, G. McIvor, & C. Trotter (Eds.), *What works with women offenders*. Devon, UK: Willan Publishing.

Siponen, M., & Vance, A. (2010). Neutralization: New insights into the problem of employee information systems security policy violations. *MIS Quarterly, 34*(3), 487–502.

Smith, R. (2009). Understanding entrepreneurial behavior in organized criminals. *Journal of Enterprising Communities: People and Places in the Global Economy, 3*(3), 256–268.

Steffensmeier, D., & Allan, E. (1996). Gender and crime: Toward a gendered theory of female offending. *Annual Review of Sociology, 22*, 459–487.

Sullivan, N. (2012). The somatechnics of perception and the matter of the non/human: A critical response to the new materialism. *European Journal of Women's Studies, 19*(3), 299–313.

Sykes, G., & Matza, D. (1957). Techniques of neutralization: A theory of delinquency. *American Sociological Review, 22*(6), 664–670.

Wheeler, S. (1992). The problem of white collar crime motivation. In K. Schlegel, & D. Weisburd (Eds.), *White collar crime reconsidered* (pp. 108–123). Boston: Northeastern University Press.

Worthen, M. G. F. (2011). Gender differences in parent-child bonding: Implications for understanding the gender gap in delinquency. *Journal of Crime and Justice, 34*(1), 3–23.

Yusuf, T. O., & Babalola, A. R. (2009). Control of insurance fraud in Nigeria: An exploratory study. *Journal of Financial Crime, 16*(4), 418–435.

Management Positions in Crime

6

While research on the effect of chief executive officer (CEO) behavior on the company's performance is still inconclusive (Lieberson & O'Connor, 1972; Mackey, 2008; Thomas, 1988), the investment in top leadership performance and accountability has reached unprecedented highs. In 2005, the average U.S. CEO's pay for one day was almost equivalent to the average worker's pay for one year. Citing this figure, Ranft, Ferris, and Perryman (2007) call for more research on the job demands of CEOs. When evaluating the effect of CEOs on company performance in terms of leadership skills, we argue that a one-dimensional, more or less, perspective is too simple. Just as some CEOs may be related to spectacular growth, as in the case of Steve Jobs (Isaacson, 2011), some CEOs may expose the company to spectacular downsides and risks by committing white-collar crime.

Chief Executives

Porter, Lorsch, and Nohria (2004) argue that this comes as a surprise to CEOs who are new to the job. Is it possible that CEOs are more likely than other managers and professionals to develop mindsets that are conducive to white-collar crime? This study addresses the following research question: What differences might be found between white-collar criminals in the position of chief executive officers versus white-collar criminals in other positions?

This study investigates the special case of CEOs as white-collar criminals. While CEOs are seen as the classic representatives of the level of a white-collar criminal, this kind of crime is committed by all sorts of people. Building on principal-agent theory and research on mindset development, we argue that the job characteristics of CEOs are likely to give rise to a special type of mindset, detecting and capitalizing on business opportunities. Mindsets are automatic pattern recognition responses in the brain that evolve after repeated exposure to tasks. Most mindsets are not readily accessible to conscious reflection, and because they are not, in themselves, related to legal or ethical issues, they will exert their influence on behavior also in illegal circumstances. Increased pressure on accountability for CEOs has paradoxically reduced the possibility of monitoring their behavior, creating expanded discretion, more secrecy, and an even stronger pressure on profitability. In adverse times, the resulting CEO

155

mindsets may turn into liabilities, capturing opportunities for personal maximizing of gains instead of gains for other stakeholders.

There is probably no single occupation in the world that has met with a more systematic suspiciousness from its employers than the chief executive. Dating back to the viewpoints of Smith (2008), the motives behind the decisions of chief executives have been under continuous scrutiny and subjected to systematic influence. Smith's point is that if man is indeed economically rational, any shopkeeper standing in for the true owner will face incentives to improve his own fortune instead of serving the interests of the owner. The shopkeeper's self-interested actions range all the way from being softhearted toward employees and local environments to outright theft and embezzlement. With the advent of the joint stock company act of 1844, the shopkeeper's role changed into that of the chief executive, the CEO. Because a shareholding company with limited liability often has not one but several owners, the decisions and dispositions of the CEO are even less obvious to the individual owner. This viewpoint has been turned into academic mainstream with the introduction of Williamson's (1975) principal-agent theory and turned into a systematic instrument for assuring motives with the compensation systems of corporate governance since the 1990s (Eisenhardt, 1985; Ranft et al., 2007).

The chief executive officer is the only executive at level 1 in the hierarchy of an organization (Carpenter & Wade, 2002). All other executives in the organization are at lower levels. At level 2, we find the most senior executives. If the organization is of a substantial size in terms of employees, then level 3 includes the next tier of executives.

Being a CEO involves handling exceptional circumstances and developing a high level of tacit knowledge and expertise; these characteristics and experiences contribute to the accumulation of firm-specific human capital. The time a CEO spends in the position represents a significant investment in firm-specific human capital for both the individual and the firm. The firm is investing its resources to compensate the CEO, and the CEO is investing his or her productive time. Both make these investments with the expectation of future return, so age is a major factor determining the level of firm-specific human capital investment (Buchholtz, Ribbens, & Houle, 2003).

Being the CEO means being accountable and bearing full responsibility for a company's success or failure but being unable to control most of what will determine it and having more authority than anyone else in the organization but being unable to wield it without unhappy consequences (Stacey, Griffin, & Shaw, 2000). Porter et al. (2004) make this sound like a very tough job. They argue that this comes as a surprise to CEOs who are new to the job.

Some of the surprises for new CEOs arise from time and knowledge limitations—there is so much to do in complex new areas with imperfect information and never enough time. Others stem from unexpected and unfamiliar new roles and altered professional relationships. Still others crop up because of the paradox that the more power you have, the harder it is to use. While several of the challenges may appear familiar, Porter et al. (2004) discovered that nothing in a leader's background, even running a large business within his or her company, fully prepares him or her to be a CEO.

CEOs have long been recognized as the principal architects of corporate strategy and major catalysts of organizational change, and the extent to which CEOs can effect change in corporate strategy is thought to be determined largely by the power they possess and how they decide to wield it (Bigley & Wiersema, 2002).

When assuming the position of CEO, the new accountabilities arise from several sources, such as time and knowledge limitations, unexpected and unfamiliar new roles, and altered professional relationships, because of the power paradox—the more power you have, the harder it is to use. And last but not least, the lack of group identity may make it hard to stay in tune with the values of the larger society. A CEO is normally not an owner and not quite an employee either, but a wielder of powers that need to keep a certain distance from almost all stakeholders. A number of these potential difficulties may seem common; however, Porter et al. (2004) purports that a leader's previous experience, including managing a major division or the like within his or her corporation, still cannot fully prepare a person to become a chief executive. The only certain thing is the purpose of the task: to maximize return on investments, keeping the employed capital as lean as possible. But as Ranft et al. (2007) comment:

> Holding people accountable for outcomes is quite different from holding them accountable for the behaviors demonstrated to achieve those outcomes. (p. 677)

The focus on accountability is, paradoxically, a way of giving the CEO more discretion to act because the board trusts the CEO to find a way. In this setting, declarative knowledge has been shown to be of critical but limited value (Khurana, 2007; Livingston, 1971). The industry of leadership theories and leadership development gain their legitimization from the need to develop dynamic mindsets, rather than formal, declarative knowledge (Petriglieri & Petriglieri, 2010). A look at the nature of mindsets will show how and why these mindsets may facilitate criminal transgressions in CEOs.

Mindsets are conceived as distinct cognitive operations that facilitate problem solving (Torelli & Kaikati, 2009). The concept goes back to the experimental psychologist Oswald Külpe at the end of the 19th century, who showed that most of human thinking happens without images (imageless thoughts) and that most of it also occurs outside of our awareness. They named it *Bewusstseinslage*, literally a "state of mind," which was later translated into the concept of mindsets: *Einstellung* (Humphrey, 1951).

Külpe showed that subjects would single out the features related to their tasks, and unimportant features were rejected from attention. For example, with the task of observing a number of letters, subjects may be totally unable to report on color and may deny that color has been experienced at all. This is the original meaning of the term "mindset": the brain is "set" to perceive the world according to predefined criteria. They observed that while given tasks were conscious initially, with a few repetitions the tasks would gradually disappear from consciousness. With increased practice, the awareness about the task waned, but the task kept being completed even if there was no awareness of it. Subjects had no phenomenological awareness of inner speech at the time of study, that is, there was no longer conscious reflection about the tasks. The original purpose is forgotten, and appearance of the stimulus automatically activated the prescribed conduct (Humphrey, 1951).

The word "set" in "mindset" describes how the actor is perceptually prepared or "set" to detect and respond to a given situation (Cohen-Kdoshay & Meiran, 2007), a cognitive pattern recognition that is automatically evoked when scanning the environment. The core point is that mindsets are (a) caused by repetitive tasks, (b) automatic behaviors released with little or no awareness, and (c) replacing personality-based dispositions with mindset content. Mindsets can be extremely effective in capturing business opportunity but are in themselves neither lawful nor unlawful because the ethical implications may not be a part of the mindset. Instead, they may be seen as automated recognition of opportunity with instrumental value as profit maximizing in a competitive setting.

Bigley and Wiersema (2002) argue that CEOs' cognitive orientations should influence how they wield their power to affect corporate strategy. On the one hand, predictions about a CEO's use of power require an understanding of the CEO's cognitive orientation toward his or her firm's strategy because power is simply the ability to bring about a preferred or intended effect. On the other hand, hypothesized associations between a CEO's cognitive orientation and corporate strategy presuppose that the CEO has sufficient power to bring about the preferred or intended effects.

CEOs' strategic beliefs are likely to be instantiated to a significant degree in their firms' current strategies. When a top executive seeking advice confirms and/or restores his or her confidence in the correctness of strategic beliefs, the CEO will be less likely to change firm strategy. The mindsets of CEOs cause them to be the principal architects of corporate strategy and major catalysts of organizational change (Bigley & Wiersema, 2002). Belonging to their mindsets is how to use power and secrecy, building alliances with some people and keeping others in the dark about their dispositions, as shown by Bigley and Wiersema. CEOs' mindsets or strategic beliefs are likely to be instantiated to a significant degree in their firms' current strategies. McDonald and Westphal (2003) theorized that relatively poor firm performance can prompt CEOs to seek more advice from executives of other firms who are their friends or similar to them and less advice from acquaintances or dissimilar others, and suggest how and why this pattern of advice seeking could reduce firms' propensity to change corporate strategy in response to poor performance.

McDonald and Westphal (2003) tested their hypotheses with a large sample. The results confirm their hypotheses and show that executives' social network ties can influence firms' responses to economic adversity, in particular by inhibiting strategic change in response to relatively poor firm performance. Additional findings indicate that CEOs' advice seeking in response to low performance may ultimately have negative consequences for subsequent performance, suggesting how CEOs' social network ties could play an indirect role in organizational decline and downward spirals in firm performance.

We argue that the recent decades of strengthened focus on CEO accountability has relied on compensation to keep the interest of the CEO aligned with that of the board. However, it is possible that the same practice has also strengthened the profit-maximizing mindsets of the CEO. In times of poor firm performance, these mindsets may be torn loose from the loyalty toward other stakeholders and focus entirely on the possibilities for short-term gains for the executive himself or herself. If this assumption is right, then we would expect to find the following characteristics of CEOs as white-collar criminals:

1. There will be significantly more CEOs than any other profession or management level involved in white-collar crime.
2. Success in business will be positively related to the scope of criminal "success," that is, the monetary volumes involved in the crime.
3. Success in business and personal income will be positively related such that more successful CEOs are also engaged in white-collar crime—they don't need the money but the success in capitalizing on their mindsets.
4. White-collar crime committed by CEOs will show a lack of identification with stakeholders, such that they more often than other people betray their own organizations (other criminals more often rely on social networks to betray victims on the outside of the network).
5. CEOs will be more likely to commit white-collar crime when their companies are facing difficulties, obstructing even bigger gains from capturing business success on behalf of the crime. In this sense, CEOs committing white-collar crimes are applying their mindsets on surrogates rather than on the original business objects, that of their company.

It has been argued that goal-oriented management in itself is a management approach that can cause more white-collar crime. Especially when goals are ambitious and the CEO is personally responsible for goal achievement with negative personal consequences of nonachievement, the CEO might tend to apply both legal and illegal means in a struggle to achieve goals. This is in line with the theory of profit-driven crime.

Crime that is motivated by financial gain can best be comprehended primarily under economic instead of sociological or criminological conditions. In an effort to create an overview of financial crime, Naylor (2003) recommended a system of classification that looks at the crimes rather than the criminals. It makes distinctions, drawing lines between market crime, predatory crime, and commercial crime. This theory supposes that financially motivated crimes are also motivated by opportunity as executives and managers recognize the propects for illicit monetary gain. "Opportunity" is a variable concept when it comes to financial crime, and it is contingent on the sort of criminals concerned (Michel, 2008). An alternative to goal-oriented management is rule-based or value-based management (Jonnergård, Stafsudd, & Elg, 2010), in which pressures to commit white-collar crime are less likely.

Johnson (2002) phrased the question, do CEOs matter? To answer this, he cites two critical dimensions that influence the magnitude of a CEO's impact on a company. First is resource availability, which is dependent upon an organization's level of debt (higher debt means less cash available to direct toward investments or acquisitions) and level of slack (e.g., the number of extra people or amount of assets that the CEO can easily redeploy to take advantage of an opportunity). Second, there is opportunity availability, which is determined by independence, concentration, and growth. CEOs at the helms of companies with low debt levels and high slack levels—thus high resource availability—will exert more powerful impact on their organizations, and CEO impact increases as opportunities become scarcer.

Most CEO research has tended to take a rather one-sided view of leadership, emphasizing its positive and constructive aspects while avoiding its darker sides. A possible reason for this one-sided attention may be that leadership research has primarily focused on leader effectiveness, strategic thinking, and those factors contributing to optimal performance and results (Glasø, Einarsen, Matthiesen, & Skogstad, 2010). However, there are several dark sides of leadership that need attention by researchers. One of the darkest sides of leadership is white-collar crime, when the CEO exploits criminal options for corporate and/or personal gain. This is the main topic of our statistical analysis.

However, dark sides of leadership might be found in less severe forms. One example is bullying and harassment, which may or may not be linked to crime. Bullying and harassment by CEOs are reported to happen on a regular basis in many work organizations. Bullying and harassment at work may be defined as repeated behavior, actions, and practices directed at one or more colleagues, which may be carried out deliberately or unconsciously, but which are unwanted by the targets, causing humiliation, offense, and distress and which may interfere with job performance and/or cause an unpleasant working environment (Hoel, Glasø, Hetland, Cooper, & Einarsen, 2010).

Earlier, we conducted a survey among chief financial officers (CFOs) in the largest companies in Norway about white-collar crime. There was an open-ended question in the questionnaire concerned with executive positions and leader types vulnerable to white-collar crime. The question was formulated like this: What position categories and leader types are in your opinion most attracted to commit white-collar crime?

Here are some of the responses to position categories that we obtained in our survey:

- *"Management and trusted persons, purchasers, and those who sign contracts"*
- *"Top management and persons with access to and control over assets"*
- *"Brokers and banks, that is, finance acrobats"*
- *"Managers who have the authority to commit the company financially"*
- *"Top executives who manipulate accounting to achieve extra bonuses"*
- *"Leaders at the top who would like the company to avoid paying taxes"*
- *"Persons with close relationships to vendors and customers who handle large contracts"*
- *"Ambitious top executives who are exposed to great pressure and potential income by success"*

Here are some of the responses to leader types that we obtained in our survey:

- *"Leader types with low integrity and morals"*
- *"Persons who are independent and without perception of values"*
- *"Individuals for personal gain or subject to pressure"*
- *"Leadership types who are dominating and authoritarian, who subordinates do not dare to oppose"*
- *"Persons who have been in the business for a long time, who have a wide network but have little hope to make progress in their career and are dissatisfied with their current condition"*
- *"Those with a big ego, who implement military commands and do not accept critical questions"*
- *"Persons with a disorganized and messy private financial household"*

- *"Chief executives who have established good relationships over time with key employees by providing them favors so that they become part of the 'team' without really knowing it"*
- *"Those charismatic ones who are dependent on success and who are assigned to make 'great' decisions on behalf of the corporation"*

For executive positions, most respondents wrote text indicating procurement management, marketing management, and top management, thereby confirming the CEO frequency in this study. For leader types, a number of characteristics were mentioned, including low integrity, no morals, dominating, authoritarian, dissatisfied, big ego, private financial problems, charismatic, and no ethics.

Heroic Criminals

The likelihood that a person you meet by coincidence will be sentenced to prison during the next year is 2.7% in the United States or 0.08% in Norway, but this rate will diminish rapidly if the person is white, affluent, and 40 years of age or older. It is thus baffling why organizations handing out awards to outstanding leaders and business people who are mostly white, affluent, and mature men must be vigilantly aware of the risk that a leader being celebrated today will be indicted and convicted tomorrow. Yet, judging from our numbers, this risk seems very real.

Leaders as heroic figures have been central to leadership theory since the days of Carlyle (2001) and Weber (1922), stimulating modern-day neo-charismatic theories, such as transformational theory. A growing concern about dangerous and derailed leadership in the 1980s led to sharp criticism of this heroic picture of leaders. Omnipotent, self-centered leaders are prone to destructive leadership behaviors and bad decision-making, targeted by criticism. This almost unanimous rejection of heroic leadership has led to the so-called "post-heroic" view on leadership, which, in recent years, has been shown to predict value creation and business growth better than the heroic perspective (Day, Gronn, & Salas, 2006). In fact, the heroic perspective on leadership has been shown to be part of a frequent romantic illusion of leadership, which, in turn, has been argued to attract people with narcissistic personality. Leadership positions are tempting to narcissists because they provide legitimate exposure to attention from others, a sense of importance and power as well as gratification of the sense of entitlement that narcissists seem particularly prone to.

The sense of importance and entitlement already inherent in leadership positions is enhanced by the attention that popular media in general, and the financial press in particular, gives to leaders of all kinds. Leaders are frequently credited for their companies' performance and importance to society, visible in awards, medals, or even having made statues and monuments in praise of leaders still very much alive (Treadway, Adams, Ranft, & Ferris, 2009). In accordance with the critical perspective on heroic leadership above, research on so-called leadership celebrities indicates a CEO who becomes a leadership celebrity will experience a long-term increase in personal compensation but a slight decrease in company performance. Becoming a leadership celebrity creates social leverage for the leader in question but not necessarily for the company.

According to Treadway et al. (2009), the creation of leadership celebrities is based on the perception that individuals can build an attractive social identity, which might be a product of media creation. In particular, CEOs must generate powerful attributions of consistency in their stakeholder groups to increase the likelihood that their celebrity will be seen as a result of their ability rather than a product of their situation. The creation of leadership celebrities is a mutual process between media workers and the leader, focusing on brief, simple, and appealing explanations of complex outcomes. There is a real risk that the leader starts believing his own press, thereby becoming more susceptible to being overconfident about his ability and the accuracy of his judgment. In short, celebrity leadership consists of a public manifestation of the heroic illusion of leadership, including a strong sense of personal agency and special powers, including insight.

We believe this publically staged heroic identity may be an identifying instance for a particular and spectacular subgroup of white-collar criminals. We call this phenomenon negative heroism and define it as the onset of criminal behavior in an individual that has hitherto not been indicted or convicted of any crimes, but who starts engaging in white-collar crime late in life in conjunction with media exposure as a leadership celebrity.

As discussed in the section above, definitions of white-collar crime differ as to whether this is limited to individuals in high status positions or if it is merely another arena of crime, committed by those that simply have access to values and instruments that are blocked to normal criminals. We argue that negative heroism is not only limited to status positions, but may be even released or enhanced by status positions because of the mechanisms involved in becoming a heroic leadership celebrity. Dating more than a century back, discussions of heroic leadership (Carlyle, 2001; Weber, 1922) have documented that heroes are often given leeway to break rules and instigate a new order. They and their followers see themselves not so much as subjected to rules as innovative creators of rules, parallel to the saying that "managers do things right, but leaders do the right things."

Most ordinary criminals begin their criminal careers in early adulthood, and to many of them, the criminal transgressions appear in patterns that coincide with a lack of ability to lead an organized life, postpone gratification, and achieve social success through normal means (DeLisi, 2009). With a subset of white-collar criminals, neurotic personality traits seem to predict recidivism (Listwan, Piquero, & Van Voorhis, 2010). Heroic leaders are, to the contrary, characterized by an almost life-long ability to not only play by the rules, but almost to excel in doing it, achieving success in education, business, and social affairs.

Even if there may be personality antecedents to negative heroism (probably related to narcissism), our contribution is to show that assuming the identity of heroic leadership in public increases rather than decreases the risk for transgressing laws. The process involves (a) success in business or leadership, (b) public recognition with exaggeration of personal focus and reification of heroic leadership, and (c) the lifetime onset of criminal behavior appears simultaneously at or after the onset of celebrity construction. We therefore hypothesize that within a population of white-collar criminals, there will be a sizeable subset characterized by the following: (1) holding public status as celebrity; (2) later onset of criminal behavior; (3) significant business success prior to crime; (4) occupying a position of CEO, chairman, or similar; (5) not part of an extensive criminal society; and (6) always also the leader and not the follower in their perpetrated crimes.

The concept of negative heroism has to be advanced to how the behavioral profile of these offenders may contribute to their negativity, especially those who may display psychopathic tendencies (Babiak, Neumann, & Hare, 2010). Leaders sometimes receive accolades, such as awards, charitable giving, and praise. Negative heroism implies that such leaders use these attributes as a way to create the image that if they engage in such altruistic activities, they are not capable of committing fraud.

Boddy, Ladyshewsky, and Galvin (2010) studied the influence of corporate psychopaths on corporate social responsibility and organizational commitment to employees. They found that when corporate psychopaths are present in leadership positions within organizations, employees are less likely to agree with views that the organization does business in an environmentally friendly manner.

While the literature on the dark side of leadership commonly portrays derailed leaders as victims of their narcissistic personalities, present research on white-collar crime, alcoholism, and terrorism show that deviant behavior can be explained by path-dependent situational mechanisms. Narcissism as a potential trigger for white-collar crime in leadership positions was studied by Maccoby (2000) and Perri (2011). Executives may display a heroic persona, but there are criminal thinking patterns that long have been present predating the behavior at issue, and these thinking patterns express themselves at a moment of opportunity; the crime may very much be within the character of the offender.

Maccoby (2000) wrote about narcissistic leaders:

> Because they are extraordinarily sensitive, narcissistic leaders shun emotions as a whole. Indeed, perhaps one of the greatest paradoxes in this age of teamwork and partnering is that the best corporate leader in the contemporary world is the type of person who is emotionally isolated. Narcissistic leaders typically keep others at arm's length. They can put up a wall of defense as thick as the Pentagon. And given their difficulty with knowing or acknowledging their own feelings, they are uncomfortable with other people expressing theirs—especially their negative feelings.

Our contribution is to show that assuming the identity of heroic leadership in public increases rather than decreases the risk for transgressing laws. The process involves (a) success in business or leadership; (b) public recognition with exaggeration of personal focus and reification of heroic leadership; and (c) subsequent perception of threat to a continuing success trajectory, leading to (d) a heightened will to gamble with a sense of personal agency, entitlement, and externalization of guilt by blaming others, assuming a right to bend rules. We call this negative heroism and argue that it is a corollary to the frequent illusion of heroic leadership.

An example of a heroic leader in our sample is Robert Hermansen as presented earlier in this book. The former Norwegian chairman and chief executive officer of the world's northernmost mining company, Store Norske Spitsbergen Kullkompani, was sentenced to two years in prison for his role in a bribery scandal at the Svalbard firm. Robert Hermansen, age 72 when convicted in 2011, also faced huge debt after being ordered to repay nearly NOK 4 million in what the court in Nord-Troms viewed as bribes from the Bergen-based shipping company Kristian Jebsens Rederi. Jebsens enjoyed long-term, expensive contracts to ship ore from the mines that were tied to the payments to Hermansen. Hermansen, who had enjoyed a long career as a businessman before the bribery charges were filed, had confessed to receiving the money from Jebsens but told newspaper *Dagens Næringsliv (DN)* that he thought his sentence was much too strict. He was considering an appeal but said he didn't fear going to jail. "I've never been in prison before; it will be a new experience," he told *DN*. "Most experiences are worth something." A monument of Robert Hermansen as a hero on the Island of Spitsbergen was put up many years before his white-collar crime was revealed. Because many locals do not think of Hermansen as a bad guy, the monument still remains in place.

It is important not to confuse leadership with behavioral characteristics of white-collar offenders. High-level executives can display psychopathic traits, and such behavior should not be confused with leadership traits, such as being charismatic, visionaries, and adept at impression management, which is creating a persona by building walls of false integrity. This impression management may take the form of contributing to charities, admirable corporate mission statements, ethical guidelines that look great on paper but do not represent the internal reality of the organization that violates their own ethical guidelines. Often with these celebrity leaders, we get a very narrow view of who they really are because they engage in impression management and control information about themselves to outsiders.

Crime Theories

The *theory of double-bind leadership* suggests that mixed messages from a leader creates a double bind for a colleague or subordinate. Individuals are caught in double-bind situations in organizational relationships when the criminal leader is expressing two orders of message and one of these denies the other. Individuals are unable to comment on the message being expressed to correct their discrimination in terms of which order of messages to respond to because the situation in double-bind leadership is such that they cannot make a meta-communicative statement (Hennestad, 1990).

An individual is not able to comment on the ambiguity of the message by being critical in an assessment of the consequences of a double bind because it cements the ambiguity of the situation. A simple example of a double bind is a child being exposed to signals of both love and hate from a parent. The child is trapped:

> If the situation is defined as one of hate, the child could be punished for her reaction. On the other hand, if the child defines the signal as one of love, the reaction could be rejection of her affection. (Hennestad, 1990, p. 268)

A double bind is a dilemma in communication in which an individual receives conflicting messages with one message negating the other. This creates a situation in which a successful response to one message results in a failed response to the other message, so the person might be wrong regardless of response. The nature of a double bind is that the person is unable to confront the sender of the messages with the inherent dilemma. The double-bind theory is seen as part of the human experience of communication that involves intense relationships and the necessity to discriminate between orders of messages (Gibney, 2006).

The double-bind theory can be applied to both individuals and organizations. A double-bind organization is a social system in which mixed messages are the rule rather than an exception. An organizational schizophrenia occurs in the organization, in which mixed messages cannot be revealed, which has a negative effect on an employee's initiatives and learning situation. The result is a lack of authentic dialogue, which can freeze the horizon of meaning in the organization, thereby rendering infertile the soil of growth of vitality of organizational dynamics (Hennestad, 1990).

Social contract theory assumes that ethical dilemmas in business overlay a universe of economic transactions involving actors whose ability to comprehend their moral implications is inherently limited. Criminal social contracts at macro and micro levels constitute the basis for analyzing how individuals and organizations avoid fulfilling ethical obligations through consent and through conformity to unethical social norms (Barry & Stephens, 1998).

For some criminals, the choice of crime might be based on a rational decision. *Rational choice theory* argues that it is indeed rational to be a criminal providing two conditions are satisfied: The potential profit is great, and the likelihood of punishment is small:

> Rational choice theory suggests that people who commit crimes do so after considering the risks of detection and punishment for the crimes (risk assessment), as well as the rewards (personal, financial, etc.) of completing these acts successfully. On the other hand, persons who do not commit crime decide that completing the act successfully is too risky or not worth the benefits. (Lyman & Potter, 2007, p. 62)

Rational choice theory suggests that people who commit crimes do so after considering the risks of detection and punishment for the crimes alongside the rewards of successfully completing criminal acts. Examples of this theory include a man who discovers that his wife is having an affair and chooses to kill her, her lover, or both; the bank teller who is experiencing personal financial difficulty and decides to embezzle funds from the bank to substantially increase her earnings; and an inner-city youth who decides that social opportunities are minimal and that it would be easier to make money by dealing crack cocaine (Lyman & Potter, 2007).

Weismann (2009) applied rational choice theory to study normative ethical corporate behaviors:

> Rational choice theory as a basis for predicting corporate behaviors in the marketplace from an institutional perspective relies on two key assumptions. First, corporations will achieve regulatory compliance through an internal system of checks and balances, which can be relied upon by the regulators. Second, the least intrusion by regulators into internal corporate affairs provides the most efficient and effective means of corporate governance and internal control practices. (p. 627)

In organized crime, Shvarts (2001) suggests that rational choice theory can explain the growth of the Russian Mafia. Because of low income and financial difficulties at the individual level, combined with a corrupt police force, it seems rational to move into organized crime to improve the standard of living for members joining the criminal organization.

Rational choice theory suggests that humans are selfish, focused on achieving their own individual happiness as the highest moral purpose of rational existence. Altruism, in contrast, is thereby irrational and, therefore, determinative of undesirable outcomes. By placing others above oneself in altruism, one denies self-sufficiency, eschews personal happiness, and compromises individual rights. Here, sacrifice is the antithesis of rationality, when the individual surrenders the right to the wrong, good to evil. Self-interest is defended in the rational choice theory by contrasting it with irrational sacrifice (Barry & Stephens, 1998).

Dobash et al. (2009) used rational choice theory to describe white-collar crime as perpetrated by both males and females, saying that rationalizations of crime can happen when people experience troublesome financial conditions. Dobash et al. cite crisis, stress, and opportunity as three reasons why people might commit fraud. Circumstances such as problematic upbringings and hardships as an adult are not helpful. Within this context, middle-class, white-collar offenders can be seen as people making justifiable choices to commit crime from the perspective of being mired in an emergency situation.

Rational choice theory finds support in an empirical study by Bucy, Formby, Raspanti, and Rooney (2008), who identified a number of motives for white-collar crime. According to their empirical study, greed is the most common reason for white-collar criminal acts. Money and other forms of financial gain were found to be a frequent motivator. Criminals pursue desired goals, weigh up likely consequences, and make selections from various options. When criminal opportunity is attractive as a means of responding to desires, rational actors will choose it.

Similarly, rational choice theory found support in an empirical study of white-collar criminals by Goldstraw-White (2012), in which planning actors may be seen as those individuals who look for opportunities to advance and execute their criminal acts in an organized and intentional way. These planners exhibit a higher degree of rationality compared to opportunists. In adopting a rational approach to their crimes, individuals are perceived as reasoned, purposeful, and calculating. They will usually have investigated as many aspects of their potential criminal acts as possible, including weighing up the costs and benefits of all the factors involved, and assessing where known internal controls serve or do not serve as sufficient deterrents to prevent them from carrying out their plans.

Heroic criminals are well known, and some may be politically exposed. The *theory of politically exposed persons* is a behavioral theory related to the role that the criminal or potential criminal occupies at that point in time. A politically exposed person is an individual who is entrusted with prominent public functions. It is argued by Gilligan (2009) that, as such individuals pose a potential reputation risk to regulated entities, financial institutions must track them. Most of the high-profile media politically exposed person-related coverage in recent years relates to persons such as former president of the Philippines, Ferdinand Marcos, and former president of Nigeria, Sani Abacha, who were accused of fostering corruption within their countries and transferring millions of dollars of public funds out of their home countries into bank accounts overseas.

Criminal Sample

Before our sample reached the number of 305 convicted white-collar criminals, statistical analysis was conducted on CEO versus non-CEO individuals. The sample size at that time was 179 white-collar criminals, consisting of 78 CEO criminals and 101 non-CEO criminals as listed in Table 6.1.

As listed in the table, there are some interesting differences between CEO-criminals and other white-collar criminals. Firstly, CEOs receive a significantly longer jail sentence (2.6 years) compared to other criminals (2.0 years). Furthermore, there are significantly fewer persons involved in CEO crime (4.0 persons) when compared to other types (5.3 persons). Organizational size is, on average, smaller in CEO cases, in which the average size is only 58 employees (as opposed to 168).

When looking at five different main categories for financial crime in Table 6.2, there are few differences between CEO criminals and other white-collar criminals. CEOs seem to be slightly more involved in manipulation, such as fixing of accounting, and slightly less in corruption.

Table 6.1   Comparison of Chief Executive Officers versus Other White-Collar Criminals

Total 179 White-Collar Criminals	78 CEO Criminals	101 Non-CEO Criminals	Significant Difference?
Age at which convicted	48 years	49 years	No
Age at which crime committed	43 years	44 years	No
Years in prison	2.6 years	2.0 years	Yes
Crime amount	66 million kr	76 million kr	No
Personal income	479,000 kr	346,000 kr	No
Personal tax	177,000 kr	165,000 kr	No
Personal wealth	1.9 million kr	1.7 million kr	No
Involved persons	4.0 persons	5.3 persons	Yes
Business revenue	160 million kr	265 million kr	No
Business employees	58 persons	168 persons	Yes
Sector private/public	1.1 most private	1.1 most private	No
Crime detection	1.7 some media	1.8 most others	Yes

Table 6.2   Comparison of Crime Categories of CEOs' Share of White-Collar Crime Cases

Category	Total Number in Each Crime Category	CEO Number in Each Crime Category	CEO Fraction in Each Crime Category
Fraud	80	35	44%
Theft	1	1	100%
Manipulation	47	23	49%
Corruption	36	13	36%
Embezzlement	15	6	40%
Total	179	78	44%

Chief executive officer is the top position in a company. Almost half of our sample is CEOs. It is interesting to compare this finding with an earlier survey we conducted. We conducted a survey about white-collar crime among chief financial officers (CFOs) in the largest companies in Norway. There was an open-ended question in the questionnaire concerned with executive positions and leader types vulnerable to white-collar crime. The question was formulated like this: What position categories and leader types are in your opinion most attracted to commit white-collar crime?

Before our sample reached the number of 305 convicted white-collar criminals, statistical analysis was conducted on heroic leaders versus nonheroic individuals. The sample size at that time was 179 white-collar criminals, consisting of 26 heroic criminals and 153 nonheroic criminals as listed in Table 6.3.

There are several significant differences to be found in the table. First, the heroic leaders are older than the regular ones. Heroic leaders as white-collar criminals receive a significantly longer jail sentence. Perhaps this is because their criminal transgression is significantly more substantial in terms of

Table 6.3   Comparison of Characteristics of Heroic and Regular White-Collar Criminals

Total 179 White-Collar Criminals	26 Heroic White-Collar Criminals	153 Regular White-Collar Criminals	Significant Difference?
Age when convicted	55 years	48 years	Yes
Years in prison	3.0 years	2.2 years	Yes
Crime amount	184 million kr	52 million kr	Yes
Personal income	943,000 kr	313,000 kr	Yes
Personal tax	320,000 kr	146,000 kr	Yes
Personal wealth	3.2 million kr	1.6 million kr	No
Involved persons	3 persons	5 persons	Yes
Business revenue	414 million kr	187 million kr	Yes
Business employees	159 persons	114 persons	Yes

the amount of money abused. Heroic leader criminals report a significantly higher income to the public revenue service. Heroic leader criminals involve significantly fewer persons in their crime. Heroic leader criminals operate in larger organizations in terms of business revenue and number of employees.

Before our sample reached 305 convicted white-collar criminals, the following analysis was carried out based on 255 criminals. As previously mentioned, we define three white-collar levels. The first level is owners of companies, board members of companies, and chief executive officers of companies. The second level is lawyers, consultants, investors, and brokers. The third level is middle managers, independent contractors, and single working individuals. In our

Table 6.4 Comparison of Management Positions in Crime

Total 255 White-Collar Criminals	76 Top Level Executives 1	106 Middle Level Executives 2	73 Basic Level Executives 3	Significant Differences
Age convicted	50 years	49 years	43 years	1–2 1.00 1–3 .001 2–3 .001
Age crime committed	44 years	45 years	39 years	1–2 1.00 1–3 .043 2–3 .006
Years prison	2.6 years	2.1 years	2.0 years	1–2 .216 1–3 .160 2–3 1.00
Crime amount	96 million kr	56 million kr	19 million kr	1–2 .434 1–3 .032 2–3 .556
Personal income	490,000 kr	316,000 kr	175,000 kr	1–2 .101 1–3 .001 2–3 .264
Personal tax	226,000 kr	121,000 kr	60,000 kr	1–2 .004 1–3 .000 2–3 .190
Personal wealth	3.8 million kr	0.6 million kr	0.1 million kr	1–2 .001 1–3 .001 2–3 .001
Involved persons	2.9 persons	3.8 persons	6.1 persons	1–2 .239 1–3 .000 2–3 .000
Business revenue	289 million kr	242 million kr	46 million kr	1–2 1.00 1–3 .000 2–3 .002
Business employees	118 persons	194 persons	30 persons	1–2 .235 1–3 .190 2–3 .001

sample of 255 convicted white-collar criminals, we find 76 individuals (30%) at level 1, 106 individuals (41%) at level 2, and 73 individuals (29%) at level 3.

These three categories are compared in Table 6.4. One-way ANOVA statistical analysis based on post-hoc Bonferroni was applied for this analysis of four groups (Hair, Black, Babin, & Anderson, 2010).

There are a number of significant differences found between the three categories of management positions:

- Level 1 and level 2 criminals are significantly older than level 3 criminals, both when convicted and when committing crime.
- Crime amount for level 1 criminals is significantly higher than for level 3 criminals.
- Personal income for level 1 criminals is significantly higher than for level 3 criminals.
- Level 1 criminals paid significantly more tax than level 2 and 3 criminals.
- Level 1 criminals are significantly wealthier than level 2 and 3 criminals, and level 2 criminals are significantly wealthier than level 3 criminals.
- Level 1 and level 2 criminals involve significantly fewer persons in the crime when compared to level 3.
- Level 1 and level 2 criminals work in significantly larger organizations than level 3 criminals, as measured in business revenue.
- Level 2 criminals work in significantly larger organizations than level 3 criminals, as measured in business employees.

There are no significant differences in sentence in terms of years in prison that ranged from 2.6 via 2.1 to 2.0 years.

References

Babiak, P., Neumann, C. S., & Hare, R. D. (2010). Corporate psychopathy: Talking the walk. *Behavioral Science and the Law, 28*(2), 174–193.

Barry, B., & Stephens, C. U. (1998). Objections to an objectivist approach to integrity. *Academy of Management Review, 23*(1), 162–169.

Bigley, G. A., & Wiersema, M. F. (2002). New CEOs and corporate strategic refocusing: How experience as heir apparent influences the use of power. *Administrative Science Quarterly, 47*, 707–727.

Boddy, C. R., Ladyshewsky, R. K., & Galvin, P. (2010). The influence of corporate psychopaths on corporate social responsibility and organizational commitment to employees. *Journal of Business Ethics, 97*(1), 1–19.

Buchholtz, A. K., Ribbens, B. A., & Houle, I. T. (2003). The role of human capital in postacquisition CEO departure. *Academy of Management Journal, 46*(4), 506–514.

Bucy, P. H., Formby, E. P., Raspanti, M. S., & Rooney, K. E. (2008). Why do they do it? The motives, mores, and character of white collar criminals. *St. John's Law Review, 82*(2), 401–571.

Carlyle, T. (2001, orig. 1841). *On heroes, hero worship, and the heroic in history.* London: Electric Book Co.

Carpenter, M. A., & Wade, J. B. (2002). Microlevel opportunity structures as determinants of non-CEO executive pay. *Academy of Management Journal, 45*(6), 1085–1103.

Cohen-Kdoshay, O., & Meiran, N. (2007). The representation of instructions in working memory leads to autonomous response activation: Evidence from the first trials in the flanker paradigm. *Quarterly Journal of Experiment Psychology, 60*(8), 1140–1154.

Day, D. V., Gronn, P., & Salas, E. (2006). Leadership in team-based organizations: On the threshold of a new era. *Leadership Quarterly, 17*(3), 211–216.

DeLisi, M. (2009). Psychopathy is the unified theory of crime. *Youth Violence and Juvenile Justice, 7*(3), 256–273.

Dobash, R. E., Dobash, R. P., & Cavanagh, K. (2009). "Out of the blue": Men who murder an intimate partner. *Feminist Criminology, 4*(3), 194–225.

Eisenhardt, K. M. (1985). Control: Organizational and economic approaches. *Management Science, 31*(2), 134–149.

Gibney, P. (2006). The double bind theory: Still crazy-making after all these years. *Psychotherapy in Australia, 12*(3), 48–55.

Gilligan, G. (2009). PEEPing at PEPs. *Journal of Financial Crime, 16*(2), 137–143.

Glasø, L., Einarsen, S., Matthiesen, S. B., & Skogstad, A. (2010). The dark side of leaders: A representative study of interpersonal problems among leaders. *Scandinavian Journal of Organizational Psychology, 2*(2), 3–14.

Goldstraw-White, J. (2012). *White-collar crime: Accounts of offending behaviour.* London: Palgrave Macmillan.

Hair, J. F., Black, W. C., Babin, B. J., & Anderson, R. E. (2010). *Multivariate data analysis* (7th ed.). Upper Saddle River, NJ: Pearson Education.

Hennestad, B. W. (1990). The symbolic impact of double bind leadership: Double bind and the dynamics of organizational culture. *Journal of Management Studies, 27*(3), 265–280.

Hoel, H., Glasø, L., Hetland, J., Cooper, C. L., & Einarsen, S. (2010). Leadership styles as predictors of self-reported and observed workplace bullying. *British Journal of Management, 21*, 453–468.

Humphrey, G. (1951). *Thinking: An introduction to its experimental psychology.* London: Methuen.

Isaacson, W. (2011). *Steve Jobs.* London: Little, Brown.

Johnson, L. K. (2002). Do CEOs matter? *MIT Sloan Management Review*, Winter, 8–9.

Jonnergård, K., Stafsudd, A., & Elg, U. (2010). Performance evaluations as gender barriers in professional organizations: A study of auditing firms. *Gender, Work and Organization, 17*(6), 721–747.

Khurana, R. (2007). *From higher aims to hired hands: The social transformation of American business schools and the unfulfilled promise of management as a profession.* Princeton, NJ: Princeton University Press.

Lieberson, S., & O'Connor, J. F. (1972). Leadership and organizational performance: A study of large corporations. *American Sociological Review, 37*(2), 117–130.

Listwan, S. J., Piquero, N. L., & Van Voorhis, P. (2010). Recidivism among a white-collar sample: Does personality matter? *Australian and New Zealand Journal of Criminology, 43*(1), 156–174.

Livingston, J. S. (1971). Myth of the well-educated Manager. Harvard Business Review (January–February), 79–89.

Lyman, M. D., & Potter, G. W. (2007). *Organized crime* (4th ed.). Upper Saddle River, NJ: Pearson Prentice Hall.

Maccoby, M. (2000). Narcissistic leaders: The incredible pros, the inevitable cons. *Harvard Business Review*, January–February, McKinsey Award Winning Paper. Retrieved from http://www.maccoby.com/Articles/NarLeaders.shtml.

McDonald, M. L., & Westphal, J. D. (2003). Getting by with the advice of their friends: CEOs' advice networks and firms' strategic responses to poor performance. *Administrative Science Quarterly, 48*, 1–32.

Michel, P. (2008). Financial crimes: The constant challenge of seeking effective prevention solutions. *Journal of Financial Crime, 15*(4), 383–397.

Naylor, R. T. (2003). Towards a general theory of profit-driven crimes. *British Journal of Criminology, 43*, 81–101.

Perri, F. S. (2011). White collar criminals: The "kinder, gentler" offender? *Journal of Investigative Psychology and Offender Profiling, 8*, 217–241.

Petriglieri, G., & Petriglieri, J. L. (2010). Identity workspaces: The case of business schools. *Academy of Management Learning & Education, 9*(1), 44–60.

Porter, M. E., Lorsch, J. W., & Nohria, N. (2004). Seven surprises for new CEOs. *Harvard Business Review, 82*(10), 62–72.

Ranft, A. L., Ferris, G. R., & Perryman, A. A. (2007). Dealing with celebrity and accountability in the top job. *Human Resource Management, 46*(4), 671–682.

Shvarts, A. (2001). The Russian mafia: Do rational choice models apply? *Michigan Sociological Review, 15*, 29–63.

Smith, A. (2008). *An inquiry into the nature and causes of the wealth of nations.* Oxford: Oxford Univertsity Press.

Stacey, R. D., Griffin, D., & Shaw, P. (2000). *Complexity theory and management: Fad or radical challenge to systems thinking?* London: Routledge.

Thomas, A. B. (1988). Does leadership make a difference to organizational performance? *Administrative Science Quarterly, 33*, 388–400.

Torelli, C. J., & Kaikati, A. M. (2009). Values as predictors of judgments and behaviors: The role of abstract and concrete mindsets. *Journal of Personality and Social Psychology, 96*(1), 231–247.

Treadway, D. C., Adams, G. L., Ranft, A. L., & Ferris, G. R. (2009). A meso-level conceptualization of CEO celebrity effectiveness. *The Leadership Quarterly, 40*(4), 554–570.

Weber, M. (1922). Wirtschaft und Gesellschaft. In G. Albrecht (Ed.), *Grundriss der Sozialökonomik.* Tübingen, Germany: J. C. B. Mohr.

Weismann, M. F. (2009). The Foreign Corrupt Practices Act: The failure of the self-regulatory model of corporate governance in the global business environment. *Journal of Business Ethics, 88*, 615–661.

Williamson, O. E. (1975). *Markets and hierarchies: Analysis and antitrust implications.* New York: Free Press.

Victims, Detection, and Sector

7

A distinction can be made between internal victims versus external victims of crime. When a company manipulates its accounting to obtain new loans from a bank, then the bank is an external victim. When an employee approves fake invoices and takes the money, then the company is an internal victim. In one of the largest financial fraud cases in history, Bernard Madoff stole billions of dollars of savings, investment, and retirement funds from numerous individuals, businesses, and not-for-profit foundations. The size and scope of the scam resulted in both internal and external victims (Glodstein, Glodstein, & Fornaro, 2010).

Victims Criminal Characteristics

For many victims of Madoff's scam, the consequences extended beyond financial loss and included undesired media coverage and perhaps public humiliation. The victims of the Madoff fraud are constantly reminded of this scandal on television, in newspapers and magazines, and on the Internet. However, Glodstein et al. (2010) suggest that the human element of the fraud, which includes the personal pain and suffering of the victims, ultimately disappears from view.

A victim is a person or an organization that suffers a destructive or injurious action or agency, and it may be deceived or cheated. A victim of financial crime is anyone who suffers a loss. For example, criminal fraud—the offense of false pretenses—traditionally required the misrepresentation of a material fact that the victim relied upon in relinquishing his or her property. Theft can be defined as the illegal taking of another person's, group's, or organization's property without the victim's consent (Hill, 2008).

In the United States, the law recommends heavier sentences when larger numbers of victims suffer a pecuniary loss as a result of an offender's criminal conduct. This law section governs sentencing for financial identity theft and other financial crimes, such as larceny, embezzlement, fraud, and various counterfeit offenses (Anderson, 2006).

Croall (2007) studied what he called victims of white-collar and corporate crime. This form of victimization is often seen to involve a very different set of relationships between offenders and victims as there is less obvious direct harm or blood on the streets. It appears less personal as immediate victims are often employers, the government, the public health, or the environment. Victims of many of these activities are not widely recognized as crime victims and are excluded from most traditions of victim research, which have largely accepted conventional constructions of crime. Not all offenses involve indirect victimization, and victims are aware of some offenses. However, there is no such thing as victimless crime because there is always harm caused to somebody or something because of crime.

Victims Crime Theories

As our criminal sample will illustrate, external victims are more common than internal victims. For the external victim, there is an external source causing damage and loss. This is in line with *alien conspiracy theory*, which blames outsiders and outside influences for the prevalence of organized crime in society and financial crime in organizations. Over the years, unsavory images, such as well-dressed men of foreign descent standing in shadows with machine guns and living by codes of silence, have become associated with this theory. The alien conspiracy theory posits that organized crime (the Mafia) gained prominence during the 1860s in Sicily and that Sicilian immigrants are responsible for the foundations of U.S. organized crime, which is made up of 25 or so Italian-dominated crime families (Lyman & Potter, 2007).

Lyman and Potter (2007) discuss this theory as follows:

> Although some skeptics insist that the alien conspiracy theory was born out of hysteria incited by the media, it has received considerable support over the years from federal law enforcement organizations, public officials, and some researchers. It has been argued, however, that federal law enforcement organizations have self-serving reasons to promulgate this theory: It explains their inability to eliminate organized crime, it disguises the role of political and business corruption in organized crime, and it provides fertile ground for new resources, powers, and bureaucratic expansion. (p. 60)

Lombardo (2002) has challenged the alien conspiracy theory as an explanation of the origin of organized crime in America; he reviewed the history of Black Hand (organized crime group) activity in Chicago in the early 20th century, arguing that the development of Black Hand extortion was not related to the emergence of the Sicilian Mafia but rather to the social structure of American society.

Lack of market integrity is another reason that can explain external victims of crime because *market integrity theory* is concerned with the integrity of capital markets. The concept of market integrity tends to imply many statements, such as low levels of crime, efficiency in law enforcement, fairness in competitive markets, access to information for market participants, effective regulation and prevention of financial crime, and confidence among market actors. Market integrity theory suggests that the extent of market integrity can be measured in terms of the following (Fodor, 2008):

- Market misconduct: measuring changes in the prevalence of dishonest activity
- Efforts to educate, detect, and enforce: measuring changes in the enforcement and understanding of relevant laws and regulations
- Effectiveness, efficiency, and fairness of market structures: measuring changes in the operational performance of markets
- Perceptions of market integrity: quantifying changes in public confidence in the integrity of capital markets

According to Fodor's (2008) market integrity theory, a delicate interplay of perceptions, effective regulation, law enforcement actions, and extent of market misconduct determines the relative integrity of a given market over time. Inherent within this complex interaction of market forces are a series of checks and balances that suggest that market integrity may not be measured in absolute terms but rather in a relative nature that could vary according to jurisdictions and environmental conditions.

Market integrity can be influenced by government regulation in both a positive and a negative direction. Deterioration in market integrity will occur if market actors feel the need to commit financial crime in order to adapt to new regulation regimes. An example can be found in European procurement rules, under which corruption might be the only way of achieving commercial government contracts. Opportunities for both fraud and corruption could plausibly increase owing to new rules governing public procurement (Dorn, Levi, & White, 2008).

When a company bribes an employee in another company, the corruption has an external victim. *Corruption theory* maintains that the causes of corruption are complex. It recognizes that corruption is a symptom of other, deeper-seated factors, such as poorly designed economic policies, low levels of education, underdeveloped civil society, and the weak accountability of public institutions (Ksenia, 2008).

Motivation for corruption is to influence others. Motivation theory is in line with the theory of reasoned action, in which the intention of an individual is influenced by personal attitudes, social norms, and weighing up these two considerations:

These motivational factors emanate from the self (personal identity), the environment and the interaction of the two. Within organizational settings, the self could be studied using needs theory, while the environment can be studied using leadership theory. (Woodbine & Liu, 2010, p. 29)

Motivation involves personality and cultural factors that induce individuals to act in ways that neutralize the strong ethical controls of society. Specific cultural factors that lead to crime and criminal behavior include the desire to make a fast buck, the fear of losing what has already been made, defining competitive struggle as being positive rather than negative or selfish, differential association, and even the structure of the industrial economy, such as market exchange and the use of money (Aguilera & Vadera, 2008).

Aguilera and Vadera (2008) make distinctions between procedural corruption, schematic corruption, and categorical corruption. Procedural corruption results from either the lack of formalized procedures or formal rules of business conduct in the organization or from the violation of existing formal procedures for personal gain. Schematic corruption is structured and present uniformly throughout the organization, and results are due to the simultaneous involvement of multiple organizational levels in corrupt acts and at multiple points in time. Categorical corruption is the result of concentrated and delimited acts of corruption within the organization.

Victims Criminal Sample

In our sample of 305 convicted white-collar criminals, there were 58 internal victims and 247 external victims as listed in Table 7.1. While most criminals worked in the private sector, most victims could be found in the public sector as discussed earlier in this book.

Table 7.1 Comparison of Characteristics of Internal Victim Cases versus External Victim Cases

Total 305 Criminals	58 Internal Victim Cases	247 External Victim Cases	t Statistical Difference	Significance of t Statistic
Age convicted	51 years	47 years	2.187	.030
Age at time of crime	46 years	42 years	2.107	.036
Years in prison	2.5 years	2.1 years	1.791	.074
Crime amount	20 million kr	53 million kr	−1.392	.165
Personal income	494,000 kr	298,000 kr	2.408	.017
Personal tax	203,000 kr	127,000 kr	2.225	.027
Personal wealth	1.7 million kr	1.5 million kr	.236	.813
Involved persons	2.1 persons	4.2 persons	−4.189	.000
Business revenue	331 million kr	157 million kr	3.499	.001
Business employees	225 persons	100 persons	2.947	.003

Several differences in the table can be found between criminals who caused harm to internal victims versus criminals who caused harm to external victims. Because most victims are external, we concentrate on this group of criminals. White-collar criminals having external victims are significantly younger, both when they commit their crime and when they receive their jail sentence. Years in prison and crime amount do not significantly differ. Criminals with external victims have lower income and pay less tax. Criminals with external victims involve significantly more persons, and they work in significantly smaller organizations.

Classification of Victims

A victim of white-collar crime is anyone who suffers a financial loss because of financial crime committed by a white-collar criminal. As suggested by Croall (2007), victims of white-collar crime involve a very different set of relationships between offenders and victims, compared to victims of traditional street crime. White-collar crime is often less personal and immediate victims are often employers, banks, tax authorities, customers, shareholders, customs, social security agencies, or the environment. Victims, such as tax authorities or social security agencies, are not widely recognized as crime victims. Rather, it is often argued that white-collar crime is generally undermining society at large and associated institutions. However, this research attempts to identify distinct victims of white-collar crime by establishing categories of victims. After studying all 323 convicted white-collar criminals in 148 white-collar crime cases, the following categories emerge as most frequent for classification of white-collar crime victims:

1. *Employers.* Kristian Aspen (born 1977) was chief of accounting at Pratt & Whitney in Stavanger, Norway. He transferred 42 million kr (about U.S. $7 million) to his personal firm's account. Aspen was sentenced to four years and six months in prison by the district court of Stavanger in 2012. Employers are typically victims of financial crime types, such as embezzlement and theft, including theft of cash and fraud (Pickett & Pickett, 2002; Williams, 2006). Peltier-Rivest (2009) studied characteristics of organizations that are victims of occupational fraud. The most frequent category of fraud in their study in Canada was asset misappropriations (81% of cases), followed by corruption (35%), and fraudulent statements (10%). Asset misappropriations may be cash or non-cash. Cash schemes include cash larceny, skimming, or fraudulent disbursements, such as billing schemes, payroll fraud, check tampering, and expense reimbursement frauds. Noncash schemes include theft of inventory, equipment, proprietary

information, and securities. The most frequent victims of occupational fraud in the Peltier-Rivest (2009) study were private companies, followed by government entities and public companies. The mean loss suffered by private companies was U.S. $1 million. The study was based on a sample of 90 complete cases of occupational fraud investigated in Canada.

2. *Banks.* Torgeir Stensrud (born 1949) and Trond Kristoffersen (born 1949) were chairman of the board and chief executive officer, respectively, of Finance Credit. The company structure was so complex that banks continued to provide new loans even after the company was, in fact, bankrupt. After bankruptcy, several local banks lost a total of 1.2 billion kr (about U.S. $600 million). Stensrud and Kristoffersen were sentenced to seven years and nine years imprisonment, respectively. Banks are typically victims of financial crime types, such as fraud, including check fraud; credit card fraud; mortgage fraud; and identity fraud (Barker, D'Amato, & Sheridon, 2008; Fisher, 2008; Gilsinan et al., 2008; Pickett & Pickett, 2002).

3. *Tax authorities.* Henry Amundsen (born 1950) was managing his own accounting firm. More than 372 cab owners in Oslo were having their accounting work handled by Amundsen's accounting firm. Finn Fornaas (born 1960) developed for Amundsen a computer program, which made it possible for cab owners to remove most of the profit from income statements. Norwegian tax authorities lost about 600 million kr (about U.S. $100 million) in revenues. Amundsen and Fornaas were sentenced to seven and three years imprisonment, respectively. Many cab owners, mostly of Pakistani descent, were also sentenced to prison. Tax authorities are typically victims of crime types, such as bankruptcy crime, money laundering, and income tax crime based on misleading accounting (Abramova, 2007; Elvins, 2003; Malkawi & Haloush, 2008).

4. *Customers.* Svein Anders Kvarving (born 1958) was running the company Screen Communications with his brother Knut Egil Kvarving (born 1965) and Geir Kirkbak (born 1960) as sales manager in the firm. They were bribing purchasing managers at customer sites, so customers bought their equipment at higher prices. Customers were victims because they paid too much for the screens. Competitors were also victims as they might have secured the contracts if there was no corruption on behalf of Screen Communications. The Kvarving brothers were sentenced to four years and five months imprisonment, respectively. Kirkbak was sentenced to two years imprisonment. Customers are typically victims of crime types, such as corruption crime in terms of bribery and kickbacks (Martin,

Cullen, Johnson, & Parbotteeah, 2007; Misangyi, Weaver, & Elms, 2008; Pickett & Pickett, 2002; Pinto, Leana, & Pil, 2008).

5. *Shareholders.* Rune Brynhildsen (born 1965) was convicted of insider trading. Insider trading implies that insiders make a profit of stock trade at the expense of other shareholders. Brynhildsen was in charge of a PR company, Brynhildsen Woldsdal Public Relations. One of his clients was Via Travel. When he worked with the client, he learned about a merger and told his friend Dag Eriksen (born 1969). Eriksen bought shares and made a quick profit on behalf of both of them. Both Brynhildsen and Eriksen were sentenced to 10 months in jail. Shareholders are typically victims of crime types, such as insider trading (Toner, 2009; Wagner, 2011).

6. *Others.* Here we find victims such as suppliers, customs, and social security agencies. These are very fragmented and heterogeneous kinds of victims among which no single group stands out as a potential category.

As the following analysis was conducted at a later point in time, a total of 323 white-collar criminals were convicted and received jail sentences in Norwegian courts from 2009 to 2012. As listed in Table 7.2, most criminals were found in the category of employers as victims. There were 82 white-collar criminals convicted in 43 court cases that caused financial loss to their employers. On average, 2.4 persons were convicted in each case. Cases involving employers represented 29% of the total sample. In terms of number of criminals convicted, banks are the second largest category. In terms of number of crime cases, tax authorities and customers are both the second largest category. Thus, banks as victims had more persons involved in each case.

Table 7.3 lists some of the characteristics of white-collar criminals for each category of crime victims. There is little variation in the age of criminals when convicted. More variation can be found in jail sentences; banks as victims are associated with the longest average sentence of 2.7 years. There is even more variation in the amount of money involved in financial crime for

Table 7.2 Distribution of White-Collar Criminals According to Categories of Victims

#	Victims of Crime	Convicted Persons	Crime Cases in Court	Persons per Court Case	Fraction of Court Cases
1	Employers	82	43	2.4	29%
2	Banks	59	15	3.9	10%
3	Tax authorities	57	29	2.0	20%
4	Customers	51	29	1.8	20%
5	Shareholders	20	11	1.8	7%
6	Others	54	21	2.6	14%
	Total	323	148	2.2	100%

Table 7.3 Characteristics of White-Collar Criminals for Each Category of Victims

#	Victims of Crime	Offender Age Years	Jail Sentence Years	Crime Amount	Business Employees
1	Employers	52	2.3	14 million kr	192
2	Banks	46	2.7	147 million kr	73
3	Tax authorities	47	2.1	39 million kr	48
4	Customers	46	2.3	18 million kr	153
5	Shareholders	49	2.4	65 million kr	62
6	Others	46	1.5	9 million kr	121
	Average	48	2.2	46 million kr	119

different victim categories. The largest amount, on average, is found among bank victims. This is interesting because larger amounts are often associated with longer jail sentences, which is indeed the case for white-collar criminals causing financial loss to banks. Also, heavier sentences for these criminals can be explained by larger numbers of victims that suffered pecuniary loss as a result of an offender's criminal conduct, which is similar to the law in the United States (Anderson, 2006). This explanation can also be applied to both customers and shareholders, among which there will typically be many victims.

The final column in Table 7.2 lists the average size of the organization at which the white-collar criminal was employed. We see that when the organization itself is the victim as an employer, then the organization is larger than in other categories. This means that fraud and theft inside an organization is typically occurring in larger organizations, and tax fraud is occurring in smaller organizations.

It is important to remind ourselves that the sample in this research consists of all white-collar criminals in white-collar crime cases presented in Norwegian financial newspapers from 2009 to 2012. This sample is biased for two reasons. First, only cases that satisfy media criteria are included, such as famous, surprising, important, high-profile cases. Second, only detected and prosecuted cases are included. As known from other crime areas as well, the detection rate is an important variable (Silverstone & Sheetz, 2003). If, for example, it is assumed that the detection rate is 10%, that is, one out of 10 white-collar criminals are detected, then it remains an open question whether our sample represents a reliable distribution in terms of categories of crime victims. Finally, which cases to prosecute is decided by prosecution lawyers. It might be argued, for example, that cases in which customers and shareholders are victims will be more seldom prosecuted because of evidence problems. Cases involving the employer, a bank, or tax authorities might be associated with relatively easier access to evidence retrieval and presentation.

Victims of white-collar crime might be classified into five main categories of employers, banks, tax authorities, customers, and shareholders. Employers represent the largest group of victims from known cases in Norway in the years from 2009 to 2012. Banks are the second largest group of victims, and white-collar criminals in this category received the most severe jail sentences. The most severe jail sentences were associated with the most significant crime amounts.

Criminal Insiders

Insider threats entail situations in which important and critical members of an organization behave in conflict with the organization's interests: in an unethical, unacceptable, and illegal manner. The ability to identify and detect how an individual's behavior may vary over time—and how abnormal behavior might be uncovered—are important elements in fighting insider threats. Ho et al. (2010) developed a theory in order to judge and estimate the levels of trust and distrust potentially required to prevent and detect insider crime.

The theory about insider criminals is based on attribution theory, which is concerned with how one confers explanatory factors for a phenomenon. Typically, a distinction is made between internal and external explanatory factors. If a criminal act occurs, the act can be explained by internal factors that are attributed to the criminal or by external factors that are attributed to the environment and the situation.

Attribution theory is thus about identifying causality predicated on internal and external circumstances:

> Identifying the locus of causality has been at the core of attribution theory since its inception and has generated an extensive research stream in the field of organizational behavior. But the question emerges whether the "internal" and "external" categories capture the entire conceptual space of this phenomenon. (Eberly, Holley, Johnson, & Mitchell, 2011, p. 731)

Based on this argument, Eberly et al. (2011) suggest there is a third category in addition to internal and external explanations, which is labeled relational explanation. These three categories of attributes can be explored to seek causal explanations regarding how persons react in criminal situations.

Attribution theory is a part of social psychology, which studies how humans spontaneously attribute reasons, guilt, and responsibility in situations that arise. The fundamental attribution error is a term used to designate overemphasis on personal factors rather than situational factors in order to explain behavior.

Ho et al. (2010) explain their theory of insider trustworthiness based on attribution theory in the following way:

> The theoretical framework we propose examines basic mechanisms for detecting changes in the trustworthiness of an individual who holds a key position in an organization, by observing overt behavior—including communication behavior—over time. Since Steinke (1975) suggests that it is possible to detect cheating behavior without directly observing the individual, the overarching question is: What changes of behaviors can reflect a downward shift in the trustworthiness of a critical member in a virtual organization which might signal possible insider threats?
>
> Three comparison stages of behavioral observables are needed to answer this question. First, the actual trustworthiness of the actor is hypothesized to be reflected in the actor's behavior. We hypothesize that the downward shift in a person's actual trustworthiness can be reflected in her behavior. Second, actor's behavioral changes can be observed and attributed, as the perceived trustworthiness of the actor, by the observers. We hypothesize that the inconsistency and unreliability in this actor's unexpected behaviors when compared to her communicated intentions can be detected by the observers' subjective perceptions over time. The observers refer to the members of her close social network. Third, it is possible that perceived trustworthiness may differ from the actual trustworthiness of the actor. Depending on the sensitivity of each group, we hypothesize that the perceived trustworthiness can be closely related to the actual trustworthiness, and thus be utilized as a precursor to insider threats. (p. 10)

Thus, this theory consists of three steps:

1. Judge and estimate trustworthiness of the individual
2. Judge and estimate changes in individual trustworthiness caused by changes in behavior
3. Identify a possible discrepancy between perceived trustworthiness and actual trustworthiness

An example of a criminal insider in the Norwegian sample of convicted white-collar criminals is Fakhir Munir who was convicted to 5.5 years in prison after having acted as an insider in a bank owned by Nordea. Together with outsiders, he was able to exploit the bank account of one of Norway's richest women, the late widow of a rich Norwegian construction entrepreneur. Insider Munir and several outsiders were able to transfer U.S. $10 million (63 million kr) from the widow's account to an account in Dubai. The fraud was discovered in late 2010 when they attempted to transfer another U.S. $4 million to banks in Dubai and the Nordea bank initiated a request for the widow to confirm the large single transfer of U.S. $4 million.

Among the outsiders was a 50-year old woman, Inger Aamodt, who entered the bank and purported to be the widow. This happened after Munir had identified the widow's account as a very attractive fraud target because there was a large sum of money permanently available in that account. Inger Aamodt, was able to successfully play the widow role in the bank several times.

In addition to insider Munir and outsider Aamodt, there were several other outsiders. Usman Zahoor and Edmond Thaqi, both second generation Pakistanis in Norway, helped to establish the accounts in Dubai and aided the subsequent transfer of the money to other accounts that the police were unable to trace. Also alongside Inger Aamodt, two native Norwegians, Lars-Erik Martinsen and Rolf Erik Fredriksen, were also involved in the fraud.

While Munir was sentenced to 5.5 years imprisonment, Usman Zahoor received the longest jail sentence of 10 years because he was found to be the leader of organized crime, and Fredriksen got 5 years, Martinsen 4.8 years, Aamodt 4.5 years, and Thaqi 4 years.

Insider, as a term, is widely known from insider trading, in which shares in a company are traded illegally based on inside information. This is not our topic here. Generally, however, insider is also applied in insider theory to identify criminals who operate from inside the organization, either in collaboration with outsiders or alone. For some crime categories, such as computer crime, insiders represent the greatest threat. It is estimated that more than 50% of all computer crime is carried out by permanent and temporary employees in the respective companies.

Detection of White-Collar Criminals

In most criminal areas, it is expected that a combination of victim and police are the main sources of criminal detection. After crime victims suffer an injury or a loss, they tend to report the incident to the police who investigate and hopefully find the offender(s). In cases of financial crime by white-collar criminals, it is often quite different. A victim is frequently not aware of the injury or loss. For example, accounting fraud resulting in tax evasion is not a damage perceived by tax authorities.

Detection Crime Theories

Detection is thought to be a key ingredient in deterring crime according to *deterrence theory*. There are researchers who think it is possible to decrease crime levels through these deterrents. Crime prevention (which is the ultimate aim of these deterrents) concepts are centered around the idea that criminals or prospective criminals will give serious consideration to any consequences before they perpetrate a crime if it is probable that they will be apprehended and face prompt, harsh penalties. Because of this idea, general deterrence theory purports that crime can be avoided as a result of potential criminals weighing the risk of facing some very real consequences, and special deterrence theory maintains that punishments for criminal behavior should be serious enough that those with prior criminal convictions will not repeat their actions (Lyman and Potter, 2007). Deterrence theory holds that individuals commit crimes as the result of thoughtful deliberation and weighing of some apparent personal gains, and the possibility of legal penalties will dissuade people who will be afraid of these penalties (Yusuf and Babalola, 2009). Comey (2009) says deterrence functions best when imposed penalties are swift and certain. White-collar sentencing in the United States since the passing of the Sarbanes-Oxley Act, however, has not been swift, and this situation occurs around the world. In Norway, for instance, white-collar crime investigations can take more than a year.

Deterrence theory seems more appropriate for occupational crime than for corporate crime:

> Both courts and scholars have readily accepted deterrence as a justification for organizational criminal sanctioning. However, from the beginning legal scholars appeared to be uncomfortable with retribution as a goal of organizational criminal liability. Without consciousness and self-awareness, business organizations lacked the capacity to be morally blameworthy. (Robson, 2010, p. 121)

Because deterrence theory purports that severe punishment will deter potential criminals, Lyman and Potter (2007) have further theorized that criminal penalties should be serious enough to prevent recidivism (special deterrence theory). As an example, someone arrested for marijuana possession should be sentenced harshly enough that the cost of a marijuana possession arrest is not worth the pleasure of possessing it.

Crimes, however, come with a wide variety of possible punishments, and judges effectively have absolute discretion (decades versus months of incarceration, for example). In addition, in contrast to many potential criminals, those considering committing white-collar offenses often understand that, if caught, they may benefit from a lenient plea-bargain system, and they have seen or read about cases in which a judge has offered compassionate sentencing (Comey, 2009).

The opposing claim is that the best deterrent is possible penalties that are both severe and unpredictable. Comey (2009) says penalties levied somewhat arbitrarily would be a superior deterrent. Those who subscribe to this theory would see the Sarbanes-Oxley Act, which is rife with disparities, as a positive development.

Jeremy Bentham (1748–1832) and Cesare Beccaria (1738–1794) first purported that people thought through a sort of cost–benefit analysis when thinking of committing a crime, choosing to commit the crime when it is beneficial. If someone understands that the possibility of being caught is high and accompanied by definite, serious penalties, then deterrence theory claims people will decide against committing crime (Siponen and Vance, 2010).

Informal sanctions (peer-group disapproval, negative media coverage, marriage and family consequences, etc.) and shame, which can damage one's self-esteem, are also relevant sanctions.

Utility theory suggests that a criminal will attempt to maximize the utility from criminal behavior. An expected utility maximizing criminal commits an illegal act and, if he or she is neither caught nor punished, his or her total wealth thereby increases by an amount, x. His or her criminally enhanced total wealth, w + x, will be greater than his or her current wealth, w. He is caught and punished with probability p, and the punishment consists of a fine, z, which is less than or equal to his enhanced wealth, w + x. His personal assessment of any benefits to him of his criminal activity is described by a utility function linking p and z to w and x (Cain, 2009).

Cain (2009) argues that the general piece of evidence available is that criminals are more responsive to changes in the chance of being caught (p) than to changes in the consequence. Because it is sometimes said that punishment does not work; only the probability of being caught will influence the behavior in the desired direction. In certain cases, the consequence may influence the behavior in an undesired direction, whereby a crime with a longer sentence may stimulate the criminal. This is similar to a demand that increases when the price of the good increases (the Giffen effect).

Fraud theory argues that three conditions of fraud arise from fraudulent financial reporting (Ilter, 2009):

1. Incentives/pressures: Management or other employees have incentives or pressures to commit fraud.
2. Opportunities: Circumstances provide opportunities for management or employees to commit fraud.
3. Attitudes/rationalization: An attitude, character, or set of ethical values exists that allows management or employees to intentionally commit a dishonest act, or they are in an environment that imposes pressure sufficient to cause them to rationalize committing a dishonest act.

Thus, the risk of fraud is a combination of incentives/pressures, opportunities, and attitude/rationalization. The fraud examination process centers on the fraud hypothesis approach, which has four sequential steps (Ilter, 2009):

1. Analyzing the available data: An auditor gathers documentary evidence depicting all of the business.
2. Developing a fraud hypothesis: Based on what is discovered during analysis, a fraud examiner develops a hypothesis—always assuming a worst-case scenario—of what could have occurred. This hypothesis addresses one of the three major classifications of occupational (internal) fraud: asset misappropriations, corruption, or fraudulent financial statements.
3. Revising it as necessary: If, for example, the facts do not point to a kickback scheme, the fraud examiner will look for the possibility of a billing scheme. Although the two schemes have several common elements, the latter raises its own red flags.
4. Confirming it: Testing of the hypothesis by combining theoretical elements with empirical evidence.

White-Collar Crime Detection

How was crime detected? Who detected crime? In this research, we searched the source of detection and found that journalists in the media investigated and revealed a total of 80 out of 305 white-collar criminals. This represents 26%, which means that a quarter of all white-collar crime was revealed by the press. However, there is a bias in our sample toward media sources as only cases presented in the media are included. Nevertheless, it may seem surprising that journalists make such a significant contribution. After journalists we find victims of crime, who revealed 61 criminals (20%) as listed in Table 7.4.

While it may seem surprising that journalists detected as many as 80 criminals (26%), it may seem surprising as well that the police only detected four criminals (1%). It may also seem surprising that auditors, who are in charge of accounting controls in client organizations, detected very few of the white-collar crime cases.

A comparison of convicted white-collar criminals detected by journalists and convicted white-collar criminals detected by others is presented in Table 7.5. Statistically significant differences can be found for crime amount, business revenue, and business employees. This means that journalists detect financial crime cases in which there is significantly more money involved.

Table 7.4   White-Collar Crime Detectors

Rank	Crime Detecting Sources	Criminals	Fraction
1	Journalists investigating tips from readers	80	26%
2	Crime victims suffering financial loss	61	20%
3	Internal controls of transactions in organizations	28	9%
4	Lawyers identifying misconduct after bankruptcy	27	9%
5	Tax authorities carrying out controls	18	6%
6	Banks carrying out controls on accounts	18	6%
7	Auditors controlling client accounting	11	4%
8	Police investigations into financial crime	4	1%
9	Stock exchange controls of transactions	3	1%
10	Other detection sources	55	18%
	Total	305	100%

Journalists detect financial crime cases in significantly larger organizations when compared to crime cases detected by others.

When we compare financial crime categories committed by white-collar criminals, in terms of detection, results indicate that journalists tend to detect theft to a relatively larger extent than fraud and manipulation as listed in Table 7.6. It comes as no surprise that manipulation—such as accounting fraud and fake invoices—are harder to detect than theft and corruption for external investigators, such as journalists. In actual numbers, fraud cases outnumber other kinds of white-collar crime.

Table 7.5   Comparison of Journalist and Nonjournalist Detected White-Collar Criminals

Total 305 Criminals	80 Detected by Journalists	225 Detected by Others	t Statistical Difference	Significance of t Statistic
Age convicted	48 years	48 years	−.178	.859
Age crime	42 years	43 years	−.418	.676
Years prison	2.1 years	2.2 years	−.549	.583
Crime amount	114 million kr	23 million kr	4.523	.000
Involved individuals	4.4 persons	3.6 persons	1.626	.105
Personal income	268,000 kr	359,000 kr	−1.247	.213
Personal tax	112,000 kr	151,000 kr	−1.293	.197
Personal wealth	1,589,000 kr	1,488,000 kr	.122	.903
Business revenue	294 million kr	154 million kr	3.151	.002
Business employees	198 persons	98 persons	2.665	.008

Table 7.6   **Financial Crime Categories by Detection Sources**

	Total Detections	Detections by Journalists	Percentage by Journalists
Fraud	153	36	19%
Theft	21	14	40%
Manipulation	73	17	19%
Corruption	58	13	18%
Total	305	80	26%

The Role of Journalists in Crime Detection

Journalists detected 18 corporate crime scandals and 44 occupational crime scandals. There are a total of 88 corporate crime scandals and 167 occupational crime scandals in the early sample of 255 convicts. Thus, journalists detected relatively fewer corporate criminals and relatively more occupational criminals.

Journalists detected 27 criminal leaders and 35 criminal followers. There are a total of 140 leaders and 115 followers in the sample of 255 convicts. Thus, journalists detected relatively fewer criminal leaders and relatively more criminal followers.

Journalists detected 14 rotten apples and 48 individuals in rotten apple barrels. There are a total of 91 rotten apples and 164 rotten barrel persons in the sample of 255 convicts. Thus, journalists detected relatively fewer rotten apples and relatively more rotten barrel persons.

There are 20 female and 235 male criminals in the total sample of 255 convicts. Journalists detected two women and 60 men. Thus, journalists detected relatively fewer women than men.

In terms of position, the total sample consists of 76 top-level executives, 106 middle-level executives, and 73 basic-level executives. Journalists detected 20 criminals at level 1, 23 criminals at level 2, and 19 criminals at level 3. Thus, journalists detected higher-level executives slightly more often out of the total sample.

There were 54 internal victim cases and 201 external victim cases in the total sample. Journalists detected seven and 55 cases, respectively. Thus, journalists detected slightly more cases with external victims.

Journalists detected relatively more white-collar scandals in the public sector compared to the private sector. Out of 255 criminal scandals, 23 criminals emerged from the public sector, and 232 criminals emerged from the private sector as will be presented in the next chapter. Journalists detected seven criminals in the public sector and 55 criminals in the private sector.

Because a substantial fraction of white-collar criminals are detected by journalists, and very few are detected by traditional law enforcement agencies, there might be lessons learned from the media's working procedures. Journalists consider information and information sources in established and developing networks of individuals located in key areas of the economy. Journalists study accounting reports and other information and receive documents from their network of sources. They interview lawyers, competitors, police, and authorities. They let a case rest for weeks and months until new information emerges. In the meantime, they keep information top secret until they publish for the first time.

This chapter repeatedly talks about journalists "detecting" white-collar crime in the sense that they have gone public with published accounts of wrongdoing. It is important to mention sources and the use of sources. Whistleblowers, in many cases, alert journalists to serious crime and are sometimes the true "detectors," not the journalists or media. In journalism and media and communication studies, the use of sources is a major concern, as is reflected, for example, in The Norwegian Press Association's Code of Ethics ("Vær Varsom Plakaten"—Be Careful Notice). However, in this research, it was established that journalists receive so many tips and hints of potential white-collar crime and criminals, which are more often than not ungrounded in reality, that detection is defined as the work involved in separating a few suspicious leads from all kinds of rumors and allegations.

Journalists of the investigative type tend to develop hypotheses about phenomena and causality. They are very different from referring journalists who only tell what they have heard or seen. Investigative journalists develop an idea into a study of potential offenders and their victims. They apply systematic analysis and treat their sources with care and professional concern.

Based on a sample of 179 convicted white-collar criminals in Norway, among which 43 individuals were detected by journalists and 136 were detected by others, we found some interesting differences between the two groups. In statistical terms, significant differences can be found in terms of age and crime amount and organizational revenue and employees.

There seems to be a lot to learn from investigative media and their journalists. Rather than formal procedures often applied on a routine basis by auditors and internal controllers, information sources in terms of persons in networks seem to be a more fruitful approach to detection of white-collar crime.

A number of angles can be explored in the process of white-collar crime detection within news media. On the one hand, we have the news media (newspapers and online-media) that have specialized in and focused on financial information of all sorts and report on this regularly. For them, the sources of information can be traditional through tips, company reports, stock-exchange information, and press conferences as well as other sources. For regular news media spread out over the country, the situation can be quite different. The detection of white-collar crime can come as a tip-off from a whistleblower or as official information if the Economic Crime Prosecutor (ECOCRIME) performs a razzia locally. Additionally, the way the news is treated in the news media is dependent on many variables that occur at the same time: Do they have the right journalists in place at the time? Do they have an interest in the matter? Do they know anything or anyone related to this? There will also be a resource balance that takes place. Not many news media outside of the larger ones will have the possibility of setting aside journalists to work on an investigative white-collar crime for months. In the cases where they have done this, some experience among editors seems to be that there is an uncertainty as to whether this was worthwhile relative to the size and the complexity of the case. For a common, nonspecialist news media, there will always be the balance of resources against the newsworthiness of the matter at hand. If a major white-collar crime story had emerged in Norway in the weeks after the July 22 terrorist attacks in 2011, reasonable doubt can be raised if the matter would have caught much attention in the general public press.

General news media have a constant incoming flow of news on hand, and there is a constant daily priority of what is important and what should be published. For all news items, there are some general rules of journalism that comes into play: Is it important for many people? Is it really news? Is it possible to get reliable information on this? Is it possible to approach the right people with the right questions? Can both parties in a conflict be approached? And, in addition to these questions, there will be a question as to whether the news organization at this point in time has the resources to deal with it. If the journalist knowledgeable on economic matters is on holiday, doubt can be raised if the news media organization will come back to the same matter later. That will depend on the development and the newsworthiness of the case at the second point in time. If the news organization is the first to report on the crime, and it is regarded as "hot," it will probably do whatever possible to handle the matter at hand, knowing that other media, and especially online media, can report on the same matter and as such "steal" the story. There is always an internal pride in a news organization when it can report on a matter of significant interest and be cited by other news organizations.

The organizational culture also has an influence on white-collar crime detection among journalists. If you have journalists who are driven by their own interest to win investigative journalist prizes (SKUP in Norway), there is a higher possibility for such stories to emerge in publication. However, this might differ greatly among news organizations.

Øvrebø (2004) showed in a study of the Norwegian newspaper *Dagsavisen*, after a change of the editor-in-chief in 2001, that the news profile and priorities of the newspaper changed according to the principles laid down by the new editor when she took up her position. It can be argued that the personal preferences of an editor can have influence on the priorities of news in the newspaper and that this will relate to all types of editorial material, whether it is general news, sports, culture, or financial news.

For a general news organization, white-collar crime is not a big story in itself unless it has repercussions on well-known persons locally or if something happens to the organization where the crime has taken place. Nationally, it can be a big story if the person has a well-known profile or if the crime in itself is of an unusual nature. If a main employer locally has to file for bankruptcy because of a white-collar crime, then the story is more than just another white-collar crime case because it has wider consequences that turn the world upside down for ordinary people in this local area. Then the white-collar crime will take the form of another typical important news story and be followed and treated as such, and the white-collar crime element will be mixed with other elements and consequential stories, building on the starting point as a white-collar crime.

The argument of white-collar crime detection among journalists seems to be related to the story's importance in itself, and, as such, it will be treated as just another crime or news story and have the same internal process. For smaller news organizations without journalistic specialization in financial matters, the white-collar crime story will be treated according to the news prioritizing structure of that particular organization. For larger news organizations that typically have separate sections for financial and economic news, the story will be treated within the prioritizing of that particular section. And if the story is big enough in total, it will be moved from the particular section for finance into the general news of the organization. The higher the profile of the persons involved, the more likely it is that it will have more centralized coverage, that is, be moved into what is often the first section of the newspaper or the prioritized areas of a website's front page.

As shown in Table 7.4, four of the 10 categories made up 64% of the total crime-detecting sources, and out of these the two—*investigating tips from readers* and *crime victims suffering loss*—made up 46%. It can be argued that these two categories are more susceptible to journalistic interest than the others simply because it is easier to construct news stories based on these journalistic angles. Themes like manipulation and corruption are much more difficult to make into a story that is interesting for the readers simply because it is more complex and difficult to describe these matters in layman's terms. A tip from readers that is given to a news medium is, most of the time, accompanied by a subjective story from the person giving the tip that, in turn, gives the journalist clues to work on and discuss internally to assign the right news priority and angle. This is also supported by the breakdown in Table 7.6, which shows that theft is the category that has the highest percentage of journalistic detection.

White-collar crime detection and follow-up seems to be related to a number of simultaneous journalistic procedures and cultural elements. For specialized publications in the financial information area, the white-collar crime news arena is closer at hand, and the organization will typically be able to go deeper into the matter. If white-collar crime is detected by general or local news organizations, the procedure involved will more often take the form of a general news story with the resource balance that follows from that. It can also be shown that white-collar crime is more often detected by journalists if it is based on a tip from readers or if it is reported as a theft. Underlying all this are the internal news preferences and editorial guidance that are part of the policies of the news medium.

The Role of Auditors in Crime Detection

One of the surprising results of this research is the lack of crime detection by auditors: Only eight (4%) of the 179 criminals in our sample were detected by auditors. Moyes and Baker (2003) asked external, internal, and governmental auditors to evaluate the effectiveness of various standard audit procedures in detecting fraud. Although external and internal auditors differed in the types of audit procedures they recommended, the authors conclude that "the audit procedures judged more effective in detecting fraud were those which provided evidence about the existence of internal controls and those which evaluated the strength of internal controls," and that "strategic use of standard audit procedures may help auditors fulfill their responsibilities under SAS No. 99" (Moyes & Baker, 2003, p. 199).

Furthermore,

> the results of this study indicate that fraud detection might be improved through the strategic use of standard audit procedures earlier in the audit examination. ... If these audit procedures were applied during the preliminary stages of the audit, they would be more likely to indicate the potential existence of fraud, in which case the auditor would have more time to revise the audit plan and conduct other necessary investigations (Moyes & Baker, 2003, p. 216).

Similarly, Albrecht, Albrecht, and Dunn (2001) reviewed fraud detection aspects of current auditing standards and the empirical and other research that has been conducted on fraud detection. They concluded that "even though the red flag approach to detecting fraud has been endorsed by policy makers and written about widely by researchers, there is little empirical evidence that shows the red flag approach is an effective way to detect fraud, especially for fraud that has yet to be discovered" (Albrecht et al., 2001, p. 4). Their research review on the subject reveals that one of the major conclusions drawn from previous studies included the fact that only 18%–20% of frauds appear to be detected by internal and external auditors and further that only about half of the perpetrators of frauds detected are duly prosecuted. The article also calls for further fraud detection research. These detection rates are loosely corroborated by Silverstone and Sheetz (2003), who estimate that approximately 12% of initial fraud detection is through external audit, and approximately 19% arises from internal audit. (Both of these estimations apply to the American context.)

An article dealing with the responsibilities for prevention and detection of white-collar crime refers to a study undertaken to map how members of the accounting profession viewed the changing role of the external auditor following the introduction of SAS No. 82:

> Most of those answering the questionnaire disagreed that they should be responsible for searching for fraud. ... Clearly, this notion concerning the auditor's responsibility is not widely held by the public at large. ... The general public and Congress certainly sided against the CPAs and was the reason for this legislation. (Farrell & Healy, 2000, p. 25)

As to the question of whether the certified public accountants (CPAs) should act as police or detectives when performing the audit, the response was a resounding "no":

> This may also indicate that changes brought about with the implementation of the SAS No. 82 requiring a *policing component* clearly require added responsibility and may necessitate additional training and changes to job description requirements. Again, although the general public may believe policing is within the auditors' duties, even SAS No. 82 does not require this. (Farrell & Healy, 2000, p. 25)

Similarly, an investigation into fraud prevention and detection in the United States uncovered that the majority of CPAs who responded to the study believed the external auditor's responsibility for fraud detection extends only to assessing the probability of fraud and planning the audit accordingly. They ranked internal auditors as the group most effective in detecting fraud, followed by fraud examiners, and client management (Johnson & Rudesill, 2001).

Jones (2004) presents a slightly more balanced view on the auditor's role in crime detection:

> A persistent debate has dogged relationships between auditors and managers. This debate revolves around the precise roles and duties of each party in relation to fraud and corruption, and particularly who should take responsibility for investigation. Current legal and professional precedents leave little doubt that management bears the main responsibility for ensuring that reasonable measures are taken to prevent fraud and corruption. In any event it is

common practice for managers to request assistance and advice from auditors upon suspicion or discovery of fraud. The final responsibility must lie with managers unless the auditor has given specific assurance regarding particular controls or the absence of error or fraud. (pp. 12–13)

In a study in Norway by Warhuus (2011), she found that 11% of her cases of white-collar crime were detected by auditing functions, this is lower than the 4% (according to our sample) reported above and also significantly lower than the results presented by Albrecht et al. (2001), Moyes and Baker (2003), and Silverstone and Sheetz (2003). The figures of 4% and 11% in Norway indicate that Norwegian auditing has an even less pronounced role in detection of white-collar crime than the measurements performed in the United States, for example.

The role of auditing in the detection of white-collar crime is an interesting topic as it is not obvious that auditors are able to detect crime. This might have to do with the responsibilities of auditing functions as well as procedures and practices followed by auditors in their work (Warhuus, 2011). For example, Beasley (2003) is concerned with the fact that auditors seem to struggle with reducing occurrences of material misstatements due to fraud even in the light of new standards for auditing. The focus of new standards remains on fraudulent activities that lead to intentional material misstatements due to fraud, and it expands the guidance and procedures to be performed in every audit. The expanded guidance might, hopefully, lead to improvements of auditor detection of material misstatements due to fraud by strengthening the auditor's responses to identified high fraud risks.

Samociuk and Iyer (2009) argue that fraud risks need to be recorded, monitored, and reported. Such recording includes the nature of each risk, likelihood and consequences, current and suggested controls, and the owner of the risk for follow-up action.

Within the extant accounting and auditing research, a great deal of attention is devoted to how the external auditor is a primary figure in detecting irregularities and corruption, and government and standard setters also stress the importance of the responsibilities of the auditing community in this respect (Olsen, 2007; Telberg, 2004). However, there seems to be limited faith in and responsibility on the auditing function among some for this specific purpose: Only in very few cases does auditing in some form seem to be responsible for the detection, unraveling, and exposure of the offense (Ellingsen & Sky, 2005). This opinion is backed up by the work of Drage and Olstad (2008), who analyzed the role of the auditing function in relation to both preventing and detecting white-collar crime. Although their study included a look at the perceived preventative power of the auditing function as well as actual detection of criminal offenses, their findings were consistent with the above mentioned hypothesis: Many of their interviewees were skeptical regarding the auditing function having a central role in the detection of white-collar crime.

Olsen (2007) reminds us that the auditing standards that external auditors must act in compliance with also require them to uncover irregularities should they be present. However, the primary concern of the external auditor is to reduce the auditing risk (i.e., the risk that the financial statements may still contain material misstatements even after the auditor has given a positive auditor report), not the risk of irregularities. In spite of external auditors rarely being credited for the detection of financial crime, Olsen still believes that the auditing function contributes significantly to the prevention of such crime by reducing temptations and opportunities, thus corroborating the findings of Drage and Olstad (2008) on prevention.

Rendal and Westerby (2010) examined Norwegian auditors' expectations regarding their own abilities in detecting and preventing irregularities and compared these with the expectations other users of financial information have on this same issue. Their findings indicate certain gaps in terms of how the auditor is expected to perform. Auditors themselves answer that they sometimes do not act in accordance with laws and regulations, and both auditors and users of financial information feel that the auditing function should include more than what is required today through standards and regulations, for example, pertaining to companies' internal guidelines. They also uncover unrealistic expectations regarding the extent to which the auditing function is capable of uncovering irregularities. They conclude that, to a certain extent, auditors are too reserved and aloof when it comes to their responsibilities in the prevention and detection of irregularities and call for improvements.

Crime in Private versus Public Sector

The private sector typically consists of for-profit organizations, and the public sector typically consists of not-for-profit organizations. Procurement and other transactions that are potential white-collar crime areas fill a different role and rely upon different strategies in not-for-profit organizations than for-profit organizations. For example, for-profit sector procurement more often encompasses tasks related to inventory management and material flows. Not-for-profit sector procurement relies more heavily upon competition and seems to rely more on rigid contracts and more performance monitoring and less on trust than does the for-profit sector. The public sector seems more concerned with formalism, rules, bureaucracy, and procedures. The private sector seems more concerned with goals, objectives, and end results. Not-for-profit sector procurement is less concerned with efficient outcomes in terms of end results (Hawkins, Gravier, & Powley, 2011).

According to Hawkins et al. (2011), not-for-profit organizations employ different strategies for managing opportunism. For-profits frequently rely upon the expected long-term duration of the relationship between a buyer and supplier to decrease opportunism. Procurement in the public sector is highly regulated via contracting statutes and regulations that discourage either close or long-term relationships with suppliers. Trust and commitment as governance mechanisms are sparse in government procurement. The monopoly power of government agencies means that suppliers often must invest in specific assets without knowing whether they will win the contract, and the open-bidding process eliminates any significant commitment to the relationship in advance unless bribery or other kinds of financial crime have occurred. In addition to many barriers to long-term relationships, the contractual nature of not-for-profit procurement reduces the flexibility that characterizes most relational exchanges and also undermines the value of relational commitments.

Relational commitments in the private sector represent other kinds of challenges for white-collar crime detection and prevention. Because informal procedures, personal relationships, and dynamic actions often determine business conduct, other avenues for white-collar crime open up in the private sector that are closed in the public sector. All kinds of arrangements are allowed as long as they supposedly contribute to long-term success.

The need to distinguish between private and public sector organizations involves conceiving and analyzing possible differences, variations, and similarities across the two sectors. A growing body of literature has purported to study the differences between the two types of organizations in terms of variables such as job satisfaction and organizational commitment, motivation, efficiency, and effectiveness (Mouly & Sankaran, 2007).

Convicted white-collar criminals working in the private sector may differ from convicted white-collar criminals in the public sector. Also the frequency of crime may differ.

Sector Crime Theories

While private sector organizations typically are managed by goals and objectives, public sector organizations are managed by rules and regulations. Therefore, control mechanisms will be different in the two sectors. *Social control theory* argues that individuals will refrain from white-collar crime if society and the organization has processes that prevent them from doing so:

> Social control refers to those processes by which the community influences its members toward conformance with established norms of behavior. Social control theorists argue that the relevant question is not, why do persons

become involved in crime, organized or otherwise, but, rather, why do most persons conform to societal norms? If, as control theorists generally assume, most persons are sufficiently motivated by the potential rewards to commit criminal acts, why do only a few make crime a career? According to control theorists, delinquent acts result when an individual's bond to society is weak or broken. The strength of this bond is determined by internal and external restraints. In other words, internal and external restraints determine whether we move in the direction of crime or of law-abiding behavior. (Abadinsky, 2007, p. 22)

Social control theory is also concerned with relationships between individuals controlled and those that perform controls:

We define attempted control as the extent to which a controller attempts to utilize a given control mechanism to influence controlee behavior. Attempted control therefore refers to the control mechanisms that the controller implements in a given project, independent of whether or how they are exercised. We define realized control as the extent to which the controller is able to successfully exercise a given control mechanism during the systems development process. An attempted control mechanism must be effectively exercised, or realized, for it to enhance systems development performance. (Tiwana & Keil, 2009, p. 13)

Deviant culture theory argues that joining a criminal subculture in the higher class will increase the likelihood of white-collar crime:

The subculture shares a lifestyle that is often accompanied by an alternative language and culture. The lower-class lifestyle is typically characterized by being tough, taking care of one's own affairs, and rejecting any kind of governmental authority. (Lyman & Potter, 2007, p. 70)

To understand individual actions, *game theory* suggests that individuals act and react to others' actions, and white-collar crime can be both an act of action as well as an act of reaction:

Based on utility theory, game theory involves the mathematical representation of the decision making process in situations where the interests of two or more players are interconnected and interdependent. A player may be either an individual or a group that operates as a single decision making entity. Players in situations of uncertainty choose from a set of available actions called strategies, each of which offers a probability of producing a possible outcome. The choice a player makes is determined by the anticipated utility, viewed as an indication of the individual's beliefs and preferences that each alternative behavioral strategy is expected to produce. (Krebs, Costelloe, & Jenks, 2003, p. 2)

Table 7.7   Comparison of Private Sector Criminals versus Public Sector Criminals

Total of 305 Criminals	282 Convicts in Private Sector	23 Convicts in Public Sector	t Statistical Difference	Significance of t Statistic
Age convicted	47 years	57 years	−3.972	.000
Age crime	42 years	52 years	−4.226	.000
Years prison	2.1 years	2.8 years	−1.791	.074
Crime amount	49 million kr	16 million kr	.953	.342
Involved individuals	3.9 persons	2.7 persons	1.543	.124
Personal income	334,000 kr	350,000 kr	−.128	.898
Personal tax	142,000 kr	126,000 kr	.318	.751
Personal wealth	1.6 million kr	.6 million kr	.699	.485
Business revenue	173 million kr	407 million kr	−3.167	.002
Business employees	111 persons	289 persons	−2.838	.005

Sector Criminal Sample

Convicted white-collar criminals working in the public sector differ from convicted white-collar criminals in the public sector. There were 282 convicts in the private sector and 23 convicts in the public sector as listed in Table 7.7.

White-collar criminals in the public sector are significantly older than private sector criminals, both when they commit crime and when they are sentenced to jail. The other significant difference is concerned with organization size; public sector organizations are significantly larger in terms of both business revenue and business employees. There are more persons involved in each white-collar crime case in the business sector, but this difference is statistically not significant. Private sector cases involve a greater amount of money, but neither this difference nor personal wealth differences are statistically significant. It is interesting to note that although the crime amount is larger for private sector criminals, the jail sentence is nevertheless shorter than for public sector criminals. This is interesting because the total sample shows a statistically significant and positive relationship between crime amount and jail sentence in terms of years in prison.

References

Abadinsky, H. (2007). *Organized Crime* (8th ed.). Belmont, CA: Thomson Wadsworth.

Abramova, I. (2007). The funding of traditional organized crime in Russia. *Economic Affairs*, March, 18–21.

Aguilera, R. V., & Vadera, A. K. (2008). The dark side of authority: Antecedents, mechanisms, and outcomes of organizational corruption. *Journal of Business Ethics*, 77, 431–449.

Albrecht, C. C., Albrecht, W. S., & Dunn, J. G. (2001). Can auditors detect fraud: A review of the research evidence. *Journal of Forensic Accounting, II*, 1–12.

Anderson, R. M. (2006). A proposal for calculating reimbursed victims of financial identity theft under the federal sentencing guidelines. *Brooklyn Journal of Corporate, Financial & Commercial Law, 5*, 447–472.

Barker, K. J., D'Amato, J., & Sheridon, P. (2008). Credit card fraud: Awareness and prevention. *Journal of Financial Crime, 15*(4), 398–410.

Beasley, M. S. (2003). SAS no. 99: A new look at auditor detection of fraud. *Journal of Forensic Accounting, IV*, 1–20.

Cain, M. (2009). Is crime Giffen? *Journal of Financial Crime, 16*(1), 80–85.

Comey, J. B. (2009). Go directly to jail: White collar sentencing after the Sarbanes-Oxley Act. *Harvard Law Review, 122*, 1728–1749.

Croall, H. (2007). *Victims, crime and society*. Los Angeles: Sage.

Dorn, N., Levi, M., & White, S. (2008). Do European procurement rules generate or prevent crime? *Journal of Financial Crime, 15*(3), 243–260.

Drage, K., & Olstad, T. (2008). Ekstern revisor og økonomisk kriminalitet: En analyse av revisors ansvar og brukernes forventninger Regnskap og revisjon. Oslo: BI Norwegian School of Management.

Eberly, M. B., Holley, E. C., Johnson, M. D., & Mitchell, T. R. (2011). Beyond internal and external: A dyadic theory of relational attributions. *Academy of Management Review, 36*(4), 731–753.

Ellingsen, D., & Sky, V. (2005). *Virksomheter som ofre for økonomisk kriminalitet* (vol. 2005/14) *Rapporter*. Oslo: SSB.

Elvins, M. (2003). Europe's response to transnational organised crime. In A. Edwards & P. Gill (Eds.), *Crime: Perspectives on global security* (pp. 29–41). London: Routledge.

Farrell, B. R., & Healy, P. (2000). White collar crime: A profile of the perpetrator and an evaluation of the responsibilities for its prevention and detection. *Journal of Forensic Accounting, 1*, 17–34.

Fisher, J. (2008). The UK's faster payment project: Avoiding a bonanza for cybercrime fraudsters. *Journal of Financial Crime, 15*(2), 155–164.

Fodor, B. (2008). Measuring market integrity: A propsed Canadian approach. *Journal of Financial Crime, 15*(3), 261–268.

Gilsinan, J. F., Millar, J., Seitz, N., Fisher, J., Harshman, E., Islam, M., & Yeager, F. (2008). The role of private sector organizations in the control and policing of serious financial crime and abuse. *Journal of Financial Crime, 15*(2), 111–123.

Glodstein, D., Glodstein, S. L., & Fornaro, J. (2010). Fraud trauma syndrome: The victims of the Bernard Madoff scandal. *Journal of Forensic Studies in Accounting and Business*, Summer, 1–9.

Hawkins, T. G., Gravier, M. J., & Powley, E. H. (2011). Public versus private sector procurement ethics and strategy: What each sector can learn from the other. *Journal of Business Ethics, 103*, 567–586.

Hill, C. (2008). Art crime and the Wealth of Nations. *Journal of Financial Crime, 15*(4), 444–448.

Ho, S. M., Benbasat, I. og Stanton, J. M. (2010). The theory of trustworthiness attribution for countering insider threats, proceedings of JAIS theory development workshop. *Sprouts: Working Papers on Information Systems, 10*(71). http://sprouts.aisnet.org/10-71.

Ilter, C. (2009). Fraudulent money transfers: A case from Turkey. *Journal of Financial Crime, 16*(2), 125–136.

Johnson, G. G., & Rudesill, C. L. (2001). An investigation into fraud prevention and detection of small businesses in the United States: Responsibilities of auditors, managers, and business owners. *Accounting Forum, 25*(1), 56.

Jones, P. (2004). *Fraud and corruption in public services: A guide to risk and prevention.* Aldershot: Gower.

Krebs, C. P., Costelloe, M., & Jenks, D. (2003). Drug control policy and smuggling innovation: A game-theoretic analysis. *Journal of Drug Issues, 33*(1), 133–160.

Ksenia, G. (2008). Can corruption and economic crime be controlled in developing countries and if so, is it cost-effective? *Journal of Financial Crime, 15*(2), 223–233.

Lombardo, R. M. (2002). Black Hand: Terror by letter in Chicago. *Journal of Contemporary Criminal Justice, 18*(4), 394–409.

Lyman, M. D., & Potter, G. W. (2007). *Organized crime* (4th ed.). Upper Saddle River, NJ: Pearson Prentice Hall.

Malkawi, B. H., & Haloush, H. A. (2008). The case of income tax evasion in Jordan: Symptoms and solutions. *Journal of Financial Crime, 15*(3), 282–294.

Martin, K. D., Cullen, J. B., Johnson, J. L., & Parbotteeah, K. P. (2007). Deciding to bribe: A cross-level analysis of firm and home country influences on bribery activity. *Academy of Management Journal, 50*(6), 1401–1422.

Misangyi, V. F., Weaver, G. R., & Elms, H. (2008). Ending corruption: The interplay among institutional logics, resources, and institutional entrepreneurs. *The Academy of Management Review, 33*(3), 750–798.

Mouly, V. S., & Sankaran, J. K. (2007). Public- versus private-sector research and development. *International Studies in Management and Organization, 37*(1), 80–102.

Moyes, G. D., & Baker, C. R. (2003). Auditor's beliefs about the fraud detection effectiveness of standard audit procedures. *Journal of Forensic Accounting, IV*, 199–216.

Olsen, A. B. (2007). *Økonomisk kriminalitet: Avdekking, gransking og forebygging (Economic crime: Detection, investigation and prevention).* Oslo: Universitetsforlaget.

Øvrebø, T. (2004). Nyhetsproduksjon: kjønn og makt. En studie av endring i Dagsavisen 2000–2003. (News production: Sex and power. A study of change in *Dagsavisen* [Norwegian Daily Newspaper] 2000–2003). Hovedoppgave i medievitenskap (masters thesis in media science). Universitetet i Oslo (University of Oslo).

Peltier-Rivest, D. (2009). An analysis of the victims of occupational fraud: A Canadian perspective. *Journal of Financial Crime, 16*(1), 60–66.

Pickett, K. H. S., & Pickett, J. M. (2002). *Financial crime investigation and control.* New York: John Wiley & Sons.

Pinto, J., Leana, C. R., & Pil, F. K. (2008). Corrupt organizations or organizations of corrupt individuals? Two types of organization-level corruption. *The Academy of Management Review, 33*(3), 685–709.

Rendal, S., & Westerby, T. (2010). *Hvilke forventninger har revisor i forhold til brukere av finansiell informasjon når det gjelder revisors plikter til forebygging og avdekking av misligheter? (What expectations do auditors have in relation to users of financial information when it comes to auditors' duty to prevent and detect misconduct?).* (MSc thesis). BI Norwegian Business School, Oslo.

Robson, R. A. (2010). Crime and punishment: Rehabilitating retribution as a justification for organizational criminal liability. *American Business Law Journal, 47*(1), 109–144.

Samociuk, M., & Iyer, N. (2009). *A short guide to fraud risk.* Aldershot: Gower Publishing.

Silverstone, H., & Sheetz, M. (2003). *Forensic accounting and fraud investigation for non-experts.* Hoboken, NJ: Wiley.

Siponen, M., & Vance, A. (2010). Neutralization: New insights into the problem of employee information systems security policy violations. *MIS Quarterly, 34*(3), 487–502.

Telberg, R. (2004). A joint effort to fight corporate fraud. *Journal of Accountancy, 197*(4), 53–56.

Toner, G. A. (2009). New ways of thinking about old crimes: Prosecuting corruption and organized criminal groups engaged in labour-management racketeering. *Journal of Financial Crime, 16*(1), 41–59.

Wagner, R. E. (2011). Gordon Gekko to the rescue? Insider trading as a tool to combat accounting fraud. *University of Cincinnati Law Review, 79,* 973–993.

Warhuus, C. (2011). *Present principle: The role of auditing in detection of white-collar crime.* (MSc thesis). BI Norwegian Business School, Oslo, Norway.

Williams, C. C. (2006). *The hidden enterprise culture: Entrepreneurship in the underground economy.* Cheltenham: Edward Elgar Publishing.

Woodbine, G. F., & Liu, J. (2010). Leadership styles and the moral choice of internal auditors. *Electronic Journal of Business Ethics and Organization Studies, 15*(1), 28–35.

Yusuf, T. O., & Babalola, A. R. (2009). Control of insurance fraud in Nigeria: An exploratory study. *Journal of Financial Crime, 16*(4), 418–435

Statistical Analyses of Crime Sample

8

A number of variables registered for each convicted white-collar criminal may have the potential to explain variations in jail sentencing. To explore this possibility, different statistical approaches are applied in this chapter (Hair, Black, Babin, & Anderson, 2010).

This chapter presents new insights into white-collar criminals based on the Norwegian sample and statistical techniques. However, for readers mainly interested in policing aspects of white-collar crime, this chapter can be skipped because it is not linked to later chapters in the book.

Statistical Correlation Analysis

First, correlation analysis is applied, in which covariation of variables is explored. Significant correlations occur at $p < .01$ (**) and $p < .05$ (*) in the analysis (Hair et al., 2010). As listed in Tables 8.1a and 8.1b, a number of significant correlations emerge:

- *Age of offender* is positively correlated with years in prison, crime amount, personal income, personal tax, personal wealth, business revenue, and number of employees in the organization. Offender age is negatively correlated with the number of persons involved in the crime. These correlations are significant for both the criminal age when convicted and age when committing crime, except for personal wealth. Thus, an older criminal is associated with a longer jail sentence, a larger crime amount, greater personal income, more tax, more wealth, fewer involved persons in the crime, and a larger organization where he or she is employed.
- *Jail sentence*, in terms of days sentenced to prison, is positively correlated with offender age and crime amount as well as tax but negatively correlated with personal income.
- *Crime amount* is positively correlated with offender age, prison years, and organization size in terms of both business revenue and business employees.
- *Personal income* of offender is positively correlated with individual age, negatively correlated with years in prison, and negatively

Table 8.1a　Correlation Analysis of White-Collar Crime Characteristics

Total of 305 Criminals	Age When Convicted	Age When Crime	Years Prison	Crime Amount	Personal Income
Age convicted	1	.960**	.174*	.167**	.143*
Age crime		1	.146*	.162**	.124*
Years prison			1	.262**	−.140*
Crime amount				1	−.014
Personal income					1
Personal tax					
Personal wealth					
Involved persons					
Business revenue					
Business employees					

Table 8.1b　Correlation Analysis of White-Collar Crime Characteristics

Total of 255 Criminals	Personal Tax	Personal Wealth	Involved Persons	Business Revenue	Business Employees
Age convicted	.155**	.143*	−.240**	.223**	.164**
Age crime	.123*	.100	−.180**	.227**	.177**
Years prison	−.128*	−.019	−.068	.107	−.020
Crime amount	−.006	.006	−.033	.298**	.172**
Personal income	.932**	.207**	−.170**	.093	.128*
Personal tax	1	.475**	−.207**	.157**	.153**
Personal wealth		1	−.092	.189**	.038
Involved persons			1	−.116**	−.067
Business revenue				1	.887**
Business employees					1

* Significance of .05; ** Significance of .01.

correlated with the number of involved persons. Thus, poorer criminals in terms of taxable income tend to be younger, spend more time
in prison, and involve more persons in their crime. Personal income
of the offender tends to be higher in larger organizations.
- Criminals who pay more *personal tax* spend less time in prison and
involve fewer persons in their crime. Older criminals pay more tax,
and criminals in larger organizations pay more tax.
- Criminals with more *personal wealth* are working in larger organizations. Older criminals are wealthier, and more wealthy criminals
have higher personal income.
- When the number of *involved persons* in crime is larger, then criminals are younger, they have a lower income and pay less tax, and they
work in smaller organizations. The number of persons involved in
the crime is negatively correlated with a number of variables: Fewer

involved criminals are related to higher age, more income, and larger organizations.

- Criminals in larger organizations in terms of *business revenue* tend to be older and commit crimes of larger amount. They have more personal wealth, pay more taxes, and involve fewer persons in their crime.
- Criminals in larger organizations in terms of *business employees* tend to be older and commit crime of larger amount. They have higher personal income and pay more taxes.

Statistical Regression Analysis

While correlation is concerned with bivariate changes in variable values, regression is concerned with determinants or predictors with which one variable is defined as a dependent variable, and others are defined as independent variables (Hair et al., 2010).

First, regression analysis is applied here to predict jail sentences, in which imprisonment in terms of years in jail is defined as the dependent variable. We enter all other variables, a total of nine variables, as independent variables in a stepwise process, in which the most significant predictor of jail sentence is entered first.

Regression analysis results in crime amount being entered first. Thus, crime amount is the most significant predictor of jail sentence. A higher crime amount leads to a longer jail sentence. Personal income is entered second by the system. Lower personal income leads to a longer jail sentence. The third independent variable entered by the system is age when convicted. Older criminals receive a longer jail sentence. The remaining six variables turned out not to be significant as listed in Table 8.2.

Table 8.2   Stepwise Regression Analysis

Total of 255 Criminals	R Square	Significance	t Statistic for Power	Significance of t Statistic
Model	.111	.000		
Age convicted		(3)	2.297	.022
Age crime			−.687	.492
Crime amount		(1)	4.223	.000
Personal income		(2)	−2.900	.004
Personal tax			−.472	.637
Personal wealth			.165	.869
Involved persons			−.802	.423
Business revenue			.210	.834
Business employees			−.888	.375

Based on these results, we can establish the following predictor model for jail sentences as illustrated in Figure 8.1 and formulated in the following research hypotheses.

Hypothesis 1: A greater amount of money in Norwegian kroner involved in the financial crime will lead to a greater number of years in jail for the white-collar criminal.

Hypothesis 2: A greater personal income of the criminal as reported to the public revenue service will lead to a smaller number of years in jail for the white-collar criminal.

Hypothesis 3: A higher age of white-collar criminal when convicted to imprisonment will lead to a higher number of years in jail for the white-criminal.

When regression analysis is applied by entering all nine independent variables at the same time into the equation, R square improves slightly to .153 for the model. Here, crime amount is a significant predictor in addition to age when convicted, business revenue, and business employees as listed in Table 8.3.

Based on these results, we can establish the following predictor model for jail sentences as illustrated in Figure 8.2 and formulated in the following research hypotheses.

Hypothesis 1: White-collar crime committed in a larger organization with more business employees will lead to a larger number of years in jail for the white-collar criminal.

Hypothesis 2: A greater amount of money in Norwegian kroner involved in the financial crime will lead to a larger number of years in jail for the white-collar criminal.

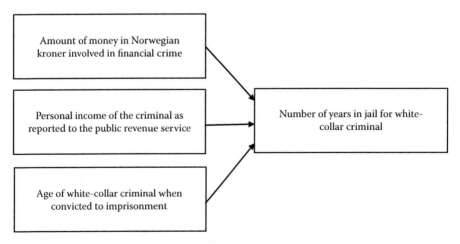

Figure 8.1 Research model for predictors of jail sentence based on stepwise regression.

Table 8.3   Complete Regression Analysis

Total of 255 Criminals	R Square	Significance	t Statistic for Power	Significance of t Statistic
Model	.153	.000		
Age convicted		(4)	1.989	.048
Age crime			−1.384	.167
Crime amount		(2)	3.182	.002
Personal income			.118	.906
Personal tax			−.767	.444
Personal wealth			.095	.925
Involved persons			−.530	.597
Business revenue		(3)	3.079	.002
Business employees		(1)	−3.213	.001

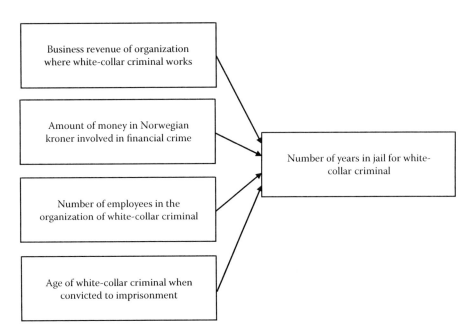

Figure 8.2 Research model for predictors of jail sentence based on complete regression.

> *Hypothesis 3: White-collar crime committed in a larger organization in terms of business revenue will lead to a larger number of years in jail for the white-collar criminal.*
>
> *Hypothesis 4: A higher age of white-collar criminal when convicted to imprisonment will lead to a larger number of years in jail for the white-criminal.*

So far, regression analysis has been applied to predict jail sentence. Other variables can be applied as dependent variables as well. For example, what predicts crime amount? When regression analysis is applied to this question, we find a model in which the size of the organization is important. Both business revenue and business employees are significant predictors of crime amount.

Hypothesis 5: White-collar crime in larger organizations, both in terms of business revenue and in terms of business employees, will lead to a greater amount of money in Norwegian kroner involved in the financial crime.

Structural Equation Modeling

In the following, potential predictors of jail sentences for white-collar criminals are studied. To carry out statistical research of this kind, there is a need to collect characteristics of each convicted person, including age when convicted, number of years in prison, amount of money involved in crime, personal income and wealth according to public income statement, organization revenue, and organization employees as documented in this book. Based on such variables, the following research hypotheses are formulated:

H1: Years of imprisonment are positively related to income.
H2: Years of imprisonment are positively related to age.
H3: Years of imprisonment are positively related to revenue.
H4: Years of imprisonment are positively related to employees.
H5: Years of imprisonment are positively related to amount.
H6: Amount is positively related to income.
H7: Amount is positively related to age.
H8: Amount is positively related to income.
H9: Amount is positively related to employees.

Structural equation modeling (SEM) has been used in almost every conceivable field of study, including psychology, sociology, and management (Hair et al., 2010). In the management field, the use of SEM has increased dramatically in recent years (e.g., Bock, Zmud, & Kim, 2005; Goles, 2001; Ho, Ang & Straub, 2003). The reasons for its attractiveness are twofold: 1) It provides a straightforward method of dealing with multiple relationships simultaneously while providing statistical efficiency, and 2) its ability to assess the relationships comprehensively has provided a transition from exploratory to confirmatory analysis.

SEM is a second-generation data analysis technique that not only assesses the structural model—the assumed causation among a set of dependent and independent constructs—but, in the same analysis, also evaluates the measurement model—loading of observed items (measurements) on their expected latent variables (constructs). The combined analysis of the measurement and the structural model enables measurement errors of the observed variables to be analyzed as an integral part of the model and the factor analysis to be combined in one operation with hypothesis testing (Gefen, Straub, & Boudreau, 2000). SEM evaluates the reliability and validity of the measurement items while simultaneously evaluating the research model within which the constructs are embedded.

Of particular interest in this study is SEM's ability to model latent variables (sometimes referred to as factors). Latent variables are unobservable variables or variables that cannot be directly measured. These latent variables are measured indirectly via the use of measurement items (also known as observed variables or manifest variables) that either reflect or form the latent variable.

A general SEM model can be broken down into two components: the measurement model and the structural model. The measurement model, sometimes called the outer model, is concerned with the relationship between latent variables and the specific set of items associated with each of them. The structural model, sometimes called the inner model, is concerned with the relationship between the various latent variables. The structural model represents the theory posited by the researcher. The measurement model provides a means to evaluate the validity of the measurement items and their relationships with their associated latent variables.

Several different techniques fall under the SEM umbrella. The best known are covariance-based approaches reflected by software such as LISREL, AMOS, and EQS (Goles, 2001). Covariance-based SEM techniques generally utilize a maximum-likelihood function and endeavor to minimize the difference between the covariances of the sample data and those implied by the estimated parameters of the theoretical model. Underlying covariance-based SEM techniques are the twin assumptions that the data follows a normal distribution and that the observations are independent of each other (Chin & Gopal, 1995). Covariance-based SEM is also subject to certain constraints relative to sample size. Minimal sample sizes range from 200 to 800, depending on the power analysis of the specific model (Chin & Newsted, 1999).

An alternative to covariance-based SEM techniques is the partial least squares approach, exemplified by PLS-Graph (hereafter referred to as PLS). This technique is a variance-based approach that is oriented toward the predictive aspects (variance explanation) of the model as opposed to covariance-based techniques that are oriented toward corroborating the overall model fit. PLS also estimates parameters separately for each block of indicators associated with a particular latent variable as opposed to the covariance-based approach of simultaneously estimating all parameters. Thus, in PLS any bias in the estimates of one parameter is less likely to affect the estimates of other parameters. Further, due to its use of an ordinary least squares algorithm, PLS is relatively immune to instances in which the sample data is not normally distributed and is not subject to the restrictions on sample size as is covariance-based SEM. Minimally acceptable samples sizes for PLS range from 30 to 100, depending on the model (Chin & Newsted, 1999; Gefen et al., 2000).

These two versions of SEM techniques, covariance-based and partial least square, differ in the orientation of their analysis and in the nature of their underlying assumptions. Consequently, each type is more appropriately used in certain situations. Covariance-based techniques are more suited when the underlying theory is strong and the overall objective is theory testing. In contrast, PLS's forte is its ability to help the researcher understand and predict the relationships of the individual latent variables among themselves. That is, when the objective is oriented more toward theory building than theory testing (Chin & Newsted, 1999; Gefen et al., 2000).

This study has several characteristics that must be taken into consideration when determining which analysis tool is appropriate. It is among the first studies to incorporate different environmental predictors of imprisonment. Consequently, it is more of an exploratory study than a confirmatory one. The theoretical model is complex and untested. In addition, the sample size of convicted white-collar criminals is just above the minimum recommendation of 200 cases for covariance-based SEM methodologies. Taking all into account, it is obvious that PLS is a more appropriate tool in this instance for data analysis than covariance-based SEM techniques. Consequently, PLS-Graph version 3.0 was selected to analyze the data and test the model.

Criminal characteristics collected for each person included gender, age when convicted, age when committing crime, number of years in prison, court level, amount of money involved in crime, number of persons involved in crime, crime type, position level, personal income, personal tax, personal wealth according to income statement, organization revenue, organization employees, private versus public sector, internal versus external detection, source of detection, corporate versus occupational crime, leader versus follower, and rotten apple versus rotten apple barrel.

Most white-collar criminals are men. This is confirmed in the sample now applied in this analysis of 259 persons, which included only 22 female criminals and 237 male criminals. Thus, less than 8% of the white-collar crime sample from newspaper articles was women—sometimes labeled pink-collar criminals.

The youngest white-collar criminal in Norway was 21 years and the oldest was 77 years old. A distinction is made between age when convicted and age when committing crime. On average, a person was convicted five years after the crime, thus the average age when committing crime is 43 years old because the average age when convicted was 48 years old.

Most anecdotal cases, such as Rajaratman and Schilling, were men in their 50s or older. This is confirmed in our sample in which the average age is 48 years old when convicted in court. These average numbers are similar to a study by Blickle, Schlegel, Fassbender, and Klein (2006) of 76 convicted German white-collar criminals. In their responding sample, there were six female criminals and 70 male criminals. The mean age of the offenders in Germany was 47 years.

The average jail sentence for 259 convicted white-collar criminals in Norwegian courts was 2.2 years with a maximum of 10 years and a minimum of 15 days. The longest jail sentence of 10 years was given to a person involved in bank fraud, in which millions were transferred from a rich widow's account in Norway to a friend's account in Dubai. Because the convicted criminal was operating in a group of criminals, he was convicted of organized crime, which, under Norwegian law, causes the jail sentence for a criminal act to be extended from a more normal level, say, six years, to 10 years in his case.

All persons in the sample received a jail sentence for white-collar crime. Compared to famous U.S. cases mentioned above, these sentences are quite modest. However, in a Norwegian context, these jail sentences are quite substantial, only passed by organized crime and murder. Also, when comparing to the sample used by Blickle et al. (2006) of white-collar criminals in Germany, there is no substantial difference as the average was 3.9 years imprisonment in Germany in their sample of 76 convicts.

A total of 259 convicted white-collar criminals in our sample resulted in relationships between variables as illustrated in Figure 8.3.

A structural modeling technique, partial least squares (PLS) was used to analyze the data and test the hypotheses (Chin, 1998). We used PLS Graph version 3.0 in our analysis. The results of the analysis are depicted in Figure 8.1 and estimates of the relationships are shown in Table 8.4.

In hypotheses 1 through 5, we examined the relationship between imprisonment and five different predictor variables: income, age, revenue, employees, and amount. In hypothesis 1, income was found to have a negative relationship with imprisonment ($\beta = -0.128$, $t = 2.8643$, $p < 0.005$). In hypothesis 2, age was found to have a positive relationship with imprisonment ($\beta = 0.094$, $t = 1.4228$, $p < 0.1$). No support was found for hypothesis 3 ($\beta = 0.219$, $t = 1.2743$). In hypothesis 4, the number of employees was found to have a negative relationship with imprisonment ($\beta = -0.224$, $t = 1.4292$, $p < 0.1$). In hypothesis 5, the amount was found to have a positive relationship with imprisonment ($\beta = 0.233$, $t = 2.2052$, $p < 0.025$).

Hypotheses 6 through 9 examined the relationship between six different predictor variables and amount. No support was found for hypothesis 6 ($\beta = -0.016$, $t = 0.4250$). In hypothesis 7, age was found to have a positive relationship with amount ($\beta = 0.065$, $t = 1.5617$, $p < 0.1$). In hypothesis 8, results indicated

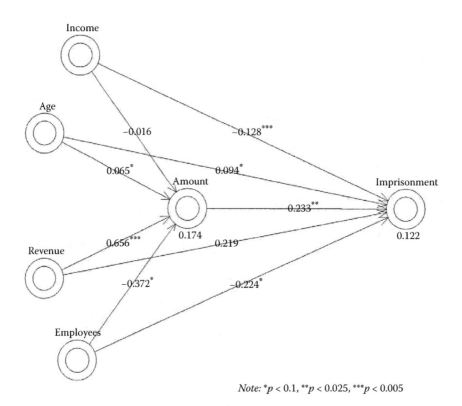

Note: *$p < 0.1$, **$p < 0.025$, ***$p < 0.005$

Figure 8.3 Path coefficients of PLS analysis.

Table 8.4   Imprisonment and Amount Estimates

Dependent Variable	Predictor Variable	Hypothesized Sign	Path Coefficients	t Value	Significance Level	R^2
Imprisonment	Income	+	−0.128	2.8643	$p < 0.005$	0.122
	Age	+	0.094	1.4228	$p < 0.1$	
	Revenue	+	0.219	1.2743	–	
	Employees	+	−0.224	1.4292	$p < 0.1$	
	Amount	+	0.233	2.2052	$p < 0.025$	
Amount	Income	+	−0.016	0.4250	–	0.174
	Age	+	0.065	1.5617	$p < 0.1$	
	Revenue	+	0.656	2.6158	$p < 0.005$	
	Employees	+	−0.372	1.4094	$p < 0.1$	

a positive relationship between revenue and amount ($\beta = 0.656$, $t = 2.6158$, $p < 0.005$). In hypothesis 8, the number of employees of the organization was found to have a negative relationship with amount ($\beta = −0.372$, $t = 1.4094$, $p < 0.1$).

Explained variance for amount was 17.4% and for imprisonment was 12.2%. There are no community standards for what is an acceptable level of explained variance (Gefen et al., 2000). In the basic research of fields like sociology, levels under 10% are commonly reported. Studies published in top-ranked IS/IT journals explain variance in the 20%–30% range (e.g., Bock et al., 2005). In this research, the explained variances found were around these levels.

Predictors of prison sentence for white-collar criminals were estimated statistically based on 259 offenders convicted in Norway. Personal income of the offender was found to have a negative relationship with imprisonment. This result seems surprising as more wealthy criminals tend to abuse larger funds, causing more severe jail sentences. On the other hand, defendant income being negatively related to imprisonment could indicate resources to buy a better legal team and thus improve case outcome. It could also be a marker of privilege that is triggering judicial focal concerns. In comparison, defendant income and punishment severity is negatively related for street crime as judges view such individuals as less dangerous to the community.

Next, age was found to have a positive relationship with imprisonment. This result is not surprising as older criminals tend to abuse larger funds, causing more severe jail sentences. Finally, there were mixed results for company size as the number of employees had a negative relationship, and company turnover in terms of revenue had no significant impact. Finally, crime amount had a negative relationship with imprisonment. Thus, results from the partial least squares analysis indicate that the income of the criminal, age of the criminal, number of employees in the organization, and money amount involved in the crime emerge as significantly related to sentence.

Results of this study might be compared to other studies of white-collar crime that examine prison sentences for white-collar offenders. For example, Schanzenbach and Yeager (2006) studied prison time, fines, and federal white-collar criminals in terms of the anatomy of racial disparity. They defined white-collar offenses as fraud, embezzlement, forgery/counterfeiting, bribery, tax offenses, and money laundering. Their sample consisted of 22,208 convicted white-collar criminals registered with the Office of Policy Analysis of the U.S. Sentencing Commission. Average prison sentence for the large sample was 11 months.

An average of 11 months in the United States is substantially lower than the average of more than two years in Norway. This difference can mainly be explained by the definitions as the U.S. sample only defined the crime, and the Norwegian sample also defines the criminal in terms of position, trust, network, and media coverage.

Income was found to be a significant predictor of prison sentence in the U.S. study. Those in the low-income level received sentences roughly six months longer than those in the high-income level. Schanzenbach and Yeager (2006) presume that some of this difference arises because income determines what quality of legal services the defendant retains and perhaps a greater ability to trade fines for prison time.

Schanzenbach and Yeager (2006) found large racial disparities using standard regression techniques. When controlling for as many relevant characteristics as possible, blacks and Hispanics received longer prison sentences than whites. When the dependent variable is the total prison sentence conditional on the final offense level, the disparities are roughly three times larger among those offenders who paid a fine. When income was considered, the prison sentence disparities decreased by roughly one third. In addition, when sentences were conditioned on base offense levels instead of final offense levels, the estimated racial disparities actually change sides. Whites, not blacks and Hispanics, were on the losing side of the disparity. The sex disparity, on the other hand, consistently disfavors men.

There are several avenues for future research based on this study. First, the empirical basis for convicted criminals might be strengthened by accessing all court records, rather than court records to supplement case material from newspapers. Then it would be possible to go back into the media for variables that are not in the court records. This will strengthen the extent to which the sample is representative of the population of white-collar offenders in Norway.

Next, the literature review might be strengthened by articulating how a study on predictors of prison length is related to previous research. For example, it might be argued that employees with higher personal income and/or from larger corporations receive shorter sentences regardless of amount stolen, which might be a conflicting perspective. It might also be argued that white-collar criminals steal more money if they have a smaller personal income, which might be a strain perspective.

In summary, structural equation modeling was applied to identify predictors of prison sentence based on an empirical study of convicted white-collar criminals in Norway from 2009 to 2012. A total of 259 criminals were mentioned in the press during those three years. The press is one of the criteria used to define white-collar criminals in this study. We examined the relationships between imprisonment and five potential predictor variables: income of the criminal according to public records, age of the criminal when convicted, revenue of the organization where the criminal worked, number of employees in the organization where the criminal worked, and money amount involved in the crime.

Income was found to have a negative relationship with imprisonment. Age was found to have a positive relationship with imprisonment. Number of employees was found to have a negative relationship with imprisonment. Crime amount was found to have a positive relationship with imprisonment. Thus, predictors of prison sentence in terms of time in jail include income, age, employees, and amount.

References

Blickle, G., Schlegel, A., Fassbender, P., & Klein, U. (2006). Some personality correlates of business white-collar crime. *Applied Psychology: An International Review, 55*(2), 220–233.

Bock, G. W., Zmud, R. W., & Kim, Y. G. (2005). Behavioural intention formation in knowledge sharing: Examining the roles of extrinsic motivators, social-psychological forces, and organizational climate. *MIS Quarterly, 29*(1), 87–111.

Chin, W. W. (1998). Issues and opinion on structural equation modeling. *MIS Quarterly, 22*(1), vii–xvi.

Chin, W. W., & Gopal, A. (1995). Adoption intention in GSS: Relative importance of beliefs. *Data Base for Advances in Information Systems, 26*(2–3), 42–64.

Chin, W. W., & Newsted, P. R. (1999). Structural equation modeling analysis with small samples using partial least squares. In R. Hoyle (Ed.), *Statistical strategies for small sample research* (pp. 307–341). Thousand Oaks, CA: Sage Publications.

Gefen, D., Straub, D. W., & Boudreau, M.-C. (2000). Structural equation modeling and regression: Guidelines for research practice. *Communications of the Association for Information Systems, 4*(7), 1–79.

Goles, T. (2001). *The impact of the client-vendor relationship on information systems outsourcing success.* PhD dissertation. University of Houston, Houston, TX.

Hair, J. F., Black, W. C., Babin, B. J., & Anderson, R. E. (2010). *Multivariate data analysis* (7th ed.). Upper Saddle River, NJ: Pearson Education.

Ho, V. T., Ang, S., & Straub, D. (2003). When subordinates become IT contractors: Persistent managerial expectations in IT outsourcing. *Information System Research, 14*(1), 66–86.

Schanzenbach, M., & Yeager, M. L. (2006). Prison time, fines and federal white-collar criminals: The anatomy of racial disparity. *Journal of Criminal Law and Criminology, 96*(2), 757–793.

Police Value Shop Configuration

9

The public expects law enforcement officers to be physically fit. It is a logical assumption that strength and stamina are necessary requirements for the job. Clearly, policing can be a physically demanding job. Officers encounter instances in which strength and endurance are an advantage. However, Bissett, Bissett, and Snell (2012) raised the question, how important are physical strength and fitness to the job?

In policing white-collar crime, financial knowledge and business insights are more important than running or fighting skills. Knowledge is applied in the value configuration of a value shop to solve crime cases. The value shop concept within a learning organization (LO) is presented in this chapter. However, for some readers this may not be of particular interest. Therefore, it is indeed possible to skip this chapter as well without any loss when reading later chapters.

Typically most physical activity in policing is conducted by a small percentage of the force. More officers spend their time doing knowledge work. Over the past decade, police executives have investigated methods for improving organizational performance by providing police officers with better ways of accessing one another's knowledge. Such knowledge management efforts often rely on information technology (Durcikova & Gray, 2009).

Bissett et al. (2012) conducted a survey among officers in the Houston police department on the importance of 11 competencies for law enforcement officers. Integrity was rated as the most important competence, followed by self-control, dependability, situational reasoning, and interpersonal skills. Within each competence, there is a core of knowledge as competence is referred to as the sum of knowledge, skills, abilities, and attitudes. At the bottom of the list, physical agility could be found, again stressing the importance of law enforcement being more knowledge work and less physical work.

Traditionally, the primary purpose of the police has been to prevent and respond to crime and emergencies. More recently, security has become important. Increased emphasis on homeland security has widened the responsibilities of local police officers (Wilson, 2012). Security issues are frequently linked to financial crime because security threats are based on a black economy. Button (2012) studied policing of cross-border fraud. He argues the need for creation of an international body to lead the fight. Such an organization will require knowledge resources.

Police Culture

Police culture has been studied for many years (Fielding, 1984; Reuss-Ianni, 1993; Moir & Eijkman, 1992; Miller, 1995; Vickers & Kouzmin, 2001) and has received increased attention in recent years. For example, Christensen and Crank (2001) studied police work and culture in a nonurban setting in the United States. They found a police culture that emphasized secrecy, self-protection, violence, and maintenance of respect. Lahneman (2004) studied knowledge sharing in the international intelligence community after 9/11, and Granér (2004) studied uniformed police officers' occupational culture. Barton (2004) found that the English and Welsh police epitomize organizations that are steeped in tradition, and Reuss-Ianni (1993) made a distinction between street cops and management cops. Moir and Eijkman (1992) find a hierarchic police culture based on authority, and Vickers and Kouzmin (2001) find that police forces remain fundamentally unchanged as an authoritarian organization.

These examples of police cultures appear contradictory to that of a learning culture, which is essential for a learning organization (DiBella, 2003). Within a learning culture, shared cultural values will act as premises for performance and people continually expanding their capacity to create desired results (Senge, 1990). Watkins and Marsick (1992) focus on employees' total involvement in processes of collaboration with collective accountable changes that are directed toward shared values within a learning organization.

A police culture must be understood in relation to the characteristics of an organizational culture and will involve more than just values. It is a question of a set of shared norms, values, and perceptions, representing a shared system of interrelated understanding that is shaped by its members' shared history and expectations (Veiga, Lubatkin, Calori, & Very, 2000). It is holistic, historically determined, socially constructed, and, therefore, difficult to change (Hofstede, Neuijen, Ohayv, & Sanders, 1990). Also, organizational culture might determine how the "organization" thinks, feels, and acts as it defines the "shoulds" and "oughts" of organizational life (Veiga et al., 2000). However, the "organization" as such can never be known or rationally defined, but it might learn, develop, and unfold as crucial for becoming a learning organization (Clegg, Kornberger, & Rhodes, 2005). This is important as organizations are about being pragmatic, creative, and constructive (Chia, 1998) with the potential of changing the organizational culture.

We approach police culture as socially constructed within the particular police force (Christensen & Crank, 2001). Hence, police culture is embedded in the tradition and the history of policing; police culture contains accepted practices, rules, values, and principles of conduct that are applied to a variety of practical situations at work and on generalized rationales and beliefs. For instance, studies of cultural values among Norwegian police officers show that their interpretation of their own police culture is that it is more based on collective work and cooperation than working individually in their professional performances.

Schein (1990) distinguishes between three fundamental levels at which any culture manifests itself: (a) observable artifacts, (b) values, and (c) basic underlying assumptions. This indicates that when investigating the police culture, police values represent one important characteristic as values define social principles, goals, norms, and what is considered important within this particular police culture. Accordingly, Hofstede et al. (1990) argue that values comprise the core of any culture as values are emotional perceptions of what is appreciated and preferred. In other words, police values are essential for police officers' perception of right and wrong and what is desirable and valuable in professional work. Consequently, it is believed that police force values dictate the behavior of its officers. For instance, when Kiely and Peek (2002) used a shared value perspective to understand British police culture, they found values such as honesty, morality, and integrity regarded as important, resulting in self-discipline, commitment, and fairness in police work.

Hatch (2001) focuses on the dynamics among artifacts, values, and basic assumptions and how they are interrelated instead of being hierarchical with different levels and dimensions of organizational culture as described by Schein (1990). Also, she does not agree with Schein's argument that when organizations are effective and well-functioning, there is no need to change basic assumptions and values. This is problematic related to organizational learning (Hatch, 2001). A learning organization suggests a changing, dynamic, and complex understanding of both culture and learning (Gleerup, 2008) in which learning is integrated in the culture as a learning culture, not just from detection of error, but in which learning and knowledge development are continuing processes of past inquiries and reflection in and on action (Schön, 1987).

To be able to address police values, we need to be specific about which values are believed to support a learning organization and, as a result, highlight what police values should be investigated in our studies. Our choice of police values is related to both the literature on police culture and on learning organizations. In Argyris and Schön's (1996) double-loop learning, the authors differentiate between espoused values and values used and enacted in practice as theories-in-use. Hence, theories-in-use might differ from espoused values, and enacted values represent the characteristics and possibilities of becoming a learning organization. Consequently, espoused values are used here to clarify the distinction between what we have studied and what values people hold (Kabanoff & Daly, 2002) as values that are enacted and explain practice.

First, the police culture is traditionally characterized as bureaucratic and closed, not open and creative (Steinheider & Wuestewald, 2008), and a learning organization needs enabling structures (Pedler, Buoydell, & Burgoyne, 1991) that promote empowerment (Gardiner & Whiting, 1997) and openness (Watkins & Marsick, 1992). Accordingly, we explore the following values:

1. Equality and empowerment versus hierarchy that is, short distance between layers versus hierarchy in status
2. Open versus closed that is, communication with the environment during investigation or secrecy, loyalty, and no communication outside the force
3. Freedom versus control that is, being creative versus controlled behavior
4. Privacy versus openness that is, how the social condition in the unit is characterized as private or more intimate and open. This last value is also in accordance to the Christensen and Crank (2001) characterization of a police culture being closed with secrecy and self-protection

Second, Barton (2004) and Vickers and Kouzmin (2001) expose a traditional and unchanging police culture, and a learning organization requires continuous learning (Watkins & Marsick, 1992) and openness to new ideas (Tannenbaum, 1997) and experimentation (Pedler et al., 1991). Hence, the following values are explored:

5. Change versus tradition that is, encouraging new methods versus holding on to how tasks were solved in the past
6. Security versus challenge that is, adapting to security versus possibilities of challenges
7. Stability versus instability that is, harmony and predictability versus unpredictability and some confusion
8. Firm leadership versus individual creativity that is, practicing strong leadership versus facilitating individual creativity
9. Practical versus philosophical that is, having a practical and pragmatic orientation versus a theoretical and philosophical orientation
10. Security and integrity versus effectiveness and productivity that is, focus on integrity and accountability versus being effective by preventing crime in accordance with each officers' consideration of best practice
11. Traditional organization versus knowledge organization that is, further establishing of a traditional police organization versus a knowledge organization

Third, it is believed that the police culture is more collectivistic than individualistic. This is in accordance with a learning organization, which focuses on collaboration, team learning, and participatory decision making (Pedler et al., 1991; Watkins & Marsick, 1992). Accordingly, the following values are explored:

12. Individualism versus group orientation that is, strong individual responsibilities versus cooperation in teams and partnerships
13. Individual competition versus cooperation that is, competing individually versus cooperation in solving police work
14. Task versus relationship that is, focusing on task versus being more relational oriented
15. Informal versus formal that is, communicating and interacting informally versus mostly relying on formal communication

Finally, a learning organization must provide a platform that facilitates learning opportunities and information flow (Griego, Geroy, & Wright, 2000) as well as tolerance of error and mistakes to ensure creativity and knowledge performances in its future (Tannenbaum, 1997; Pedler et al., 1991). Hence, our final choice of values is as follows:

16. Short-term versus long-term that is, fast solutions and results or a long-term perspective
17. Work versus balance that is, work being most important versus creating a balance between work and private life
18. Direct versus indirect that is, using an open and direct communication style versus communicating more indirectly
19. Act versus plan that is, focus on action and practice versus more focus and planning and "paperwork"
20. Time firm versus time float that is, punctuality or less time consciousness
21. Learning versus nonlearning organization that is, fulfill necessary requirements characteristic of a learning organization versus not practicing learning and knowledge sharing

Obviously, dichotomizing values as being "either/or" is problematic and, in relation to organizational learning, can often be a question of having values that include, for instance, being both individualistic and group-oriented. These issues will be addressed in our discussions of how the espoused police values of police managers represent a potential for becoming a learning organization.

Norwegian police are described in the following as a case for police culture study. Norway has one police force. There are 27 local police districts, each under the command of a chief of police. In addition to the police districts, there are five central police institutions. About 13,000 personnel work in the Norwegian police force; approximately 9000 are trained police officers, and almost 800 are lawyers, and 3200 are civilian employees.

One chief of police has full responsibility within each police district. A police district has its own headquarters as well as several police stations. All police officers in Norway are trained to fulfill every aspect of ordinary police work, including criminal investigations, maintaining public order, and community policing.

Two police districts were selected for this research. Both of these districts have several towns and rural areas with a similar geography, demography, and crime statistics. In both police districts, executive training programs were carried out in 2008, 2009, and 2010. Participants in these programs were selected for this research: 60 and 70 managers respectively. Recognizing the biases of asking police managers about their values might give contradictions between espoused and enacted police values. Hence, we account for these possible contradictions in our analysis. Also, our study of espoused values represent a first study for further investigations of addressing both espoused and enacting values in the Norwegian police force.

A questionnaire was conducted. The questionnaire was first tested on 15 police managers at different leadership levels from different police districts. Seven of them provided written comments, and some others made verbal comments on the telephone. All comments from the pretest were considered, and several changes were made to the questionnaire. The study is based on a convenience sample. All participants from the two police districts were asked by email as well as encouraged by their chief constable to fill in the online survey. The study was carried out in 2010 with a response rate of 50%. Forty-nine percent were first-line managers, 27% middle managers, and 22% top managers. Thirty-eight percent had been managers for more than 11 years.

The value scales applied give a measurement of one as, for instance, very individualistic versus seven as very group-oriented. The measurements are listed in Table 9.1. We find that by creating a middle of four, the values are believed by the respondents to be "either/or" but also more a combination of both. Actually, many of the measurement scores can be found around four.

Our findings indicate that police values are not very prominent and that the dichotomy can be problematic. Also, it can be a result of police managers not being conscious of police values, and thus, they are more neutral in espousing them. Consequently, with regard to a learning organization, respondents' answers show a largely "neither/nor" interpretation of whether or not the police force is a learning organization. Only a few measurement scores indicate significant values:

- Cooperation is considered to be more important than individual competition in policing.
- Informal communication is more common than formal communication in policing.

Table 9.1   Measurement of Police Values

Scale	Police Culture Value	Measurement
1	Time firm versus time floats	3.03
2	Change versus tradition	3.97
3	Individualism versus group orientation	4.40
4	Freedom versus control	3.21
5	Privacy versus openness	4.14
6	Informal versus formal	2.98
7	Individual competition versus cooperation	5.12
8	Equality and empowerment versus hierarchy	2.91
9	Short term versus long term	3.14
10	Work versus balance	4.16
11	Task versus relationships	3.42
12	Direct versus indirect	3.84
13	Act versus plan	2.95
14	Practical versus philosophical	2.35
15	Security versus challenge	2.54
16	Integrity versus effectiveness	2.23
17	Firm leadership versus individual creativity	4.05
18	Open versus closed	3.14
19	Traditional versus knowledge organization	3.44
20	Stability versus instability	3.55
21	Learning versus nonlearning organization	3.78

- Equality and empowerment are more prominent than hierarchy and authority.
- To act is considered to be more important than to plan in the police force.
- Cooperation is more prominent than competition.
- Police officers are more practical and less philosophical.
- Security and integrity are more important than challenge and productivity in the police force.

We then ran a correlation of coefficients linking espoused police values to those of a learning organization, as listed in Table 9.2.

These 20 espoused values are correlated with important characteristics of a learning organization (value 21) and intended to explain the police managers espoused values of the police force being a learning organization or not, which was quite neutral (3.78).

Accordingly, a number of significant correlations emerge in Table 9.2 on whether those values we measured were in accordance to those of a learning organization.

Table 9.2 Correlation Coefficients Linking Values and Learning Organization

Scale	Occupational Culture Value	Correlation
1	Time firm versus time floats	.186
2	Change versus tradition	.388**
3	Individualism versus group orientation	−.019
4	Freedom versus control	.239
5	Privacy versus openness	−.182
6	Informal versus formal	.355**
7	Individual competition versus cooperation	−.212
8	Equality and empowerment versus hierarchy	.372**
9	Short term versus long term	−.101
10	Work versus balance	−.045
11	Task versus relationships	−.358**
12	Direct versus indirect	.372**
13	Act versus plan	−.038
14	Practical versus philosophical	.025
15	Security versus challenge	.192
16	Integrity versus effectiveness	.062
17	Firm leadership versus individual creativity	−.069
18	Open versus closed	.491**
19	Traditional versus knowledge organization	−.303*
20	Stability versus instability	.384**

* Significance of .05; ** Significance of .01.

1. A learning organization is related to change rather than tradition and to a stable rather than an instable organization.
2. A learning organization is related to informal rather than formal communication and a direct rather than an indirect form.
3. A learning organization is related to equality and empowerment rather than hierarchy and an open rather than closed culture.
4. A learning organization is related to relationships rather than tasks and is a knowledge organization rather than a traditional organization.

Our results show that the only espoused values reported by police managers, which represent significant correlation with those of a learning organization, are informality and equality/empowerment over a formal and hierarchic police force. This indicates two important police values characterizing the Norwegian police force, which give way to a learning organization. However, due to the number of neutrally correlated police values, we also believe that the police managers are not necessarily aware of their own police culture, especially related to values such as change, stability, directness, and openness as crucial for a learning organization. As a result, the police force does not espouse all of the values that have been characterized within the total set of necessary values of knowledge or learning organizations. In other words, we find some espoused police values that simply represent the potential for becoming a learning organization.

Van Beek, Ter Huurne, Van Vierssen, and Vinter (2005) argue that the police officers must be responsible for their continuous learning throughout their career. It is believed, however, that the police forces cannot be alienated from the process as they should create necessary conditions to allow and to encourage the self-learning of their police officers (Felgueiras, 2011). Police officers face adverse and violent social conditions and vulnerable individuals, and they are supposed to find and reestablish the equilibrium, overcome difficulties, and maintain trust in themselves and in justice (Felgueiras, 2011). Consequently, Felgueiras argues that training and education is elaborated, and the police force has the responsibility and supervision of the process so that employees are led through an assimilation process of culture, knowledge, and competence the police force consider most important. The police officers are autonomous in their learning process and encourage self-learning, making clear the police officers' responsibilities to create a learning culture that has the fundamental and transversal role in the learning processes within the police force.

Linking our studies of the police force potential for becoming a learning organization is based on our belief that it is all about creating a strong learning culture. The police force must act upon (not just espouse) values that are believed to develop a maturity level in accordance with a learning organization. We would argue that these values are very much focused upon within the learning organization concept. It is argued that a learning organization needs enabling structures (Pedler et al., 1991) for empowerment (Gardiner & Whiting, 1997), involving all employees in decisions (Watkins & Marsick, 1992), which supports the values of equality, empowerment, and openness. Also, a learning organization requires continuous learning (Watkins & Marsick, 1992) and openness to new ideas and experimentation (Tannenbaum, 1997; Pedler et al., 1991), which supports values of change, stability, and knowledge-orientation. Finally, a learning organization must focus on collaboration, team learning, and facilitation of learning opportunities (Griego et al., 2000; Pedler et al., 1991; Watkins & Marsick, 1992) and should support relational orientation and informal, direct, and open communication.

When police managers only recognize a police culture characterized as informal and empowering, the importance of the other values that facilitate the learning organization, such as change, relational-orientation, directness, openness, stability, and knowledge-orientation, are overlooked. It can be that the police managers are not necessarily conscious of the importance of their police values and how they relate to police work and consequently their possibilities of being a learning organization. This is even more critical as being a learning organization is part of their overall goal and vision, and how to accomplish that and creating a common understanding of what it means is crucial for creating a strong learning culture (Filstad, 2010). Also, is it possible that a profession such as policing should provide other criteria for a learning organization, providing the argument that each learning organization is different? For instance, it would be common to question whether the more cooperative and collectivistic culture characterizing the Norwegian police force is related to the particular occupation of policing itself. Police officers must follow rules and regulations to ensure their own and their partners' security in dangerous situations. Thus, accountability and collective work is crucial (Edelbacher and Ivkovic, 2004) within police culture, and creativity and individual solutions can provide difficulties and even danger although the question remains as to whether these occupational factors hinder learning, knowledge development, and change.

Security and integrity are considered more important than challenges and proactivity in our study, confirming previous studies of police culture. Within a learning organization, managers must facilitate challenges and change through their own participation in an environment characterized by equality and empowerment (Watkins & Marsick, 1992; Conner & Clawson, 2004) but in which change and openness for new ideas are victims of a more neutral interpretation from the police managers. Equality and empowerment, however, meaning a short distance between layers, is found to be an important value in our two police districts. This is confirmed by previous studies in Norwegian police forces, but only among counter-terrorism officers and not among criminal investigators, as espoused values. Criminal investigators claim safety versus challenge to be equal; thus safety is not believed to be a more dominant value than challenge. Security is also linked to integrity when informal communication is more common than formal and when police officers prefer not to communicate with the environment when working on police investigations.

Even when reporting on a police culture characterized by empowerment and equality, the police managers espouse values of a traditional organization. Within a learning organization, management is supposed to participate on all levels in the organization, relying on a short distance between layers, minor differences in status, and a tight social environment; thus a learning organization relies on empowerment and equality. This is not in accordance with previous studies finding that the police force has a strong hierarchical and authoritarian organization form (Moir & Eijkman, 1992; Vickers & Kouzmin, 2001). Hence, our studies are not sufficient to claim that the Norwegian police force is less hierarchical and authoritarian as no additional research can confirm this.

Police managers espouse neither change nor stability. A learning organization is supposed to change as employees learn and transform themselves within a learning organization (Senge, 1990; Pedler et al., 1991). We would approach change as more than learning, justifying that learning is the goal, not just the mean for change, also because change alone tends to amplify stability (Antonacopoulou, Jarvis, Andersen, Elkjaer, & Høyrup, 2006). Our interpretation is therefore in accordance with Gherardi and Nicolini's (2000) arguing that learning and knowledge is as important to both facilitate continuity and stability as it is to facilitate change (Gherardi & Nicolini, 2000). This is due to the fact that change and flux are the natural state of an organization, and therefore, stability is not a natural state within an organization but an accomplishment (Tsoukas & Chia, 2002; Clegg et al., 2005). Consequently, a learning organization characterized by change versus an organization characterized as stable is not a contradiction. Rather, organizing is a process of increasing complexity and reducing it (Clegg et al., 2005). Organizational learning qualifies as an oxymoron because learning is to disorganize and increase variety, and organizing reduces this variety (Weick & Westley, 1996). This is in accordance to our idea of a learning organization.

Experimentation, continuous improvement, teamwork, and participating decision making provide equality and empowerment over hierarchy (Pedler et al., 1991; Alegre & Chiva, 2008). This is a call for an open, knowledge-intensive organization as a precondition of a learning organization (Uretsky, 2001; Örtenblad, 2004; Rebelo & Gomes, 2008). Accordingly, Moir and Eijkman (1992) argue that policing must learn to live with the stress of experimentation and innovation through openness and allowing trial and error as well as risk as a natural element of police work instead of a police culture characterized as closed and by feelings of solidarity and "us versus them" (Miller, 1995).

Whether or not the police force should be a learning organization remains unanswered as it depends upon what type of organization the police force actually is and also has the potential to be. This is in accordance with idea of a learning organization and its contributors arguing that each organization must create its own version of the learning organization (Örtenblad, 2011).

Clearly, experimentation is not often an option in police work. Furthermore, total involvement in processes of collaboration is seldom a feasible prospect in police work. It, however, depends on the kind of police work that is in question. This leads to the essence of our police force studies and analysis. To be or not to be a learning organization is dependent upon what functions or sections of law enforcement are being studied. We find two extremes in antiterror police officers versus investigating detectives. In antiterror, there is little or no room for experimentation. When Osama bin Laden was killed in Pakistan or the Norwegian terrorist Anders Behring Breivik was caught on the island of Utøya in Norway, there was no room for experimentation. However, it might be, as related to the critics of these two incidents, that the routines and organization of these complex situations were not sufficient and therefore should be critically analyzed, scrutinized, and discussed within the police force so as to better be prepared for the unexpected.

When a murder investigation or online grooming investigation is going on without much evidence, then there is certainly room for creative experimentation to produce more case evidence. Therefore, in accordance to our stage model, we find police units such as the antiterror police as "activity" type organizations, and senior investigating officers and their staff are more closely related to a learning organization. Traffic police, for example, might however be found in the middle as "problem" or "value" type organizations. This being said, the potential of being a learning organization does not only rely upon what kind of police tasks are being executed. Openness, experience-based learning, the creation of new ideas through empowerment, questioning established values, teamwork, trial for the case of change, and a more knowledge-intensive police force will make way for a stronger learning culture within the police force and push forward the Norwegian police force toward the goal of becoming a learning organization.

Value Shop Work

Investigation and prevention of white-collar crime has the value configuration of a value shop. As can be seen in Figure 9.1, the five activities of a value shop are interlocking, and although they follow a logical sequence (much like the management of any project), the difference from a knowledge management perspective arises in terms of the manner in which knowledge is used

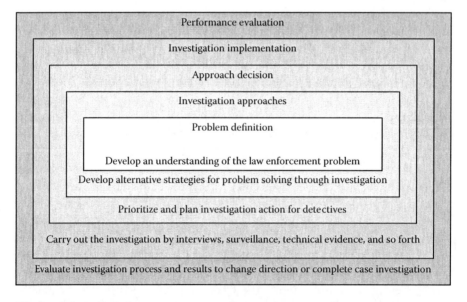

Performance evaluation

Investigation implementation

Approach decision

Investigation approaches

Problem definition

Develop an understanding of the law enforcement problem

Develop alternative strategies for problem solving through investigation

Prioritize and plan investigation action for detectives

Carry out the investigation by interviews, surveillance, technical evidence, and so forth

Evaluate investigation process and results to change direction or complete case investigation

Figure 9.1 Knowledge organization of investigation and prevention units as value shop activities.

as a resource to create value in terms of results for the organization. Hence, the logic of the five interlocking value shop activities in this example pertains to a policing unit and the manner in which it carries out its core business of conducting reactive and proactive investigations.

The sequence of activities commences with problem understanding; moves into alternative investigation approaches, investigation decision, and investigation implementation; and ends up with criminal investigation evaluation. However, these five sequential activities tend to overlap and link back to earlier activities, especially in relation to activity 5 (control and evaluation) in policing units, when the need for control and command structures are a daily necessity due to the legal obligations that policing unit authority entails. Hence, the diagram is meant to illustrate the reiterative and cyclical nature of these five primary activities when it comes to managing the knowledge collected during and applied to a specific investigation in a value shop manner.

Furthermore, the figure illustrates the expanding domain of the knowledge work performed in financial crime investigations, starting in the center with problem understanding and ending at the periphery with evaluation of all parts of the investigation process.

The five primary activities depicted above of the value shop in relation to a financial crime investigation and prevention unit can be outlined as follows:

1. *Problem Definition.* This involves working with parties to determine the exact nature of the crime and hence how it is to be defined. For example, depending on how responding officers perceive and/or choose to define it, a physical assault in a domestic violence situation can be either upgraded to the status of grievous bodily harm to the spousal victim or it may be downgraded to a less serious, common assault and defined as a case in which a bit of rough handling took place toward the spouse. This concept of making crime, a term denoting how detectives choose to make incidents into a crime or not, is highly relevant here and accounts for why this first activity has been changed from the original problem-finding term used in the business management realm to a problem definition process here in relation to policing work. Moreover, this first investigative activity involves deciding on the overall investigative approach for the case not only in terms of information acquisition but also (as indicated in Figure 9.1) in terms of undertaking the key task, usually by a senior investigative officer in a serious or major incident, of forming an appropriate investigative team to handle the case.

2. *Investigation Approaches.* This second activity of identifying problem-solving approaches involves the actual generation of ideas and action plans for the investigation. As such, it is a key process as it establishes the direction and tone of the investigation and is very much influenced by the composition of the members of the investigative team.

For example, the experience level of investigators and their preferred investigative thinking style might be a critical success factor in this second primary activity of the value shop.

3. *Approach Decision.* This solution choice activity represents the decision of choosing between alternatives generated in the second activity. Despite being the least important primary activity of the value shop in terms of time and effort, it might be the most important in terms of value. In this case, trying to ensure as far as is possible that what is decided upon is the best option to follow to achieve an effective investigative result. A successful solution choice is dependent on two requirements. First, that alternative investigation steps were identified in the problem-solving approaches activity. It is important to think in terms of alternatives; otherwise, no choices can be made. Second, the criteria for decision making have to be known and applied to the specific investigation.

4. *Investigation Implementation.* As the name implies, solution execution entails communicating, organizing, investigating, and implementing decisions. This is an equally important process or phase in an investigation as it involves sorting through the mass of information coming into the incident room concerning a case and directing the lines of inquiry as well as establishing the criteria used to eliminate a possible suspect from further scrutiny in the investigation. A miscalculation here can stall or even ruin the whole investigation. Most of the resources expended on an investigation are used here in this fourth activity of the value shop.

5. *Performance Evaluation.* Control and evaluation involves monitoring activities and the measurement of how well the solution solved the original problem or met the original need. This is where the command and control chain of authority comes into play for investigation and prevention units and where the determination of the quality and quantity of the evidence is made in terms of whether or not to charge and prosecute an identified offender in a court of law.

Learning Organization

We expect the police to protect our society against threats as they pursue, detect, investigate, and stop crime. We also trust the police to perform honestly, fairly, efficiently, and in a lawful manner (Graham, 2006). These responsibilities are increasingly becoming more challenging and complex; thus, many countries give the police comprehensive powers. For complaints commissions mandated to monitor the police, these comprehensive powers and new challenges call for the police force to develop a knowledge-intensive organization as opposed to a bureaucratic and even quasimilitary organization (Steinheider & Wuestewald, 2008; Kelley, 2005). In the process of establishing a knowledge-based organization, current practices emphasize the use of ideas and capabilities of the employees to improve decision making and organizational effectiveness, and in bureaucratic setups, autocratic decision making by senior leadership with unquestioned execution by the workforce is practiced (Bennet & Bennet, 2005a). A knowledge-intensive organization tends to produce better quality and more effective procedures to deal with violations of law, whether terrorist or mere traffic violations, because the continued knowledge development in police work to meet new demands and obligations tends to build trust and cooperation from the public (Graham, 2006). This dynamic knowledge-based practice continuously improves performances in the police force's practical work (Schafer, 2009).

In transitioning the police force from the traditional bureaucratic structure to that of a knowledge-based institution, it is imperative to address the culture of a traditional police force (Fielding, 1984; Reuss-Ianni, 1993). Similarly, it is crucial to understand its socially constructed behavior (Hofstede et al., 1990) and to explore its ability to become a knowledge-intensive and learning organization that focuses on flexibility and openness (Watkins & Marsick, 1992; Tannenbaum, 1997) as opposed to a static bureaucratic culture that focuses mainly on stability, accuracy, and repetitiveness of internal processes (Barton, 2004; Steinheider and Wuestewald, 2008). A significant characteristic of learning and knowledge-based police organizations is that of the dynamic relationship between the different layers of decision making in the organization, which is largely based on the communication and the ideas and capabilities of employees, both of which play a role in creating a more effective police force. On the other hand, hierarchical bureaucracies utilize autocratic decision making by senior leadership with unquestioned execution by the workforce (Bennet & Bennet, 2005b). To better understand the transition from a hierarchical to a knowledge-based police force, we use the Norwegian Police force case study to introduce a learning theory that delineates stages for developing a learning organization as illustrated in Figure 9.2.

According to their study, the Norwegian Bureau of the Investigation of Police Affairs has identified as the problem that an organization needs to go through a timely and intensive process of education to promote a more effective and mature level of practice. This four-stage learning program takes place over time to reach a higher maturity level. The four stages utilize normative learning models and methodologies (Easterby-Smith, Burgoyne, & Araujo, 1999), starting with the activities (practice), then moving to the problem solving, to challenging and changing values, and lastly, leading to the creation of the learning organization based on new ideas and evolving experiences that ensure change and innovation.

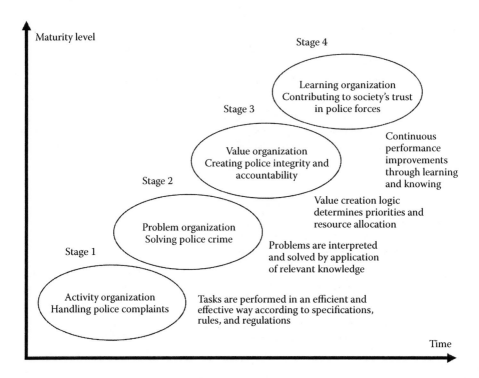

Figure 9.2 Stages of growth in police oversight agencies.

The learning organization is based on a dynamic system. It is an organization that promotes continuous learning (Senge, 1990) in response to various pressures (Grieves, 2008) and, among all its employees, transforming itself into a learning unit (Pedler et al., 1991).

A learning organization is different from organizational learning. Although the LO literature draws heavily on ideas developed within organizational learning, the LO is based selectively on the grounds of utility (Easterby-Smith et al., 1999) with a focus on change as the goal, not change as integrated in learning—when learning typically includes much more than change (Antonacopoulou et al., 2006). Consequently, the key point for LOs is outcomes, rather than mechanisms and processes of learning, with a focus on normative assumptions for change and reconstructions of organizations (Laursen, 2006). LOs enable such learning for their members, which, in turn, create positively valued outcomes, such as innovation, efficiency, and competitive advantage. Also, learning organizations must have a learning culture and establish normative conditions as essential for learning to take place (DiBella, 2003).

The learning organization can be incriminating, not sufficiently addressing how and why learning occurs (Senge & Kofman, 1995). Hence, LOs tend to suffer from a unilateral focus on normative models for learning opportunities and best practices (Laursen, 2006; Elkjaer & Wahlgren, 2006). Rebelo and Gomes (2008) argue that the learning organization perspective is more prescriptive than practical as it is oriented toward models that help organizations enhance learning and benefit from it.

It is also important to add that the literature on learning organizations describes a set of actions that are supposed to ensure learning capabilities, such as experimentation, continuous improvement, team work, and group problem-solving (Pedler et al., 1991; Alegre & Chiva, 2008). However, when Argyris and Schön (1996) outline the goal of double-loop learning, they believe that organizations must learn by continuously questioning and changing basic values, also arguing that the concept of a learning organization is not just normative and practice-oriented. Other scholars believe that a learning organization brings valuable insight on processes and context for institutions to prove and reflect upon their incapacity (Örtenblad, 2011).

Many scholars claim that the concept of the learning organization is quite ambiguous (Örtenblad, 2004) and suffers from a lack of clear definition (Garvin, 2000) that can be tested, probed, and contested (Grieves, 2008). However, we still believe that it is imperative to investigate whether the characteristics of a police culture, more specifically the espoused cultural values of police managers, result in the potential of the police force becoming a learning organization.

Most scholars agree that transitioning into a learning organization is challenging (Bui & Baruch, 2010). Each unique organization must be given the necessary flexibility to develop its own individual version of the learning organization (Pedler et al., 1991; Senge, Roberts, Ross, Smith, & Kleiner, 1994). Accordingly, Rebelo and Gomes (2008) call for more empirical research on organizational factors that promote and facilitate learning in and by each organization.

We aim to explore these challenges, recognizing that police values are difficult to change as they are socially constructed within this particular profession (Hofstede et al., 1990) and also that the police values will effect and determine their professional behavior and therefore police performance (Veiga et al., 2000).

Jaschke et al. (2007) found that the style of policing varies enormously from country to country and within local police forces. In some countries, inhabitants tend to fear the police as corrupt, brutal, and untrustworthy. In other countries, as in the case in Norway, police enjoy trust and confidence. However, due to possible cultural variances between countries, regions, and police districts, an investigation of local police districts is undertaken in this chapter so as to sufficiently grasp the Norwegian police culture and its consequences for police practice.

References

Alegre, J., & Chiva, R. (2008). Assessing the impact of organizational learning capability on product innovation performance: An empirical test. *Technovation, 28,* 315–326.

Antonacopoulou, E., Jarvis, P., Andersen, V., Elkjaer, B., and Høyrup, S. (2006). *Learning, working and living: Mapping the terrain of working life learning.* New York: Palgrave Macmillan.

Argyris, C., & Schön, D. A. (1996). *Organizational learning IT: Theory, method and practice.* Reading, MA: Addison-Wesley.

Barton, H. (2004). Cultural reformation: A case for intervention within the police service. *International Journal of Human Resources Development and Management, 4*(2), 191–199.

Bennet, A., & Bennet, D. (2005a). Designing the knowledge organization of the future: The intelligent complex adaptive system. In C. W. Holsapple (Ed.), *Handbook of knowledge management* (vol. 2) (pp. 623–638). Amsterdam: Springer Science & Business Media.

Bennet, D., & Bennet, A. (2005b). The rise of the knowledge organization. In C. W. Holsapple (Ed.), *Handbook of knowledge management* (vol. 1) (pp. 5–20). Amsterdam: Springer Science & Business Media.

Bissett, D., Bissett, J., & Snell, C. (2012). Physical agility tests and fitness standards: Perceptions of law enforcement officers. *Police Practice and Research, 13*(3), 208–223.

Bui, H., & Baruch, Y. (2010). Creating learning organizations: A systems perspective. *The Learning Organization, 17*(3), 208–227.

Button, M. (2012). Cross-border fraud and the case for an "Interfraud." *Policing: An International Journal of Police Strategies and Management, 35*(2), 285–303.

Chia, R. (1998). From complexity science to complex thinking: Organization as simple location. *Organization, 5,* 341–369.

Christensen, W., & Crank, J. P. (2001). Police work and culture in a nonurban setting: An ethnographical analysis. *Police Quarterly, 4*(1), 69–98.

Clegg, S. R., Kornberger, M., & Rhodes C. (2005). Learning/becoming/organizing. *Organization, 12*(2), 147–167.

Conner, M. L., & Clawson, J. G. (2004). *Creating a learning culture: Strategy, technology and practice.* Cambridge: Cambridge University Press.

DiBella, A. J. (2003). Managing organisations as learning portfolios. *The Systems Thinker, 14*(6), 2–6.

Durcikova, A., & Gray, P. (2009). How knowledge validation processes affect knowledge contribution. *Journal of Management Information Systems, 25*(4), 81–107.

Easterby-Smith, M., Burgoyne, J., & Araujo, L. (Eds.). (1999). *Organizational learning and the learning organization.* Thousand Oaks, CA: Sage.

Edelbacher, M., & Ivkovic, S. K. (2004). Ethics and the police: Studying police integrity in Austria. In C. B. Klockars, S. K. Ivkovic, and M. R. Haberfeld (Eds.), *The contours of police integrity* (pp. 19–39). Thousand Oaks, CA: Sage Publishing.

Elkjær, B., & Wahlgren, B. (2006). Organizational learning and workplace learning: Similarities and differences. In E. Antonacopoulou, P. Jarvis, V. Andersen, B. Elkjaer & S. Høyrup (Eds.), *Learning, working and living: Mapping the terrain of working life learning*. New York: Palgrave Macmillan.

Felgueiras, S. (2011). Police learning strategies. In B. Akhgar & S. Yates (Eds.), *Intelligence management: Knowledge driven frameworks for combating terrorism and organized crime*. London: Springer Verlag.

Fielding, N. (1984). Police socialization and police competence. *The British Journal of Sociology, 35*(4), 568–590.

Filstad, C. (2010). *Organisasjonslæring: Fra kunnskap til kompetanse (Organizational learning: From knowledge to competence)*. Bergen, Norway: Fagbokforlaget.

Gardiner, P., & Whiting, P. (1997). Success factors in learning organisation: An empirical study. *Industrial and Commercial Training, 29*(2), 41–48.

Garvin, D. A. (2000). *Learning in action: A guide to putting the learning organization at work*. Boston: Havard Business School Press.

Gherardi, S., & Nicolini, D. (2000). To transfer is to transform: The circulation of safety knowledge. *Organization, 7*, 329–348.

Gleerup, J. (2008). Ledelse af kultur i organisationer. In E. E. Sørensen, L. Hounsgaard, B. Ryberg & F. B. Andersen, (Eds.), *Ledelsen og læring: I organisasjoner*. Aarhus: Hans Reitzels Forlag.

Graham, A. (2006). Standards in public life: The challenge of enhancing public trust. *Public Money and Management, 26*(1) 3–5.

Granér, R. (2004). *Patruljerande polisers yrkeskultur*. Lund Dissertations in Social Work, University of Lund, Sweden.

Griego, O. V., Geroy, G. D., & Wright, P. C. (2000). Predictors of learning organizations: The human resource development practitioner's perspective. *The Learning Organization, 7*(1), 5–12.

Grieves, J. (2008). Why we should abandon the idea of the learning organization? *The Learning Organization, 15*(6), 463–473.

Hatch, M. J. (2001). *Organisasjonsteori: Moderne, symbolske og postmoderne perspektiver*. Oslo: Abstrakt Forlag.

Hofstede, G., Neuijen, B., Ohayv, D. D., & Sanders, G. (1990). Measuring organizational cultures: A qualitative and quantitative study across twenty cases. *Administrative Science Quarterly, 35*(2), 286–316.

Jaschke, H. G., Bjørgo, T., Romero, F. del B., Kwanten, C., Mawby, R., & Pogan, M. (2007). *Perspectives of Police Science in Europe*. Final Report, European Police College, CEPOL, Collège Européen de Police, Hampshire, England.

Kabanoff, B., & Daly, J. (2002). Espoused values of organisations. *Australian Journal of Management, 27* (special issue), 89–104.

Kelley, T. M. (2005). Mental health and prospective police professionals. *Policing: An International Journal of Police Strategies & Management, 28*(1), 6–29.

Kiely, J. A., & Peek, G. S. (2002). The culture of the British police: Views of police officers. *The Service Industries Journal, 22*(1), 167–183.

Lahneman, W. J. (2004). Knowledge-sharing in the intelligence community after 9/11. *International Journal of Intelligence and Counterintelligence, 17*, 614–633.

Laursen, E. (2006). Knowledge, progression and the understanding of workplace learning. In E. Antonacopoulou, P. Jarvis, V. Andersen, B. Elkjaer & S. Høyrup (Eds.), *Learning, working and living: Mapping the terrain of working life learning.* New York: Palgrave Macmillan.

Miller, S. (1995). The moral basis of the policing profession: Three issues. In S. Miller (Ed.), *Professional ethics: Proceedings of the professional ethics workshop.* Riverina: Keon Publications.

Moir, P., & Eijkman, H. (1992). *Policing Australia: Old issues, new perspective.* South Melbourne: Macmillan.

Örtenblad, A. (2004). The learning organization: Towards an integrated model. *The Learning Orghanization, 11*(2), 129–144.

Örtenblad, A. (2011). *Making sense of the learning organization: What is it and who needs it?* Kuala Lumpur, Malaysia: Yayasan Ilmuwan.

Pedler, M., Buoydell, T., & Burgoyne, J. (1991). Towards the learning company. *Management Education & Development, 21*(1), 1–8.

Rebelo, T. M., & Gomes, A. D. (2008). Organizational learning and the learning organization: Reviewing evolution for prospecting the future. *The Learning Organization, 15*(4), 294–308.

Reuss-Ianni, E. (1993). *Two cultures of policing: Street cops and management cops.* New Brunswick, NJ: Transaction.

Schafer, J. A. (2009). Enhancing effective leadership in policing: Perils, pitfalls, and paths forward. *Policing: An International Journal of Police Strategies and Management, 32*, 238–260.

Schein, E. H. (1990). Organizational culture. *American Psychologist, 45*(2), 109–119.

Schön, D. (1987). *Educating the reflective practitioner.* San Francisco: Jossey Bass.

Senge, P. (1990). *The fifth discipline: The art and practice of the learning organization.* New York: Doubleday.

Senge, P. M., & Kofman, F. (1995). Communities of commitment: The heart of learning organizations. In S. Chawla & J. Renesch (Eds.), *Learning organizations: Developing cultures for tomorrow's workplace.* Portland, OR: Productivity Press.

Senge, P. M., Roberts, C., Ross, R. B., Smith, B. J., & Kleiner, A. (1994). *The fifth discipline fieldbook: Strategies and tools for building a learning organization.* London: Nicholas Brealey.

Steinheider, B., & Wuestewald, T. (2008). From the bottom up: Sharing leadership in a police agency. *Police Practice and Research, 9*(2), 145–163.

Tannenbaum, S. I. (1997). Enhancing continuous learning: Diagnostic findings from multiple companies. *Human Resource Management, 36*(4), 437–452.

Tsoukas, H., & Chia, R. (2002). On organizational becoming: Rethinking organizational change. *Organizational Science, 13*, 567–582.

Uretsky, M. (2001). Preparing for the real knowledge organization. *Journal of Organizational Excellence, 21*(1), 87–93.

Van Beek, M., Ter Huurne, J., Van Vierssen, D., & Vinter, E. (2005). *Palette for teachers, learning methods for use.* Ubbergen: Tandem Felix Publishers.

Veiga, J., Lubatkin, M., Calori, R., & Very, P. (2000). "Measuring organizational culture clashes: A two-nation post-hoc analysis of a cultural compatibility index. *Human Relations, 53*(4), 539–557.

Vickers, M. H., & Kouzmin, A. (2001). New managerialism and Australian police
    organizations: A cautionary research note. *International Journal of Public Sector
    Management, 14*(1), 7–26.
Weick, K. E., & Westley, F. (1996). Organizational learning: Affirming an oxymoron.
    In S. R. Clegg, C. Hardy & W. Nord (Eds.), *Handbook of organizational studies*.
    London: Routledge.

Police Information Management Strategy 10

Information is of key importance when policing white-collar crime. Information management strategy is one of several strategies that law enforcement organizations develop and implement to improve white-collar crime detection and prevention. Police intelligence is an important element of the strategy. An information management strategy defines management approaches to the organization, control, and application of police information resources through coordination of people and technology resources in order to support policing strategy and processes. While knowledge management strategy focuses on personnel resources and information systems strategy focuses on technology resources, information management strategy focuses on the identification, retrieval, storage, and application of information resources. Important issues in this strategy are information relevance and timeliness (Chaffey & White, 2011).

Managed together, the three resources of information, personnel, and technology must support organizational strategy, which typically is concerned with safety and security in society. For information strategy, Chaffey and White (2011) cite the following 10 strategic issues in guidelines from the Hawley Committee:

1. Information relevancy
2. Organizational significance of information management
3. Legal and ethical compliance
4. Assessing information value
5. Information quality
6. Legal and ethical compliance with specific reference to information lifecycle management
7. Information management skills of employees
8. Information security including risk management
9. Maximizing value from information
10. Information systems strategy

Information systems strategy is treated as a separate strategy field later in this book. For information management strategy, distinctions can be made between information policy, information audit, and information strategy. Information policy is concerned with "what should be" as it defines principles for how information is to be managed. Information audit is concerned with "what is" as it provides an evaluation of current practice. Information strategy is concerned with the future "for a defined period ahead" as it defines objectives, targets, and actions to achieve them (Chaffey & White, 2011).

Criminal Intelligence

A key feature of the process of growth in local and global financial crime has been a steep increase in the complexity involved, brought about, among other things, by numerous innovative mechanisms and instruments that have repeatedly blurred the boundaries between financial sectors:

> Innovative financial products and practices have more often than not generated new linkages among financial agents in different financial sectors. For example, the past 12 years have witnessed a steady growth in cross-sectorial risk transfer between reinsurance and capital markets. (Kattan, King, & Ramella, 2009, p. 353)

New and complicated interrelations among financial sectors have a wide variety of consequences. On the one hand, they may enable and promote efficiency and effectiveness in the allocation of resources, both locally and globally. On the other hand, new connections often bind agents with competing interests with differing degrees of access to information as well as different insights regarding the content of a variety of transactions. Intelligence is needed—both inside and from outside the financial sector—to combat financial crime occurring in novel and complicated interrelations among financial sectors.

Strategic criminal intelligence analysis aims to weigh a variety of crimes against each other in order to base priorities on a calculus of social harm. According to Sheptycki (2007), this implies that strategic analysis attempts to compare different types of criminal activity, including violence, drug distribution and consumption, intellectual property theft, car theft and burglary, smuggling of guns, child pornography, trafficking in humans, stock market fraud, and the avoidance of health and safety legislation in food production.

Chaffey and White (2011) distinguish between the following six information management themes:

1. *Information value* representing importance. Information can be prioritized in importance and better-quality sources identified so that improved information is delivered. Information value can be assessed in terms of its fitness for policing purposes. Once information has been identified as valuable, plans can then be put in

place to protect it from deletion or modification, share it within a defined audience, and improve its quality. Lower-value information can either be improved to increase its relevance to police officers or removed from detailed reports to produce summaries.

2. *Information quality* in terms of content, time, and form. The content dimension is concerned with accuracy (information correct), relevance (information can support decision making), completeness (no data items missing), conciseness (information is not too detailed), and scope (may be broad or narrow, internal or external to the organization). The time dimension is concerned with timeliness (available when needed, immediate or real-time information is a common requirement, alerts are also a requirement), currency (information is up to date), frequency (information supplied at appropriate regular intervals), and time period (a time series covers the right period of time). The form dimension is concerned with clarity (information readily interpreted), detail (both summary "dashboard" views and detailed "drill-down" views may be required), order (data sorted in a logical order and can be modified), presentation (tabulations and graphs), and media (hard copy from printouts, and soft copy electronically stored and displayed).

3. *Information security* to safeguard from accidental or deliberate modification or deletion by people and events. Information and the media, on which it is held, may be destroyed by security breaches. Information security refers to protection of information and the systems and hardware that use, store, and transmit that information. The key features of information security are availability (only to those eligible), confidentiality (only to those eligible), and authenticity and integrity (safeguarding accuracy of information).

4. *Legal and ethical compliance* to handle sensitivity. Information is held about individuals on computer systems. Governments have developed many laws both to protect individuals and to give government agencies access to information that may be needed for law enforcement.

5. *Information resource* for knowledge management. The police are collections of individuals who possess knowledge. Information becomes knowledge when it is interpreted by individuals and put into context. Knowledge is information combined with reflection, interpretation, and context, in which skills and opinions are added to make sense to new insights. Knowledge becomes information when it is codified and stored in information systems.

6. *Information requirement* to technology. Information is handled electronically by computer systems. Technology support to achieve the objectives of the information management strategy involves selecting relevant information systems applications and infrastructure.

Furthermore, Chaffey and White (2011) distinguish between the following five information management approaches:

1. *Structuring the information management function.* The need for a separate organizational structure with a clearly defined information management unit provides a focus for improving information management that everyone in the organization is aware of. The creation of this unit demonstrates a commitment by senior management to information management because they have empowered the group with the resources and responsibility to improve information management.

2. *Responsibilities.* In addition to creation of distinct overall responsibility for information management as a whole, there is a need for governance, stewardship, infrastructure, and usage. Governance responsibility represents management actions for overall direction. Stewardship responsibility involves activities such as information capture or creation, dissemination, and deletion. Infrastructure responsibility is concerned with creating the right environment for using information. Usage responsibility includes assessing information for quality and highlighting problems with quality.

3. *Resource analysis* includes information audit and information mapping. The purpose of information audit is for the organizational information resource to identify actual and potential users of information, information quality requirements for these users, types of information available, where information is held, how information is used, and cost of information usage. The purpose of information mapping is to help the police manage information as a resource by cataloguing, understanding, organizing, and navigating within information sources.

4. *Information policy* highlights the importance of information management to staff and details personnel responsibilities. It is a brief statement of intent of how information should be managed and used within an organization.

5. *Risk management* is used to identify potential risks in a range of situations and then take actions to minimize the risks. Risk management typically has these four steps: (a) identify risks, including their probabilities and impacts; (b) identify possible solutions to these risks; (c) implement the solutions targeting the highest-impact, most likely risks; and (d) monitor the risks to learn for future risk assessment.

Distinct information management strategy is developed in the police to help exploit and protect information assets. An information management strategy may include six themes and five approaches as presented above.

Strategy Characteristics

Traditionally, intelligence was understood to mean information from criminals about criminal activity by a covert source. Today, intelligence is a systematic approach to collecting information with the purpose of tracking and predicting crime to improve law enforcement (Brown, Cannings, & Sherriff, 2004). Intelligence analysts investigate who is committing crimes, how, when, where, and why. They then provide recommendations on how to stop or curb the offenses. As part of this, analysts produce profiles of crime problems and individual targets and produce both strategic (overall, long-term) and tactical (specific, short-term) assessments within the confines set by the policing unit.

The aim of intelligence strategy is to continue to develop intelligence-led policing in all parts of a nation and in all regions of the world. An intelligence strategy provides a framework for a structured problem-solving and partnership-enhanced approach, based around a common model. For example, the National Intelligence Model in the United Kingdom is a structured approach to improving intelligence-led policing both centrally and locally in policing districts such as the South Yorkshire Police (SYPIS, 2007).

Intelligence-led policing is carried out in many law enforcement areas. For example, intelligence-led vehicle crime reduction was carried out in the West Surrey police area in the United Kingdom. Analysis of vehicle crime included identifying the following (Brown et al., 2004):

- Locations (hot spots, streets, parking lots, zip codes, wards, etc.) of vehicle crime
- Sites where vehicles were dumped
- Times of offenses
- Prolific vehicle crime offenders
- Areas where prolific offenders were identified as offending
- Models of vehicles targeted for vehicle crime
- Type of property stolen in theft from vehicle offenses

The analysis resulted in problem profiles, which identified emerging patterns of crime. These patterns included vehicle crime occurring in beauty spot parking lots and the theft of badges from cars. Such information was disseminated to local officers to act upon.

Intelligence-led policing is defined as a business model and a management philosophy according to Ratcliffe (2008):

Intelligence-led policing is a business model and managerial philosophy where data analysis and crime intelligence are pivotal to an objective, decision-making framework that facilitates crime and problem reduction, disruption and prevention through both strategic management and effective enforcement strategies that target prolific and serious offenders. (p. 89)

An interesting case of intelligence-led policing in the United Kingdom was the project called "Operation Gallant" that lead to a reduction of 17% in car thefts. Operation Gallant involved all basic command units (BCU) in the collection and analysis of information:

> In the case of Operation Gallant, the intelligence-led vehicle crime reduction approach involved the activity of officers from across a BCU. A crime analyst, dedicated solely to examine vehicle crime patterns and trends, developed a detailed picture of vehicle crime in the area, including analysis of time, location, vehicle type and known offenders. As a result of this strategic analysis, a number of interventions were planned, drawing heavily upon the Operation Igneous tactical menu. The most significant, in terms of resources devoted to the operation, involved a program of prolific offender targeting and crime prevention advice targeted towards the owners of high-risk vehicles. (Brown et al., 2004, p. 2)

The substantial decline in car crimes was accounted for in terms of the increased attention paid to this crime sector:

> Given the fact that the first reduction coincides with the commencement of the planning process for Operation Gallant, this may also reflect an anticipatory effect in which the very act of planning and talking about an operation leads to a decline. (Brown et al., 2004, p. 16)

Classification of Information Sources

In intelligence work pertaining to investigating and preventing white-collar crime, a variety of information sources are available. Sheptycki (2007) lists the following information sources in policing for general corporate social responsibility work: victim reports, witness reports, police reports, crime scene examinations, historical data held by police agencies (such as criminal records), prisoner debriefings, technical or human surveillance products, suspicious financial transaction reporting, and reports emanating from undercover police operations. Similarly, internal investigation units in business organizations can apply intelligence sources. Intelligence analysis may also refer to the governmental records of other governmental departments and agencies and other, more open, sources of information may also be used in elaborate intelligence assessment. Most of the information used to prevent and investigate financial crime is sensitive, complex, and the result of a time-consuming process (Wilhelmsen, 2009).

However, Sheptycki (2007) found that most crime analysis is organized around existing investigation and prevention sector data. Intelligence analysis is typically framed in terms of preexisting institutional ways of thinking.

He argues that organized crime notification, classification, and measurement schemes tend to reify preexisting notions of traditional policing practice.

According to this perspective, it is important for strategic criminal analysts to be aware of the variety of information sources available. In this book we have chosen to classify information sources into the following categories:

1. *Interview.* By means of *interrogation* of witnesses, suspects, reference persons, and experts, information is collected on crimes, criminals, times and places, organizations, criminal projects, activities, roles, and so forth.
2. *Network.* By means of *informants* in the criminal underworld as well as in legal businesses, information is collected on actors, plans, competitors, markets, customers, and so forth. Informants often have connections with persons that an investigating colleague would be unable to formally approach.
3. *Location.* By analyzing potential and actual *crime scenes* and potential criminal scenes, information is collected on criminal procedures, preferences, crime evolution, and so forth. Hot spots and traces are found. Secret ransacking of suspicious places is one aspect of this information source. Pictures, in terms of crime scene photographs, are important information elements.
4. *Documents.* Studying documents obtained through *confiscation* may provide information on ownership, transactions, accounts, and so forth. One such example is forensic accounting, which is the application of accounting tasks for an evidentiary purpose. Forensic accounting is the action of identifying, recording, settling, extracting, sorting, reporting, and verifying past financial data or other accounting activities for settling current or prospective legal disputes or using such past financial data to project future financial data in order to settle legal disputes (Curtis, 2008).
5. *Observation.* By means of *anonymous personal presence*, both individuals and activities can be observed. Both in the physical and the virtual world, observation is important in financial crime intelligence. An example is digital forensics, in which successful cybercrime intelligence requires computer skills and modern systems in policing. Digital forensics is the art and science of applying computer science to aid the legal process. It amounts to more than the technological, systematic inspection of electronic systems and their contents for evidence or supportive evidence of a criminal act; digital forensics requires specialized expertise and tools when applied to intelligence in important areas, such as the online victimization of children.

6. *Action.* For example, *provocation* and actions conducted by the investigating unit to cause reactions that yield intelligence information. In the case of the online victimization of children, online grooming offenders in a pedophile ring are identified, and their reaction to provocation leads intelligence officers to new nodes (persons, computers) and new actual and potential victims. While the individual pedophile is mainly concerned with combining indecent image impression and personal fantasy to achieve personal satisfaction, online organizers of sexual abuse of children do so for profit. Police initiate contact with criminal business enterprises making money from pedophile customers by claiming online to be a child of nine years, for example. Undercover operations by police officers also belong to the action category of information sources.

7. *Surveillance.* Surveillance (visual and auditory) of places by means of *video cameras* and microphones belong to this information source. Many business organizations have surveillance cameras on their premises to control entrants and also other critical areas. It is possible for the police to listen in on discussions in a room without the participants knowing. For example, police in a district identified the room used by local Hells Angels members for crime planning and installed listening devices in the room. Harfield (2008, p. 64) argues that when surveillance is employed to produce evidence, the product is often considered incontrovertible (hence defense lawyers' focus on process rather than product when cross-examining surveillance officers): "An essentially covert activity, by definition surveillance lacks transparency and is therefore vulnerable to abuse by over-zealous investigators."

8. *Communication control.* Wiretapping in terms of *interception* belongs to this information source. Police listen in on what is discussed on a telephone or transmitted via a data line without the participants being aware. In the United Kingdom, the interception of communications (telephone calls, emails, letters, etc.), while generating intelligence to identify more conventional evidential opportunities, is excluded from trial evidence by law—to the evident incredulity of foreign law enforcement colleagues (Harfield, 2008).

9. *Physical material.* This is the investigation of material in order to identify, for example, *fingerprints* on doors or bags, or material to investigate blood splatters and identify blood type. Another example is legal visitation; this is an approach to identify illegal material. DNA is emerging as an important information source and is derived from physical material, such as hair or saliva from a person. One approach to physical material collection is police search.

10. *Internet.* As an *open source*, the Internet is as important for general information and specific happenings to corporate crime intelligence as

to everyone else. It is important to note that use of open sources is by no means a new activity and nor is it a new phenomenon of the Internet, which is in itself not a source; rather it is a tool used for finding sources. Also, there are risks of using open sources such as self-corroboration.

11. *Policing systems. Police records* are readily available in most police agencies. For example, DNA records may prove helpful when DNA material from new suspects is collected. Similarly, corporate social responsibility units may collate and develop records that do not violate privacy rights.

12. *Employees.* Information from the *local community* is often supplied in the form of tips to local police, using law enforcement tip lines. Similarly, a corporate social responsibility unit can receive tips from employees in various departments.

13. *Accusations.* Victimized persons and goods file a *claim* with the corporate investigation unit or the unit for corporate social responsibility.

14. *Exchange.* International *policing cooperation* includes exchange of intelligence information. International partners for national police include national police in other countries as well as multinational organizations, such as Europol and Interpol. Similarly, trade organizations and other entities for business organizations create exchanges for financial crime intelligence.

15. *Media.* Intelligence officers are exposed to the *news* by reading newspapers and watching TV.

16. *Control authorities.* Cartel agencies, stock exchanges, tax authorities, and other control authorities are *suppliers of information* to the corporate executives in the event of suspicious transactions.

17. *External data storage.* A number of business and government organizations store information that may prove useful in financial crime intelligence. For example, telecom firms store data about traffic, in which both the sender and the recipient are registered with date and time of communication.

All these information sources have different characteristics. For example, information sources can be distinguished in terms of the extent of trustworthiness and accessibility.

Prisons and other correctional environments are potential places for several information sources and production of intelligence useful to law enforcement. The total prison environment, including the physical plant, the schedule regimens of both staff and inmates, and all points of ingress and egress can be legitimately tapped for intelligence purposes in countries such as the United States (Maghan, 1994). Because organized criminals are often sophisticated in terms of using, or exploiting, the correction environment to their advantage, police and correction personnel need to be immersed in the intelligence operations and strategies of their respective agencies. Legal visitation and escape attempts are sources of information. Prisoners are reluctant to testify, and their credibility is easily attacked. Communication control is derived from inmate use of phones, visits, mail, and other contacts.

The 17 information sources can be classified into two main categories. The first category includes all person-oriented information sources, with which the challenge in corporate intelligence is communication with individuals. The second category includes all media-oriented information sources, with which the challenge in corporate intelligence is the management and use of different technological and other media. This distinction into two main categories leads to the following classification of 17 information sources:

A. Person-oriented information sources
  1 Interrogation in interview
  2 Informants in network
  5 Anonymous, individual presence undercover for observation
  6 Provocation through action
  12 Tips from citizens in local community
  13 Claims in accusations
  14 Information exchange in interorganizational cooperation
B. Media-oriented information sources
  3 Crime scenes at location
  4 Confiscated documents
  7 Video cameras for surveillance
  8 Interception for communication control
  9 Physical material, such as fingerprints
  10 Open sources, such as the Internet
  11 Internal records in policing systems
  15 News in the media
  16 Supply of information from control authorities
  17 External data storage

Combinations of information sources are selected in investigation and intelligence according to the subject of white-collar crime. When forensic accounting is applied as document study, it is typically combined with interviews and observations, thereby integrating behavioral aspects into forensic accounting (Ramamoorti, 2008).

Forensic Accounting

Forensic accounting is concerned with identifying, recording, settling, extracting, sorting, reporting, and verifying past financial data. The focus of forensic accounting is upon evidence revealed by the examination of financial documents. The evidence collected or prepared by a forensic accountant may be applied in different contexts. For example, forensic accounting results can serve as evidence in an internal corporate investigation that leads either only to internal discipline or no action whatsoever (Curtis, 2008).

Forensic accounting as a discipline has its own models and methodologies of investigative procedures, which search for assurance, attestation, and advisory perspectives in order to produce legal evidence. It is concerned with the evidentiary nature of accounting data and, as a practical field, is concerned with accounting fraud and forensic auditing; compliance, due diligence, and risk assessment; and detection of financial statement misrepresentation and financial statement fraud (Skousen & Wright, 2008) as well as tax evasion, bankruptcy and valuation studies, violations of accounting regulations, nonstandard entries, structured transactions, records tampering, and earnings mismanagement.

Forensic accountants apply decision aids as well as professional judgment in their work (Chan, Lowe, & Yao, 2008). Decision aids comprise technology and systems that offer the potential to improve detection of white-collar crime in accounting. Hughes, Louwers, and Reynolds (2008) argue that strong corporate control environments are critical to responsible and reliable detection of misconduct.

Forensic results can also serve as evidence in a professional disciplinary hearing or other administrative proceedings, such as an administrative enforcement procedure by financial authorities. As with evidence in some phases of a criminal action, the weight that a testimony carries will depend on a number of factors, the most important, according to Curtis (2008), being whether the forensic accountant can be qualified as an expert and thus whether the opinion of the accountant actually qualifies as an expert opinion. Forensic accounting is often used in conjunction with interviews and inspections, which incorporates some psychological characteristics into the practice (Ramamoorti, 2008). Forensic accounting is emerging as a specialist discipline (Kranacher, Morris, Pearson, & Riley, 2008).

Financial crime, such as fraud, can be subject to forensic accounting because fraud encompasses the acquisition of property or economic advantage by means of deception through either misrepresentation or concealment. Forensic examinations include consideration of digital evidence, including communications (Curtis, 2008).

To develop investigative knowledge in the area of forensic accounting, Kranacher et al. (2008) suggest a model curriculum consisting of several concepts, such as basic accounting, basic auditing, transaction processing, business law, business communication, and computer skills. The purpose of such a curriculum is to build up knowledge, skills, and abilities in forensic accounting in order to combat white-collar crime.

Accounting, in general, and forensic accounting, in particular (Baird & Zelin, 2009), are important investigative tools for the detection of white-collar crime. However, Carnegie and Napier (2010) found that society's perception of the legitimacy of the accounting profession and accounting professionals has suffered following scandals such as Enron:

> The unexpected collapse of Enron and the bewildering demise of Arthur Andersen in the aftermath sent shock waves through the accounting profession worldwide. The impact of Enron's collapse was greater because it was closely followed by the bankruptcy of WorldCom in the USA, while scandals and collapses involving companies such as HIH Insurance in Australia, Parmalat in Italy, Royal Ahold in the Netherlands and Equitable Life Assurance Society in the UK showed that this was not just a U.S. phenomenon. "Enronitis" became a label associated with highly questionable accounting and auditing practices. Although these practices were widely condemned as they became public knowledge, they sharply undermined confidence in corporate financial reporting and auditing as well as corporate regulation. (p. 360)

As a consequence, accountants have to deal with an increasing variety of new rules on corporate governance, audit independence, and financial reporting. Carnegie and Napier (2010) applied legitimacy and social contract theory to portray the consequences of this for the accounting profession after Enron. According to legitimacy theory, business organizations are part of a broader social system and do not possess an inherent right to own or use resources or even to exist. Society confers legitimacy upon an organization whereby legitimacy is defined as a condition or status that exists when an entity's value system is congruent with the value system of the larger social system that the entity is a part of. Under social contract theory, the basic morality is adherence to uniform social accords that serve the best interests of those entering into agreement. Social contract theory is concerned with showing how individual and social group rights and liberties are founded on mutually advantageous agreements between members of society.

Forensic accounting is dependent on a link between accounting information and intelligence management. Despite calls that management accounting should generally be linked more closely to management, Hall (2010) found that there is still a great deal to be learned concerning the role of accounting information in managerial work. Similarly, there is much to be learned about the role of forensic accounting in white-collar detection, prevention, and strategy in business enterprises.

Crime Intelligence Analysis

For Innes, Fielding, and Cope (2005), crime analysis is concerned with insight and understanding:

There has been a move away from an ad hoc, intuitive and largely unstructured mode of analytic work, to a more ordered, rationalized approach, based upon specific methodologies, on the basis that this provides a more "objective" perspective on patterns of crime and offending. This has raised the profile and status of intelligence analysis within policing, and seen new techniques and technologies introduced, which should, at least in theory, allow police a better understanding of how, when and why crimes are occurring. (p. 41)

The Council of Europe (2002) described crime analysis as a law enforcement function whereby data relating to crime are collected, collated, analyzed, and disseminated. Crime analysis is the study of crime patterns and trends in an attempt to solve crimes or prevent their repeat occurrence.

A distinction can be made between operational/tactical analysis and strategic analysis. Operational analysis is directed toward a short-term law enforcement goal with an immediate impact in mind (e.g., arrest, seizure, and forfeiture). The goal of strategic crime analysis is to develop or implement a policy or to evaluate a policy based on insights regarding the nature of a type of crime or criminal and the scope and projections of growth in types of criminal activities. However, strategic analyses need not be restricted to crime; methods of strategic analysis can be used, in principle, for all kinds of security and safety issues. Strategic analysis can deal with crime as well as with other security issues, such as traffic problems and public order maintenance. According to the Council of Europe (2002), it departs from the question of which information is needed and which data is lacking. A structured plan has to be developed and discussed. The next steps are the detection of a problem, the consideration of a new phenomenon, and the gathering of information.

Examples of strategic crime analysis include the following:

- *Crime pattern analysis*: Examination of the nature and distribution of crime within an area in order to identify emerging and current trends and patterns, linked crimes or incidents, and hot spots of activity. This includes crime trend identification, crime series identification, general profile analysis, and hot spot analysis alongside examination of the nature and scale of crime within a defined area and within a time frame.
- *Crime control methods analysis*: Evaluation of investigative or preventive methods and techniques with the aim of establishing their future usefulness.
- *General profile analysis*: Identification of the typical characteristics of perpetrators of certain crimes.
- *Results analysis*: Evaluation of the effectiveness of law enforcement activities.

- *Demographic/social trends analysis*: Examination of the nature of demographic changes and their impact on criminality as well as the analysis of social factors (e.g., unemployment), which might underlie changing trends in offending patterns. Also, statistical description of the constitution of the population of a given area and the associated economic indicators with reference to law enforcement requirements.
- *Criminal business analysis/profile*: The examination of how illegal operations/businesses and techniques work in detail.
- *Market profile*: A survey of the criminal market around a given commodity (e.g., illicit drugs, stolen vehicles). It can include crime pattern analysis and network analysis.
- *Strategic analysis*: A category of types of crime analysis designed to aid the formation or evaluation of crime policy. The aims are to provide information that can depict a phenomenon and which can identify trends in criminality upon which management can base their decisions.

The United Nations has made illicit businesses a target of law enforcement. This is important because, besides violating human rights, illicit businesses preclude proper economic development and collectively make up as much as 10% of the global economy. Byrne (2011) argues that given the scope of this complex ethical problem, it is fortuitous that law-making institutions, including the UN, have been clarifying the issues at stake.

Examples of tactical/operational crime analysis include the following:

- *Specific profile analysis*: Identification of the specific characteristics of perpetrators of certain crimes. This entails construction of a hypothetical picture of the perpetrator of a serious crime or series of offenses on the basis of crime scene data, witness statements, and other available information.
- *Offender group analysis*: Examination of the structure of a group of suspects, the significance of each member and their involvement with criminal activities.
- *Investigations/operations analysis*: Evaluation of the effectiveness of activities that are undertaken within the context of an investigation.
- *Case analysis*: Establishment of the course of events immediately before, during, and after a serious offense.
- *Comparative case analysis*: Identification of a series of crimes with common offenders by seeking similarities between offenses.
- *Operational crime analysis*: Category of types of crime analysis designed to support the investigation of one particular crime or one

specific series of crimes with common offender(s). It aims to provide an understanding of the information collected during a specific investigation.

- *Network analysis*: Provision of a detailed picture of the roles played by individuals, the nature and significance of the links between people and the strengths and weaknesses of the criminal network.

References

Baird, J. E., & Zelin, R. C. (2009). An examination of the impact of obedience pressure on perceptions of fraudulent acts and the likelihood of committing occupational fraud. *Journal of Forensic Studies in Accounting and Business, 1*(1), 1–14.

Brown, R., Cannings, A., & Sherriff, J. (2004). *Intelligence-led vehicle crime reduction: an evaluation of Operation Gallant*, Home Office Online Report 47/04. Retrieved from http://www.homeoffice.gov.uk/rds/pdfs04/rdsolr4704.pdf.

Byrne, E. F. (2011). Business ethics should study illicit businesses: To advance respect for human rights. *Journal of Business Ethics, 103*, 497–509.

Carnegie, G. D., & Napier, C. J. (2010). Traditional accountants and business professionals: Portraying the accounting profession after Enron. *Accounting, Organizations and Society, 35*, 360–376.

Chaffey, D., & White, G. (2011). *Business information management* (2nd ed.). London: Prentice Hall.

Chan, S. H., Lowe, D. J., & Yao, L. J. (2008). The legal implications of auditors using a fraud decision aid vs. professional judgment. *Journal of Forensic Accounting, 9*, 63–82.

Council of Europe. (2002). *Crime analysis: Organized crime—Best practice survey no. 4*, Economic Crime Division, Department of Crime Problems, Directorate General I—Legal Affairs, Council of Europe, Strasbourg, France.

Curtis, G. E. (2008). Legal and regulatory environments and ethics: Essential components of a fraud and forensic accounting curriculum. *Issues in Accounting Education, 23*(4), 535–543.

Hall, M. (2010). Accounting information and managerial work. *Accounting, Organizations and Society, 35*, 301–315.

Harfield, C. (2008). Paradigms, pathologies, and practicalities: Policing organized crime in England and Wales. *Policing, 2*(1), 63–73.

Hughes, K. E., Louwers, T. J., & Reynolds, J. K. (2008). Toward an expanded control environment framework. *Journal of Forensic Accounting, 9*, 115–128.

Innes, M., Fielding, N., & Cope, N. (2005). The appliance of science: The theory and practice of crime intelligence analysis. *British Journal of Criminology, 45*, 39–57.

Kattan, W., King, W., & Ramella, M. (2009). Handling conflicts of interest within financial innovation: The case of regulation and supervision of Bermuda sidecars. *Journal of Financial Crime, 16*(4), 353–363.

Kranacher, M. J., Morris, B. W., Pearson, T. A., & Riley, A. (2008). A model curriculum for education in fraud and forensic accounting. *Issues in Accounting Education, 23*(4), 505–519.

Maghan, J. (1994). Intelligence gathering approaches in prisons. *Low Intensity Conflict & Law Enforcement, 3*(3), 548–557.

Ramamoorti, S. (2008). The psychology and sociology of fraud: Integrating the behavioral sciences component into fraud and forensic accounting curricula. *Issues in Accounting Education, 23*(4), 521–533.

Ratcliffe, J. H. (2008). *Intelligence-led policing.* Devon, UK: Willan Publishing.

Sheptycki, J. (2007). Police ethnography in the house of serious and organized crime. In A. Henry & D. J. Smith (Eds.), *Transformations of policing* (pp. 51–77). Oxford: Ashgate Publishing.

Skousen, C. J., & Wright, C. J. (2008). Contemporaneous risk factors and the prediction of financial statement fraud. *Journal of Forensic Accounting, 9,* 37–62.

SYPIS (2007). *South Yorkshire Police Intelligence Strategy 2007—Breaking the chain,* South Yorkshire Police, UK. Retrieved from www.policereform.gov.uk.

Wilhelmsen, S. (2009). *Maximising organizational information sharing and effective intelligence analysis in critical data sets.* PhD dissertation. University of Bergen, Norway.

Police Knowledge Management Strategy 11

Knowledge is of key importance when policing white-collar crime. In policing, performance risk and execution risk reflect the knowledge deficits impeding process performance. Where knowledge deficits exist, incomplete information and know-how give rise to uncertainties that obscure prediction and execution. Performance risk and execution risk are lowered through knowledge transfer mechanisms developed to avoid and handle uncertainties. Such knowledge transfer permits knowledge reuse, and the recombination of existing knowledge is an important antecedent of uncertainty resolution (Mitchell, 2006).

Knowledge management strategy focuses on personnel resources, and the knowledge of each police officer as well as the combined knowledge in the police represents resources that are to be explored and exploited for better police work. The knowledge management strategy process includes developing a working definition of knowledge, developing a working definition of knowledge management, doing a knowledge audit, defining knowledge management objectives and strategy approaches, and implementing a strategy with quality measures (Chaffey & White, 2011).

Intelligence for Knowledge

In 2008, the office of the director of national intelligence in the United States published Vision 2015, which expands upon the notion of an intelligence enterprise. It was first introduced in the National Intelligence Strategy and later in the 100- and 500-Day Plans (ODNI, 2008). It charts a new path for a globally networked and integrated intelligence enterprise for the 21st century, founded on the principles of integration, collaboration, and innovation.

The vision is focused on knowledge management:

> By 2015, the focus should shift from information sharing (e.g., interoperable systems, information discovery and access) to knowledge sharing (e.g., capturing and disseminating both explicit and tacit knowledge). Just as we are dismantling today's information "silos," we will need to bridge the knowledge "archipelagos" of tomorrow in a systematic way that combines both content and context in an on-demand environment. Robust social networking capabilities will be required—expertise location, ubiquitous collaboration services,

integrated e-learning solutions, visualization tools, and enterprise content management systems. More importantly, a strategic approach to knowledge sharing and management must be incorporated that includes lessons learned and concept and doctrine development. (ODNI, 2008, p. 15)

When discussing implementation of the vision, ODNI (2008) stresses the importance of adaptability, alignment, and agility. Adaptability is an organization's aptitude for anticipating, sensing, and responding successfully to changes in the environment. Alignment is the degree of consistency and coherence among an institution's core strategy, systems, processes, and communications. Agility is an organization's ability to reconfigure processes and structures quickly—with minimal effort and resources—to seize opportunities and address strategic risks.

Management Approaches

Collier (2006) argues that effective knowledge management is as important to investigating and preventing crime as it is to any other public or private sector organization in terms of improving performance. Over the past 10 years, there has been a shift from a reactive, response-led approach to a proactive, intelligence-led style of law enforcement. In the UK, Norway, Sweden, and many other countries, the intelligence-led approach has been developed into a systematic approach, such as NIM by national criminal intelligence services. The intelligence used in both strategic and tactical assessments is derived from a number of knowledge and information sources, and the production of assessments represents knowledge work as well.

Wilhelmsen (2009) found that "since knowledge and experience often are obtained with great personal and work related costs, the individual or the organization can develop emotional ownership to the information and not be willing to share all they know." However, sharing knowledge in suspected crime cases is vital because misleading or false information can have unfortunate and harmful consequences.

The working definition of knowledge suggested by Chaffey and White (2011) is as follows:

The combination of data and information, to which is added expert opinion, skills and experience, to result in a valuable asset which can be used to aid decision making. Knowledge may be explicit and/or tacit, individual and/or collective. (p. 209)

Explicit knowledge refers to details of processes or procedures that have been codified or captured and recorded. Explicit knowledge can be readily detailed in procedural manuals and databases. Examples include records of meetings, records of interviews with suspected white-collar criminals, and management reports. Tacit knowledge is less tangible than explicit knowledge. It refers to experience on how to react to a policing situation when many different variables are involved. It is more difficult to encapsulate this knowledge, which often resides in the heads of employees. Techniques for sharing this knowledge include learning stories and histories. Examples include knowing how to react when changes occur in a police interview or in a terrorist attack (Chaffey & White, 2011).

Knowledge work refers to organizational activities and occupations that are characterized by an emphasis on theoretical knowledge, creativity, and use of analytical and social skills. Knowledge work encompasses both what is traditionally referred to as professional work and also more contemporary types of work. In these kinds of work, knowledge acts as the main input into the work, the major way of achieving the work, and the major output (Newell, Robertson, Scarbrough, & Swan, 2009).

The term "knowledge worker" encompasses, then, both professionals and those with other discipline-based knowledge or more esoteric expertise and skills, whose major work tasks involve the creation of new knowledge or the application of existing knowledge in new ways. Knowledge workers typically have high levels of education and specialized skills combined with the ability to apply these skills in practice to identify and solve problems (Newell et al., 2009).

Knowledge collaboration is defined as the sharing, transfer, recombination, and reuse of knowledge among parties. Collaboration is a process that allows parties to leverage their differences in interests, concerns, and knowledge (Jarvenpaa & Majchrzak, 2012).

In knowledge collaboration, teams are considered to be an important building block in today's knowledge-based police organizations. An important factor affecting team performance is socio-cognitive processes. A key problem underlying the socio-cognitive process in teams is the uneven distribution of knowledge among individuals in the team. In particular, Choi, Lee, and Yoo (2010) argue that a socio-cognitive structure called the transactive memory system plays a particularly important role in a team's ability to leverage team members' knowledge in team performance. A transactive memory system refers to a specialized division of cognitive labor that develops within a team with respect to the encoding, storage, and retrieval of knowledge from different domains. The cognitive labor implies that team members know who knows what and who knows who knows what.

One of the main challenges in managing an organization's knowledge is transferring knowledge from its source to its destination where it is needed. Unlike tangible assets, such as police cars and arms, the police organization often does not know if they have relevant knowledge and where it potentially is located. Furthermore, they do not know how much it is worth to them as compared to a big military-type car versus a police motorcycle (Liu, Ray, & Whinston, 2010).

A distinction is often made between knowledge exploitation and knowledge exploration. Exploitation refers to solution reuse while exploration refers to solution innovation. Exploitation leverages existing knowledge through the application of pre-established procedures, technologies, and policing approaches. Exploration can lead to new investigative approaches and new policing procedures (Durcikova, Fadel, Butler, & Galletta, 2011).

Police Knowledge

Policing is heavily dependent on information, intelligence, and knowledge. The amount of information police officers come in contact with in the course of their work is often astounding. With a more proactive and preventive approach to crime reduction, police forces have increasingly relied on information and knowledge and associated information technology in terms of knowledge management systems to improve their performance. Accordingly, the management of knowledge is a crucial aspect of policing work to promote knowledge development and sharing.

Knowledge is indispensable to modern policing. Police ability to create, identify, share, and apply knowledge directly affects its competitive advantage (Choi et al., 2010). Of special importance is financial crime knowledge among corporate executives. Investigation and prevention of financial crime requires that board members and executive managers have knowledge about crime categories and motives. Executives need to be knowledgeable about contexts, complexities, and also connections. Bevan and Gitsham (2009) argue that such knowledge can be developed through leadership development programs whereby the appropriate knowledge and skills are sought when recruiting new talent into the organization, and the knowledge and skills are subsequently built upon through career development planning and succession planning while ensuring that performance management and incentive systems enable and reward the building and acquisition of such knowledge and that such knowledge is developed through individual as well as collective competency frameworks.

Knowledge management has also become important in corporate social responsibility work. Companies increasingly find themselves under pressure to adopt socially responsible forms of operation to prevent financial crime. Preuss and Cordoba-Pachon (2009) distinguish between the element view and the process view of corporate social responsibility knowledge. Elements of knowledge are technical knowledge and knowledge held by other functions. Processes of knowledge are new ways of working with internal and external stakeholders.

Knowledge management implies that an organization has adopted a structured approach to utilizing knowledge. A structured approach typically includes knowledge identification, new knowledge generation, knowledge storage, knowledge distribution, and knowledge application. Both individual and organizational knowledge capabilities have to be taken into account. Individual knowledge capabilities include ambition, skills, behavior, tools, and time. Organizational knowledge capabilities include mission, vision, strategy, culture, process and organization, measurement, and assets (Chaffey & White, 2011).

Knowledge Integration

In knowledge management, the *theory of absorptive capacity* is important. Absorptive capacity is viewed as a dynamic capability of processing knowledge that enhances organizational innovation (Joshi, Chi, Datta, & Han, 2010). More specifically, absorptive capacity is an organization's ability to identify, assimilate, transform, and apply valuable external knowledge (Roberts, Galluch, Dinger, & Grover, 2012). Through their law enforcement activities, the police develop collective knowledge about certain areas of crime, criminals, behaviors, and motives. This knowledge base enhances the organization's ability to identify and value external knowledge. However, sheer exposure to related external knowledge is not sufficient to ensure that the police organization will absorb it successfully. The knowledge must be assimilated or transformed into the organization's knowledge base. While a knowledge base enables the associative connections needed for insights into new white-collar crime cases, the organizational assimilation of new knowledge depends more upon the transfer of knowledge across and within policing units. The police apply their newly absorbed knowledge in a variety of ways, for example, to replenish their knowledge base, to forecast crime trends, to reconfigure existing capabilities, and to create innovative policing services.

Access to external knowledge enables the importation of new knowledge coupled with the recombination of existing knowledge. Recombination avoids the inside view, which refers to an insular approach to policing, in which intuition and knowledge of current cases are used to forecast future case outcomes. Bold forecasts are reduced when police executives adopt an outside view, which refers to an active search of complementing and contradicting knowledge. The outside view avoids distortion related to historical bias (Mitchell, 2006).

There are three assumptions underlying absorptive capacity (Roberts et al., 2012):

- Absorptive capacity depends on prior related knowledge. Without some prior related knowledge, the police will not be able to accurately determine the potential value of external knowledge. This implies that absorptive capacity is domain-specific.
- An organization's absorptive capacity depends on the absorptive capabilities of its individual members. However, it is not simply the

sum of its members' absorptive capacities. Rather, it depends on the links between individuals as well. Thus, the organization's absorptive capacity is formed from an overlap in individual members' knowledge across and within police units. These overlaps imply that absorptive capacity is unit-specific and police-specific.

- An organization's absorptive capacity is path-dependent. Accumulating absorptive capacity in one period will permit its more efficient accumulation in the next. Likewise, in an uncertain environment, absorptive capacity affects expectation formation, permitting the police to predict more accurately the nature and potential of new knowledge. These two features of absorptive capacity—cumulativeness and its effect on expectation formation—imply that its development is path-dependent.

According to Roberts et al. (2012), organizational scholars have viewed absorptive capacity from two general perspectives: as a stock of prior related knowledge and as an ability to understand new knowledge. When viewed as an asset, absorptive capacity is referred to as the level of relevant prior knowledge possessed by the police unit. When viewed as ability, absorptive capacity is referred to as the extent to which the police unit is able to change according to new knowledge.

Within absorptive capacity Mitchell (2006) stresses the importance of knowledge integration. The knowledge integration process involves social interactions among individuals using internal communication channels for knowledge transfer to arrive at a common perspective for problem solving. Where organizational units hold specialized knowledge, inter-unit linkages are the primary means of transferring knowledge.

Transferring knowledge among experts in the police is not the only possible approach to knowledge integration. An alternative approach is combination of specialized, differentiated, but complementary knowledge. As the problem of knowledge integration is usually conceived as a consequence of the benefits of specialization, Tell (2011) finds it not surprising that many definitions characterize knowledge integration as a process/activity whereby such specialized knowledge is combined—rather than shared and transferred. This means that when studying and conceptualizing knowledge integration at the level of people and processes, projects and partnerships, and strategies and outcomes, the fundamental problem of knowledge integration lies in understanding the process involving the combination of specialized knowledge bases embodied in individuals. To be successful, a minimum of common knowledge has to be present to enable knowledge integration of completely specialized knowledge.

When integration of knowledge is conceptualized as combination of expert knowledge, the core argument developed by Söderlund and Bredin (2011) is that knowledge integration depends on the individual actors' abilities to participate in knowledge integration processes and, hence, that the individuals' behavior and skills are central for the analysis of such processes. It is at this level that different areas of expertise and problem-solving cycles typically are being integrated. This is perhaps especially true for complex crime investigations such as white-collar crime, in which expert knowledge of finance, organization, management, psychology, law, communication, and sociology is often needed in a well-integrated process. If knowledge collectivities are playing an increasingly important role for knowledge integration and problem-solving in police work, it seems imperative to address how individual officers relate to less developed groups and new organizational context and how they cope with increasingly higher demands for flexibility and mobility.

Knowledge Categories

A number of approaches to knowledge management are available in the literature. Wang (2009) describes these approaches as schools of knowledge management strategy. First, the systems school strategies aim to capture and store information based on knowledge of individuals in knowledge support repositories. This implies that the fundamental concerns of the system school are the creation and codification of knowledge. Next, the cartographic school strategies focus on mapping knowledge by creating yellow pages or directories of knowledge owners. When people need certain kinds of knowledge, they look in the yellow pages to find who has the knowledge needed and how this person can be reached.

Third, the process school strategies aim to provide people not only with the knowledge they request but also with the most useful knowledge that is relevant to their current tasks. This implies an approach to equip individuals with the knowledge they need to effectively perform their tasks. Next, the commercial school strategies support the concept of managing knowledge as an asset and stress the importance of organizations' capability of recognizing the economic value of their knowledge. Fifth, the organizational school strategies aim to facilitate knowledge management activities by designing organizational structures or interorganizational networks that connect knowledge owners for sharing knowledge. Sixth, the spatial school strategies take advantage of the use of space to facilitate knowledge exchange. Socialization, such as face-to-face contact, is critical because it accounts for a significant proportion of the transferred knowledge. Seventh, and finally, the strategic school strategies aim to examine the knowledge, as a key organizational resource, preserved by an organization in order to determine what competitive advantages the organization can generate by utilizing its knowledge (Wang, 2009).

According to all these schools of knowledge management strategies, knowledge has to be identified in terms of categories and levels. One identification approach suggested here is the knowledge matrix approach. A knowledge matrix is a table that lists knowledge needs. The matrix shows knowledge categories and knowledge levels.

Here we make distinctions between the following knowledge categories for investigating and preventing financial crime:

1. *Administrative knowledge* is knowledge about the role of management and executive leadership. It is knowledge about procedures, rules, and regulations.
2. *Organizational knowledge* is knowledge about how the business is organized and management as a law enforcement role. This is knowledge at the organizational level.
3. *Employee knowledge* is knowledge about where employees spend their working hours, what they do, and why they do it. This is knowledge at the individual level.
4. *Process knowledge* is knowledge about work processes and practices in business work when committing financial crime. Process knowledge is based on police science, which includes all aspects of policing, internally as well as externally (Jaschke et al., 2007). It includes external factors that influence the role and behavior of policing in society.
5. *Investigative knowledge* is knowledge based on the case-specific and case-oriented collection of information to confirm or disconfirm whether an act or no act is criminal. Included here are case documents and evidence in such a form that they prove useful in a court case.
6. *Intelligence knowledge* is knowledge based on a systematic collection of information concerned with a certain topic, a certain domain, certain persons, or any other focused scope. Collected information is transformed and processed according to a transparent methodology to discover criminal capacity, dispositions and goals. Transformation and processing generate new insights into criminality that guide the effectiveness and efficiency of prevention and investigation. Included in intelligence knowledge is phenomenological knowledge, which is defined as knowledge about a phenomenon, in terms of what it is about (know-what), how it works (know-how), and why it works (know-why). Phenomenological knowledge enables intelligence workers to "see" what "something" is about by understanding and not overlooking information that emerges.
7. *Legal knowledge* is knowledge of the law, regulations, and legal procedures. It is based on access to a variety of legal sources both nationally and internationally, including court decisions. Legal knowledge is composed of declarative, procedural, and analytical knowledge. Declarative knowledge is law and other regulations. Procedural knowledge is the practice of law. Analytical knowledge is the link between case information and laws.

8. *Technological knowledge* is knowledge about the development, use, exploitation, and exploration of information and communication technology. It is knowledge about applications, systems, networks, and databases.

9. *Analytical knowledge* is knowledge about the strategies, tactics, and actions that executive managers and investigators can implement to reach desired goals.

An example of investigative knowledge in financial crime investigations is forensic accounting. Forensic accounting is concerned with identifying, recording, settling, extracting, sorting, reporting, and verifying past financial data. The focus of forensic accounting is on evidence revealed by the examination of financial documents. Financial crime, such as fraud, can be subject to forensic accounting because fraud encompasses the acquisition of property or economic advantage by means of deception through either a misrepresentation or concealment. Forensic examinations include consideration of digital evidence, including communications (Curtis, 2008).

To develop investigative knowledge in the area of forensic accounting, Kranacher, Morris, Pearson, and Riley (2008) suggest a model curriculum consisting of several concepts, such as basic accounting, basic auditing, transaction processing, business law, business communication, and computer skills. The purpose of such a curriculum is to build knowledge, skills, and abilities in forensic accounting to combat white-collar crime.

In addition to the above classification into knowledge categories, we also make distinctions between knowledge levels:

1. *Basic knowledge* is knowledge necessary to get work done. Basic knowledge is required for an intelligence officer and investigator (i.e., a knowledge worker) to understand and interpret information. It is also required for an intelligence and investigation unit as a knowledge organization to receive and process incoming information and produce output. However, basic knowledge alone yields only elementary and basic results of little value and low quality.

2. *Advanced knowledge* is knowledge necessary to get good work done. Advanced knowledge is required for an intelligence officer and investigator as a knowledge worker to achieve satisfactory work performance. It is also required for an intelligence and investigation unit as a knowledge organization to produce intelligence reports and crime analysis as well as charges that prove useful in investigation and prevention of financial crime. When advanced knowledge is combined with basic knowledge, professional knowledge workers and professional knowledge organizations in law enforcement emerge.

3. *Innovative knowledge* is knowledge that makes a real difference. When intelligence officers and investigators apply innovative knowledge in intelligence and analysis of incoming and available information, then new insights are generated in terms of crime patterns, criminal profiles, and prevention and investigation strategies. The application of innovative knowledge by intelligence units, along with the introduction of new methodologies in intelligence and analysis, enables learning in corporate management.

Based on these categories and levels, our knowledge matrix in Table 11.1 consists of nine knowledge categories and three knowledge levels as illustrated in the table. The purpose of the table is to illustrate that there are a total of 27 knowledge needs in investigating and preventing financial crime. Based on the table, each intelligence unit and investigation unit should identify and fill in the table according to knowledge needs.

Table 11.1 Knowledge Management Matrix for Knowledge Needs in Investigation and Prevention of Financial Crime in Organizations

#	Category	Basic Knowledge	Advanced Knowledge	Innovative Knowledge
1	Administrative knowledge	The role of a complaints and whistle-blowing investigator	Sources of information	Best practice in complaints and crime investigations
2	Organizational knowledge	How the business is organized and managed	How internal misconduct and crime is solved	Power structures in the organization and links to the criminal world
3	Employee knowledge	Where employees spend their working hours	What employees do in their working hours	Why employees do what they do in their working hours
4	Process knowledge	Information sources in investigation and prevention	Analysis techniques in investigation and prevention	Behavior in investigative and preventive work
5	Investigative knowledge	Investigative procedures	Contingent approaches to investigations	Hypothesis and causality in crime
6	Intelligence knowledge	Intelligence procedures	Contingent approaches to intelligence	Hypotheses and causality in potential crime
7	Legal knowledge	What investigators can do	What investigators cannot do	Expected outcome of court procedure
8	Technological knowledge	Equipment in investigative work	Equipment in analysis work	Artificial intelligence and expert systems
9	Analytical knowledge	Analytical methods	Analytical procedures	Analytical creativity

Knowledge levels are defined here as basic knowledge, advanced knowledge, and innovative knowledge. An alternative approach is to define knowledge levels in terms of knowledge depth: know-what, know-how, and know-why as listed in Table 11.2. These knowledge depth levels represent the extent of insight and understanding regarding a phenomenon. While know-what is the simple perception concerning what is going on, know-why entails complicated insight about cause-and-effect relationships in terms of why it is going on:

1. *Know-what* is knowledge about what is happening and what is going on whereby an executive perceives that something is going on that might need his or her attention. The executive's insight is limited to perception of something happening. The executive neither understands how nor why it is happening.

Table 11.2 Alternative Knowledge Management Matrix for Knowledge Needs in Investigation and Prevention of Financial Crime in Organizations

#	Category	Know-What	Know-How	Know-Why
1	Administrative knowledge	What investigating colleagues is all about	How investigating colleagues is conducted	Why investigation and prevention of financial crime is carried out
2	Organization knowledge	What employees do	How employees do the things they do	Why employees do the things they do
3	Employee knowledge	What colleagues do during their working hours	How colleagues do their work	Why colleagues do what they do
4	Process knowledge	Which kinds of financial crime occurs	How financial crime occurs	Why financial crime occurs
5	Investigative knowledge	Which investigative procedures are available	How investigative procedures work	Why investigative procedures work the way they do
6	Intelligence knowledge	Which intelligence procedures are available	How intelligence procedures work	Why investigative procedures work the way they do
7	Legal knowledge	Which laws and regulations are relevant for financial crime	How these laws and regulations are relevant for financial crime	Why these laws and regulations are relevant for financial crime
8	Technological knowledge	Which technological means are available to enforce law on criminal employees	How these technological means enable law enforcement	Why these technological means enable law enforcement
9	Analytical knowledge	Which approaches are successful in enforcing law on criminal employees	How are these approaches successful	Why these approaches are successful

2. *Know-how* is knowledge about how financial crime develops, how a criminal behaves, or how a criminal activity is organized. The insight of the executive or investigator is not limited to a perception that something is happening; he or she also understands how it is happening or how the situation is.

3. *Know-why* is the knowledge representing the deepest form of understanding and insight into a phenomenon. The executive or investigator not only knows what is occurring and how it occurs, he or she also has developed an understanding of why it occurs or why it is as it is. Developing hypotheses about cause-and-effect relationships and empirically validating causality are important characteristics of know-why knowledge.

One aspect of the knowledge work entails investigating a crime when a colleague is a suspect. This form of internal policing is described above. It seems easy to forget another part of internal policing as well—not only executives, but other colleagues also have a responsibility to prevent other colleagues becoming involved in illegal actions in the course of business. In order to succeed, executives and colleagues require the knowledge discussed above; it is also important that internal police officers have an interest and dare to take action in the prevention of or reaction to illegal actions committed by colleagues at work.

From Data to Wisdom

While data are numbers and letters without meaning, information is data in a context that makes sense. When combined with interpretation and reflection, information becomes knowledge, and knowledge accumulated over time, as learning, is wisdom. In this hierarchical structure, we find that intelligence amounts to more than information and less than knowledge. Intelligence is analyzed information as illustrated in Figure 11.1.

The word "intelligence" can refer to a product, a process, the individual organization that shapes raw data into a finished intelligence product, and also the larger community containing these organizations. The word intelligence also often refers to the military or to agencies such as MI5 (The Security Service) or MI6 (Secret Intelligence Service) in the United Kingdom. However, in this book, intelligence relates to criminal actions and is defined as a goal-oriented gathering, systematization, and analysis of information (Wilhelmsen, 2009).

Data is considered the raw material from which information develops. As is the case with notes, information is data endowed with relevance and purpose. The same can be said of intelligence in that it is a form of insight to

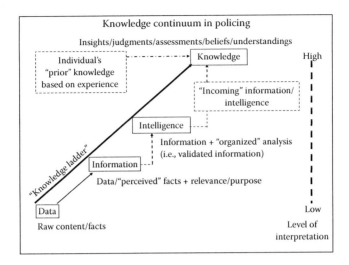

Figure 11.1 Hierarchy of investigation and prevention insight expressed as a continuum.

which some relevance has been attached through an attempt to offer an organized analysis of the information received by a crime analyst/intelligence officer. Accordingly, on the above continuum, intelligence is placed between information and knowledge, as ideally (as argued) intelligence represents a form of validated information.

A core process of policing and law enforcement is investigation—it is a truism in policing that information is the lifeblood of an investigation. An investigation goes nowhere if information is not forthcoming concerning an incident. Information is the raw data that breathes life into an investigation. It comprises ordinary rank-and-file employees either working in human resource departments and accounting departments or sitting at a computer conducting searches, background checks, or more sophisticated crime mapping and intelligence analysis reports and collecting and collating information.

Information and, to a similar extent, intelligence thereby consist of facts and other data that is organized to characterize or profile a particular situation, incident, or crime and the individual or group of individuals presumed to be involved. This organizing of data into meaningful information necessarily involves some level of interpretation of the facts as presented. However, the role of interpretation here in information is relatively minor in comparison to its role in terms of knowledge construction. In this regard, the role of interpretation in intelligence is greater and more explicit than it is in terms of information but not as extensive as in the making of knowledge.

Knowledge helps one develop relevant meaning to information in intelligence work:

The distinction between information and intelligence is well established, but can be difficult to grasp. Information consists of bits of data that, when combined and viewed together with relevant background knowledge, may be used to produce intelligence, which informs the actions and decisions of policing organizations. (Innes & Sheptycki, 2004, p. 6)

As implied, knowledge operates at a higher level of abstraction and consists of judgments and assessments based on personal beliefs, truths, and expectations regarding the information received and how it should be analyzed, evaluated and synthesized—in short interpreted—so that it may be used and implemented into some form of action.

References

Bevan, D., & Gitsham, M. (2009). Context, complexity and connectedness: Dimensions of globalization revealed. *Corporate Governance, 9*(4), 435–447.

Chaffey, D., & White, G. (2011). *Business information management* (2nd ed.). London: Prentice Hall.

Choi, S. Y., Lee, H., & Yoo, Y. (2010). The impact of information technology and transactive memory systems on knowledge sharing, application, and team performance: A field study. *MIS Quarterly, 34*(4), 855–870.

Collier, P. M. (2006). Policing and the intelligent application of knowledge. *Public Money & Management*, April, 109–116.

Curtis, G. E. (2008). Legal and regulatory environments and ethics: Essential components of a fraud and forensic accounting curriculum. *Issues in Accounting Education, 23*(4), 535–543.

Durcikova, A., Fadel, K. J., Butler, B. S., & Galletta, D. F. (2011). Knowledge exploration and exploitation: The impacts of psychological climate and knowledge management system access. *Information Systems Research, 22*(4), 855–866.

Innes, M., & Sheptycki, J. W. E. (2004). From detection to disruption: Intelligence and the changing logic of police crime control in the United Kingdom. *International Criminal Justice Review, 14*, 1–24.

Jaschke, H. G., Bjørgo, T., del Romero, F. B., Kwanten, C., Mawby, R., & Pogan, M. (2007). *Perspectives of police science in Europe*, Final Report, European Police College, CEPOL, Collège Européen de Police, Hampshire, England.

Joshi, K. D., Chi, L., Datta, A., & Han, S. (2010). Changing the competitive landscape: Continuous innovation through IT-enabled knowledge capabilities. *Information Systems Research, 21*(3), 472–495.

Kranacher, M. J., Morris, B. W., Pearson, T. A., & Riley, A. (2008). A model curriculum for education in fraud and forensic accounting. *Issues in Accounting Education, 23*(4), 505–519.

Liu, D., Ray, G., & Whinston, A. B. (2010). The interaction between knowledge codification and knowledge-sharing networks. *Information Systems Research, 21*(4), 892–906.

Mitchell, V. L. (2006). Knowledge integration and information technology project performance. *MIS Quarterly, 30*(4), 919–939.

Newell, S., Robertson, M., Scarbrough, H., & Swan, J. (2009). *Managing knowledge work and innovation* (2nd ed.). London: Palgrave Macmillan.

ODNI (2008). Vision 2015 – A Globally Networked and Integrated Intelligence Enterprise, Office of the Director of National Intelligence (ODNI), Washington, DC. Retrieved from www.odni.gov

Preuss, L., & Cordoba-Pachon, J. R. (2009). A knowledge management perspective of corporate social responsibility. *Corporate Governance, 9*(4), 517–527.

Roberts, N., Galluch, P. S., Dinger, M., & Grover, V. (2012). Absorptive capacity and information systems research: Review, synthesis, and directions for future research. *MIS Quarterly, 36*(2), 625–648.

Söderlund, J., & Bredin, K. (2011). Participants in the process of knowledge integration. In C. Berggren, A. Bergek, L. Bengtsson, M. Hobday & J. Söderlund (Eds.), *Knowledge integration & innovation: Critical challenges facing international technology-based firms* (pp. 96–121). Oxford: Oxford University Press.

Tell, F. (2011). Knowledge integration and innovation: A survey of the field. In C. Berggren, A. Bergek, L. Bengtsson, M. Hobday & J. Söderlund (Eds.), *Knowledge integration & innovation: Critical challenges facing international technology-based firms* (pp. 20–58). Oxford: Oxford University Press.

Wang, W. T. (2009). Knowledge management adoption in times of crisis. *Industrial Management & Data Systems, 109*(4), 445–462.

Wilhelmsen, S. (2009). *Maximising Organizational Information Sharing and Effective Intelligence Analysis in Critical Data Sets*. PhD dissertation. University of Bergen, Norway.

Police Information Systems Strategy

12

Computer systems are of key importance when policing white-collar crime. Information systems are needed to support investigation and prevention of white-collar crime. Information technology is applied to organize intelligence and analyses in electronic format and to enable easy retrieval, combination, and sharing among executives and colleagues.

Information technology is identified as an effective enabler in promoting information sharing and knowledge management in organizations. Information systems strategy is concerned with defining how information systems will be used to support and impact police work. It is a portfolio of computer-based applications to be implemented. It brings together the business aims of the police and understanding of the information needed to support those aims and the implementation of computer systems to provide that information (Chaffey & White, 2011). The emphasis is on delivering an applications portfolio of appropriate software tools and systems to support the future direction of an organization in general and knowledge work within the police in particular.

Information technology can play an important role in leveraging knowledge resources in organizations. Organizations often implement information systems that are specifically designed to support various aspects of knowledge management in organizations. These systems include features such as intranets, search engines, document repositories, and collaboration tools that allow virtual communities of practice to be organized (Choi, Lee, & Yoo, 2010).

Knowledge Management Systems

Knowledge management systems are information systems coupled with knowledge-sharing practices that support knowledge management efforts within an organization (Durcikova, Fadel, Butler, & Galletta, 2011).

To be more successful in policing white-collar crime, the police increasingly depend on their knowledge capabilities to continuously innovate. Innovation is defined as the design, invention, development, and implementation of new processes for the purpose of creating new value for society. Information technology is critical for supporting knowledge management initiatives and nurturing innovation. IT has the potential of enabling the creation, dissemination, and use of knowledge, thus greatly augmenting and enabling firms' knowledge capabilities, which Joshi, Chi, Datta, and Han (2010) refer to as IT-enabled knowledge capabilities.

IT's contribution and assistance in augmenting, building, and strengthening firms' knowledge capabilities have been recognized, and the link between knowledge capabilities and innovation has also been emphasized. Joshi et al. (2010) studied the link between IT-enabled knowledge capabilities and firm innovation. They introduced the theory of absorptive capacity for their study. Their study's findings provide strong support for the main assertion that knowledge capabilities that are enhanced through the use of IT contribute to firm innovation.

Organizations invest in knowledge management systems for the same reason they invest in other information systems: They believe that the value derived by the individuals using the system will exceed its cost (Ko & Dennis, 2011).

Knowledge management is concerned with simplifying and improving the process of sharing, distributing, creating, capturing, and understanding knowledge. Information and communication technology can play an important role in successful knowledge management initiatives. The extent of information technology can be defined in terms of growth stages for knowledge management systems. In this chapter, a model consisting of four stages is presented: investigator-to-technology systems, investigator-to-investigator systems, investigator-to-information systems, and investigator-to-application systems, respectively.

Collier (2006) argues that technology is clearly a major impediment to progress in the intelligent application of knowledge in policing. Traditionally, inadequacies in computer systems have been evidenced in most countries in terms of the lack of national police information strategy, the inability of systems in use by different forces to communicate with each other, and the lack of integration between computer systems in any one force. Internal investigators in intelligence systems have also displayed a lack of confidence in such practices, suggesting that tacit rather than explicit knowledge remained fundamental to the manner in which many internal police officers work. This is not surprising, when one bears in mind that many police officers consider their work to primarily entail handicraft rather than knowledge. The only way an inexperienced officer could learn a new policing field was to observe and join an experienced officer in his or her work (as craftsmen).

The potential of knowledge management systems in terms of enabling new organizational forms as well as interorganizational relationships and partnerships useful in policing will be demonstrated in this chapter. Partnership working is an increasingly common methodology in the public sector, deployed when addressing complex social issues, such as poverty, economic development, and crime. According to Wastell, Kawalek, Langmead-Jones, and Ormerod (2004), information systems have a vital role to play in enabling such interorganizational networks and in facilitating the multidisciplinary collaboration that is essential to joint collaboration when fighting financial crime.

Knowledge management systems refer to a class of information systems applied to the management of organizational knowledge. These systems are IT applications to support and enhance the organizational processes of knowledge creation, storage and retrieval, transfer, and application. Knowledge management and collaboration systems are among the fastest-growing areas of corporate and government software investments (Laudon & Laudon, 2010).

Knowledge management and collaboration are closely related. Laudon and Laudon (2010) argue that knowledge that cannot be communicated and shared with others is virtually useless. Knowledge becomes useful and actionable when shared throughout an organization and between collaborating organizations.

The knowledge management technology stage model presented in this chapter is a multistage model proposed for organizational evolution over time. Stages of knowledge management technology are a relative concept concerned with information and communication technology's (ICT) ability to process information for knowledge work. The knowledge management technology stage model consists of four stages. In terms of the application to law enforcement in this chapter, the stages are labeled investigator-to-technology, investigator-to-investigator, investigator-to-information, and investigator-to-application as illustrated in Figure 12.1.

Stages of knowledge management technology are such that ICT, in its later stages, is more useful to knowledge work than it is at earlier stages. The relative concept implies that ICT is more directly involved in knowledge work at higher stages and that ICT is able to support more advanced knowledge work at higher stages as illustrated in Figure 12.1.

Stage 1: Investigator to Technology

Investigator-to-Technology Stage: Tools for end users are made available to knowledge workers. In the simplest stage, this means a capable networked PC on every desk or a laptop in every briefcase with standardized personal productivity tools (word processing, presentation software) so that documents can be exchanged easily throughout a company. More complex and functional desktop infrastructures can also be the basis for the same types of knowledge support. Stage 1 is characterized by widespread dissemination

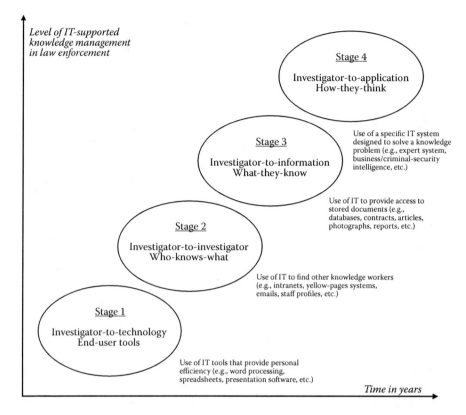

Figure 12.1 Knowledge management systems stage model for policing.

and use of end-user tools among knowledge workers in the company. For example, in this stage, lawyers in a law firm will use word processing, spreadsheets, legal databases, presentation software, and scheduling programs.

Advances in computer technology partly account for the transformation that has occurred in report writing and recordkeeping in financial crime investigations. Every policing activity or crime incident demands a report in some form. Most business organizations have computer information systems that can store reports electronically. Today, investigators can write reports on small notebook computers. Cursor keys and spell-check functions in these report programs are also useful timesaving features that increase efficiency.

An example of a specialized investigator-to-technology system is a fraud examination process tool that centers on the fraud hypothesis approach, which has four sequential steps (Ilter, 2009):

a. Analyzing the available data: An auditor gathers document evidence depicting all of the business.
b. Developing a fraud hypothesis: Based on what is discovered during analysis, a fraud examiner develops a hypothesis—always assuming

a worst-case scenario—of what could have occurred. The hypothesis addresses one of the three major classifications of occupational (internal) fraud: asset misappropriations, corruption, or fraudulent financial statements.

c. Revising it as necessary: If, for example, the facts do not point to a kickback scheme, the fraud examiner will look for the possibility of a billing scheme. Although the two schemes have several common elements, the latter raises red flags.

d. Confirming it: Testing the hypothesis by combining theoretical elements with empirical evidence.

An example of a generalized investigator-to-technology system is the Major Incident Policy Document in the United Kingdom. This document is maintained whenever a major incident room using the HOLMES system is in operation. Decisions that should be recorded are those that affect the practical or administrative features of the enquiry, and each entry must clearly show the reasoning for the decision. When the HOLMES system is used, the SIO directs which policy decisions are recorded on the system.

The basic information entered into HOLMES comprises location of incident, data and time of incident, victim(s), the senior investigating executive, and date the enquiry commenced. In the course of the enquiry, which is duly run on the HOLMES system, a closing report is prepared and registered as another document linked to a category of closing reports. The report will contain the following information: introduction, scene, the victim, and miscellaneous.

Most knowledge workers rely on office systems, such as word processors, voice mail, email, and presentation tools, which are designed to increase worker productivity. Some knowledge workers require highly specialized knowledge work systems with powerful graphics, analytical tools, and document management capabilities (Laudon & Laudon, 2010). Stage 1 can be labeled *end-user tools* or *people to technology*, as information technology that provides knowledge workers with tools that improve personal efficiency.

Stage 2: Investigator to Investigator

Investigator-to-Investigator Stage: Information about who knows what is made available to all people in the firm and to target outside partners. Search engines should normally facilitate work with a thesaurus because the terminology in which expertise is sought may not always match the terms (and hence the search words) the expert uses to classify that expertise.

The creation of corporate directories, also referred to as the mapping of internal expertise, is a common application of knowledge management technology. Because a great deal of knowledge in an organization remains not codified, mapping the internal expertise is a potentially useful application of technology to enable easy identification of knowledgeable persons.

Here we find the cartographic school of knowledge management, which is concerned with mapping organizational knowledge. It aims to record and disclose who knows what in the organization by compiling knowledge directories. Often called Yellow Pages, the principal idea is to ensure that knowledgeable people in the organization are accessible to others for advice, consultation, or knowledge exchange. Knowledge-oriented directories are not so much repositories of knowledge-based information as gateways to knowledge, and the knowledge is as likely to be tacit as explicit.

At stage 2, firms apply the personalization strategy in knowledge management. The personalization strategy implies that knowledge is tied to the person who developed it, and it is mainly shared through direct person-to-person contact. This strategy focuses on dialogue between individuals: Knowledge is transferred mainly in the form of personal emails, meetings, and one-on-one conversations.

Electronic networks of practice are computer-mediated discussion forums focused on problems of practice that enable individuals to exchange advice and ideas with others on the basis of common interests. Electronic networks have been found to support organizational knowledge flows between geographically dispersed coworkers and distributed research and development efforts. These networks also assist cooperative open-source software development and open congregation on the Internet for individuals interested in a specific practice. Electronic networks make it possible to share information quickly, globally, and with large numbers of individuals.

Information systems at stage 2 are knowledge network systems; they are also known as expertise location and management systems. These systems address the problem that arises when the appropriate knowledge is not represented as information in the form of a digital document at stages 1 or 3. Instead, knowledge resides in the memory of expert individuals in the organization:

> Knowledge network systems provide an online directory of corporate experts in well-defined knowledge domains and use communication technologies to make it easy for employees to find the appropriate expert in the organization. (Laudon & Laudon, 2010, p. 448)

Some knowledge network systems overcome this by systematizing the solutions developed by experts and then storing the solutions in a knowledge support database, either as best practices or frequently asked questions (FAQ) repositories at stage 3.

An example of a stage 2 system in policing financial crime is a knowledge network system, exchanging information about self-regulation in the private sector. Governance in the form of clear policies and procedures and formalized cross-company communication along with performance-based salary for board members and employees reduces incidences of white-collar crime within corporations (Hansen, 2009).

The typical system at stage 2 of knowledge management technology in investigation and prevention of financial crime is the intranet. Intranets provide a rich set of tools for creating collaborative environments in which members of an organization can exchange ideas, share information, and work together on common projects and assignments, regardless of their physical location. Information from many different sources and media, including text, graphics, video, audio, and even digital slides, can be displayed, shared, and accessed across an enterprise through a simple common interface.

Person-to-person systems in terms of online participation expose individuals to new ideas, prospective ties, and the thrill of fast-paced knowledge collaboration. Digital interactions between persons can take place on discussion boards; open source development; wiki sites; social media sites, such as Facebook; and online knowledge management systems that expose individuals as sources of information (Jarvenpaa & Majchrzak, 2012).

Jarvenpaa and Majchrzak (2012) emphasize that online participation in such person-to-person systems engenders both the benefits of knowledge sharing and the risks of harm. They introduce the term "vigilant interaction." Vigilant interaction in knowledge collaboration refers to an interactive emergent dialogue in which knowledge is shared while it is protected, which requires deep appraisals of mutual and individual actions in order to determine how each action may influence the outcomes of the collaboration. They argue that vigilant interactions are critical in online knowledge collaborations under ambivalent relationships in which users collaborate to gain benefits but, at the same time, protect it to avoid harm from perceived vulnerabilities.

Knowledge collaboration online refers to the use of digital media to facilitate the sharing, transfer, recombination, and reuse of knowledge among parties. Much online collaboration occurs in public forums, including practice networks and online communities. As argued by Jarvenpaa and Majchrzak (2012), online knowledge collaboration can take many forms. It could involve an individual posting a question to a discussion forum and then engaging in a process of reflecting on incoming responses and posting clarifying questions. The collaboration could involve parties engaging each other in surfacing contested assumptions, and it could be intended to help coordinate subprojects as in the case of open-source software development. Collaborations online typically take the form of a dialogic interaction style, variously referred to as expertise sharing, help seeking, or hermeneutic inquiry.

When Jarvenpaa and Majchrzak (2012) emphasize the risks of harm, they list a range of factors that create the possibility of vulnerabilities. For example, vulnerabilities are made possible when social identities are socially ambiguous as individuals share only partial information about their identities. Collaborating parties may have competing interests even though they are contributing to the same online forum. If, for example two business consultants from two different consulting firms are entering into knowledge collaboration, they may both be driven by self-interest for exploitation of the other party in addition to causing harm to a competitor.

Potential vulnerabilities increase in the online context because of limited social cues that are provided online as well as the lack of alternative information sources. Common ground for trustworthy knowledge collaboration can be missing, leading to miscommunication and misattribution. Jarvenpaa and Majchrzak (2012) define online knowledge collaborations as ambivalent relationships. Collaborations are ambivalent because persons approach the community or other parties with a promise of collective and private benefits but are concerned about the perceived vulnerabilities that such collaboration creates.

Stage 2 is in line with what has been labeled personalization strategy in knowledge management. With a personalization strategy, knowledge is shared through person-to-person contacts (Ko & Dennis, 2011). The personalization approach, sometimes also referred to as the network approach, centers on facilitating interpersonal knowledge sharing through networks of people. Knowledge workers remain owners of their knowledge and are rewarded by reciprocity, attention, and identification as knowledgeable persons. A network tie can be a self-enforcing sharing agreement between two knowledge workers. Knowledge sharing within a network tie is enforced through the benefits of future reciprocity and respect from one's sharing partner if one shares according to the sharing agreement and the withdrawal of such benefits if one defaults (Liu, Ray, & Whinston, 2010).

Some systems at this stage are labeled online communities. An online community describes a group of people who communicate and interact, develop relationships, and collectively and individually seek to attain some knowledge goals in an IT-supported virtual space. As pointed out by Ma and Agarwal (2007), mediation by technology creates several challenges for effective social interaction. Mediated communication suffers from social cue deficiencies because the transmission of important contextual cues, such as body language and physical surroundings, cannot easily and conveniently be realized through computer channels. In the disembodied virtual environment, a lack of synchronicity and immediacy can attenuate the effect of social norms on behavior and result in more social loafing.

Nevertheless, individuals engage in content contribution in online communities. A variety of drivers motivate this behavior, such as the anticipation of extrinsic benefits (economic rewards), intrinsic benefits (sense of self-worth, social norms, and social affiliation), and social capital. Maybe the most important driver, according to a study by Ma and Agarwal (2007), is the perceived identity verification in knowledge contribution. People prefer interacting with partners who verify their identities. Acknowledgment from group members increases a person's contribution. When an individual believes that other members of the online community understand and confirm his self-view, this engenders feelings of cognitive consonance in the interpersonal discourse and motivates the focal individual to continue interaction and contribute to it.

A special kind of system at stage 2 is knowledge-intensive service delivery networks. These networks not only connect knowledge workers, they also provide services from knowledge workers to users and customers. In our policing context, a knowledge-intensive service delivery network can provide internal services, such as knowledge from national police units to district police units, and external services to the public. These networks are concerned with knowledge delivery from multiple locations to multiple locations. Police officers providing such services may be at different locations and interact with each other to form a knowledge-intensive service delivery network. Dong, Johar, and Kumar (2012) define a knowledge-intensive service delivery network as connections of knowledge workers who use their expertise and professional relationships with other experts in an IT-intensive environment to perform knowledge-intensive service tasks.

Professionals, such as police detectives, are known to seek knowledge from their own personal networks—ego-centered networks, which extend beyond the formal organizational police structures in response to the need for rapid ad hoc knowledge collaboration. Ego-centered networks are comprised of ties between professionals. In a survey by Jarvenpaa and Majchrzak (2008), FBI agents provided data about their perceptions of their ego-centered networks. The 104 FBI respondents reported networks with sizes ranging from four to 500 with a mean of 103. On average, 16%–30% of the members in the networks were new each year. On average, half of the members of the networks were geographically local (within driving distance). Despite the geographical closeness, the most common media for interaction among network members were one-on-one email and group email lists, followed by phone calling. Face-to-face meetings were the least-used mode of interaction, occurring on average a few times per year.

In the study by Jarvenpaa and Majchrzak (2008), they integrated research on knowledge networks, trust, and distribution cognition to delineate the semi-structures that build awareness of others' expertise and improve interorganizational collaborations involving security professionals, such as police officers. The semi-structures encompass practices and procedures that affect how other parties interpret shared knowledge, whether other parties own the knowledge, and whether other parties agree to privacy, dissemination, and sensitivity protocols.

If the police enter into collaboration with outsiders, it can be a risky business. Outsiders can misuse information obtained in the exchange. To reduce this risk, the police need to manage the dialogue. Managed dialogue by collaborations with other parties in risky environments is implemented to ensure that sensitive information, if shared, is properly used and handled. Managed dialogue involves devoting cognitive and physical resources to monitoring or attending to potential vulnerabilities. Preemptions set up a secure social area for the interactions to take place by constraining, compartmentalizing, or regulating behavior during the interaction (Majchrzak & Jarvenpaa, 2010).

In research by Majchrzak and Jarvenpaa (2010), they suggest three safe context factors for interorganizational collaborations that can be applied to the individual security professional level in the police. These factors help to protect against inappropriate information release and, as such, allow security professionals to collaborate in a way that successfully resolves the threat. The three safe context factors that the researchers suggest are as follows: (1) degree to which the security professional interdependently relies on others to solve the security threat, (2) rules promoted by the police about what information can be released to external parties, and (3) selection of different network members with which to collaborate for each new threat event.

First, interdependency refers to the job requirement to interact with others in a reciprocal manner. An individual who feels interdependent with others is more likely to seek out common goals that require the participation of both parties. These common goals then help to protect against inappropriate information release because harming one party ends up harming the other party (Majchrzak & Jarvenpaa, 2010).

Second, rules limit what types of information are released to external parties. When parties follow rules restricting release, this promotes cautious sharing and creates a safe context for successful collaborations. Restrictive rules validate that some information can be shared. The lack of rules—or using rules that are too liberal—would not yield a strong signal of what can or cannot be shared.

Third, selection of different collaborators can create a safe context for collaborating with network members. Using different collaborators for different tasks provides insurance that no one informant sees enough of the police task's situation at any one time to understand it fully and exploit the understanding opportunistically. Another advantage is the ability to cross check information from one source with information from another source. Using different collaborators allows the police officer to feel protected from questionable behavior by a network member because the police officer can more easily shift to alternative collaborators (Majchrzak & Jarvenpaa, 2010).

As illustrated by these factors, there is a need at stage 2 for a safe context because stage 2 systems not only provide access to knowledgeable persons, but also the use of interorganizational systems applied to information exchange. Collaboration with insecure outsiders requires protection against potential risks. The police often have no choice as the force is dependent on information and collaboration with the public to solve security obligations. Faced with a difficult problem, police professionals must be able to engage others in ad hoc collaborations and quickly combine knowledge from these sources to solve the problem (Jarvenpaa & Majchrzak, 2008).

Stage 2 can be labeled *who knows what* or *people to people* as knowledge workers use information technology to find other knowledge workers.

Stage 3: Investigator to Information

Investigator-to-Information Stage: Information from knowledge workers is stored and made available to everyone in the firm and to designated external partners. Data mining techniques can be applied here to find relevant information and combine information in data warehouses (as discussed earlier in this book).

In broader terms, search engines are web browsers and server software that operate with a thesaurus because the terminology in which expertise is sought may not always match the terms used by the expert to classify that expertise.

At Stage 3, firms apply the codification strategy in knowledge management. The codification strategy centers on information technology: knowledge is carefully codified and stored in knowledge databases whereupon it can be accessed and used by anyone. With a codification strategy, knowledge is extracted from the person who developed it, made independent from that individual, and stored in the form of interview guides, work schedules, benchmark data, and so forth. It is subsequently searched and information is retrieved and used by many employees.

Two examples of knowledge management systems at stage 3 in law enforcement are COPLINK and geo-demographics. COPLINK has a relational database system for crime-specific cases, such as gang-related incidents, and serious crimes, such as homicide, aggravated assault, and sexual assault. Deliberately targeting these criminal areas allows a manageable amount of information to be entered into a database. Geo-demographic profiles of the characteristics of individuals and small areas are central to efficient and effective deployment of law enforcement resources. Geo-computation is based on geographical information systems.

A third example of a stage 3 system in policing is business intelligence systems. Business intelligence (BI) systems provide the ability to analyze business information in order to support and improve management decision making across a broad range of business activities (Elbashir, Collier, & Davern, 2008). For example, the Staffordshire Police in Great Britain uses a series of custom-made applications, including crime recording, custody recording, file preparation, court administration, and an intelligence system. A small number of criminals commit most of the crime and detailed BI analysis of data reveals information about offenders and leads to their eventual prosecution. Functions in the system include general queries, property queries, statistical searches, crime profiling queries, and prolific offender queries.

An important part of stage 3 systems are enterprise content management systems that belong to enterprise-wide knowledge management systems. Enterprise-wide knowledge management systems are general-purpose business-wide efforts to collect, store, distribute, and apply digital content. Enterprise content management systems help organizations manage business-wide content. Such systems include agency repositories of documents, reports, presentations, and best practices as well as the capabilities for collecting and organizing semi-structured information, such as email (Laudon & Laudon, 2010). A tool at stage 1, email is also developing into a content provider of information for knowledge sharing at stage 3.

A fourth example of a level 3 system is CompStat, which is a policing approach involving the generation of as much real-time data as possible about crime and the frequent evaluation of the data to develop strategies to reduce crime as quickly and effectively as possible. CompStat stands for "computer statistics" or "comparative statistics." It includes computer-enabled crime statistics to identify where and when specific types of crime and disorder problems are happening. A key element in the CompStat approach is frequent evaluation of the intelligence collected, so police can develop plans for moving quickly and effectively to reduce crime. Before CompStat, statistical crime reports were available at the end of each month instead of in real time. By gathering real-time information, police agencies can deploy personnel and other resources rapidly to areas where crimes are occurring. As such, this approach has helped create a sense of urgency for suppressing crime and apprehending suspects, and it has enabled police agencies to focus their resources more sharply on where those resources are needed most (Ortmeier & Davis, 2012).

An important source of information for stage 3 policing systems is private sector organization's contribution in the control of financial crime. Gilsinan et al. (2008) identified this contribution in terms of five distinct roles with each role having its own dynamics and implications for successful suppression of unlawful conduct. The five roles are the grudging informant, the enthusiastic intelligence operative, the agent provocateur, the cop on the take, and the investigator friendly:

- The *grudging informant* is an organization that complies with the requirement to produce information for public sector enforcement activity.
- The *enthusiastic intelligence operative* is an organization that finds it profitable to have a partnership with the government.

- The *agent provocateur* is an organization that adheres to the provision requiring the chief operating and financial executives to certify that the firm's internal controls provide transparency to the financial processes of the company.
- The *cop on the take* is an organization in which corporate entities have the primary responsibility for policing their own ranks to ensure compliance with regulatory strictures.
- The *investigator friendly* is an organization that acts from different motives than the government and with different abilities although both end up engaging in a kind of token enforcement strategy.

Gilsinan et al. (2008) argue that a calculus of incentives and disincentives determines which role will be adopted by the private sector. For the grudging informant, a disincentive can be found in the form of customers who demand secrecy in their financial dealings. For the enthusiastic intelligence operative, however, an incentive is technology that allows private brokers to gather large amounts of information and package these data as a commodity for sale to governments. For the agent provocateur, an incentive is to better manage risk and thereby increase the market appeal of its stock. For the cop on the take, a disincentive is a potential stock market bubble that encourages risk-taking with the lure of enormous, quickly realized profits. For the investigator friendly, an incentive is external business threats from fraudulent activity by competitors.

Gilsinan et al. (2008) further argue that the temptation toward malfeasance is high when the private sector is responsible for both the provision and production of industry regulation. Behaviors change when such provision and production is linked to fraudulent activity perpetrated by individuals external to the organization and when either government resources or the likelihood of success are in short supply. In these kinds of situations, the government tends to be laid back, and businesses tend to optimize their own utility.

Tellechea (2008) proposes the introduction of reverse corruption whereby individuals and entities are attracted to incentives to uncover and report misconduct by quickly and efficiently giving them a share of any seized funds. There is precedent for this type of approach in the United States: Should an individual provide sufficiently detailed information on a tax evader, then the Internal Revenue Service may award up to 15% of the amount recovered in taxes and penalties (up to a maximum of $2 million). In 2003, whistleblowers in the United States received $4.1 million in such rewards. In 2002, the IRS paid $7.7 million and recovered $66.9 million in taxes, fines, penalties, and interest. The record year was 2000, when $10.8 million was paid out. Such incentives might stimulate the flow of information into stage 3 systems.

While stage 2 is in line with what has been labeled personalization strategy, stage 3 is in line with codification strategy. This is one of the most fundamental dichotomies in terms of knowledge management strategy adopted by organizations whether codification or personalization. With a codification strategy, the police's knowledge is carefully organized into reusable knowledge documents that are stored in a formal knowledge management system, and knowledge is shared through the reuse of these documents. The knowledge management system plays a much smaller role in the personalization strategy than it does in the codification strategy (Ko & Dennis, 2011).

Ko and Dennis (2011) argue that neither strategy is inherently better or worse than the other; it depends on the fit of the strategy to the needs of the organization. A codification strategy, for example, is best suited to organizations that reuse the same information repeatedly and where the source of information in terms of a person is not always easy to identify or contact. Liu et al. (2010) argue that organizations should use codification for sharing explicit knowledge and the personalization approach for sharing tacit knowledge. Codification enjoys the effect of scale economies in knowledge reuse when the knowledge source is not bothered when the knowledge destination is absorbing and applying the knowledge. Personalization enjoys the effect of expert economies in knowledge reuse, in which the knowledge destination is obtaining value-added customized solutions from the knowledge source. Therefore, organizations that focus on providing standard solutions should follow the codification approach while organizations that focus on providing highly specialized and contingent services should follow the network approach.

Obviously, different parts of the police force are in different situations at different points in time, requiring, over time, both the application of the codification strategy and the network strategy. For example, antiterror intelligence may have to rest mainly on the personalization strategy, and speed controls may rest mainly on the codification strategy.

A codification strategy is essentially a people-to-documents or person-to-document approach at stage 3 in which the organization expects to derive performance benefits through reusing knowledge documents. Managing these codified knowledge documents means careful planning of knowledge captures, such as the codifying and storing of knowledge in databases where it can be made available for others to access. It also requires careful monitoring of the knowledge to ensure that it is valid within the intended target context. Because the goal is to reuse the knowledge as often and as long as possible, the organization is likely to invest in acquiring and validating knowledge of high relevance to many persons (Ko & Dennis, 2011).

The codification approach involves codifying knowledge into electronic repositories that are made accessible to all knowledge workers in the organization (Liu et al., 2010).

In an empirical study by Ko and Dennis (2011), they found that a codification-based knowledge management system had significant positive impacts on individual performance among sales representatives and that these performance benefits grew over time. The more a sales representative used the system, the more likely he or she was to meet or exceed the sales quota. Those sales representatives with greater systems experience derived immediate value from the system use in the same month they used the system, and all users derived significant value in the second, third, and fourth month after use.

Ko and Dennis (2011) found that knowledge management use affects performance when users can selectively find the new knowledge they need, recognize its relevance, absorb it into their mental models, and effectively translate and apply it to change their behavior. However, once an individual acquires new knowledge, initial performance may drop before the individual develops ways to effectively apply this knowledge. This is because change—even a change for the better—can decrease performance until the person has successfully integrated it into his or her new work processes.

Ko and Dennis (2011) found that knowledge workers with more experience were able to more quickly absorb and apply the knowledge from the knowledge management system than those with less experience, who took longer to benefit from system use.

Codification versus personalization provides different incentives for knowledge workers to codify or share their knowledge. In codification, the knowledge is transferred from knowledge workers to the organization, and knowledge workers are rewarded by the firm in the form of prizes, bonuses, salary increases, promotions, or special roles. In network sharing, knowledge workers remain owners and the only source of their knowledge and are rewarded by their peers through reciprocity or by altruism, with which they are recognized as very knowledgeable persons receiving special status inside and possibly outside the organization. Thus, the two approaches can also be viewed as two distinctive incentive systems for knowledge transfer (Liu et al., 2010).

By separately studying the network approach at stage 2 and the codification strategy at stage 3, it seems that the two approaches work independently of each other. However, the two systems approaches as well as associated incentive systems for knowledge workers interact. The personalization approach is preceding the codification approach because knowledge sources have to be identified before their knowledge can be codified. Therefore, personalization is located at stage 2, and codification is located at stage 3. In terms of incentive systems, some knowledge workers may prefer direct personalization rewards, and others may prefer indirect codification rewards. Organizations introducing explicit rewards for codifying knowledge can experience effects on network sharing among knowledge workers. Therefore, one may not view network sharing or codification sharing as independent. Rather, there are interdependencies as well as a progression line from personalization to codification (Liu et al., 2010).

Liu et al. (2010) modeled interactions between network and codification sharing. In their model, knowledge sharing within a network tie is enforced through the benefits of future reciprocity from sharing partner(s). Network sharing interacts with codification because codification provides knowledge workers with outside options of availability and triangulation of information. The model uses a formal game-theoretical framework to provide an initial account of how the knowledge-sharing network at stage 2 and knowledge codification at stage 3 interact with each other. They found that codification sometimes threatens the extent of knowledge-sharing ties by increasing knowledge workers outside options. This is in line with theoretical foundations of stage models, in which a higher stage both builds on and partly replaces activities at the lower stages. Specifically, person-to-person network communication is partly replaced by person-to-information systems when the codification approach has been successfully applied in an organization.

As more and more information is stored and accessible at stage 3, search engines become critical to retrieving relevant information. The ability to effectively search and analyze information is a key issue at stage 3. New technology is emerging to make search engines more effective. One example of such technology is nanotechnology. Nanotechnology is a dynamic interdisciplinary domain that has brought about significant effects in different areas. An example is presented by Dong et al. (2012), who developed Nano Mapper with functions that allow users to perform statistical analyses, citation network analyses, and topic content analyses against document corpus extracted from source databases.

Information stored at stage 3 in databases and other systems needs to be trustworthy and needs to be trusted. One activity to create trust is knowledge validation. To ensure that knowledge repositories contain high-quality knowledge, Durcikova and Gray (2009) recommend that contributions to a repository undergo stringent validation processes. A repository must contain knowledge that will prove useful for employees looking for answers to their questions and solutions to their problems. Knowledge validation processes need to reject contributions to repositories that are redundant, incorrect, ineffective, outdated, or otherwise unhelpful.

As pointed out by Durcikova and Gray (2009), knowledge validation processes may have the unintended effect of being perceived as an obstacle for contributing. Individuals may grow discouraged if their contributions are often rejected, if they do not understand the processes that lead to rejection, and if decisions occur long after the initial submission. Validation processes that minimize the effort required from expert reviewers and that lead to high rejection rates may unintentionally choke off the flow of new knowledge to a repository. Without new contributions, a repository grows stale, and users soon abandon it. People will not contribute to a repository where few people are looking, and people will not look where few people are contributing.

Therefore, review processes need to be transparent and developmentally oriented as a way of encouraging knowledge contributions.

Valuable knowledge, located inside people's heads can be identified, captured, and processed via the use of information technology tools so that it can be applied in new contexts. The aim is to make the knowledge inside people's heads or knowledge embedded in successful routines widely available (Newell, Robertson, Scarbrough, & Swan, 2009).

Access to information at stage 3 is not limited to information stored within the police organization. Access to external information is included as well. An example is the Internet, which is an open source for crime investigations. Both open and undercover investigations on the Internet can be conducted in a variety of ways. Online undercover investigators may target offenders who offer bribes or engage in money laundering, tax evasion, or other kinds of financial crime. Online undercover operations, mostly applied by the police for sex offenders (Mitchell, Wolak, Finkelhor, & Jones, 2012), have a great potential for policing white-collar criminals as well.

When the police implement knowledge management systems as described in the stages of growth model, then the organization makes itself more vulnerable, both because of the systems as such and, more importantly, because of all the information stored in the systems. Therefore, managing information security becomes a key issue in the police when implementing information systems. Incidences of cyber-attacks and information breaches should be a major concern. Information security is inseparable from information systems in general and knowledge management systems in particular because such systems include sensitive information about persons and activities. It is a vital issue for all organizations that store and exchange information electronically (Mookerjee, Mookerjee, Bensoussan, & Yue, 2011).

While managing information security for an organization could involve different tasks, such as prevention, detection, and response, Mookerjee et al. (2011), in their research, focused on the detection component of information security. They argue that a detection system (e.g., firewalls, intrusion detection systems, internal intelligence, etc.) to identify attack traffic that could originate from internal as well as external sources is a critical issue in information management. One of the challenges for a detection system is to allow normal traffic to pass through without obstacles. The detection system's ability to discriminate between attackers and normal users is referred to as its discrimination ability. Discrimination ability is represented by the possible tradeoffs that the detection system can achieve between its detection ability and its false-positive rate. A detection system that has a higher detection ability for the same false-positive rate is considered to possess higher discrimination ability.

Mookerjee et al. (2011) suggest that the discrimination ability of a detection system could gradually deteriorate because of changes in the environment in which it operates, causing a drift toward a lower detection ability. On the other hand, there could also be events that abruptly degrade the discrimination ability in terms of shocks. As the discrimination ability deteriorates, hackers could intensify attacks on the organization. In response, the organization needs to continuously expend efforts to optimally maintain the detection system so as to balance the cost of maintaining the system with the cost of detection errors. A detection error occurs when a normal user is classified as malicious, and a malicious user is classified as normal.

In their research, Mookerjee et al. (2011) set themselves the task of determining the optimal maintenance effort and configuration of a detection system over time. The main parameters are traffic conditions, productivity, costs of maintenance effort, error costs, drift occurrence, and dissemination speed. The objective was to optimize the effort applied to maintain the system. The effort affects discrimination ability, which, in turn, affects the detection rate and false-positive rate of the system. An optimal approach was identified in the research, in which a steady-state solution implies that the values of effort and discrimination ability are constant.

In research by Durcikova et al. (2011), impacts of knowledge management system access and organizational climate on knowledge exploration and exploitation were studied. Their analysis shows that a climate for innovation encourages exploitation whereas a climate for autonomy encourages exploration. Additionally, their results suggest that knowledge management system access does not directly influence individuals' exploration exploitation behaviors, but neither enhances nor diminishes the effects of certain climate variables on these behaviors.

Climate is a manifestation of organizational culture that can be measured through perceptions of observable practices and procedures as well as shared values among organizational members (Durcikova et al., 2011), which is part of the police culture discussed earlier.

Stage 3 can be labeled *what they know* or *people to docs* as information technology affords knowledge workers access to information that is typically stored in documents. Examples of documents include contracts and agreements, reports, manuals and handbooks, business forms, letters, memos, articles, drawings, blueprints, photographs, email and voice mail messages, video clips, scripts and visuals from presentations, policy statements, computer printouts, and transcripts from meetings.

Stage 4: Investigator to Application

Investigator-to-Application Stage: Information systems solving knowledge problems are made available to knowledge workers and solution seekers. Artificial intelligence is applied in these systems. For example, neural networks are statistically oriented tools that excel at the application of data to classify cases into categories. Another example is expert systems that can enable the knowledge of one or a few experts to be used by a much broader group of workers. Investigator-to-application systems will only be successful if they are built on a thorough understanding of law enforcement.

An example of a stage 4 system not yet implemented is a system for evaluation of compliance levels according to recommendations by the Financial Action Task Force (FATF). The FATF was formed in 1989 by the G-7 group of countries. It was motivated by the General Assembly of the United Nations' adoption of a universal pledge to cease money laundering, fuelled largely at that time by the laundering of illegal drug trade money. Accordingly, one of the FATF's first tasks was to develop measures to combat money laundering (Johnson, 2008).

A set of 40 recommendations was issued by the FATF that were designed to provide a comprehensive strategy for action against money laundering. FATF members have been evaluated over a number of years against these recommendations and, more recently, against the nine special recommendations using self-assessment/mutual assessment procedures. Self-assessment is an annual questionnaire-based exercise. Mutual evaluation involves an onsite visit by experts from other member countries in the fields of law, financial regulation, law enforcement, and international cooperation (Johnson, 2008).

A mutual evaluation may result in one of the following compliance levels (Johnson, 2008):

1. Noncompliant (NC): There are major shortcomings with a large majority of the essential criteria not being met.
2. Partially Compliant (PC): Some substantive action has been taken, and there is compliance with some of the essential criteria.
3. Largely Compliant (LC): Only minor shortcomings with a large majority of the essential criteria being fully met.
4. Fully Compliant (FC): The recommendation is fully observed with respect to all essential criteria.

To be able to compare compliance across countries, each compliance level was assigned a numerical level: NC = 0, PC = 0.33, LC = 0.67, and FC = 1.0. The following countries achieved the highest compliance scores (Johnson, 2008):

Belgium	0.77
United Kingdom	0.70
United States	0.69
Portugal	0.69
Norway	0.68
Switzerland	0.64
Ireland	0.63

Johnson (2008) argues that the results here should be used as a guide only to the ranking and compliance of countries rather than as an exact measurement of compliance. This is because compliance levels are very broad whereby substituting a single value for each compliance level provides only a crude measure of compliance for comparisons to be made against. Only a future system based on artificial intelligence could provide an exact measure of compliance.

Another example of a stage-four system is based on artificial intelligence (AI), this is an area of computer science that endeavors to build machines exhibiting human-like cognitive capabilities. Most modern AI systems are founded on the realization that intelligence is tightly intertwined with knowledge; knowledge, in turn, is associated with the symbols we manipulate. The example is a system for auditing insurance fraud. The hybrid knowledge- and statistics-based system employs knowledge discovery techniques to, first, integrate expert knowledge with statistical information assessment to identify cases of unusual provider behavior and, second, use machine learning to develop new rules and to improve identification processes (Yusuf & Babalola, 2009).

Artificial intelligence and database technology provide a number of intelligent techniques that organizations can use to capture individual and collective knowledge and to extend their knowledge base. Expert systems, case-based reasoning, and fuzzy logic are used to harness knowledge from knowledge workers and make information representations and procedures available to other knowledge workers. Neural networks and data mining are used for knowledge discovery. They can discover underlying patterns, categories, and behaviors in large data sets that could not be discovered by intelligence officers alone or simply through experience (Laudon & Laudon, 2010).

Knowledge-based systems deal with solving problems by exercising knowledge. The most important parts of these systems are the knowledge base and the inference engine. The former holds the domain-specific knowledge whereas the latter contains the functions to exercise the knowledge in the knowledge base. Knowledge can be represented as either rules or frames. Rules are a natural choice for representing conditional knowledge, which is in the form of if-when statements. Inference engines supply the motive power to the knowledge. There are several ways to exercise knowledge, depending on the nature of the knowledge. For example, backward-chaining systems work backward from the conclusion to the inputs; these systems attempt to validate the conclusions by finding evidence to support them. In law enforcement, this is an important system feature, as evidence determines whether or not a person is charged for a crime.

Case-based reasoning systems are a different way to represent knowledge through explicit historical cases. This approach differs from the rule-based approach because the knowledge is not compiled and interpreted by an expert; instead, the experiences that possibly shaped the expert's knowledge are directly used to make decisions. Learning is an important issue in case-based reasoning because with the mere addition of new cases to the library, the system learns. In law enforcement, police officers are looking for similar cases to learn how they were handled in the past, making case-based reasoning systems an attractive application in policing.

An example of a stage 4 system in policing is the dynamic emergency response information system (DERMIS), conceptually introduced by Turoff, Walle, Chumer, and Yao (2006). They developed a set of general and supporting design principles and specifications for DERMIS by identifying design premises resulting from the use of indices. The principles are based on the assumption that, inherent in crises of varying scope and proportion, are communication and information needs that can be addressed by today's information and communication technologies. What is required, however, is organizing the premises and concepts that can be mapped into a set of generic design principles.

Turoff et al. (2006) identified the following eight design premises for the DERMIS design:

1. System training and simulation: An emergency system that is not in use on a regular basis before an emergency will never be useful in an actual emergency.
2. Information focus: People responding to an emergency are working 14- to 18-hour days and have no tolerance or time for things unrelated to dealing with the crisis.
3. Crisis memory: Learning and understanding what actually happened before, during, and after the crisis is extremely important for the improvement of the response process.
4. Exceptions as norms: Almost everything in a crisis is an exception to the norm.
5. Scope and nature of crisis: The critical problem of the moment is the nature of the crisis, a primary factor requiring people, authorities, and resources to be brought together at a specific period of time for a specific purpose.
6. Role transferability: It is impossible to predict who will undertake what specific role in a crisis situation. The actions and privileges of the role need to be well defined in the system software and people must be trained for the possibility of assuming multiple or changing roles.
7. Information validity and timelines: Establishing and supporting confidence in a decision by supplying the best possible up-to-date information is critical to those whose actions may risk lives and resources.

8. Free exchange of information: Crises involve the necessity for many hundreds of individuals from different organizations to be able to exchange information freely, delegate authority, and conduct oversight without the side effect of information overload.

Some of the premises are reminiscent of stage 2, in which communication and information exchange between people is the most important feature. Thus, a DERMIS may be developed according to the stage model by first including communication aspects at stage 2, then moving into information bases at stage 3, and finally combining systems users and information sources into information services in emergency situation in stage 4.

At this stage, information systems for detection of deception and lies can be found. Such systems apply linguistic means to separate true and false statements. The fundamental premise of linguistic approaches to the detection of deception in statements is that when we are being deceptive, certain linguistic aspects of our speech or our writing differ nonrandomly and observably from those same aspects when we are being truthful. Computer-based linguistic analysis techniques can assist law enforcement in determining veracity of statements (Armistead, 2012).

Telling lies by a suspect or a witness often requires creating a story about an experience or attitude that does not exist. As a result, false stories may be qualitatively different from true stories. When individuals provide accounts of an event, they include important linguistic and structural features. One approach to analyze statements is known as SCAN—Scientific Content Analysis. In experiments, SCAN has been able to differentiate between probably accurate statements and likely false statements (Armistead, 2012).

Among the statistically most promising linguistic variables related to deception are expression of negative emotions, fewer unique sensory details, inconsistency in use of pronouns, relative infrequency in the use of "I" and "me," use of general rather than particular descriptions, failure to deny allegation(s), presence of equivocation or avoidance words, relative lack of logical structure and plausibility, length of the statement, expressions of tension or of disinterest in cooperating, evidence (such as slowing of speech tempo) of more difficult cognitive work, and longer relative length of the "prologue" part of the statement compared to the critical-incident part. When a few of these variables are combined in a single protocol, they are percentage rates beyond laypersons' ability to do so as well as beyond chance levels (Armistead, 2012).

As mentioned earlier, transactive memory is important in teams. Choi et al. (2010) found that information technology that is designed to support knowledge management practice in organizations facilitates the development of transactive memory. Typical IT tools to support knowledge management practice include knowledge repositories (storage), bulletin boards (communication and coordination), and search engines (search and access of information).

Stage 4 can be labeled *how they think* or *people to systems*, in which the system is intended to help solve a knowledge problem.

Knowledge Work

Information technology to support knowledge work of internal investigators is improving. For example, new information systems supporting investigation processes are evolving. A criminal investigation is an information-rich and knowledge-intensive practice. Its success depends on turning information into evidence. However, the process of turning information into evidence is neither simple nor straightforward. The raw information that is gathered through the investigative process often needs to be transformed into usable knowledge before its value as potential evidence can be realized. Hence, in an investigative context, knowledge acts as an intervening variable in this transformative process of converting information via knowledge into evidence.

The extent to which knowledge management systems, as described above, are used by internal investigators is dependent on a number of factors. One important factor, frequently discussed in the research literature, is the task technology fit. Task technology theory argues that the use of a technology may result in different outcomes, depending upon its configuration and the task for which it is used. Four elements are part of this theory: task characteristics and technology characteristics, which combine to affect the fit and which affect the outcome in terms of performance or utilization. Tasks are broadly defined as the actions carried out in turning inputs into outputs in order to satisfy information needs. Perceived technology fit depends on the agreement between the perceived capabilities of the technology, the needs of the task, and the competence of the users (Lin & Huang, 2008).

Kappos and Rivard (2008) argue that culture plays an increasingly important role in information systems initiatives. Depending on cultural values, information systems initiatives can be either stimulated or prevented. For example, if legality is more important than effectiveness, and if formal is more important than informal, then initiatives will emerge more easily.

Knowledge management systems have created incentives for promoting knowledge sharing among organizational members and for fostering innovation within public and private institutions. Knowledge management systems can support four knowledge management processes (Hsiao, 2008):

(i) Knowledge creation, a process of proactively determining what knowledge is desired and needed

(ii) Knowledge development, the process of establishing valuable knowledge

(iii) Knowledge reuse, the process of putting knowledge in a reusable form
(iv) Knowledge transfer, the process of disseminating knowledge effectively

It is important to stress here that stages of growth models are very different from lifecycle models. While stage models define and describe accumulated improvements in knowledge management technology to support policing the business organization, life cycle models represent a cycle of birth, growth, decline, and eventually death, of information technology.

In future research, there is a need to validate the stage model both theoretically and empirically. Furthermore, there is a need for benchmark variables that will have different content for different stages. In the current presentation of our model, the stages lack both theoretical background and practical situations. Although stage 4 may seem understandable and viable, the remaining stages are in need of further conceptual work. Core questions in future research will be whether investigator-to-technology, investigator-to-investigator, investigator-to-information, and investigator-to-application concepts are valid, practicable, and reliable.

In future research, pros (strengths) and cons (weaknesses) of the suggested model have to be taken into account. We need to provide a more critical analysis of a stage model like the one suggested. It is far from intuitively obvious that the progression over time is from end-user tools, via who knows what and what they know to how they think. Why not what they know via who knows what and end-user tools to how they think or end-user tools via what they know and who knows what to how they think? The conceptual research presented here is lacking empirical evidence. Only a questionnaire based on Guttman scaling rather than Likert scaling can verify the suggested sequence or alternatively identify another sequence.

The important contribution of this chapter is the introduction of the stage hypothesis to knowledge management technology in policing the business organization. Rather than thinking of knowledge management technology in terms of alternative strategies, we suggest an evolutionary approach in which the future is building on the past, rather than being a divergent path from the past. Rather than thinking that what was done in the past is wrong, past actions are the only available foundation for future actions. If past actions are not on the path to success, direction is changed without history being reversed.

References

Armistead, T. W. (2012). The detection of deception by linguistic means. *Policing: An International Journal of Police Strategies & Management, 35*(2), 304–326.

Chaffey, D., & White, G. (2011). *Business information management* (2nd ed.). London: Prentice Hall.

Choi, S. Y., Lee, H., & Yoo, Y. (2010). The impact of information technology and transactive memory systems on knowledge sharing, application, and team performance: A field study. *MIS Quarterly, 34*(4), 855–870.

Collier, P. M. (2006). Policing and the intelligent application of knowledge. *Public Money & Management*, April, 109–116.

Dong, S., Johar, M. S., & Kumar, R. L. (2012). A benchmark model for management of knowledge-intensive service delivery networks. *Journal of Management Information Systems, 28*(3), 127–160.

Durcikova, A., & Gray, P. (2009). How knowledge validation processes affect knowledge contribution. *Journal of Management Information Systems, 25*(4), 81–107.

Durcikova, A., Fadel, K. J., Butler, B. S., & Galletta, D. F. (2011). Knowledge exploration and exploitation: The impacts of psychological climate and knowledge management system access. *Information Systems Research, 22*(4), 855–866.

Elbashir, M. Z., Collier, P. A., & Davern, M. J. (2008). Measuring the effects of business intelligence systems: The relationship between business process and organizational performance. *International Journal of Accounting Information Systems, 9*, 135–153.

Gilsinan, J. F., Millar, J., Seitz, N., Fisher, J., Harshman, E., Islam, M., & Yeager, F. (2008). The role of private sector organizations in the control and policing of serious financial crime and abuse. *Journal of Financial Crime, 15*(2), 111–123.

Hansen, L. L. (2009). Corporate financial crime: Social diagnosis and treatment. *Journal of Financial Crime, 16*(1), 28–40.

Hsiao, R. L. (2008). Knowledge sharing in a global professional service firm. *MIS Quarterly Executive, 7*(3), 123–137.

Ilter, C. (2009). Fraudulent money transfers: A case from Turkey. *Journal of Financial Crime, 16*(2), 125–136.

Jarvenpaa, S. L., & Majchrzak, A. (2008). Knowledge collaboration among professionals protecting national security: Role of transactive memories in ego-centered knowledge networks. *Organization Science, 19*(2), 260–276.

Johnson, J. (2008). Is the global financial system AML/CFT prepared? *Journal of Financial Crime, 15*(1), 7–21.

Joshi, K. D., Chi, L., Datta, A., & Han, S. (2010). Changing the competitive landscape: Continuous innovation through IT-enabled knowledge capabilities. *Information Systems Research, 21*(3), 472–495.

Kappos, A., & Rivard, S. (2008). A three-perspective model of culture, information systems, and their development and use. *MIS Quarterly, 32*(3), 601–634.

Ko, D. G., & Dennis, A. R. (2011). Profiting from knowledge management: The impact of time and experience. *Information Systems Research, 22*(1), 134–152.

Laudon, K. C., & Laudon, J. P. (2010). *Management information systems: Managing the digital firm* (11th ed.). London: Pearson Education.

Lin, T. C., & Huang, C. C. (2008). Understanding knowledge management system usage antecedents: An integration of social cognitive theory and task technology fit. *Information & Management, 45*, 410–417.

Liu, D., Ray, G., & Whinston, A. B. (2010). The interaction between knowledge codification and knowledge-sharing networks. *Information Systems Research, 21*(4), 892–906.

Ma, M., & Agarwal, R. (2007). Through a glass darkly: Information technology design, identity verification, and knowledge contribution in online communities. *Information Systems Research, 18*(1), 42–67.

Majchrzak, A., & Jarvenpaa, S. L. (2010). Safe contexts for interorganizational collaborations among homeland security professionals. *Journal of Management Information Systems*, 27(2), 55–86.

Mitchell, K. J., Wolak, J., Finkelhor, D., & Jones, L. (2012). Investigators using the Internet to apprehend sex offenders: Findings from the Second National Juvenile Online Victimization Study. *Police Practice and Research*, 13(3), 267–281.

Mookerjee, V., Mookerjee, R., Bensoussan, A., & Yue, W. T. (2011). When hackers talk: Managing information security under variable attack rates and knowledge dissemination. *Information Systems Research*, 22(3), 606–623.

Newell, S., Robertson, M., Scarbrough, H., & Swan, J. (2009). *Managing knowledge work and innovation* (2nd ed.). London: Palgrave Macmillan.

Ortmeier, P. J., & Davis, J. J. (2012). *Police administration: A leadership approach*. New York: McGraw Hill.

Tellechea, A. F. (2008). Economic crimes in the capital markets. *Journal of Financial Crime*, 15(2), 214–222.

Turoff, M., Walle, B. V. D., Chumer, M., & Yao, X. (2006). The design of a dynamic emergency response management information system (DERMIS). *Annual Review of Network Management and Security*, 1, 101–121.

Wastell, D., Kawalek, P., Langmead-Jones, P., & Ormerod, R. (2004). Information systems and partnership in multi-agency networks: an action research project in crime reduction. *Information and Organization*, 14, 189–210.

Yusuf, T. O., & Babalola, A. R. (2009). Control of insurance fraud in Nigeria: An exploratory study. *Journal of Financial Crime*, 16(4), 418–435.

Conclusion

Rather than anecdotal evidence of famous white-collar cases, this book has applied a systematic approach to study a large sample of convicted criminals. The sample has enabled analysis of corporate versus occupational criminals, criminals as rotten apples versus criminals as members of rotten barrels, female (pink-collar) criminals, and other important aspects. A variety of statistical analysis in this book has provided new insights into white-collar criminals.

Characteristics of white-collar criminals provided a relevant background for key strategies in policing white-collar crime:

1. Information management strategy defines management tactics for organizing, controlling, and using police information resources through the management of both staff and technological resources for the purpose of assisting with policing processes and policy. Knowledge management strategy is centered around personnel resources, information systems strategy is concentrated on technology resources, and information management strategy is directed at the identification, retrieval, storage, and application of information resources. Key matters in this strategy are information significance and timeliness.

2. When policing white-collar crime, knowledge is of primary significance. Performance risk and execution risk are indicative of the knowledge deficits that can hinder process performance. When these knowledge shortfalls occur, inadequate data and knowledge prompt reservations that can obfuscate prediction and execution. Performance risk and execution risk are lessened through knowledge transfer mechanisms that have been created to prevent or to manage these doubts. Such knowledge transfer allows knowledge reprocessing, and the combination of all current knowledge is a key precursor to uncertainty resolution. Knowledge management strategy brings together personnel resources, among which are the knowledge of every police officer and the mutually held knowledge of the police, which all represents resources that are to be examined and exploited for improved police work. The knowledge management strategy process includes creating working definitions of knowledge and knowledge management, doing a knowledge audit, defining knowledge

management objectives and strategy approaches, and implementing a strategy with the ability to measure effectiveness.

3. Computer systems are very valuable when it comes to policing white-collar crime. Information systems are required to support the investigation and prevention of white-collar crime. Information technology is used when organizing intelligence and its analysis in electronic format and to allow for quick and easy retrieval, combination, and distribution among executives and colleagues. Information technology is recognized as an efficient way to support information sharing and knowledge management in organizations. Information systems strategy is focused on describing the ways in which information systems will be employed to reinforce and influence police work. It is a collection of computer-based applications to be applied. It combines the goals of the police with an understanding of the information necessary to support those objectives and the implementation of computer systems to supply that information. The emphasis is on producing an applications portfolio of suitable software systems and tools to support the future direction of an organization in general and knowledge work within the police more specifically. Information technology has an important role to play in leveraging knowledge resources in organizations. Organizations often execute information systems that are designed especially to support numerous different aspects of knowledge management in organizations. These systems include features such as intranets, search engines, document storage, and teamwork tools that permit virtual communities of practice to be organized (Choi et al., 2010).

In addition to these three core strategies, the value shop configuration is a framework within which information, knowledge, and systems are applied to prevent and solve white-collar crime cases.

4. The order of activities in the value shop starts with understanding the problem. It then goes on to alternate investigation methods, investigation decisions, and investigation applications. Finally, it ends with criminal investigation assessment. However, these successive activities can often intersect and link back to previous activities, especially in relation to management and assessment in policing departments, when the need for control and command arrangements are necessary every day owing to the legal duties that the policing unit's authority encompasses.

There are different software tools available for information systems to study white-collar crime. An example is Analyst Notebook. It is a computer tool that tries to identify connections, patterns, and trends in data sets. It provides visual analytics. Data are created in the notebook via drag-and-drop functionality. Charts are generated by dragging and dropping data in the form of entities, links, and attributes onto the chart. Volume data can be imported from structured data files via the wizard style, which creates import specifications that can be saved to help import additional information into a chart.

Analyst Notebook provides a data model that helps generate a visualization of links and attributes. Items can be represented as entities, links, events, timelines, and attributes in order to present the type of data and allow analysis and visualization.

Reference

Choi, S. Y., Lee, H., & Yoo, Y. (2010). The impact of information technology and transactive memory systems on knowledge sharing, application, and team performance: A field study. *MIS Quarterly, 34*(4), 855–870.

A Call for Authors
Advances in Police Theory and Practice

AIMS AND SCOPE:

This cutting-edge series is designed to promote publication of books on contemporary advances in police theory and practice. We are especially interested in volumes that focus on the nexus between research and practice, with the end goal of disseminating innovations in policing. We will consider collections of expert contributions as well as individually authored works. Books in this series will be marketed internationally to both academic and professional audiences. This series also seeks to —

- Bridge the gap in knowledge about advances in theory and practice regarding who the police are, what they do, and how they maintain order, administer laws, and serve their communities
- Improve cooperation between those who are active in the field and those who are involved in academic research so as to facilitate the application of innovative advances in theory and practice

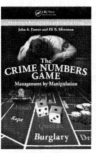

Police Reform in China

Mission-Based Policing

The International Trafficking of Human Organs
A Multidisciplinary Perspective

The series especially encourages the contribution of works coauthored by police practitioners and researchers. We are also interested in works comparing policing approaches and methods globally, examining such areas as the policing of transitional states, democratic policing, policing and minorities, preventive policing, investigation, patrolling and response, terrorism, organized crime and drug enforcement. In fact, every aspect of policing, public safety, and security, as well as public order is relevant for the series. Manuscripts should be between 300 and 600 printed pages. If you have a proposal for an original work or for a contributed volume, please be in touch.

Series Editor
Dilip Das, Ph.D., Ph: 802-598-3680
E-mail: dilipkd@aol.com

Dr. Das is a professor of criminal justice and Human Rights Consultant to the United Nations. He is a former chief of police and, founding president of the International Police Executive Symposium, IPES, www.ipes.info. He is also founding editor-in-chief of *Police Practice and Research: An International Journal* (PPR), (Routledge/Taylor & Francis), www.tandf.co.uk/journals. In addition to editing the *World Police Encyclopedia* (Taylor & Francis, 2006), Dr. Das has published numerous books and articles during his many years of involve-ment in police practice, research, writing, and education.

Proposals for the series may be submitted to the series editor or directly to –
Carolyn Spence
Senior Editor • CRC Press / Taylor & Francis Group
561-998-2515 • 561-997-7249 (fax)
carolyn.spence@taylorandfrancis.com • www.crcpress.com
6000 Broken Sound Parkway NW, Suite 300, Boca Raton, FL 33487

Index

Page numbers followed by f and t indicate figures and tables, respectively.

A

Aamodt, I., 185
Absorptive capacity theory, 261, 262
Abuse of public authority, 14
Acceptable mistake, neutralization theory, 81–82
Accountability, 157
Accounting, 251
Accusations, 249
Action, provocation and, 248
Adaptability, 258
Administrative knowledge, 264
Advanced knowledge, 265
Advance fee fraud, 5. *See also* Fraud crime
Aftenposten, 38, 49
Age
  and imprisonment, 215, 216
  of offender, 205
  white-collar crime and, 42–43
Agency theory, 68–70, 131
Agent provocateur, 285
Agility, 258
Aker industrial group, 49
Alien conspiracy theory, 176
Alignment, 258
Alliance theory, 140
Altruism, 168
America Online (AOL), 6
Amundsen, H., 180
Analyst Notebook (example), 301
Analytical knowledge, 264, 265
Appeal to higher loyalties, neutralization theory, 81
Artificial intelligence (AI), 292
Art theft, 10–11. *See also* Theft crime
Aspen, K., 179
Asset misappropriations, 10, 179

Association of Certified Fraud Examiners (ACFE), 10
Attempted control, defined, 199
Attitudes, 140
Attribution theory, 183
Auditors in crime detection, 194–197. *See also* Detection of white-collar criminals
Authority
  defined, 115
  white-collar crime, 31–37
Average jail sentence, white-collar crime, 45–47

B

Bank fraud, 2, 5–6. *See also* Financial crime; Fraud crime
  in China, 6
Bankruptcy crime, 13. *See also* Manipulation crime
Banks as victims, 180
Basic knowledge, 265
Bayou Funds, 8, 9
Beccaria, C., 137, 187
Bentham, J., 137, 187
Bias, press coverage, 40
Bid rigging, 13. *See also* Manipulation crime
Black Hand (organized crime group), 176
Bribery, 18–19. *See also* Corruption crime
Brynhildsen, R., 181
Bullying and harassment, 160–161
Business corruption
  defined, 2
  examples, 2–4. *See also* Financial crime
Business crime *vs.* organized crime, 57–58
Business intelligence (BI) systems, 283–284
Businessman gangster, 104
Business revenue/employees, 207

C

Care work, 103
Cartographic school strategy, 263, 278
Case-based reasoning systems, 292–293
Case studies
  white-collar crime
    Hermansen at Spitsbergen, 47–48
    Røkke at Aker, 48–49
Cash schemes, 179
Cash theft, 11. *See also* Theft crime
Categorical corruption, 178
Cauffman, E., 110, 142
Charts, 301
Check fraud, 6. *See also* Fraud crime
Chief executive officer (CEO), 155–162. *See also* Management positions in crime
  share of crime cases, 170t
  and white-collar criminals, 169t
Chief financial officers (CFO), 161
Chinese criminal law, 2
Claim to entitlement, neutralization theory, 81
Clandestine banking, 1
Click fraud, 6. *See also* Fraud crime
Codification strategy, 283, 286
Coercion, 14
Collaboration, knowledge, 259
Colluders, 74–75
Comey, J.B., 136, 137
Commercial school strategy, 263
Communication, 223, 224
  control, 248, 250
  technology, 274
Comparative case analysis, 254
Competition crime, 13. *See also* Manipulation crime
Competitive environment, 131
Complementary knowledge, 262
Complete regression analysis, 209f, 209t
Compliance levels, 291
CompStat approach, 284
Computer-based linguistic analysis, 294
Computer crime, 13. *See also* Manipulation crime
Computer systems, 273, 300
Condemnation of the condemners, neutralization theory, 81
Conformers, 74
Conscientiousness, white-collar crime and, 31

Construction industry, 102
Consumer fraud, 6–7. *See also* Fraud crime
Context of offending, 102, 113
Control authorities, 249
Control balance theory, 72
Conviction, 124
Cooperation, 224
COPLINK, 283
Core competence theory, 133
Corporate crime, 45
  theories, 58–62
  vs. occupational, 55–58
Corporate criminals, 88–91
  sample, 62–64
Corporate strategy, 158
Correctional environments, 249
Correlation analysis of white-collar crime. *See also* Statistical analyses
  age of offender, 205
  business revenue/employees, 207
  crime amount, 205
  jail sentence, 205
  personal income, 205–206
  personal tax/wealth, 206
Correlation coefficients, 226t
Corruption
  on business, 3
  business (examples), 2–4
  defined, 2, 18
  organizational, 19
  public, 19–20
Corruption crime. *See also* White-collar crime typologies
  bribery, 18–19
  defined, 17–18
  kickbacks, 19
  organizational corruption, 19
  public corruption, 19–20
Corruption theory, 177
Council of Europe (2002), 253
Counterfeit currency, 13–14. *See also* Manipulation crime
Cracker, 13
Credit card fraud, 7–8. *See also* Fraud crime
Crime
  acceptance of, 128
  analysis, 253
  detection, 136, 148. *See* Detection of white-collar criminals
  prevention, 136, 185
  in private *versus* public sector, 197–198
  profit-driven, 160

Crime amount, 205
  and imprisonment, 215
Crime control methods analysis, 253
Crime fraction
  to detection fraction, 145–148
  from needs fraction to, 128
Crime intelligence analysis, 252–255.
      See also Police information
      management strategy
Crime of trust, financial, 27–31
Crime pattern analysis, 253
Crime star for women, 144–145, 144f.
      See also Stage model for female
      criminals
Crime theories, 112–116, 166–169. *See also*
      Management positions in crime;
      White-collar crime by women
  feminist theory, 115–116
  labeling theory, 115
  obedience theory, 113–114
  opportunity theory, 112
  Quinney's Social Reality of Crime, 115
Criminal behavior, 143
Criminal business analysis/profile, 254
Criminal characteristics, 104–111. *See also*
      White-collar crime by women
  white-collar crime, 42–49
Criminal entrepreneurs, 20, 87–88
Criminal insiders, 183–185. *See also* Victims
Criminal intelligence, 242–244. *See also*
      Police information management
      strategy
Criminal investigators, 228
Criminal justice systems, modern, 19
Criminal money, 16
Criminal opportunities, 102, 113
Criminals, white-collar. *See also* White-
      collar crime
  characteristics, 36
  comparison of groups, 94–95
  corporate crime
    theories, 58–62
    vs. occupational, 55–58
  corporate criminals, 88–91
    sample, 62–64
  criminal entrepreneurs, 87–88
  criminal followers, 91–93
  female criminals, 93–94
  followers *vs.* leaders, 64–65
  groups of, 86–87
  leader crime theories, 67–72
  leader criminal characteristics, 65–67

leader criminal sample, 72–76
roles, 55–95
  rotten apples *vs.* rotten barrels, 76
  rotten crime theories, 78–82
  rotten criminal characteristics, 76–77
  rotten criminal sample, 82–86
Criminal sample, 116–119, 116t, 117t,
      169–172, 169t, 170t, 171t. *See also*
      Management positions in crime;
      White-collar crime by women
Criminal social contracts, 167
Crisis memory, 293
Cultural deviance theories, 50
Culture theory, 133
Customers as victims, 180–181
Cyber crime, 14. *See also* Manipulation
      crime

D

Dagens Næringsliv (DN), 38, 48, 49
Daly, K., 111
Data errors in press coverage, 40
Data mining, 292
Decision making, 233
Declarative knowledge, 264
Defendant income, 215
Demographic change analysis, 254
Denial of injury, neutralization theory,
      80–81
Denial of responsibility, neutralization
      theory, 80
Denial-of-service attacks, 13
Denial of victim, neutralization theory, 81
Dependent variables, 207
Detection fraction
  from crime fraction to, 145–148
  to sentence fraction, 148
Detection of white-collar criminals
  auditor, role of, 194–197
  detection crime theories, 185–188
  detectors, 188, 189t, 190t
  journalists, role of, 190–194
Detectors of crime, 188, 189t, 190t. *See
      also* Detection of white-collar
      criminals
Deterrence theory, 136, 137, 138, 185–187
Deviant culture theory, 199
Differential association theory, 71
Digital forensics, 247
Digital interactions, 279
Dilemma tradeoff, neutralization theory, 82

Discrimination ability, 289
Documents, 247
Dodge, M., 100, 126, 131
Domain-specific knowledge, 292
Double bind, defined, 166
Double-bind leadership theory, 166
Double-loop learning, 221
Dynamic emergency response information
     system (DERMIS), 293, 294
Dysfunctional network theory, 78–80

E

Ebbers, Bernhard, 29
Economic Crime Prosecutor (ECOCRIME),
     192
Economic criminals, 102
Ego-centered networks, 281
Electronic networks, 278
Embezzlement, 8, 11. *See also* Fraud crime
Empirical study, white-collar crime, 28
Employee knowledge, 264
Employees, 249
Employers as victims, 179–180
End-user tools, 277
Enron, 252
Enterprise content management systems, 284
Enthusiastic intelligence operative, 284
Entrepreneur, 104
Entrepreneurial theory, 50–51, 139
Entrepreneurs, criminal, 87–88
Esteem, 126
Evidence, 230
Exchange of intelligence information, 249
Exchange theory, 71–72
Executive management, 133
Experimentation in police work, 229
Explicit knowledge, 258
Exploitation, 260
External data storage, 249
External information, 289
External knowledge, 261
External victims, 175
     versus internal victim cases, 178t
Extortion, 14–15. *See also* Manipulation
     crime
ExxonMobil in Kazakhstan (example), 2

F

False invoicing, 15
Female crime, 102

Female criminal fraction, determinants of,
     124–125, 125f
Female criminals, 93–94. *See also* Women
     stage model for. *See* Stage model for
          female criminals
Female investigators, 108
Female white-collar criminals, 116t, 117t
Feminist theory, 115–116, 138. *See also*
     Crime theories
Financial Action Task Force (FATF), 291
Financial crime, 123, 251, 265, 266t, 267t.
     See also White-collar crime
          typologies
     bank fraud, 2
     business corruption (examples), 2–4
     categories and subcategories, 4–5, 4f
     and detection sources, 190t
Financial crime of trust, 27–31
Financial Intelligence Unit in Norway, 16
Finansavisen, 38
Fingerprints, 248
Firm leadership, 222
Followers
     criminal, 91–93
     vs. leaders, white-collar criminals,
          64–65
Forensic accountants, 251
Forensic accounting, 247, 250–252, 265.
     See also Police information
          management strategy
Fornaas, F., 180
For-profit sector procurement, 197, 198
Fraud
     defined, 2
     tax, 17
Fraud crime. *See also* White-collar crime
          typologies
     advance fee, 5
     bank, 5–6
     check, 6
     click, 6
     consumer, 6–7
     defined, 5
     embezzlement, 8
     hedge, 8–9
     hedge fund, 8–9
     identity, 9
     mortgage, 9
     occupational, 9–10
     subsidy crime, 10
Fraud hypothesis approach, 276–277
Fraud-inhibiting insider trading, 34–35

Fraud theory, 187–188
Free exchange of information, 294
Frequently asked questions (FAQ), 278
Friedrichs, D.O., 99
Fully compliant (FC) levels, 291

G

Game theory, 199
Gender, 99
　differences
　　in crime, 103, 113
　　white-collar crime, 25, 42
　organization of, 102, 112
　segregation, 103
Gendered theory, 93–94. *See also* Female
　　criminals
Gendered theory of female offending, 112
Gender gap
　and white-collar crime, 109, 112. *See also*
　　White-collar crime by women
General deterrence theory, 186
Geo-computation, 283
Ghost employees, 15. *See also* Manipulation
　　crime
Glass ceiling, 133
Goal theory, 131, 132
Goldstraw-White, J., 112, 131
Goodin, J.B., 5–6
Governance responsibility, 244
Greece-Albania remittance corridor, 1
Greed, white-collar crime and, 28
Grudging informant, 284
Guttman scaling, 296

H

Hansen, 138
Harassment, 160–161
Hawala banking, 1
Hawley Committee, guidelines from, 241
Hedge fund fraud, 8–9. *See also* Fraud
　　crime
Hedonism, white-collar crime and, 30, 31
Hermansen, Robert, 48, 165
Heroic criminals, 162–166. *See also*
　　Management positions in crime
Heroic leader criminals, 171
Heroism, negative, 163, 164
Holager, Ellen, 49
HOLMES system, 277
Hubris, white-collar crime and, 35

Human capital, 156
Human needs theory, 125
Hybrid knowledge, 292
Hypothesis testing, 211, 213

I

Identity fraud, 9. *See also* Fraud crime
Identity theft, 11–12. *See also* Theft crime
Imprisonment and amount estimates, 214t,
　　215
Income, 127
　and imprisonment, 216
Income tax crime, 17. *See also* Manipulation
　　crime
Independent variables, 207
Individual creativity, 222
Individualism, 223
Inference engines, 292
Inflated invoices, 15. *See also* Manipulation
　　crime
Informal communication, 224
Informants, 247
Information
　cross checking, 282
　defined, 241
　focus, 293
　free exchange of, 294
　and intelligence (distinction), 270
　from knowledge workers, 283
　policy, 244
　quality, 243
　as raw data, 269
　requirement, 243
　resource, 243
　security, 243
　source of, 284
　validity and timelines, 293
　value, 242
Information and communication
　　technology (ICT), 274, 275
Information management approaches.
　　See also Police information
　　management strategy
　information policy, 244
　resource analysis, 244
　responsibilities, 244
　risk management, 244
　structuring, 244
Information management strategy,
　　241–242, 299. *See also* Police
　　information management strategy

Information sources, 246–250. *See also* Police information management strategy
   accusations, 249
   action, 248
   communication control, 248
   control authorities, 249
   documents, 247
   employees, 249
   exchange, 249
   external data storage, 249
   internet, 248–249
   interview, 247
   location, 247
   media, 249
   network, 247
   observation, 247
   physical material, 248
   policing system, 249
   surveillance, 248
Information technology, 273, 300
Infrastructure responsibility, 244
Inner model, 211
Innovation, 273
Innovative knowledge, 266
Insider threats, 183
Institutional theory, 58–60, 89–91
Integrated theory, 78
Integrity, 219, 222, 228
Intellectual property crime, 12. *See also* Theft crime
Intelligence
   defined, 245
   for knowledge, 257–258. *See also* Police knowledge management strategy
Intelligence knowledge, 264
Intelligence-led policing, 245–246
Interception of communications, 248
Internal fraud, 10
Internal Revenue Service, 17
Internal victims, 175
   versus external victim cases, 178t
International policing cooperation, 249
Internet, 14, 248–249
   and fraud, 5
Interorganizational collaborations, 282
Interpol, 12
Interrogation, 247
Interview, 247
Intranets, 279
Inventory theft, 12. *See also* Theft crime
Investigations/operations analysis, 254
Investigative journalists, 191, 192

Investigative knowledge, 264, 265
Investigator-to-application stage, 290–295. *See also* Police information systems strategy
Investigator-to-information stage, 283–290. *See also* Police information systems strategy
Investigator-to-investigator stage, 277–283. *See also* Police information systems strategy
Investigator-to-technology stage, 275–277, 276f. *See also* Police information systems strategy
Investors, 6
Italian-dominated crime families, 176

J

Jail sentences, 137, 205, 213
Joint stock company act of 1844, 156
Jones, 195
Journalists in crime detection, 189t, 190–194. *See also* Detection of white-collar criminals
Justification of crime, 142

K

Kickbacks, 19. *See also* Corruption crime
Kirkbak, G., 180
Klassekampen, 38
Know-how knowledge, 268
Knowledge, 132, 257, 299
   development, 221, 222
   integration, 261–263, 262. *See also* Police knowledge management strategy
   intelligence for, 257–258
   organization of investigation, 230f
   sharing, 280, 288
   transfer, 257, 262, 278
Knowledge collaboration
   defined, 259
   online, 279, 280
Knowledge-intensive service delivery network, 281
Knowledge levels, defined, 267
Knowledge management, 243
   in corporate social responsibility work, 260
Knowledge management system, 273–275. *See also* Police information systems strategy
   stage model for policing, 276f

Knowledge matrix approach, 263, 266t, 267t
Knowledge network systems, 278
Knowledge-oriented directories, 278
Knowledge validation process, 288
Knowledge work, 295–296. *See also* Police
    information systems strategy
Knowledge workers, 259
Know-what knowledge, 267
Know-why knowledge, 268
KPMG, 44
Kristian Jebsens Rederi, 48
Külpe, O., 157, 158
Kvarving, S.A., 180

L

Labeling theory, 115. *See also* Crime theories
Labor market, 103
Lapping, 11
Largely compliant (LC) levels, 291
Law enforcement function, 253
Leaders
    crime theories, 67–72
    criminal characteristics, 65–67
    criminal sample, 72–76
    vs. followers, white-collar criminals,
        64–65
Leadership
    celebrity, 163, 166
    heroic, 162, 164, 165
    post-heroic, 162
Learning, 293
Learning organization (LO), 223, 232–235,
    234f. *See also* Police value shop
    configuration
    values and, 226t
Learning theories, 50, 140
Legal and ethical compliance, 243
Legal knowledge, 264
Legal mistake, neutralization theory, 81
Legitimacy theory, 252
Lesotho Dam project (example), 2
Licensing, white-collar crime and, 49–51
Lifecycle models, 296
Local community, 249
Location (crime scenes), 247

M

Machiavellianism, white-collar crime and,
    36
Madoff, B., 107

Madoff's scam, 175
Major Incident Policy Document (in UK),
    277
Male white-collar criminals, 116, 117t
Management positions in crime
    chief executive officer (CEO), 155–162
    comparisons, 171t, 172
    crime theories, 166–169
    criminal sample, 169–172, 169t, 170t,
        171t
    heroic criminals, 162–166
Manifest variables, 211
Manipulation crime. *See also* White-collar
        crime typologies
    bankruptcy crime, 13
    bid rigging, 13
    competition crime, 13
    computer crime, 13
    counterfeit currency, 13–14
    cyber crime, 14
    defined, 13
    extortion, 14–15
    ghost employees, 15
    income tax crime, 17
    inflated invoices, 15
    money laundering, 15–17
Market integrity theory, 176–177
Market misconduct, 177
Market profile, 254
Maslow, A., 125
Maximum-likelihood function, 211
Measurement errors, 211
Measurement model, 211
Media, 249
Media coverage of criminals, 99
Media-oriented information sources, 250
Mediated communication, 280
Messerschmidt, J.M., 99, 125
Microphones, 248
Mindsets, 155, 157
    core point, 158
Misappropriation schemes, 10, 15
Modus essendi, 139
Modus operandi, 139
Modus vivendi, 139
Money laundering, 1, 15–17. *See also*
        Manipulation crime
    as five-stage process, 16
    as three-stage process, 16
Moral collapse, 90
Moral theory, 129–130, 143
Mortgage fraud, 9. *See also* Fraud crime

Motivation, 128, 134, 138, 139
    for crime, 102, 113
Motivation theory, 177–178
Munir, F., 184
Mutual evaluation, 291

N

Nanotechnology, 288
Narcissism, 164
    white-collar crime and, 30, 31, 35
Narcissistic leaders, 164–165
Narcissists, 162
National Association of Investors
        Corporation (NAIC), 106
National Center for Women and Policing
        (NCWP), 107–108
National Intelligence Strategy, 257
Naylor, R.T., 160
Needs fraction
    to crime fraction, 128
    from population fraction to, 125–128
Negative heroism, 163, 164
Negotiation, 100, 111
Network, 247
Network analysis, 255
Network sharing, 287
Neural networks, 292
Neutralization theory, 80–82, 110, 142
News media, 192
Newspapers, 119
Noncash schemes, 10, 179
Noncompliant (NC) levels, 291
Nonjournalists in crime detection, 189t
Normality of action, neutralization theory,
        81
Normality theory, 139
Norway, 99, 108, 119, 213, 226
    tax authorities in, 180
Norwegian Bureau of the Investigation of
        Police Affairs, 233
Norwegian gender regime, 103
Norwegian police (case study), 223
Norwegian Press Association's Code of
        Ethics, 191
Not-for-profit sector procurement, 197

O

Obedience theory, 67–68, 92, 113–114. See
        also Crime theories
Observed variables, 211

Occupational crime, 45
    vs. corporate crime, 55–58
Occupational fraud, 9–10. See also Fraud
        crime
Offender age, 205
Offender group analysis, 254
Online knowledge collaborations, 279, 280
Online undercover investigators, 289
Open-bidding process, 198
Open source, 248–249
Operational analysis, 253
Operational crime analysis
    case analysis, 254
    comparative case analysis, 254
    investigations/operations analysis, 254
    network analysis, 255
    offender group analysis, 254
    specific profile analysis, 254
Operation Gallant (in UK), 246
Opportunity, 160
    in criminology, 128
    defined, 130, 131
    white-collar crime, 31–37
Opportunity theory, 112, 129. See also
        Crime theories
Organization, knowledge-intensive, 233
Organizational corruption, 19. See also
        Corruption crime
Organizational culture, 220, 221
Organizational knowledge, 261, 264
Organizational learning, 229
Organizational school strategy, 263
Organized crime vs. business crime, 57–58
Outer model, 211

P

Pacific Consultants International (PCI)
        (example), 20
Parent-child bonding, 102, 144
Partial least squares (PLS) analysis, 211,
        212, 213, 214f
Partially compliant (PC) levels, 291
Participation theory, 130
Partnership working, 274
Path coefficients of PLS analysis, 214f
Peltier-Rivest, D., 9, 10
Perceived technology, 295
Performance risk, 299
Performance scale, white-collar crime, 30
Personal income, 205–206
    of offender, 215

Personalization strategy, 278, 285, 286
Personal needs, 126
Personal tax/wealth, 206
Person-oriented information sources, 250
Person-to-person systems, 279
Physical material, 248
Pink-collar criminals, 42. *See also* White-collar crime
PLS. *See* Partial least squares (PLS) analysis
Police, primary purpose of, 219
Police information management strategy
   crime intelligence analysis, 252–255
   criminal intelligence, 242–244
   forensic accounting, 250–252
   information management strategy, 241–242
   information sources, 246–250
   strategy characteristics, 245–246
Police information systems strategy
   investigator-to-application stage, 290–295
   investigator-to-information stage, 283–290
   investigator-to-investigator stage, 277–283
   investigator-to-technology stage, 275–277, 276f
   knowledge management systems, 273–275
   knowledge work, 295–296
Police intelligence, 241
Police knowledge, 260–261. *See also* Police knowledge management strategy
Police knowledge management strategy
   data to wisdom, 268–270, 269f
   intelligence for knowledge, 257–258
   knowledge categories, 263–268, 266t, 267t
     administrative, 264
     advanced, 265
     analytical, 265
     basic, 265
     employee, 264
     innovative, 266
     intelligence, 264
     investigative, 264
     know-how, 268
     know-what, 267
     know-why, 268
     legal, 264
     organizational, 264

     process, 264
     technological, 265
   knowledge integration, 261–263
   management approaches, 258–260
   police knowledge, 260–261
Police managers, 228
Police officers, accountability of, 227
Police oversight agencies, stages of growth in, 234f
Police values, 221, 224
   measurement of, 225t
Police value shop configuration
   learning organization, 232–235, 234f
   police culture, 220–230, 225t, 226t
   value shop work, 230–232, 230f
     approach decision, 232
     investigation approaches, 231–232
     investigation implementation, 232
     performance evaluation, 232
     problem definition, 231
Policing, 108, 260
   intelligence-led, 245–246
   knowledge management systems stage model for, 276f
Policing system, 249
Politically exposed persons, 168–169
Pollak, O., 116
Pollak's theory, 149. *See also* Stage model for female criminals
Population fraction to needs fraction, 125–128
Predictor model for jail sentences, 208, 208f
PricewaterhouseCoopers (PwC), 33
Principal-agent theory, 155, 156
Prisoners, 250
Prison inmates, 148
Prisons, 249
Private sector, crime in, 197, 198, 200, 200t
Procedural corruption, 178
Procedural knowledge, 264
Proceeds of crime (POC) cases, 16
Process knowledge, 264
Process school strategy, 263
Procurement, 197
   in public sector, 198
Profile analysis, 253
Profit-driven crime, 131, 160
Provocation, 248
Psychiatrists view, white-collar crime, 34
Psychopaths, corporate, 164, 165
Public corruption, 19–20. *See also* Corruption crime

Public sector, crime in, 197, 198, 200, 200t
Punishment, 167

Q

Questionnaire, 224
Quinney's Social Reality of Crime, 115. *See also* Crime theories

R

Rational choice theory, 135, 167–168
Rationalization, 145
Recidivism, 164
Regression analysis, 207–210, 207t, 208f, 209f, 209t. *See also* Statistical analyses
Relational commitments in private sector, 198
Remittance, 1
Resource analysis, 244
Resource theory, 132
Responsibility scale, white-collar crime, 30
Risk, 141, 144
    for fraud, 128
    management, 244
Røkke, Kjell Inge, 48–49
Role transferability, 293
Rotten apples *vs.* rotten barrels, 76
Rotten crime theories, 78–82
Rotten criminal characteristics, 76–77
Rotten criminal sample, 82–86

S

Sample
    corporate criminal, 62–64
    leader criminal, 72–76
    rotten criminal, 82–86
Sample criminals, white-collar crime, 37–42
Schematic corruption, 178
Schizophrenia, organizational, 166
Scientific Content Analysis (SCAN), 294
Second-generation data analysis technique, 210
Sector crime theories
    deviant culture theory, 199
    game theory, 199
    social control theory, 198–199
Sector criminal sample, 200
    private sector criminals *versus* public sector criminals, 200t

Security, 228
Self-actualization, 126
Self-assessment, 291
Self-control, 102
    defined, 143
    white-collar crime and, 31
Self-control theory, 60, 88, 143
SEM. *See* Structural equation modeling (SEM)
Sentence fraction
    from detection fraction to, 148
    to prison fraction, 148–149
Shame, 137, 187
Shareholders as victims, 181
Slippery slope theory, 143
Smith, A., 156
Social altruism, 115
Social bonding theory, 70, 71, 138
Social contract theory, 167, 252
Social control, 102, 144
Social control theory, 198–199
Social desirability response bias, 101, 110
Social dominance, white-collar crime and, 35–36
Socialization, 263
Socialization pressures, 111
Socialization theory, 80
Social learning theory, 78
Social network theory, 78
Social role theory, 100, 101
Social status, crime and, 26. *See also* White-collar crime
Social trend analysis, 254
Socio-cognitive process, 259
Spatial school strategy, 263
Special deterrence theory, 136, 137, 186
Stage model for female criminals
    crime fraction to detection fraction, 145–148
    crime star for women, 144–145, 144f
    detection fraction to sentence fraction, 148
    female criminal fraction, determinants of, 124–125, 125f
    needs fraction to crime fraction, 128
    overview, 123–124, 124f
    Pollak's theory, 149
    population fraction to needs fraction, 125–128
    sentence fraction to prison fraction, 148–149
    women's justification of crime, 140–144

women's motivation for crime, 134–140
women's opportunity for crime, 128–134
State of mind, 157
Statistical analyses
    correlation analysis of white-collar
            crime
        age of offender, 205
        business revenue/employees, 207
        crime amount, 205
        jail sentence, 205
        personal income, 205–206
        personal tax/wealth, 206
        regression analysis, 207–210, 207t, 208f,
            209f, 209t
        structural equation modeling, 210–216,
            214f, 214t
Stensrud, T., 180
Stepwise regression analysis, 207t, 208f
Stewardship responsibility, 244
Stewart, M. (case study), 106–107
Sting operation, 1
Store Norske Spitsbergen Kullkompani, 47
Strain theory, 70
Strategic crime analysis
    crime control methods analysis, 253
    crime pattern analysis, 253
    criminal business analysis/profile, 254
    demographic/social trends analysis, 254
    general profile analysis, 253
    market profile, 254
    results analysis, 253
    strategic analysis, 254
Strategic Management Journal, 38
Structural equation modeling (SEM), 210–
        216, 214f, 214t. See also Statistical
        analyses
    covariance-based, 211, 212
Structural model, 211
Subsidy crime, 10. See also Fraud crime
Success in business, 159
Sulland, Frode, 48
Surveillance, 248
Sutherland, E., 104
Systems school strategy, 263
System training and simulation, 293

T

Tacit knowledge, 259
Tactical/operational crime analysis
    case analysis, 254
    comparative case analysis, 254
    investigations/operations analysis, 254
    network analysis, 255
    offender group analysis, 254
    operational crime analysis, 254–255
    specific profile analysis, 254
Tarling, R., 110–111
Task technology theory, 295
Tax
    avoidance, 17, 105
    compliance, 17
    evasion, defined, 17
Tax authorities as victims, 180
Technological knowledge, 265
The Criminality of Women, 116, 149
Theft, defined, 10
Theft crime
    art, 10–11
    cash, 11
    identity, 11–12
    intellectual property crime, 12
    inventory, 12
Theoretical perspectives, white-collar
        crime, 49–51
Theory of monopoly, 60–61
Theory of organizational crime, 60
Theory of profit-driven crime, 50
Theory of profit-driven crime, 131
Tolerance scale, white-collar crime, 30
Traffic police, 230
Transaction cost theory, 71, 129, 130
Transactive memory, 259, 294
Transnational crime, 11

U

Undercover operations, 248
Underground banking, 1
United States v. Booker, 46
"Upper socioeconomic class"
    crimes of, 27. See also White-collar
        crime
Usage responsibility, 244
Utility theory, 187

V

Validation processes, 288
Value added tax (VAT), 17
Value(s), 221
Value shop work, 230–232, 230f. See also
        Police value shop configuration
Vehicle crime, 245

Victims
  classification of, 179–183
    banks, 180
    characteristics of white-collar
      criminals, 182t
    customers, 180–181
    distribution of white-collar
      criminals, 181t
    employers, 179–180
    shareholders, 181
    tax authorities, 180
  crime theories, 176–178
  criminal characteristics, 175–176
  criminal insiders, 183–185
  criminal sample, 178–179, 178t
  external, 175
  internal victims, 175
Video cameras, 248
Vigilant interaction, 279

W

Wages, 127
Wall Street Journal, 38
Weismann, M.F., 167
Wheeler, S., 134
White-collar crime
  authority and opportunity, 31–37
  average jail sentence, 45–47
  criminal characteristics, 42–49
  criminals. *See* Criminals, white-collar
  definition, 25, 26, 28, 29, 32, 123
  explanatory approaches, 34
  financial crime of trust, 27–31
  fraud-inhibiting insider trading and, 34–35
  Hermansen at Spitsbergen, 47–48
  levels, 44
  media as information source for, 41
  men *vs.* women, 25, 42
  personality traits and, 35–36
  Røkke at Aker, 48–49
  sample criminals, 37–42
  theoretical perspectives, 49–51
  typologies, 25–51
White-collar crime by women
  accessing offenders, 106
  care work, 103
  crime theories, 112–116
  criminal characteristics, 104–111
  criminal sample, 116–119, 116t, 117t
  ethical perceptions, 107
  female crime (comparative study), 102

  feminist theory, 115–116
  fraction of, 125f
  gender differences, 99, 100, 109
  gender theory, 113
  labeling theory, 115
  media coverage, 99
  negotiation, 100
  Norwegian context, 103, 108
  obedience theory, 113–114
  opportunity theory, 112
  Policing, 108
  Quinney's Social Reality of Crime, 115
  social role theory, 101
  theory of white-collar criminality, 105
White-collar crime typologies
  corruption crime
    bribery, 18–19
    defined, 17–18
    kickbacks, 19
    organizational corruption, 19
    public corruption, 19–20
  financial crime
    bank fraud, 2
    business corruption (examples), 2–4
    categories and subcategories, 4–5, 4f
  fraud crime
    advance fee, 5
    bank, 5–6
    check, 6
    click, 6
    consumer, 6–7
    credit card, 7–8
    defined, 5
    embezzlement, 8
    hedge fund, 8–9
    identity, 9
    mortgage, 9
    occupational, 9–10
    subsidy crime, 10
  manipulation crime
    bankruptcy crime, 13
    bid rigging, 13
    competition crime, 13
    computer crime, 13
    counterfeit currency, 13–14
    cyber crime, 14
    defined, 13
    extortion, 14–15
    ghost employees, 15
    income tax crime, 17
    inflated invoices, 15
    money laundering, 15–17

outline of, 1–2
theft crime
    art theft, 10–11
    cash, 11
    identity theft, 11–12
    intellectual property crime, 12
    inventory theft, 12
White-collar criminals
    detection of. *See* Detection of white-
        collar criminals
    heroic/regular, 170t
Wi-Fi Protected Access (WPA), 8
Williamson, 156
Wired Equivalent Privacy (WEP)
        encryption system, 8
Wiretapping, 248
Women. *See also* Female criminals
    white-collar crime and, 25, 42

Women in crime. *See also* Stage model for
        female criminals
    crime star for, 144–145, 144f
    justification by, 140–144
    motivation for, 134–140
    opportunity for, 128–134
    in prison, 124f, 148
    stage model for criminals. *See* Stage
        model for female criminals
Women in white-collar crime. *See* White-
        collar crime by women
Women's labor participation, 103
WorldCom, 29, 34
Worthen, M.G.F., 102

Y

Yellow Pages, 278

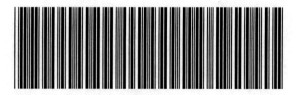